Fenix
The Museum As Metaphor

FENIX

The Museum As Metaphor

SKIRA

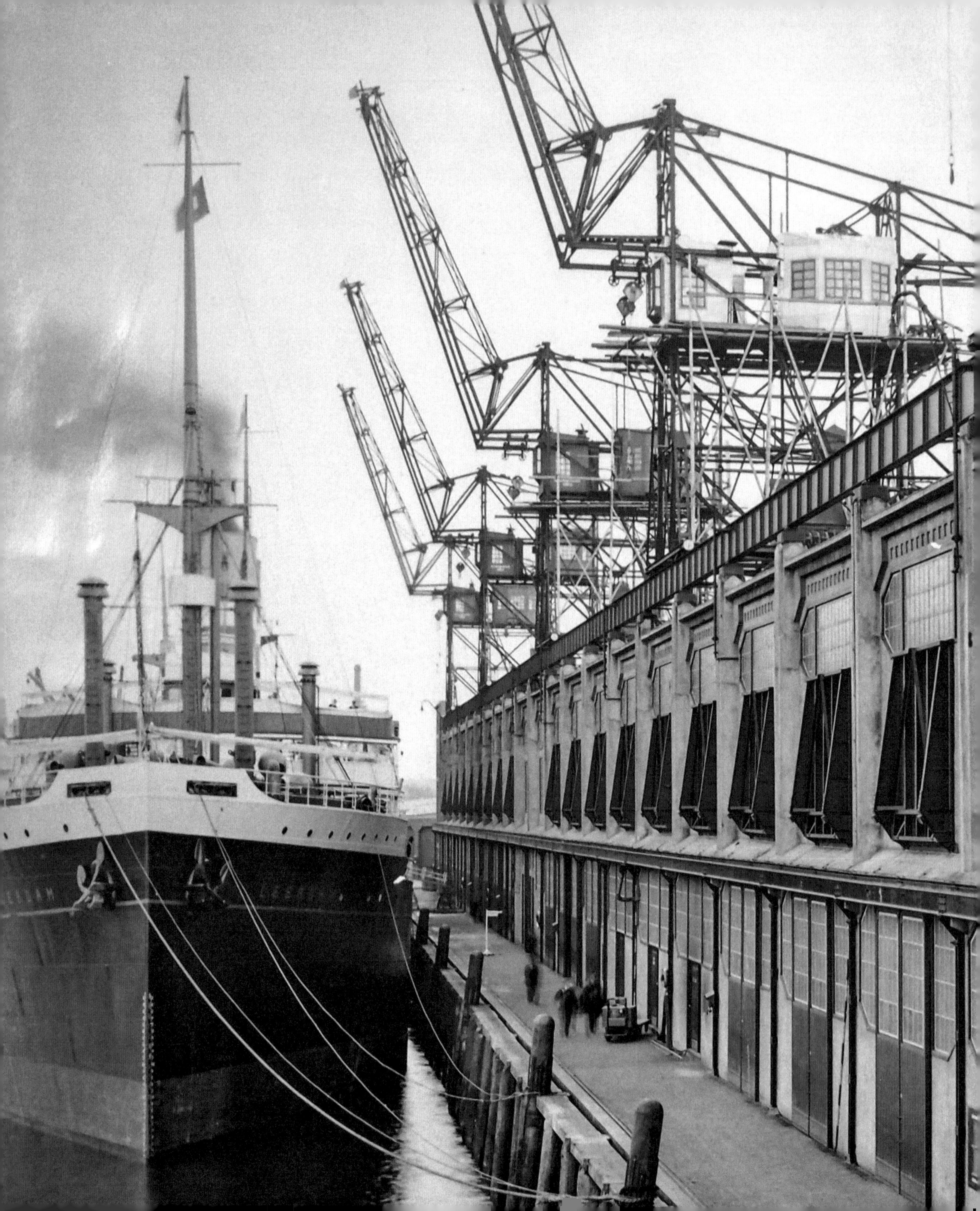

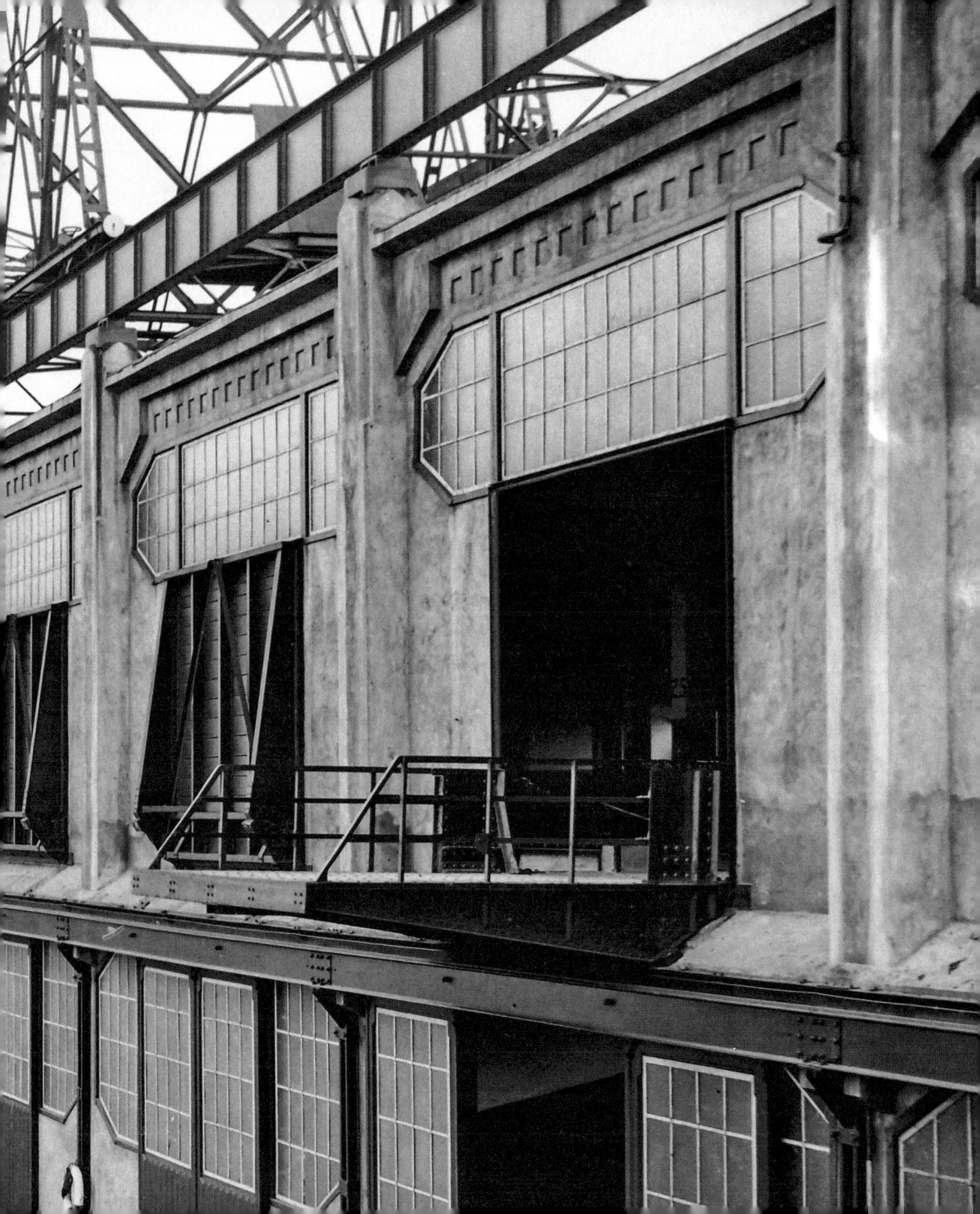

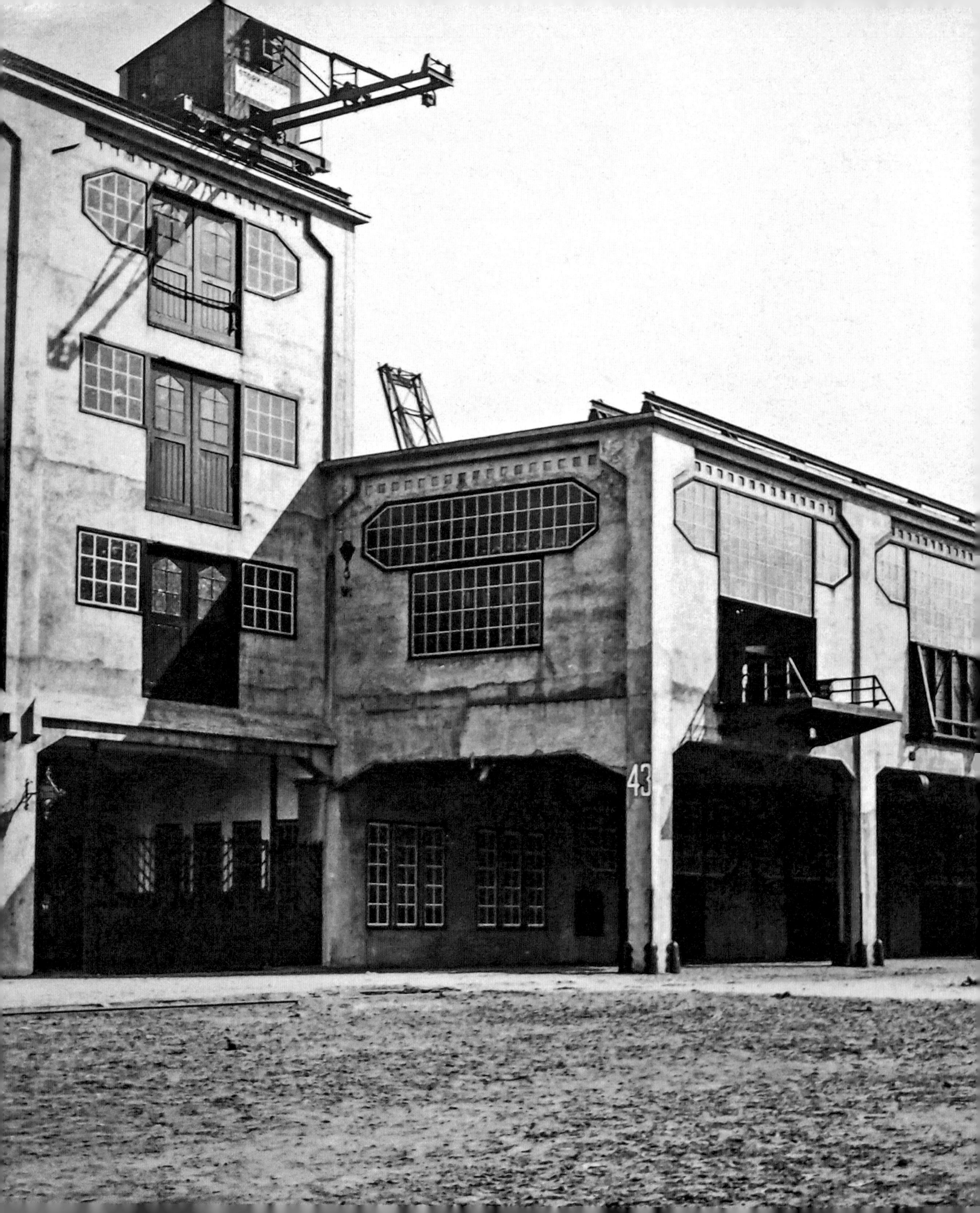
43

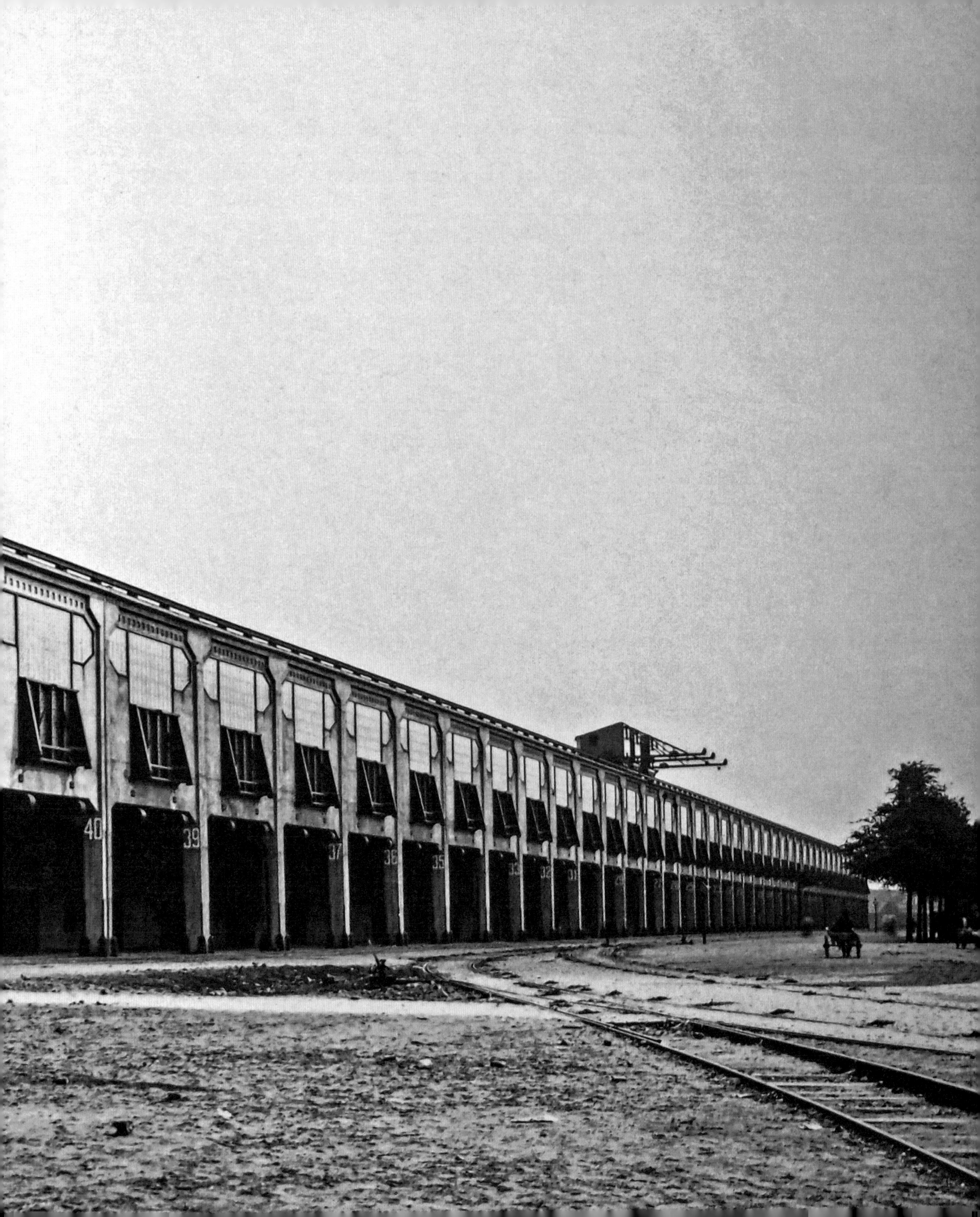
40
39
37
36
35

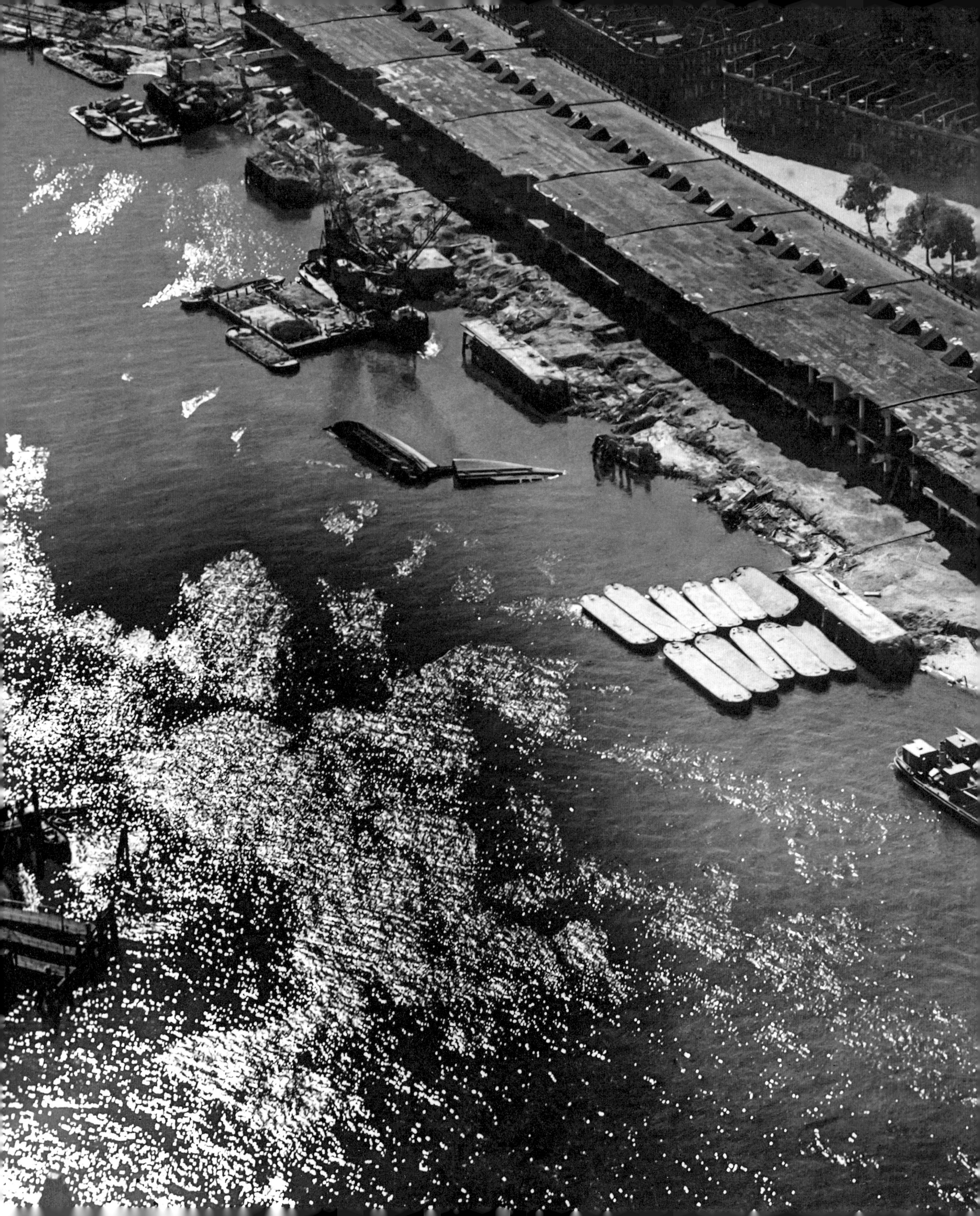

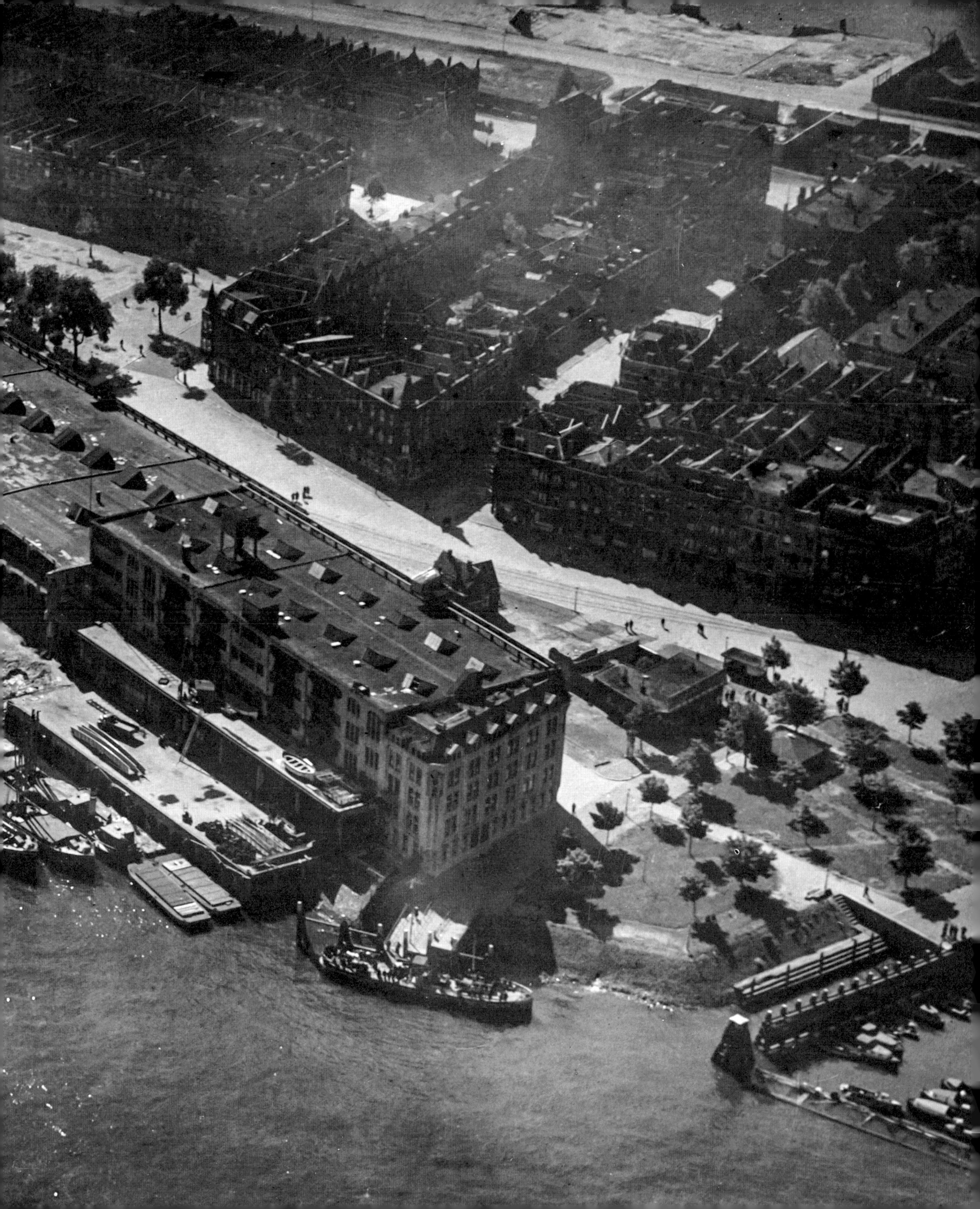

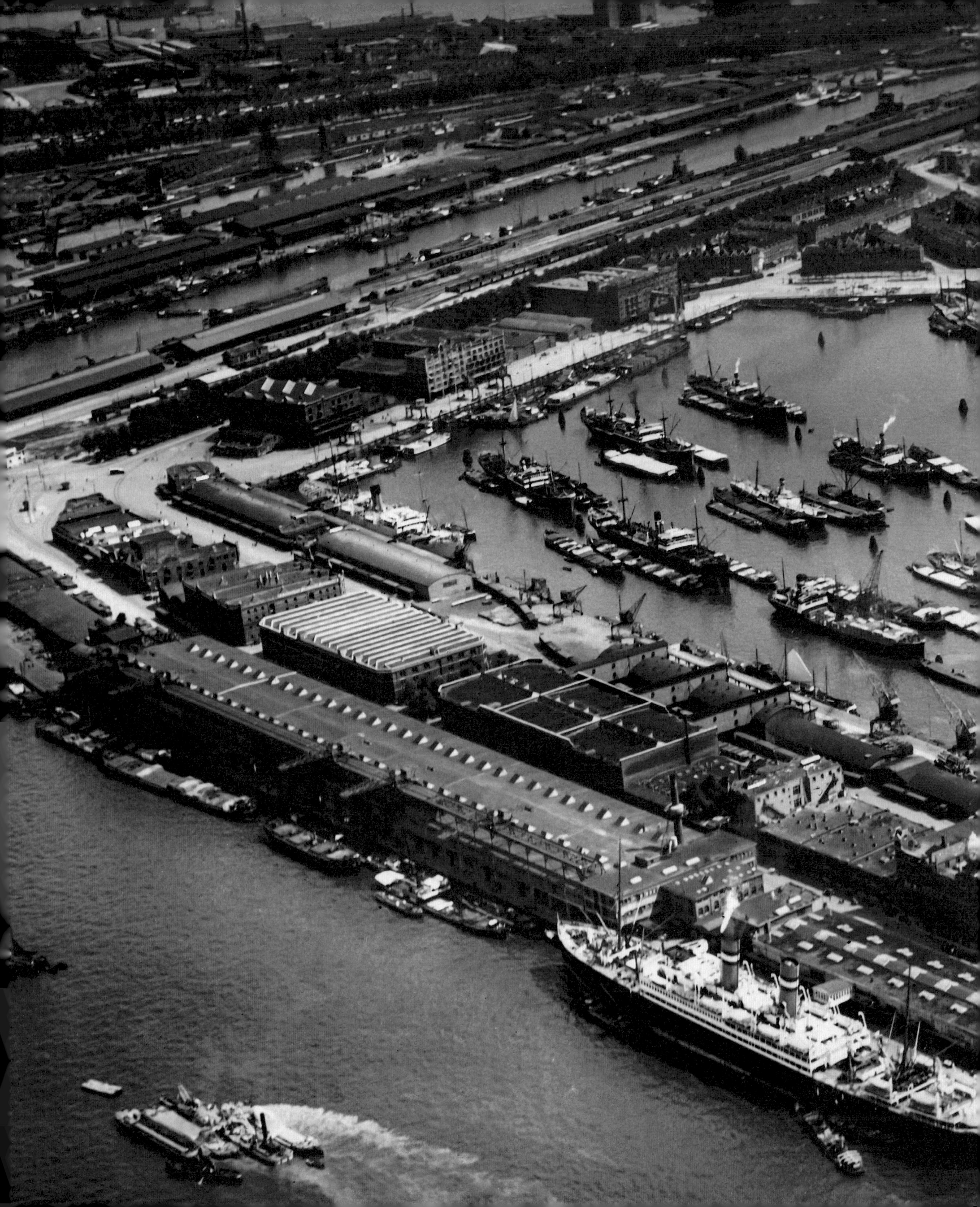

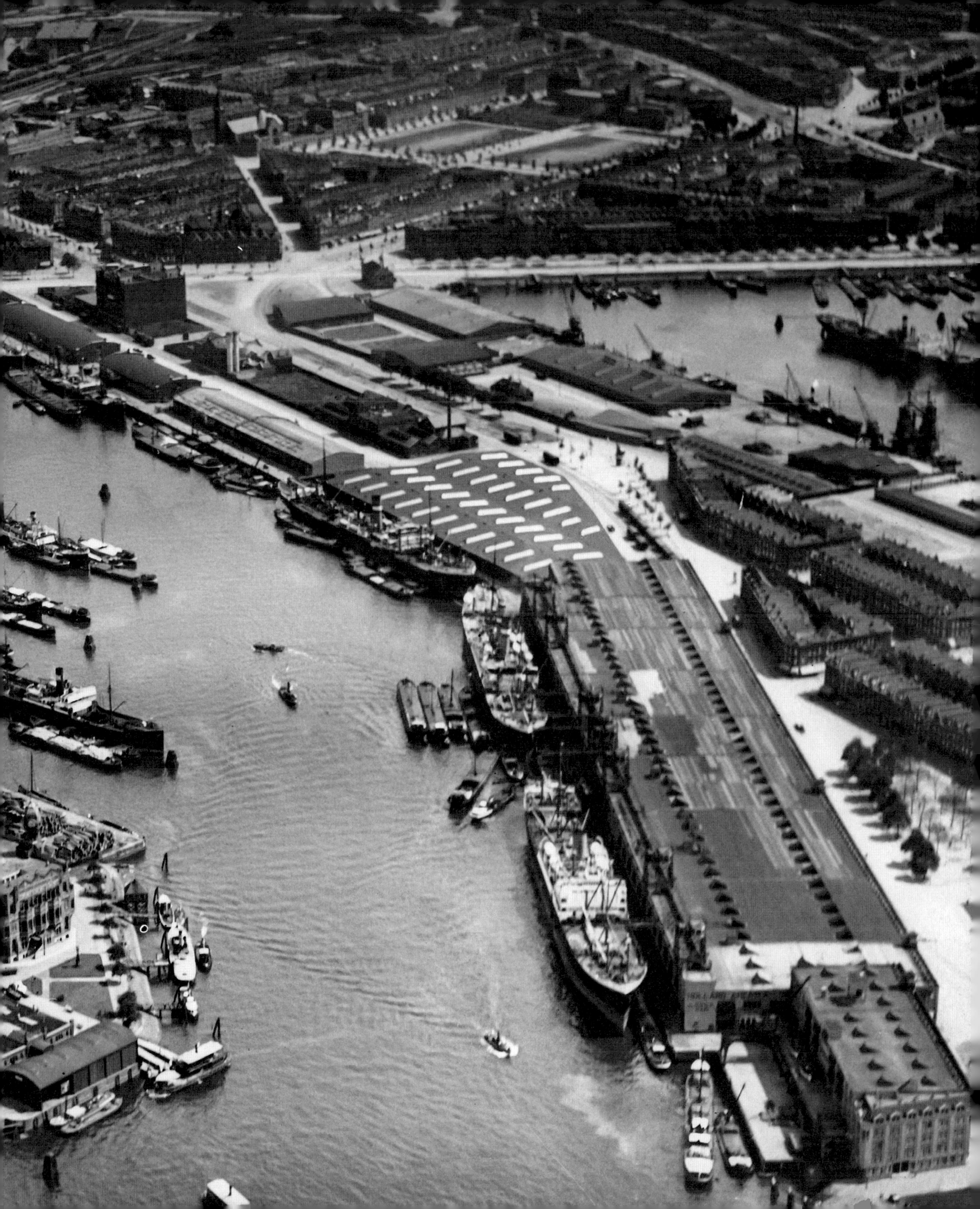

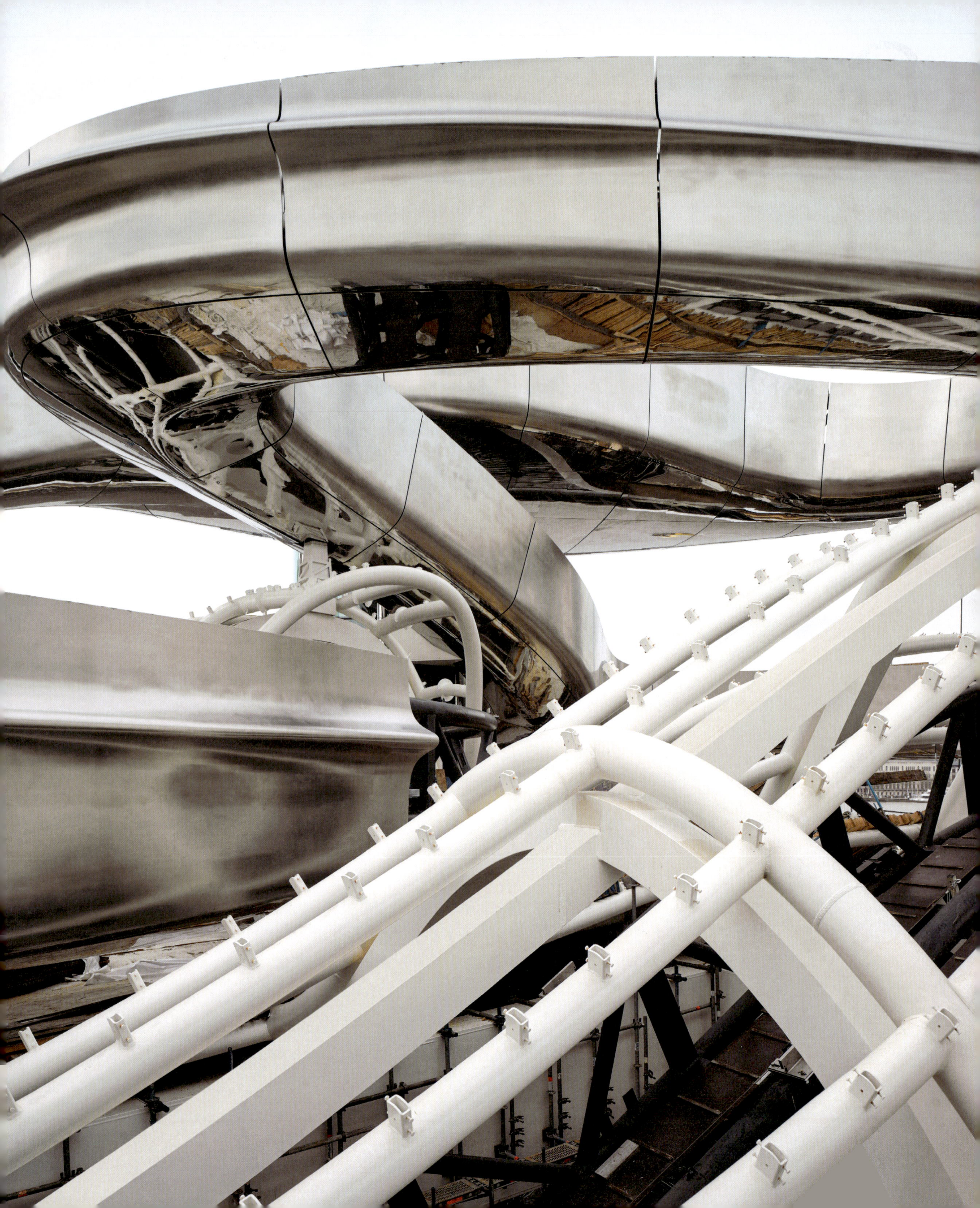

Contents

Foreword

Anne Kremers
Director of Fenix

On top of the Tornado observation platform, you have a 360-degree view over the city of Rotterdam. The largest port city in Europe and home to Rotterdammers with over 170 different nationalities. From above, you can see how the city was formed on the quays around Fenix. The lives of millions of people changed here. Some departed to the United States and Canada, others arrived from China, Cape Verde or Greece. Here, at the place of departure and arrival, Fenix opened its doors – the new international art museum devoted to the theme of migration.

In 1923, the Holland America Line built big on Katendrecht: a two-storey warehouse of 360 metres with a total surface space of 43,200 square metres. The largest of its kind. No one had ever built in concrete on such a scale. Designed by architect Cornelis Nicolaas van Goor, the new warehouse was named San Francisco. A marvel of technology and modernity: eight massive rooftop cranes on rails, huge drawbridge doors for loading on the waterfront and twelve indoor cargo lifts. Along the side of the warehouse trains crossed Katendrecht, connecting directly to Rotterdam's harbour railway, continuing to Breda, south to Germany's Ruhr Valley and the rest of Europe. Goods came and went from around the world: Washington apples from the United States, tinned salmon from Vancouver, cacao from South America and hemp and cotton from Asia. In 1944, the German occupiers blew up the quayside, causing part of the warehouse to collapse, and in 1948 a massive fire destroyed the central section. Two years later the warehouse emerged from the ashes, divided into two separate buildings: Fenix Warehouse I and Fenix Warehouse II.

Fenix is a place of departure. Here, by the river, millions of people began their journey to the other side of the world. Leaving the old, seeking the new, hoping to make a fresh start: a place of love and goodbyes. Early in the twentieth century, Uranium Steamship Company ships sailed from Maashaven, on one side of Fenix, carrying passengers from Eastern and Southern Europe. Thousands of impoverished migrants sailed to New York and Halifax. At the Brede Hilledijk, a huge hotel was built, providing space to 1,600 people. On the other side of Fenix, you look across the Wilhelminapier, also known as the Pier of Tears. From 1870 to 1960, the Holland America Line departed from here to the United States, Canada, Australia and New Zeeland. Millions said goodbye to their loved ones on that pier – most would never meet again.

Fenix is a place of arrival. It was on this quayside that many migrants first set foot on European soil. Some travelled on to other parts of the country or elsewhere in Europe. Others chose Katendrecht, “the Kaap”, as a new home. A cultural melting pot, an international neighbourhood. Chinese mariners stayed on to work for Rotterdam’s shipping companies, raising families and opening restaurants and stores: making Katendrecht the first Chinatown on the European mainland. During the war, Surinamese jazz musicians kept the Kaap’s underground nightlife buzzing. Later, repatriated Dutch and Moluccans from the Dutch East Indies arrived, and Cape Verdeans who helped rebuild the city after the war. Katendrecht and the rest of the city became a new home for many. In 2018, Droom en Daad acquired Fenix Warehouse II to transform it into a cultural venue. The warehouse was restored based on research and designs by Bureau Polderman. China’s MAD added the iconic Tornado designed by Ma Yansong. The Tornado is a double-helix staircase, artwork and experience in one. Fenix is the first museum in Europe designed by a Chinese architectural firm. This book shows the transformation of Fenix Warehouse II. Rubén Dario Kleimeer followed and photographed the construction work closely for five years. Iwan Baan took photos of the finished building.

Fenix opened in the spring of 2025. The new museum explores the theme of migration through the lens of art. The opening exhibition on the first floor, *All Directions*, features 150 artworks and objects drawn from the Fenix collection. This exhibition includes work by, among others, Steve McQueen, Rineke Dijkstra, Omar Victor Diop, Shilpa Gupta, Chiharu Shiota, and Danh Võ. The exhibition entitled *The Family of Migrants* on the ground floor of Fenix is inspired by Edward Steichen’s 1955 *The Family of Man*. *The Family of Migrants* shows striking photography on the topic of migration. The third exhibition, *The Suitcase Labyrinth*, is a monumental installation made of 2,000 donated suitcases representing countries, cultures, and communities from around the world. It is a labyrinth-like, immersive installation that visitors will encounter on the ground floor of Fenix. Then, a vast area of the ground floor of the museum represents Plein, a covered city square. It provides a space for cultural, culinary and creative encounters, with programming shaped by the communities in Rotterdam.

The architecture, artworks and objects in our museum demonstrate that migration is universal and timeless. They show how themes such as love, goodbyes, home, and happiness are connected to it. Fenix tells stories from yesterday, today and tomorrow – stories that cross borders. Art has the ability to go beyond politics and statistics to express ideas and emotions that engage the imagination.

Architects, Patrons And Directors

Wim Pijbes
Director of Droom en Daad

"Later that evening, before dinner, I ventured: So, what do you think? That's when he formulated his idea, almost as a statement: Fenix is all about movement. With this bold one-liner we immediately knew that Ma was our man."

Before starting to build a museum, it's always better first to build a good relationship between the client and the architect. Because when a visionary patron approaches the architect of their choice with a well-defined concept, things can move fast. London's Dulwich Picture Gallery, for instance. Over two centuries ago, art dealer Sir Francis Bourgeois set aside £2,000 and commissioned his friend, the prominent architect Sir John Soane, to create a permanent home for his collection – one of the first purpose-built art galleries. Complying with his friend's wishes, on 8 January 1811, a day after Bourgeois' death, Soane visits Dulwich. Only four months later, on 16 May, the architect submits his drafts, perspectives, and watercolours to the trustees of Dulwich College, showing the new building set in the landscape. In their subsequent approval on 12 July, they instruct the architect emphatically: "If possible, to carry such a plan into execution immediately". The first foundations are laid on 19 October, and Dulwich Picture Gallery opens in 1817, still one of the finest examples of gallery architecture ever built. In form, execution, and above all in its genesis, Dulwich is exemplary.

Not that progress is always this smooth, on the contrary. Most museums emerge between dream and reality. Many arise from an agonising mix of towering ambition and restrictive budgets, unrealised expectations, overspending, and deferred delivery-dates. More often than not, the architect is absent at the official festive opening of their own building. At the launch of Amsterdam's Stedelijk Museum on Saturday, 14 September 1895, one of the speakers complained that the museum had been completed "slowly, very slowly, far too slowly, I might almost add". Architect A.W. Weissman did not attend the festivities. Conclusion: even in a project enlivened by hope, kickstarted with a generous gift or legacy, things can easily go wrong. Building a museum often means that the preparations may take forever, years may pass before anyone picks up a spade, disputes may delay the construction work, resources may dry up, an economic crisis may erupt, or even a war.

A contemporary of the aforementioned Soane, Prussian architect K.F. Schinkel employed that evergreen of architectural styles, the Greek classical order, for his Altes Museum in Berlin's Museumsinsel. His confident Greek Revival design put art on a pedestal in well-lit, clear-cut galleries where visitors pass easily along a well-ordered art-historical presentation. A succession of museums followed, each with its signal Neoclassical façade, a prominent temple to the arts in the heart of the city. Schinkel's architectural programme, stately and static, would remain unchallenged for a century. All over Europe, and what was then referred to as the New World, almost identical buildings arose in Greek Revival style designed to meet their specific expectations. Comprehensible for both public, patron and architect. The role of the museum director was then still confined to the care of the collection, not the supervision of the construction process. That occurred later, when a new generation of museums emerged in the twentieth century in which it was no longer art but the general public that dominated. Willem Sandberg wanted the opposite of Schinkel and formulated his optimistic post-war vision powerfully in the 1950s:

> We want a setting
> in which the avant-garde can feel at home
> clear
> on a human scale
> no grand halls stately stairways skylights
> doors like gates uniformed attendants
> but an architecture in which people dare to talk,
> to kiss, to laugh out loud
> to be themselves
> a focus for life today.

Outspoken personalities such as Willem Sandberg, Thomas Hoving and Pontus Hultén opened their museum doors to an ever-wider audience. Hoving was the first to defile the museum space by displaying giant banners across the monumental Fifth Avenue façade of the Metropolitan and expanding the ponderous edifice with the addition of a car park. Hultén was one of the initiators of the radical accessible Centre Pompidou. Emphatically not a museum, but a centre, an elastic and open space, hosting a plethora of activities within its walls: lectures, film series, concerts, and debates. The era in which museums were the privileged preserve of white people, drinking white wine, between white walls had gone for good. With the advent of events, temporary exhibitions, and expanding audiences, the traditional definition of a museum as a home for a collection no longer sufficed. Growing demands of security, climate control, logistics, and sustainability made the requirements for a museum increasingly complex. Approachable and transparent, yet also burglar-proof and energy-efficient. Preferably iconic and distinguished, but still open to all. And if possible, within budget. All this turned commissions for new museum buildings into a miscellany of contradictions. What's a camel? A horse designed by a committee. And here comes the crucial question: how to find the right architect. Fortunately, there are plenty of good architects on all continents. They are a respectable, academically trained profession with a strong tradition. But what about the clients? There's no training for commissioning work, let alone a new museum, which makes it something of a miracle anytime a new museum emerges as a successful building.

When it comes to Fenix, the stars seemed to align. After a visit to the rundown warehouse with colleague Laura Dufour in early 2017, we saw that the building was ideally suited for a public function. With its historic location on the waterfront – the so-called Pier of Tears where millions had set foot and millions had set sail – the idea of a museum about migration began to form. Our scope soon widened: the history of migrants expanded to include migration as a universal, timeless theme. First, we came to the conclusion that in the direct neighbourhood as well as museum projects in Rotterdam, the fine fleur of Dutch architects had already realised enough projects. Our scope could be broader. And so our search started. By chance, a family member suggested: "Did you read about the new opera house at Harbin in China?" This building by MAD seemed promising, and surely capable of tempering Rotterdam's hard, angular skyline with subtle, organic forms. And a new flavour in the Dutch architectural landscape at the same time.

In June 2018, I spoke at a symposium in Berlin in memory of the late museum director Martin Roth, and architect Ma Yansong spoke there too. We discussed the idea of building a museum in the Netherlands, and so I invited him to come to Rotterdam. When we visited the warehouse, Ma took a lot of photographs but remained rather quiet. Later that evening, before dinner, I ventured: “So, what do you think?” That’s when he formulated his idea, almost as a statement: “Fenix is all about movement”. With this bold one-liner, we immediately knew that Ma was our man. Sometime later, we went to Paris to view a residential building, the first project MAD had delivered outside China. Here, Ma offered us his initial draft for Fenix, which we immediately accepted. Our requirements had been simple: an observation platform looking out over the river, restoration of the warehouse and a central entrance. Ma Yansong and MAD created the Tornado. As I later learned, Fenix is the first museum in Europe to be designed by a Chinese architectural firm. A fact that connects neatly with the site’s history. Here, along the constantly flowing waters of the river Maas, the former Chinatown on Katendrecht, the oldest in continental Europe, Ma Yansong’s double helix is a shining beacon of hope and progress, and above all, an ode to eternal movement.

Haven From The Storm

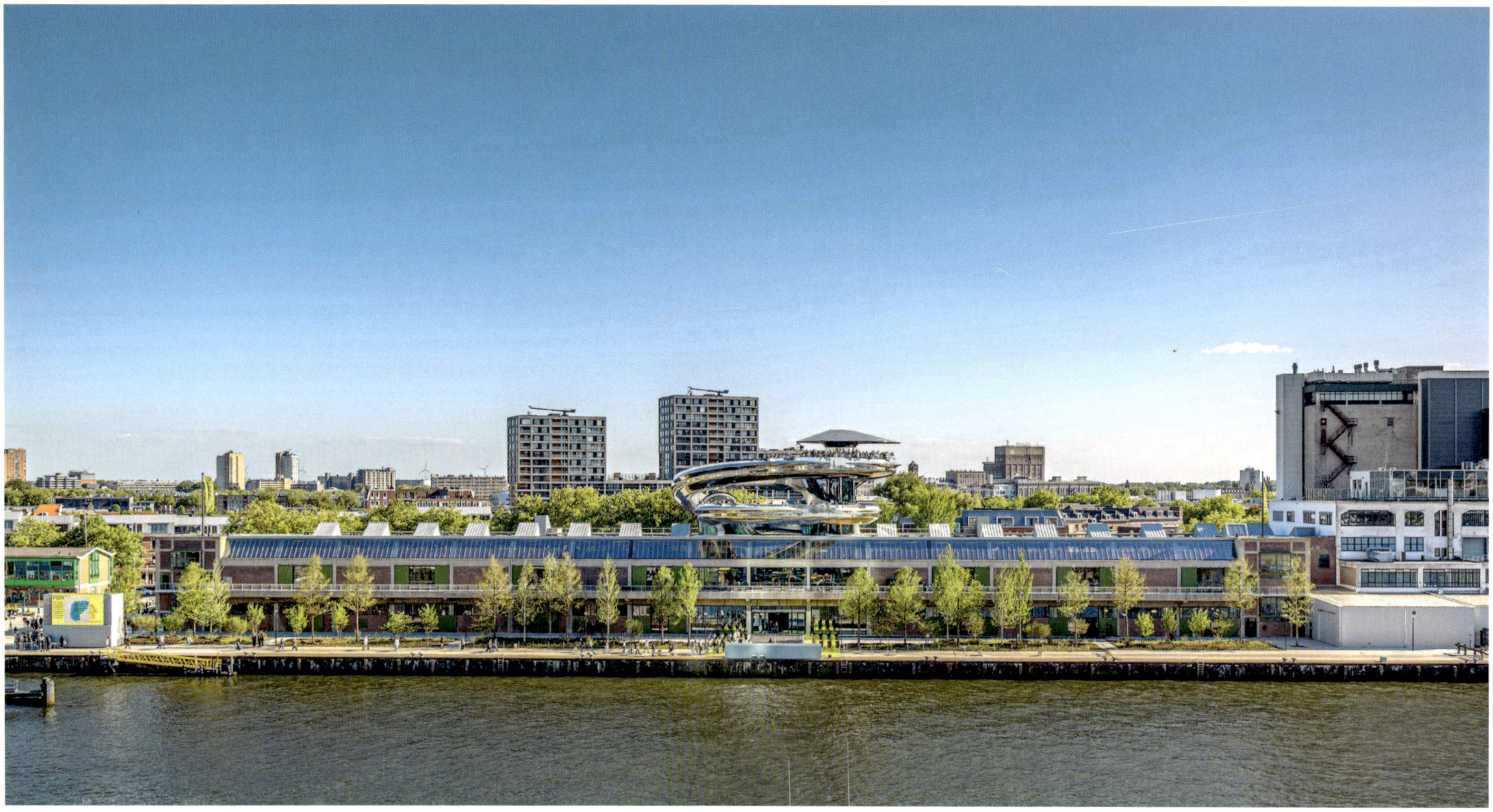

Fenix during the opening of the museum on 15 May, 2025

András Szántó
Author and Cultural Strategy Advisor

A Museum As Metaphor

Nothing prepares you for the view from Fenix, a new Rotterdam institution dedicated to telling stories about migration from around the world. You arrive on the upper deck of the muscular concrete building – a 1923 warehouse for storing grain and steel, once the largest structure of its kind in the world – via a poetic piece of architecture. It is Ma Yansong's metallic Tornado – functionally speaking, a central staircase. Having snaked through the museum, its metallic whoosh pierces the roof and morphs into an observation tower.

Then your eyes settle on that view. The museum looks down across a narrow body of water at the former headquarters of the Holland America Line, a company founded in 1873 to ship people and goods between the Netherlands and the United States. The Art Nouveau structure now houses a hotel named after the city I call home, New York. This is hallowed ground. It was from here that hundreds of thousands of migrants and refugees – including some of Europe's foremost artists and intellectuals fleeing Nazi persecution – boarded cruise liners in search of a new life.

I live on the other end of the line. On a clear day, I can spot the Statue of Liberty from the roof of my Brooklyn apartment building. And I, too, have crossed the Atlantic, albeit in search of opportunity, not to evade looming genocide.

Fenix, aptly named, has breathed new life into old infrastructure. It is a site of reinventions – from repurposing Rotterdam's hardscrabble maritime docklands to rethinking what a museum can be, especially in this precarious moment when history again seems to be churning furiously.

A signal achievement of modern life, the museum has always been a work in progress. And it has proven itself resilient in the face of historical vicissitudes. It has outlasted wars and plagues, economic meltdowns, shifting lifestyles and the disruptions of new technologies. Decade after decade, museums absorbed new ideas, invented new approaches to storytelling, harnessed new mediums, offered new platforms to exercise our citizenship and conviviality. And so it is with Fenix. This institution is adding surprising pieces to the jigsaw puzzle of the museum. In some respects, it may set a new standard.

Let's start with the typology. A museum, telling migration stories through art. The closest analogy I can think of is a similarly cavernous former warehouse in Buenos Aires. Once the world's leading destination for inbound migration, Argentina opened its arms to multitudes of Europeans in the 19th and 20th centuries, including, I suspect, many who set sail from Rotterdam. That cavernous warehouse was transformed into The Museo de la Inmigración, which, much like Fenix, deploys art as a means to convey the meaning of leaving behind where you came from.

Smaller and larger objects of historic and personal significance can be found there, side-by-side with the reflections of artists – a powerful combination. Fenix takes this approach further. As far as I know, it is the first museum to engage with migration primarily through the lens of art. It is assembling a collection of artworks, both old and new, by renowned and emerging artists, to deepen our understanding of its vexing subject.

Migration and displacement have accompanied human affairs throughout much of history, leaving behind a residue of wars, famines, pandemics, economic reconfigurations, and lately an alarmingly shifting climate. Migration is only bound to accelerate in our interconnected world. What Fenix proposes as a means to reflect on this complex social and cultural phenomenon is a hybrid: part history museum, part art museum – and arguably neither. It is a museum with a mission to share a message that demands our attention, and to do it with curiosity, creativity and empathy. If modern life gave us ever more specialised, narrowly focused institutions, we now find opportunity in institutional alloys and amalgamations. There is strength in mixing typologies. Combining different types of museum-making allows for a certain freedom, a permission to experiment that may not be available in more pure expressions of the institutional form.

Clearly, Fenix points beyond the practices of art museums, which emphasise aesthetic contemplation and learning for their own sake. An activist impulse animates it, a desire to put the museum in the service of improving deeply ingrained social attitudes. Because when it comes to migration, ignorance, prejudice, resentment and outright hatred all too often poison the public imagination. When asked what Fenix is trying to do, Anne Kremers, the museum's inaugural director, answered, "Art can create bridges between different opinions and between different views on the world; it can create bridges between people. In a polarised world, that is what we need". This desire to build connections between people of different origins and mindsets is also of great significance for the port city of Rotterdam, a melting pot of some 170 nationalities.

Social impact, in short, is not a by-product of Fenix. It is the main aim. This mission to bring people together, to foster acceptance and understanding, seeps into the museum's collections, exhibitions and programmes. It is why this museum – which could use all the fancy technology now available to buttress its storytelling – has chosen instead to emphasise direct human interactions in its welcoming spaces, from its capacious exhibition halls to its Plein, a city square open to the public.

The desire to galvanise social cohesion has led Fenix to some innovative choices regarding its programming and operating methods. From the outset, it has engaged a group of

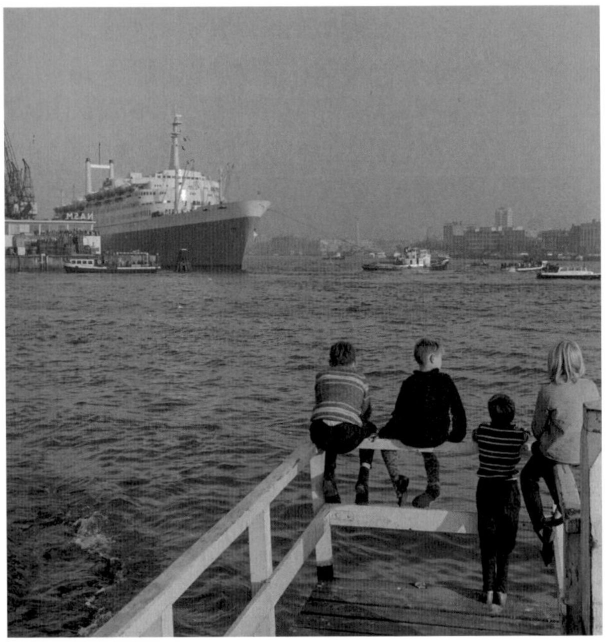

Children looking at the ss Rotterdam, moored at the head of Wilhelminakade, 1965. Collection Stadsarchief Rotterdam

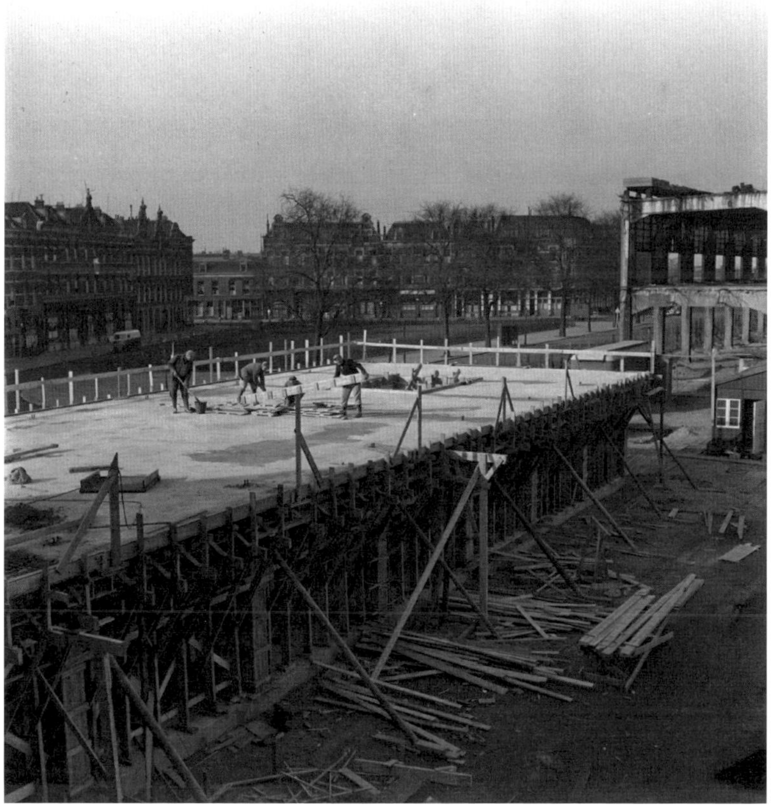

Construction on the square in between the warehouses, 1950. Collection Stadsarchief Rotterdam

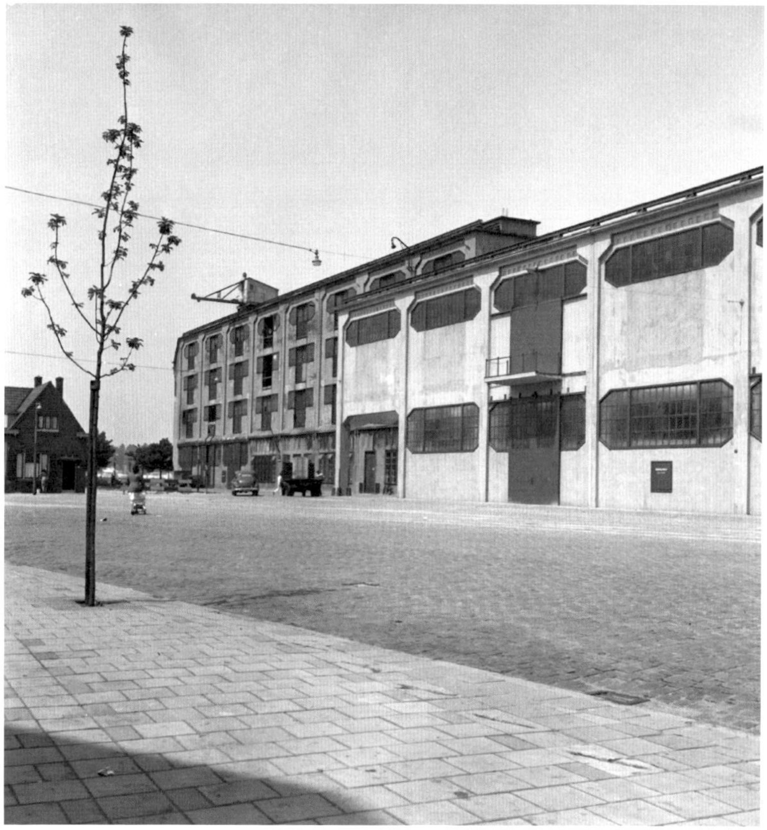

Fenix Warehouse II, 1951. Collection Stadsarchief Rotterdam

what it calls "Navigators" – eight individuals from different walks of life – to offer advice and share reflections about the museum. Incorporating their viewpoints is meant to help Fenix become a museum for everyone. Likewise, Fenix's first educational programme will not be modeled on conventional forms of museum-based learning. It will be a language programme, the first of its kind in Dutch museums, using the collection as a tool for improving language proficiency for non-Dutch speakers. Thus, the museum becomes a space for experimental and experiential learning, a pathway for connecting newcomers to the city, and ultimately a way to nurture the cultural competencies required for long-term integration into Dutch society.

Arguably the most poignant expression of Fenix's philosophy is captured in its architecture and how it apportions space inside the museum. Space is a precious resource in any institution. The way you use it reflects your priorities. At Fenix, the single largest space in the museum – and the one that will define the essence of this institution – is Plein, a vast central hall of some 2,000 square metres. It is nothing less than an extension of the city within the museum.

Plein is a dynamic forum, a covered town square, an urban nexus that reflects the open-minded, free-spirited ethos of

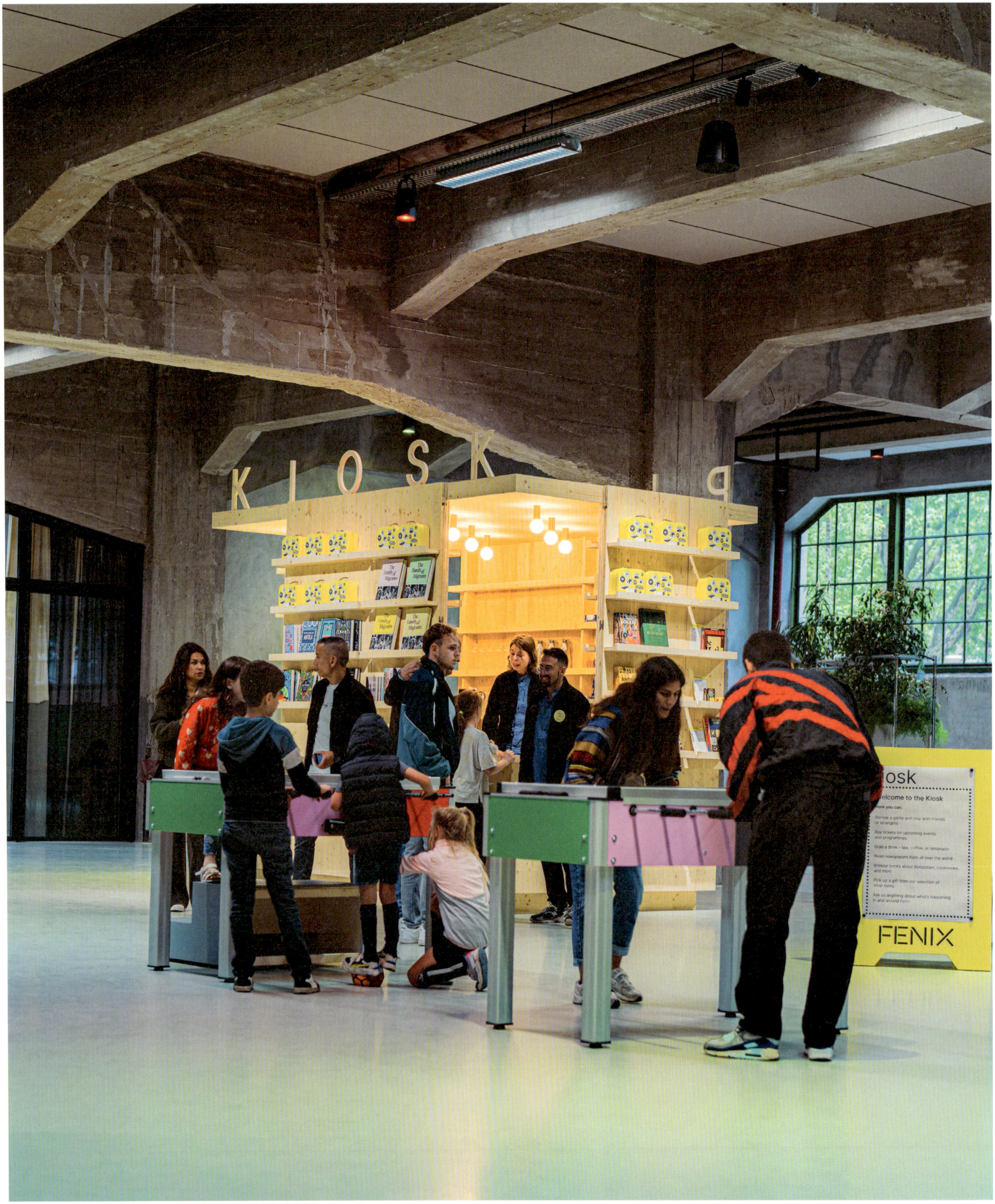
KIOSK
FENIX

Rotterdam. It invites people of all backgrounds and beliefs to spend time together, cooking, playing, relaxing, celebrating life – to not just passively receive but to co-create what it means to be inside a museum. Everyone is welcome here. There are no expectations around what people must do, other than be themselves. The atmosphere is casual. The space is open during daylight. It can be used for meetings, to set up performances in a small theater, to play board games, to work on a school assignment, or to change a baby's diapers. Like Fenix as a whole, this space caters to all kinds of cultural interests, fostering a sense of belonging. It is a staging ground for the most elusive of social rituals: participation in a community.

Plein is an embodiment of the driving intention of Fenix: a physical expression of its mission to celebrate, not to ostracize, different people. It gestures toward a more tolerant and inclusive society, where differences are accepted and embraced, where otherness is not a threat to be neutralised but a valuable resource to be cultivated.

The English word "haven", originating from northern Europe, is commonly used as a metaphor anchored in the image of the harbour. It denotes a place of safety, a refuge, where favourable conditions offer the visitor a measure of solace and security. Fenix, it should be clear by now, is likewise a metaphor. It is a paradigm of a welcoming urban space, and as such, a manifestation of the highest ideals of today's museology. It is, quite literally, a haven from the storm.

Plein in the evening

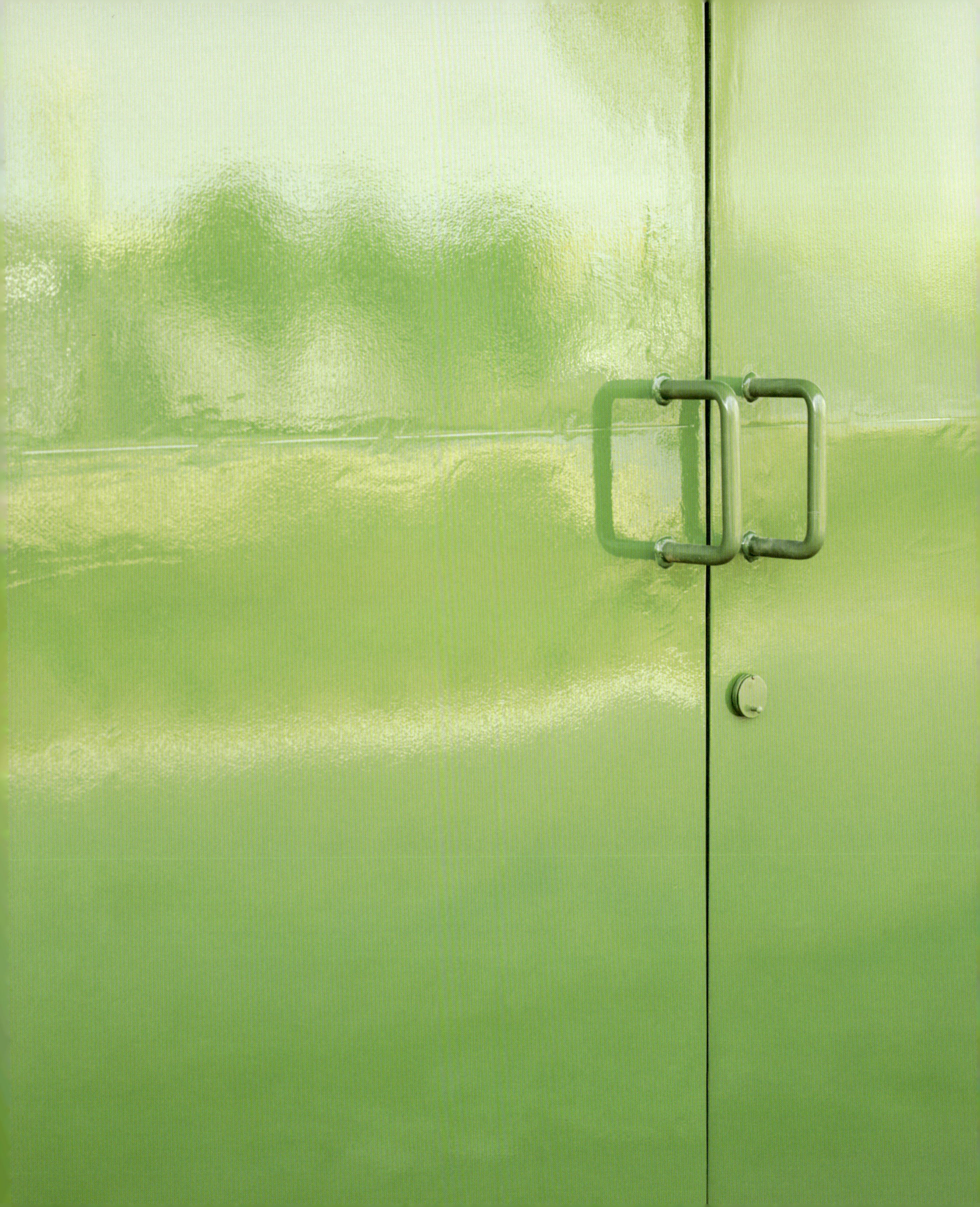

Warehouse

Restoration of the 172-metres-long façade of the former shipping and storage warehouse began in 2020 and took a year and a half to complete. Some architectural details date back to 1923 when the warehouse opened, while others were part of the 1948–1950 reconstruction plan. In the past sixty years, many additions have been made, and the building's function has changed many times. In 2020 the façade lacked uniformity. Fronts and frames were rusty. All elements along the façade have now been restored, refurbished, or rebuilt. The characteristic windows were restored to reflect the style of 1923. The 2,200 square metres expanse of the south façade was blast-cleaned, and cement stucco was reapplied by hand, showing visible strokes and crackling that reacts to changing weather. The distinctive sliding doors at street level have been restored to their post-war state, with doors and frames repainted in their original green colour. A choice made after a historic paint study, in which layers of paint were scraped off one by one. A rhythm of columns, windows, and fronts has emerged that emphasises the horizontal quality of the building. In the heart of the building, large glass windows were added on both sides, reconnecting the neighbourhood on the south side of the warehouse with the Maas River on the north side.

27

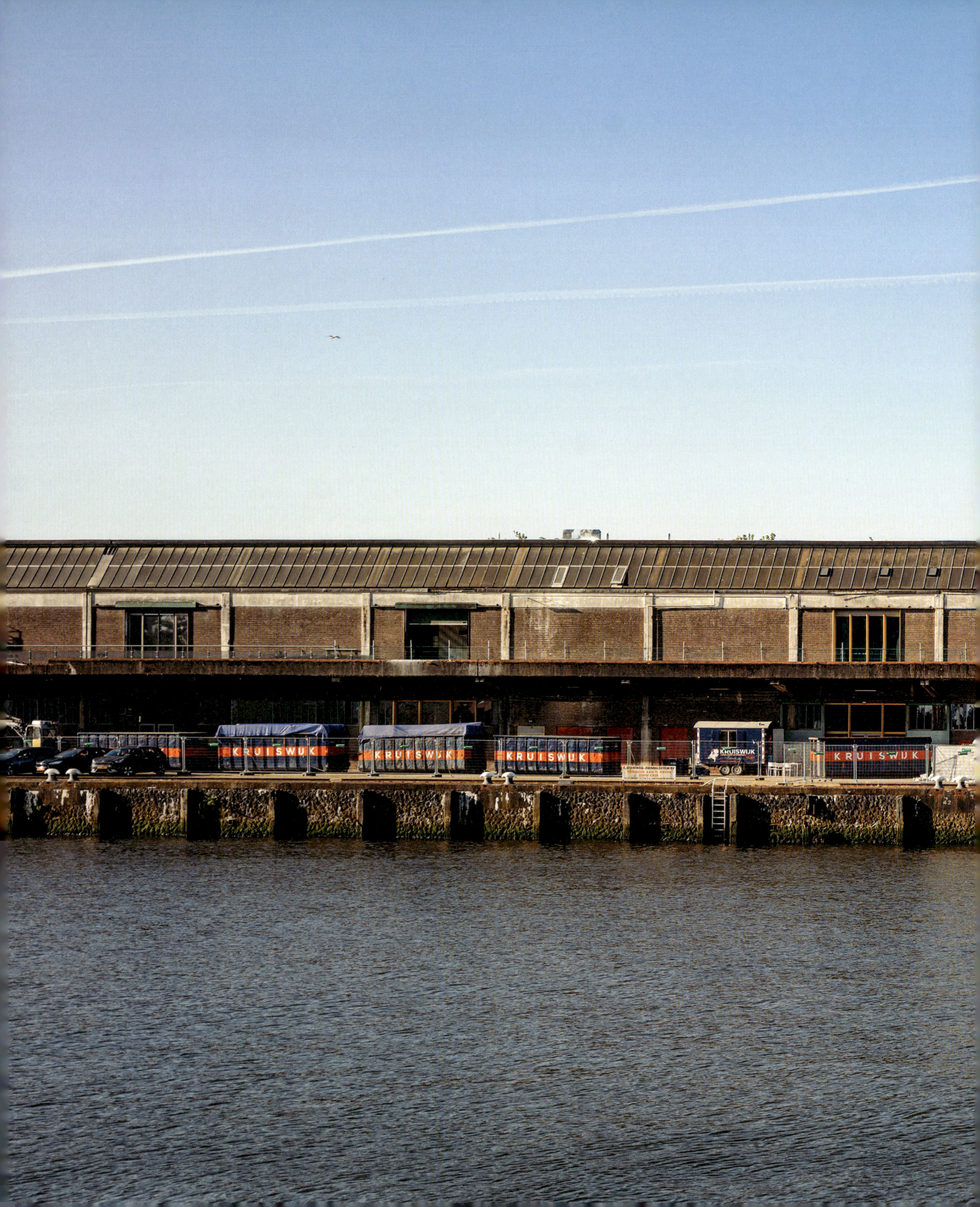
KRUISWIJK
KRUISWIJK
KRUISWIJK
KRUISWIJK
KRUISWIJK

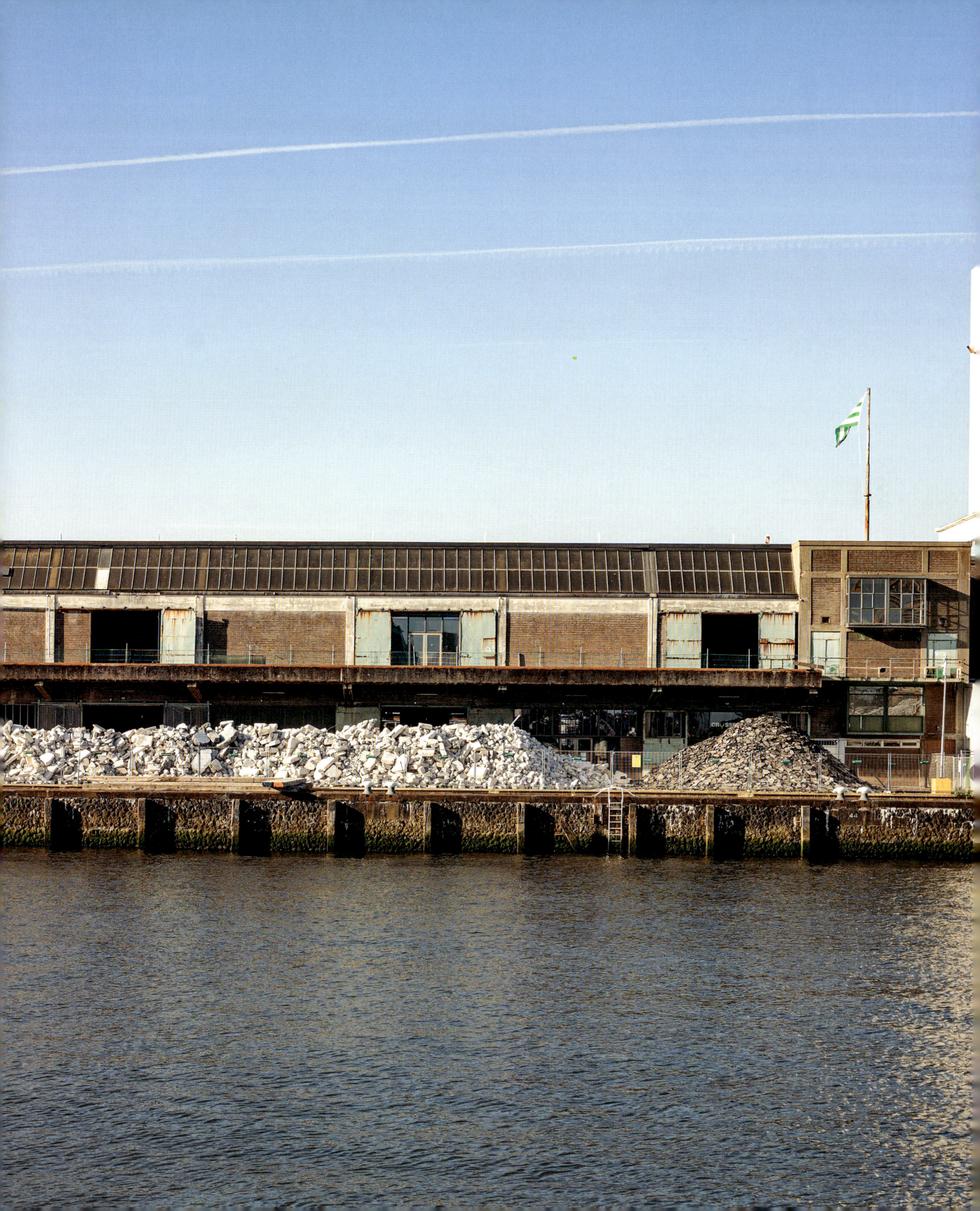

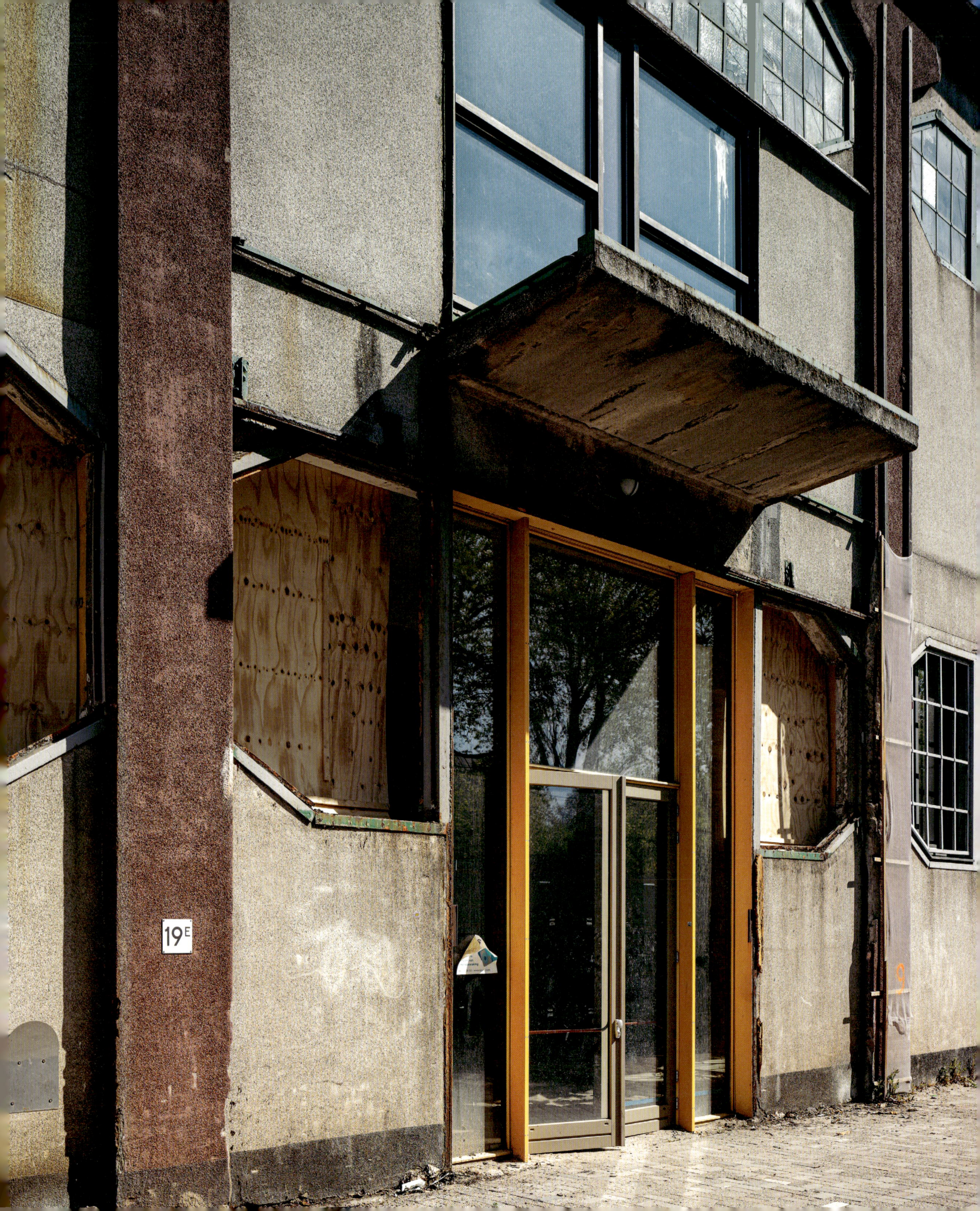
19E

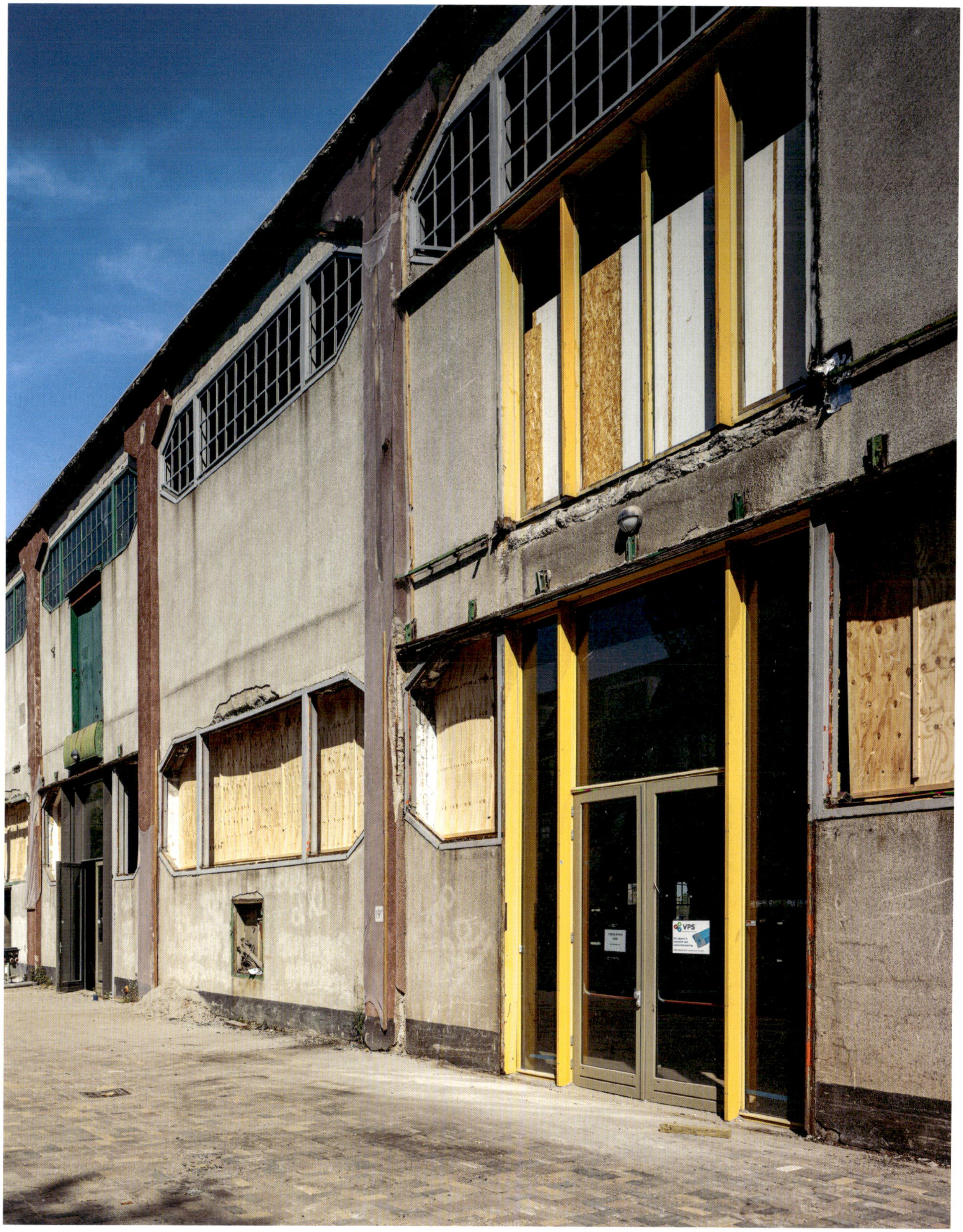

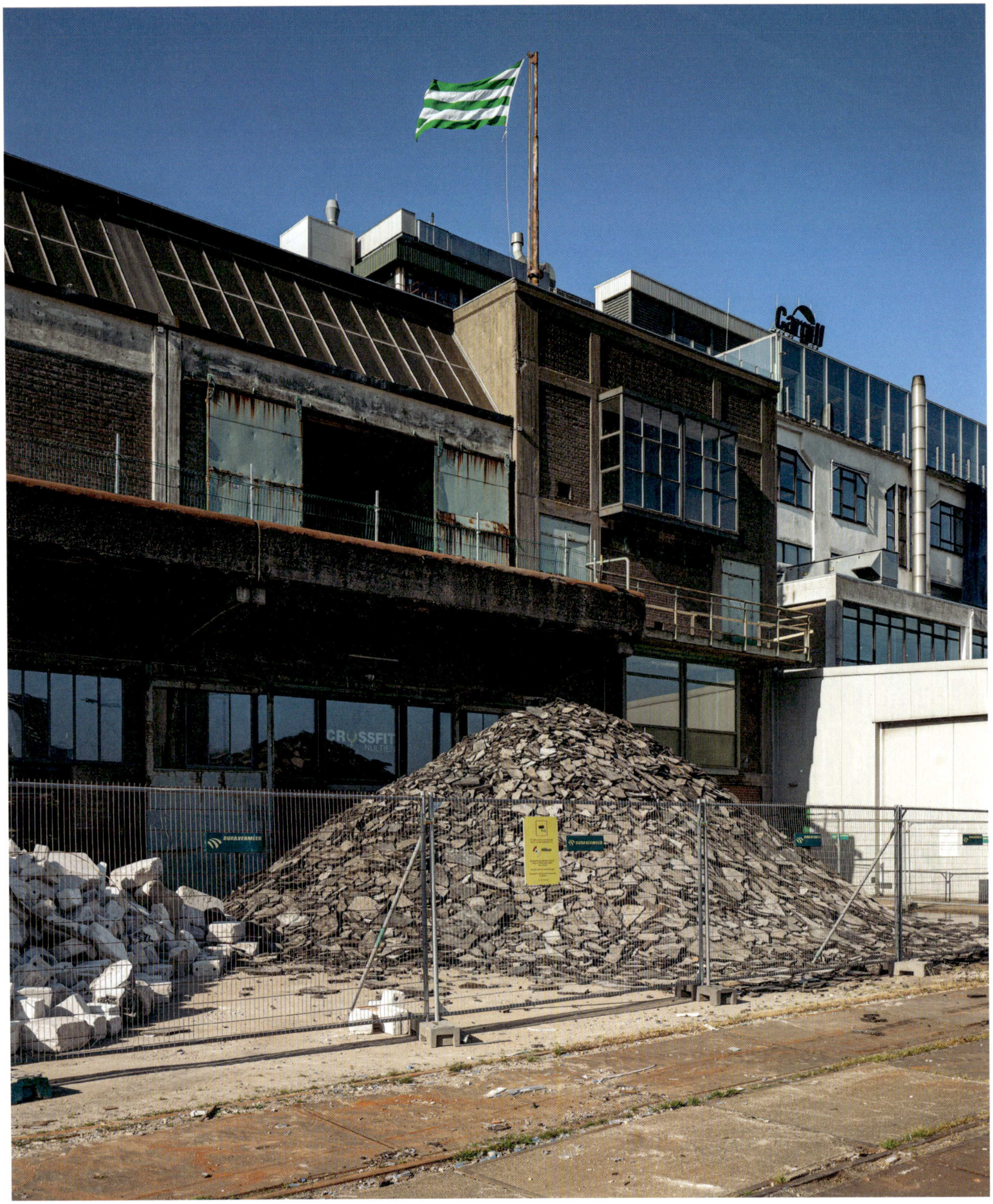
Cargill
CROSSFIT

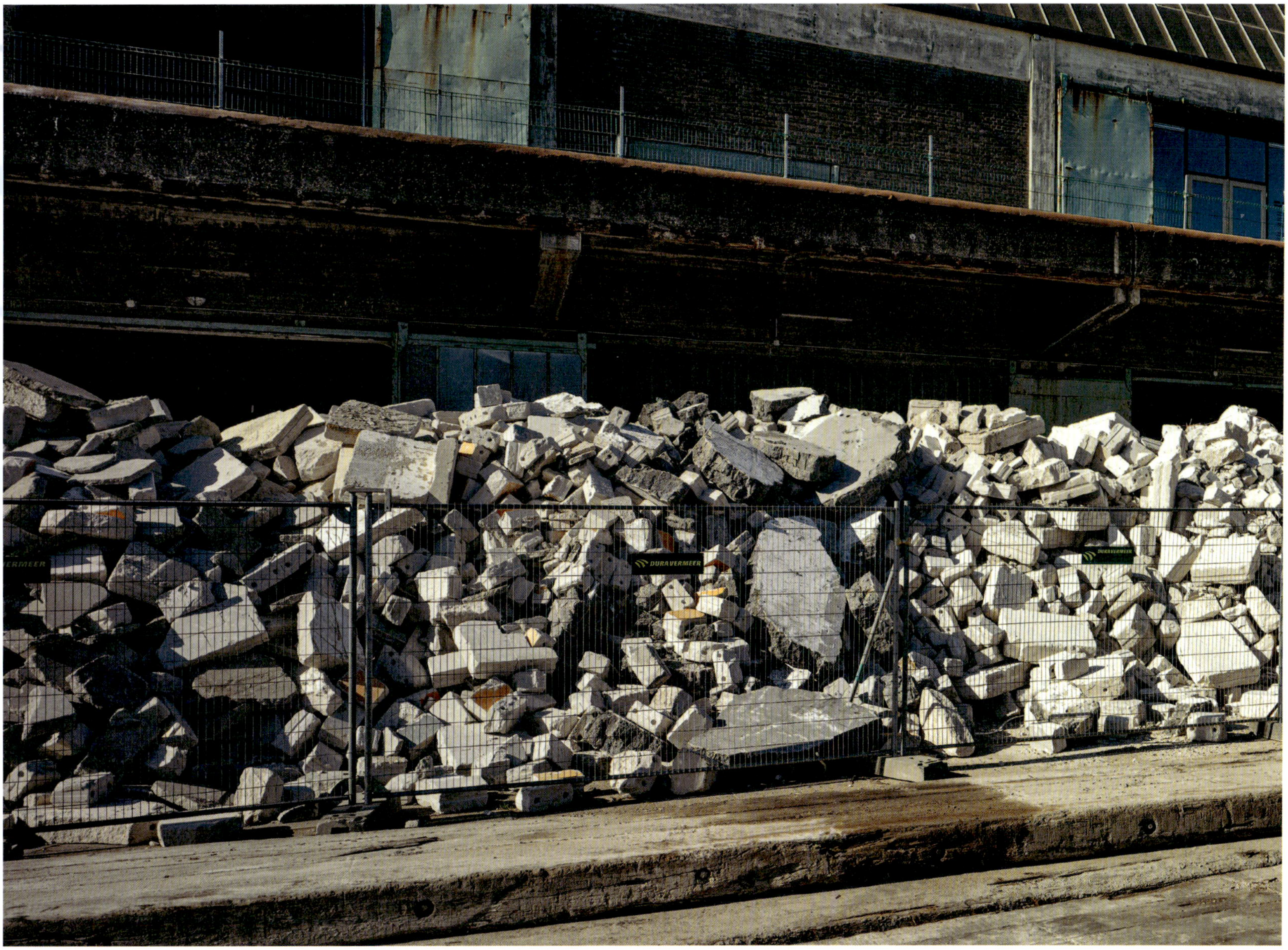
DURAVERMEER

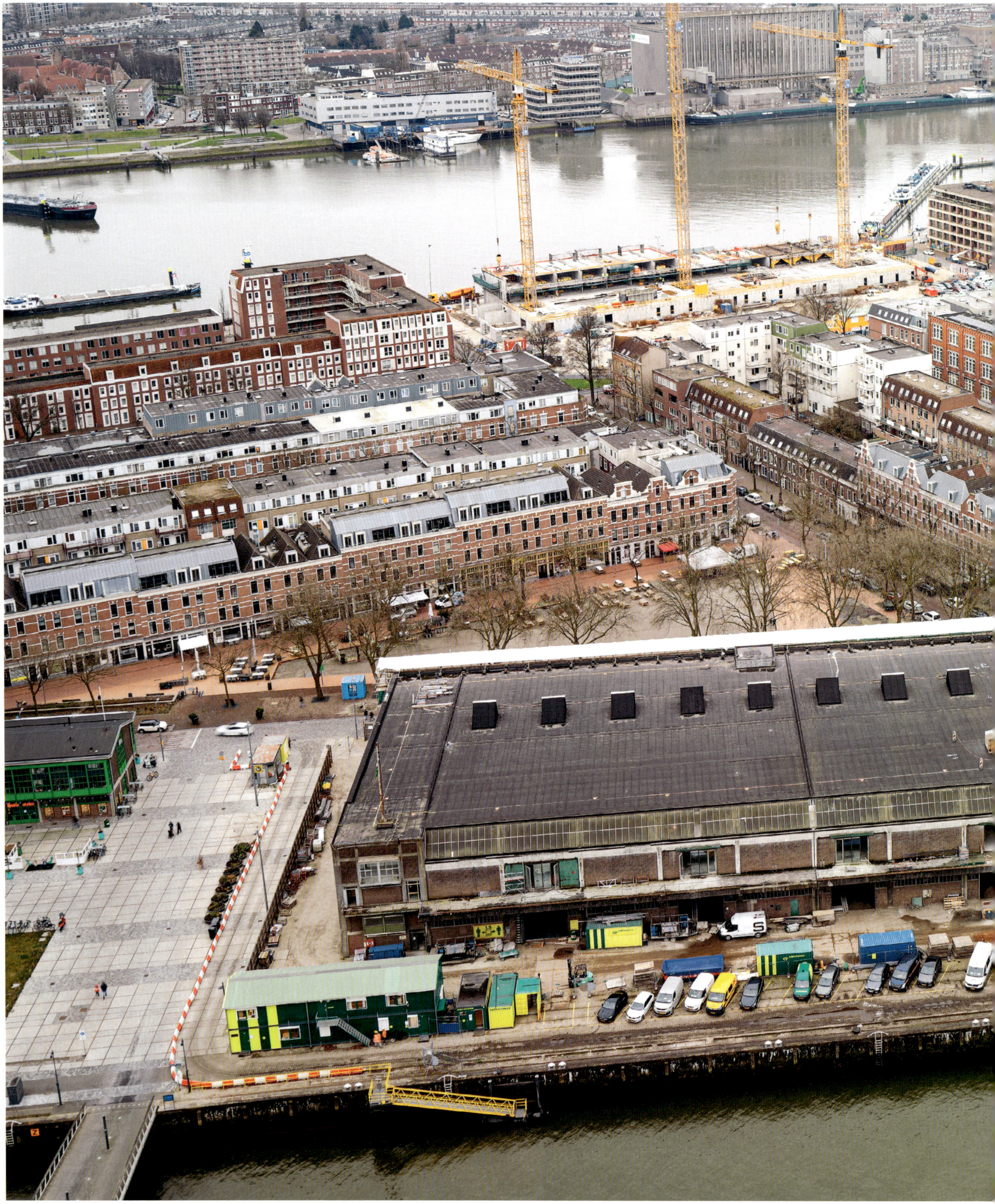

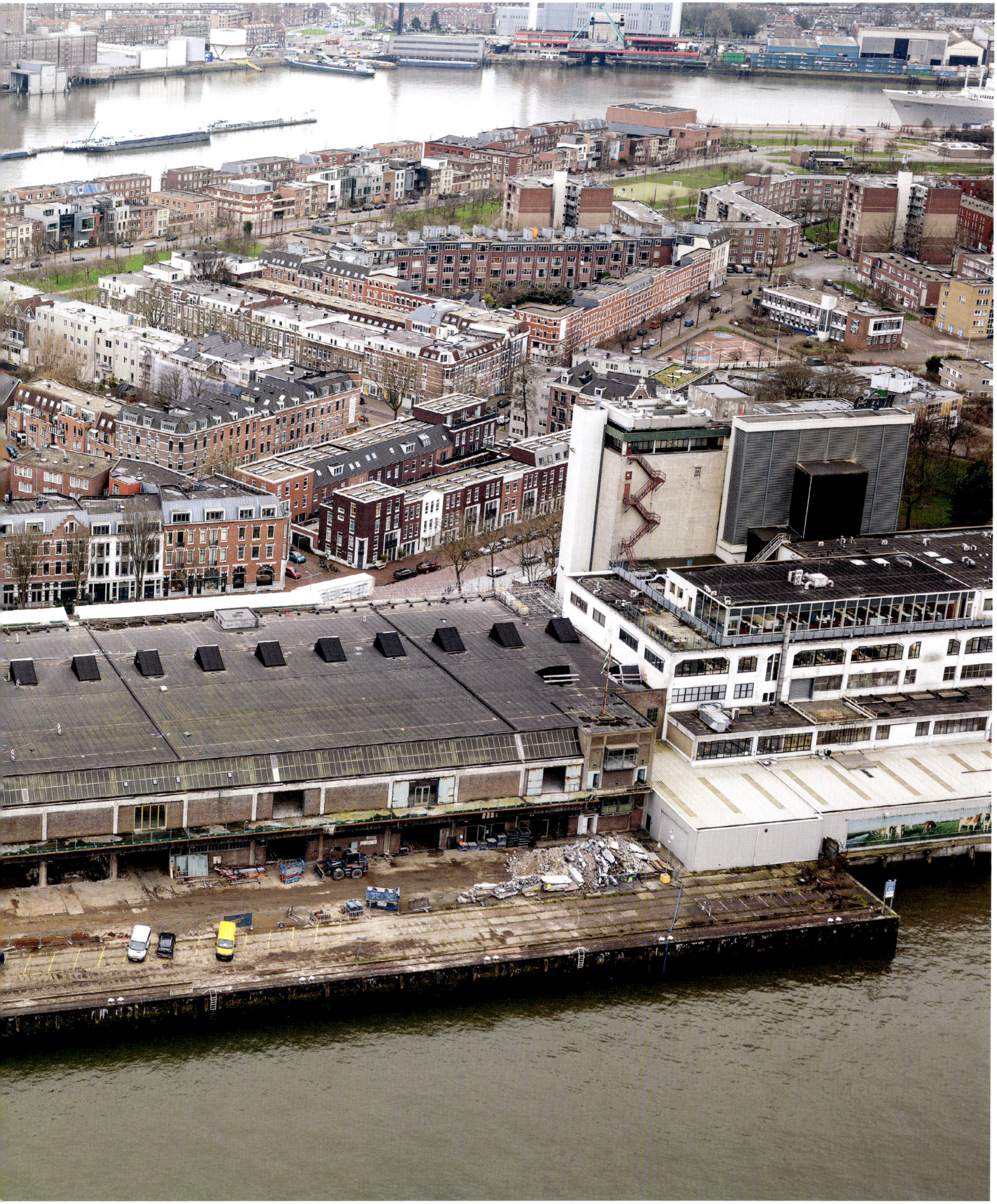

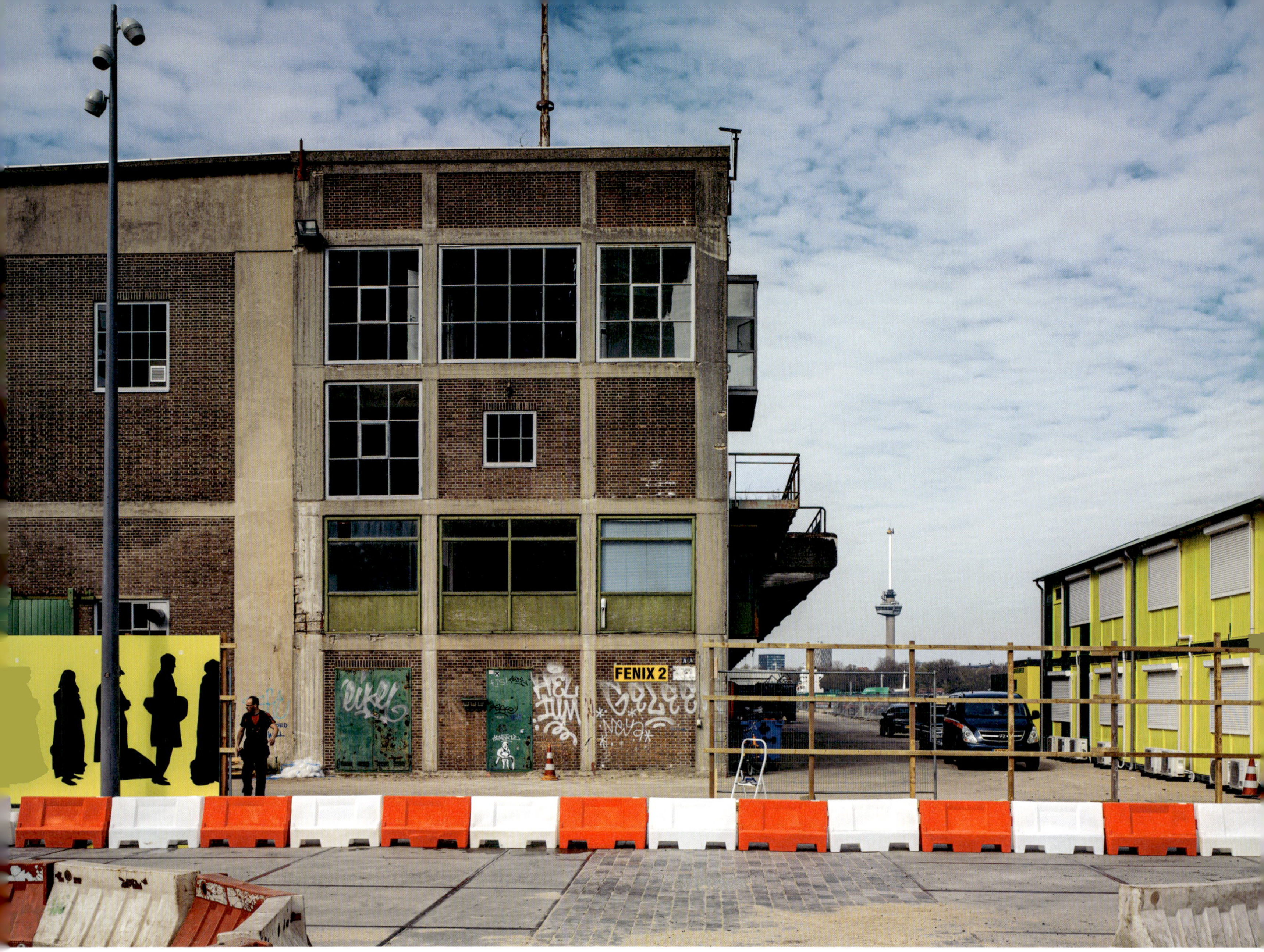
FENIX 2

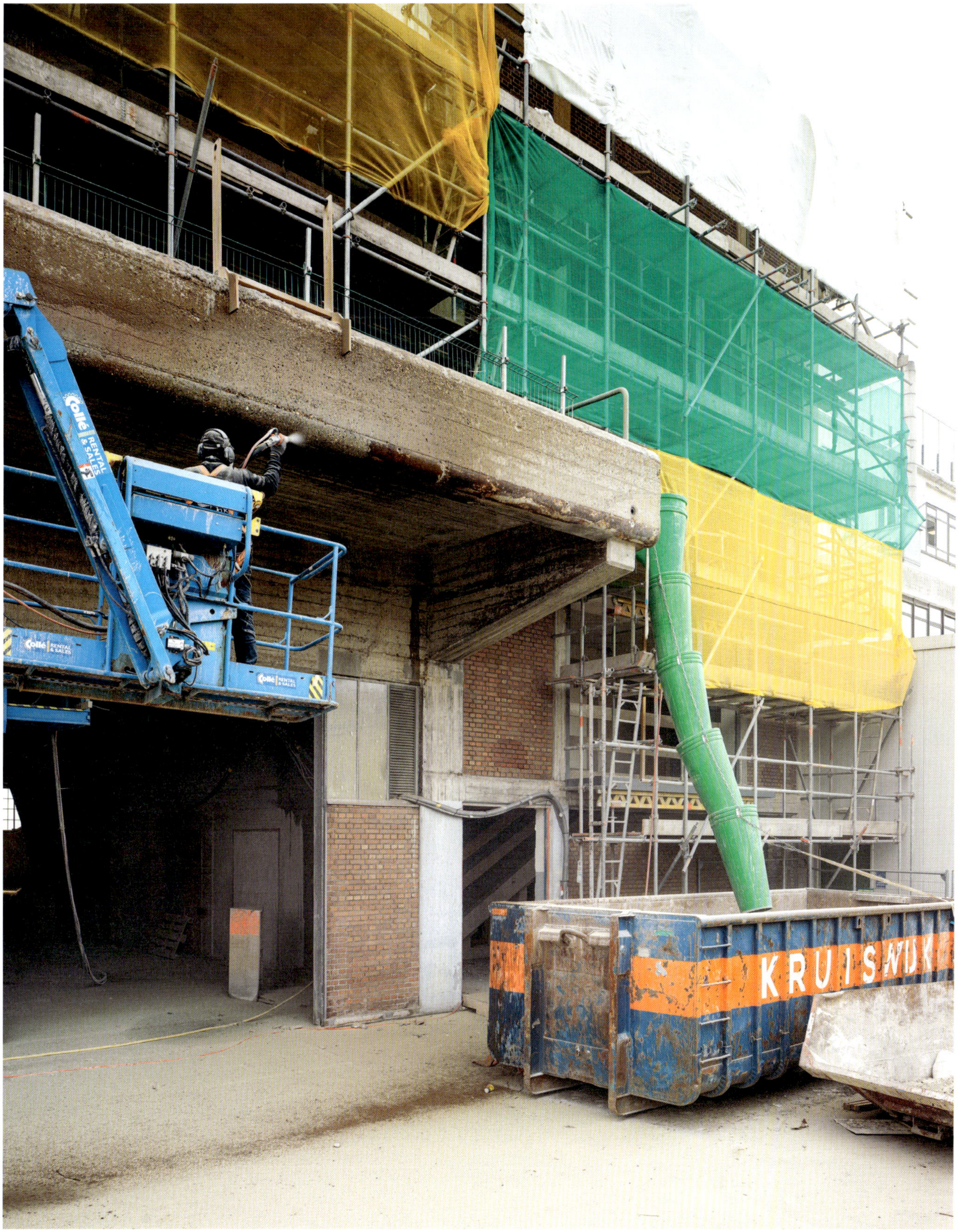
KRUISWIJK

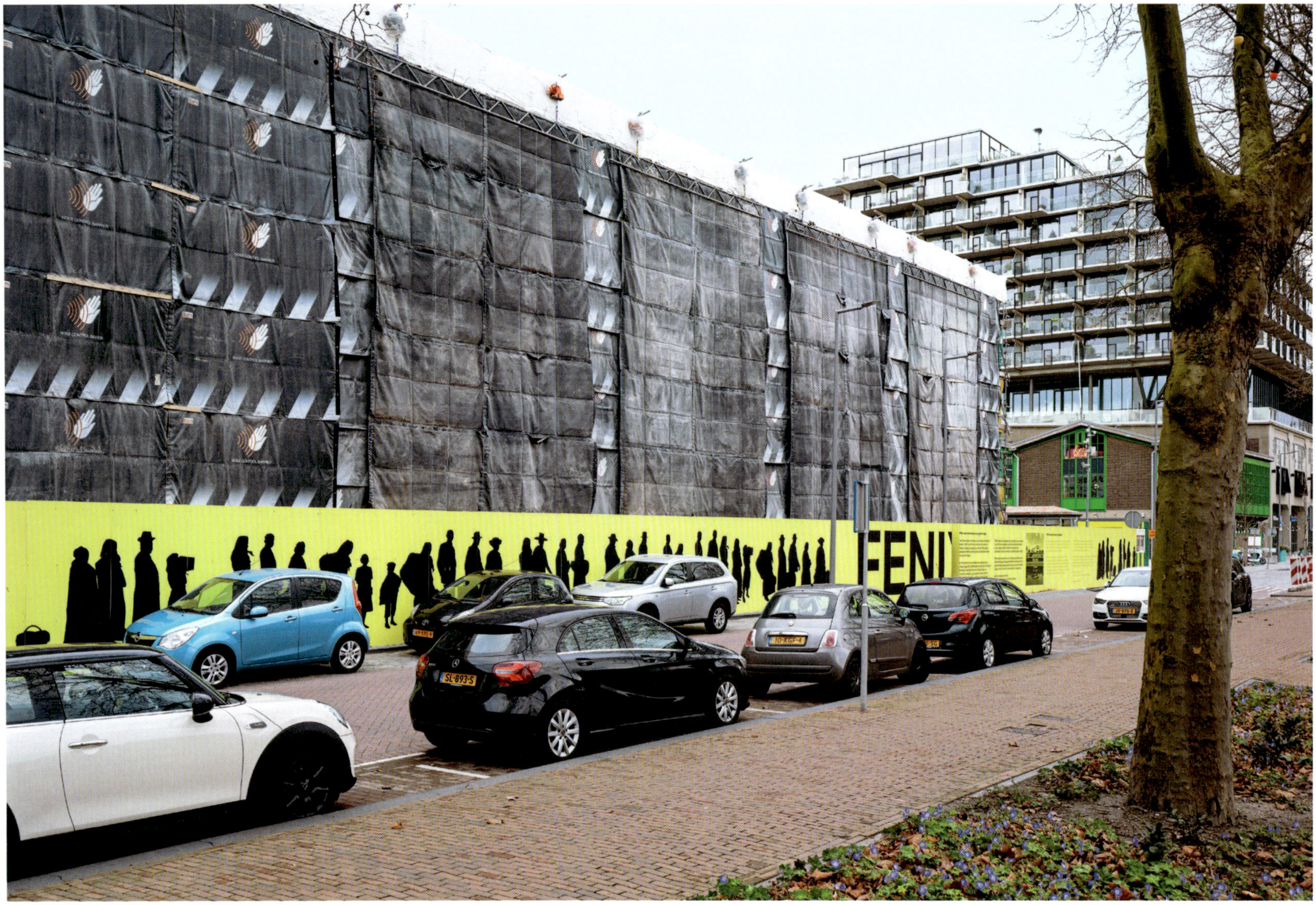

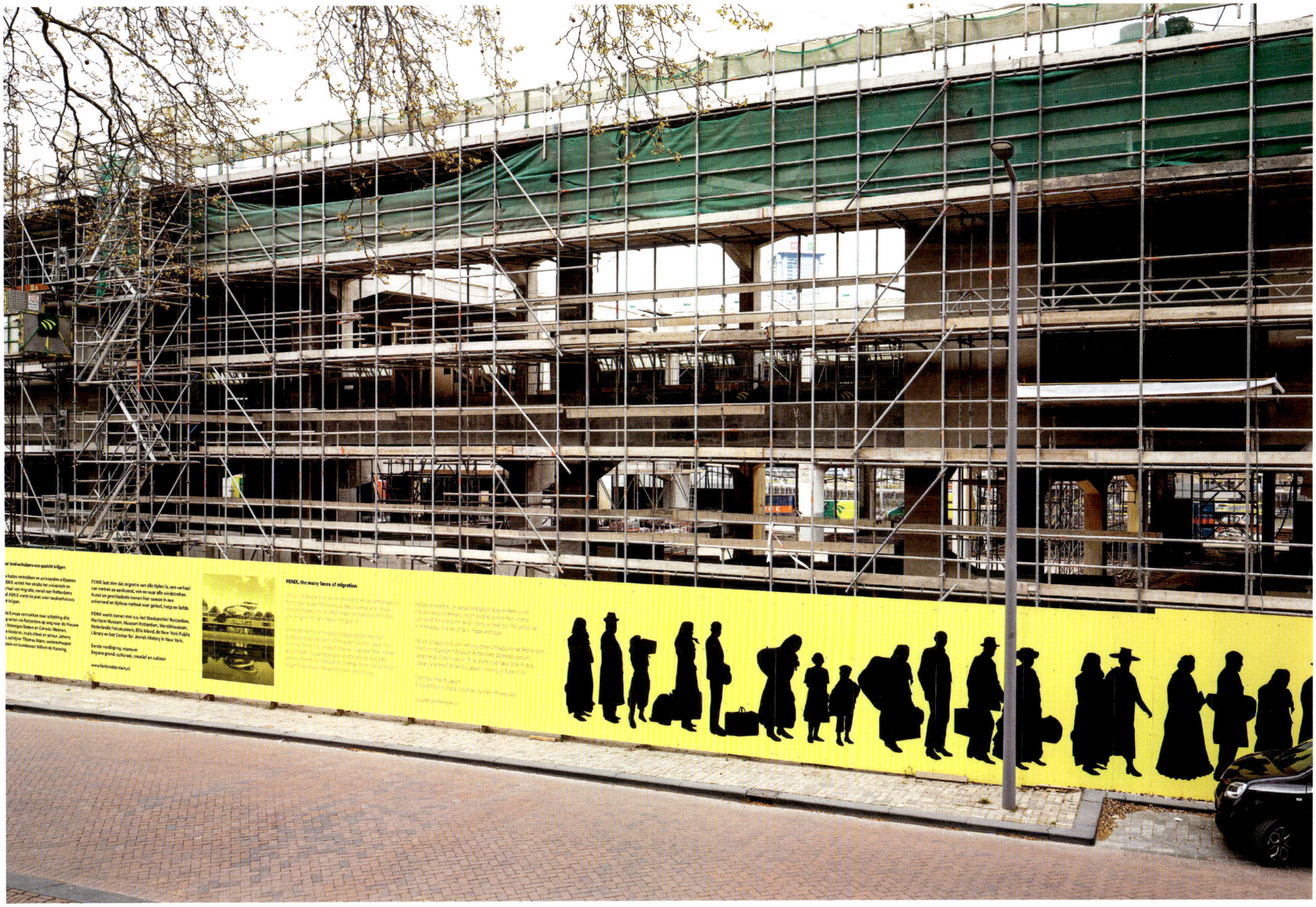
FENIX laat zien dat migratie van alle tijden is, een verhaal van vertrek en aankomst, van en naar alle windstreken. Kunst en geschiedenis komen hier samen in een universeel en tijdloos verhaal over geloof, hoop en liefde.
FENIX werkt samen met o.a. het Stadsarchief Rotterdam, Maritiem Museum, Museum Rotterdam, Wereldmuseum, Nederlands Fotomuseum, Ellis Island, de New York Public Library en het Center for Jewish History in New York.
Eerste verdieping: museum
Begane grond: cultureel, creatief en culinair
www.fenixrotterdam.nl
FENIX, the many faces of migration

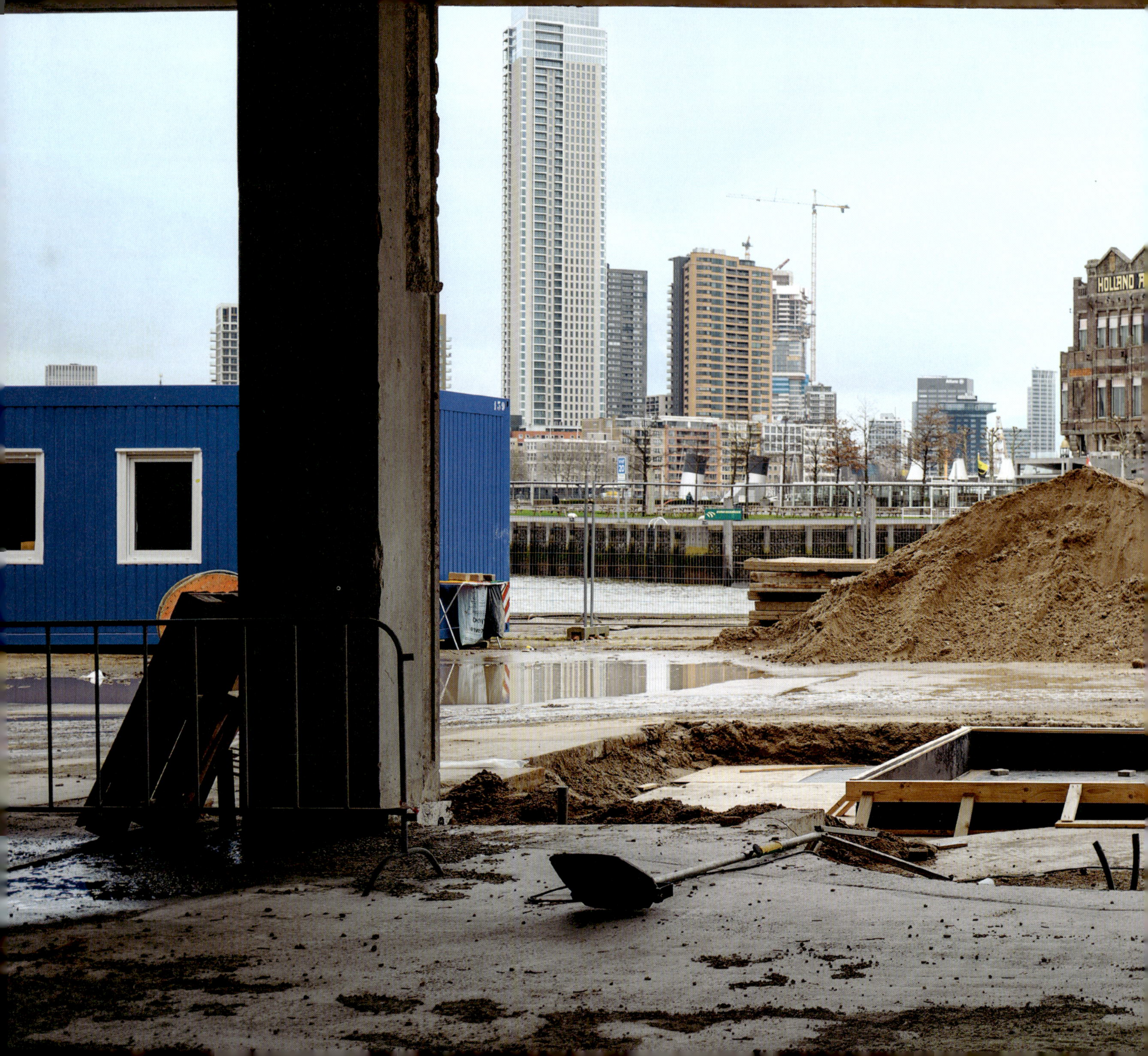
159
HOLLAND A

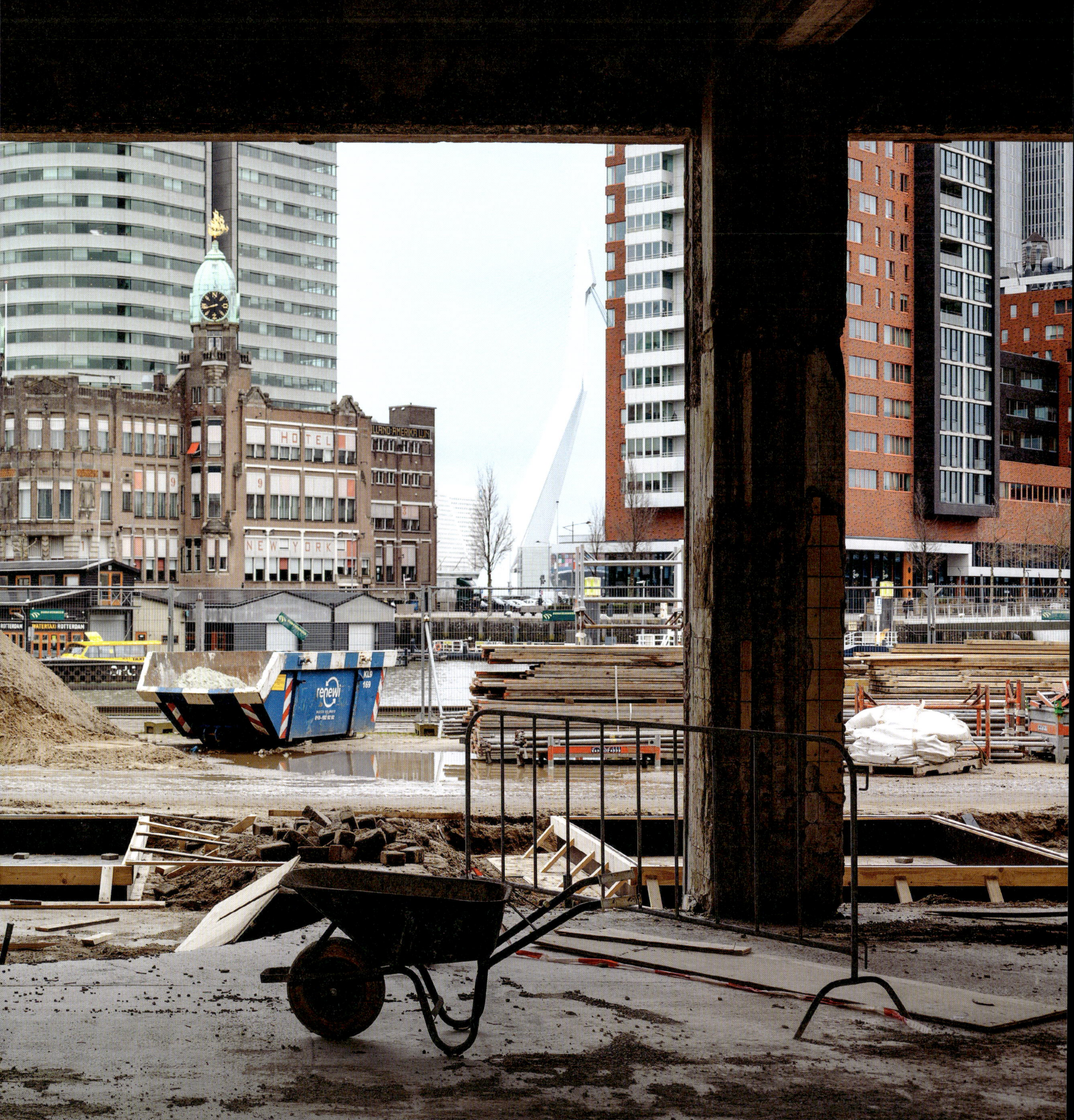

HOTEL
NEW-YORK
renewi

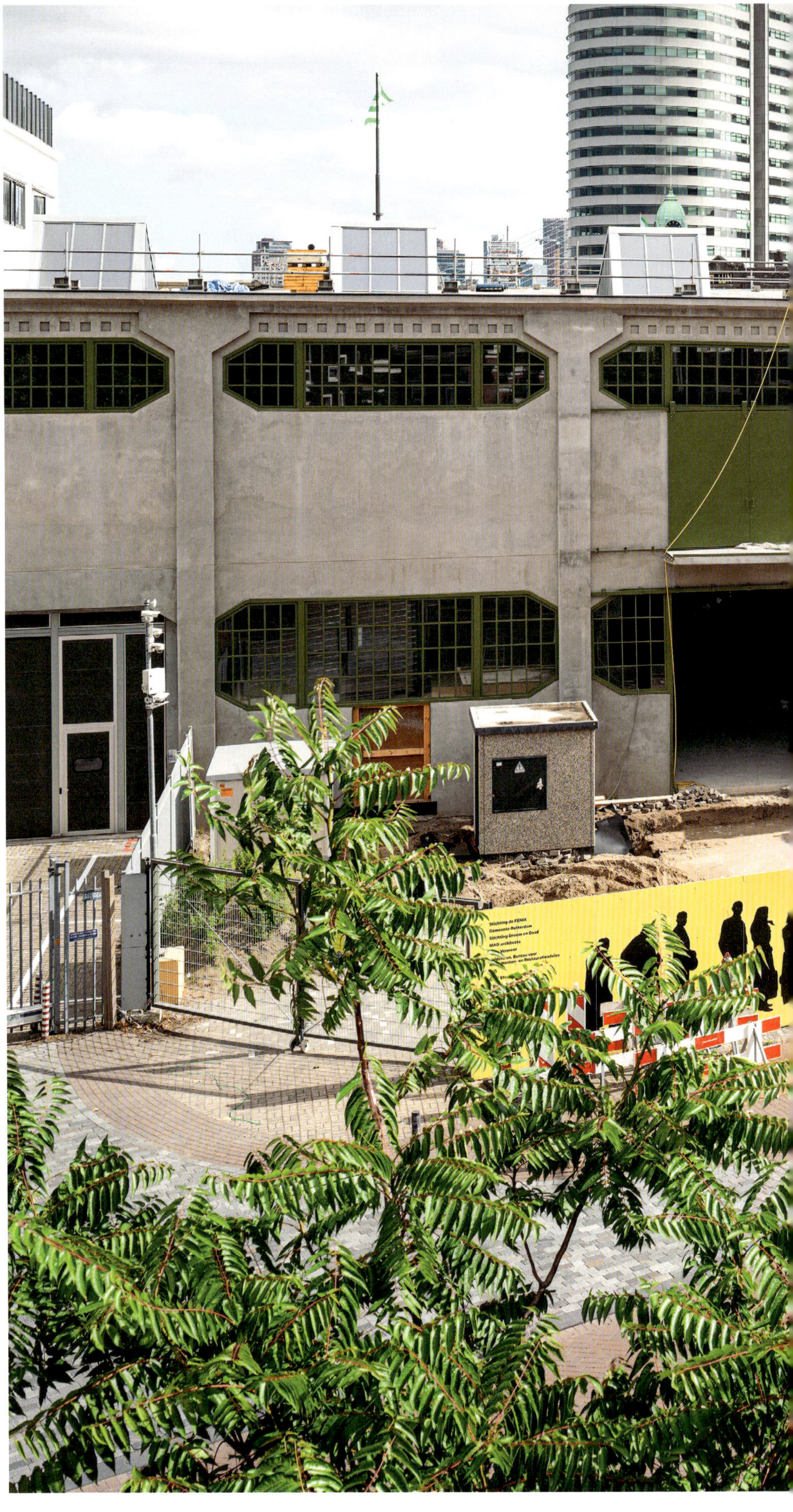
Stichting de FENIX
Gemeente Rotterdam
Stichting Droom en Daad
MAD architects

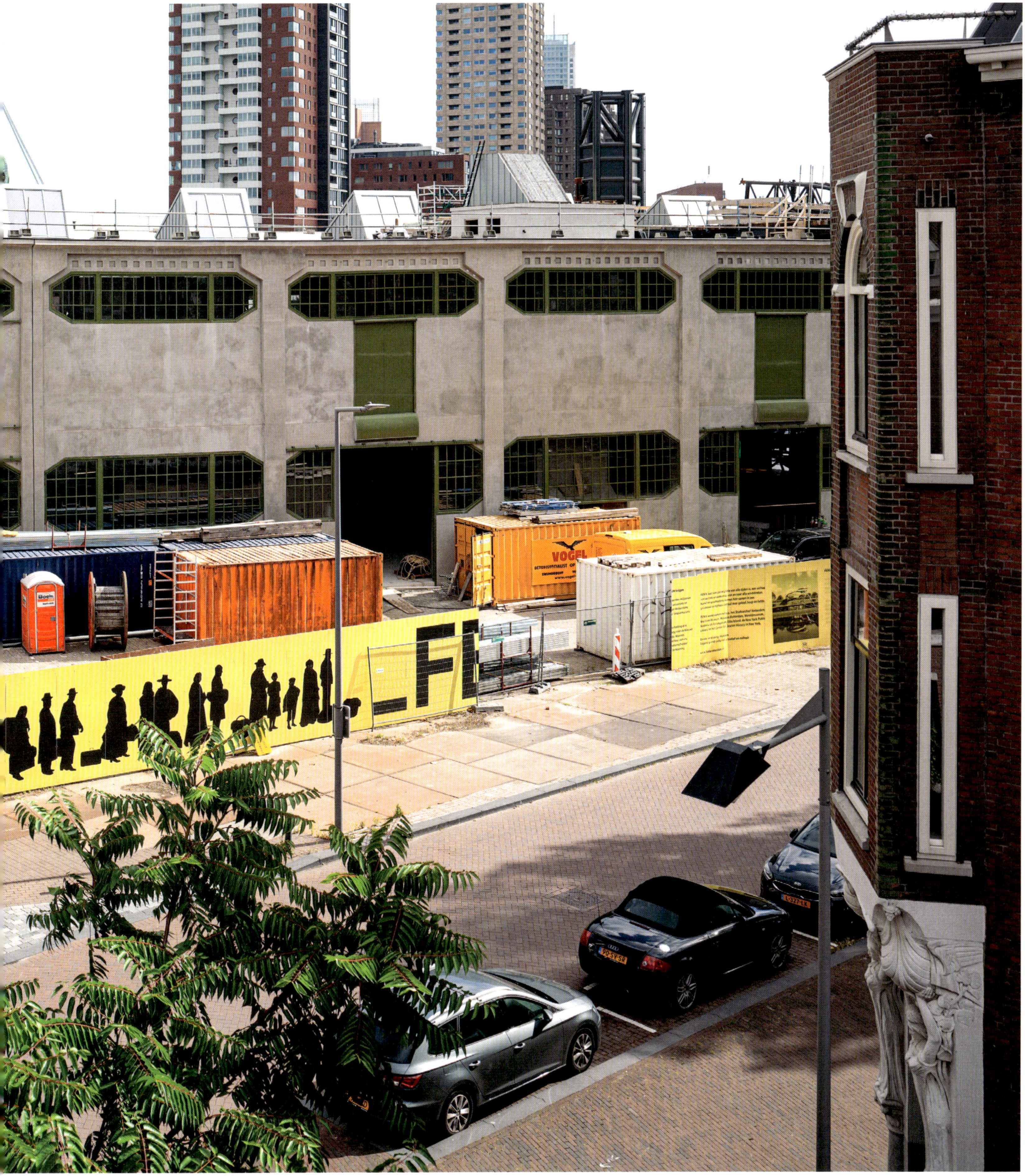
VOGEL

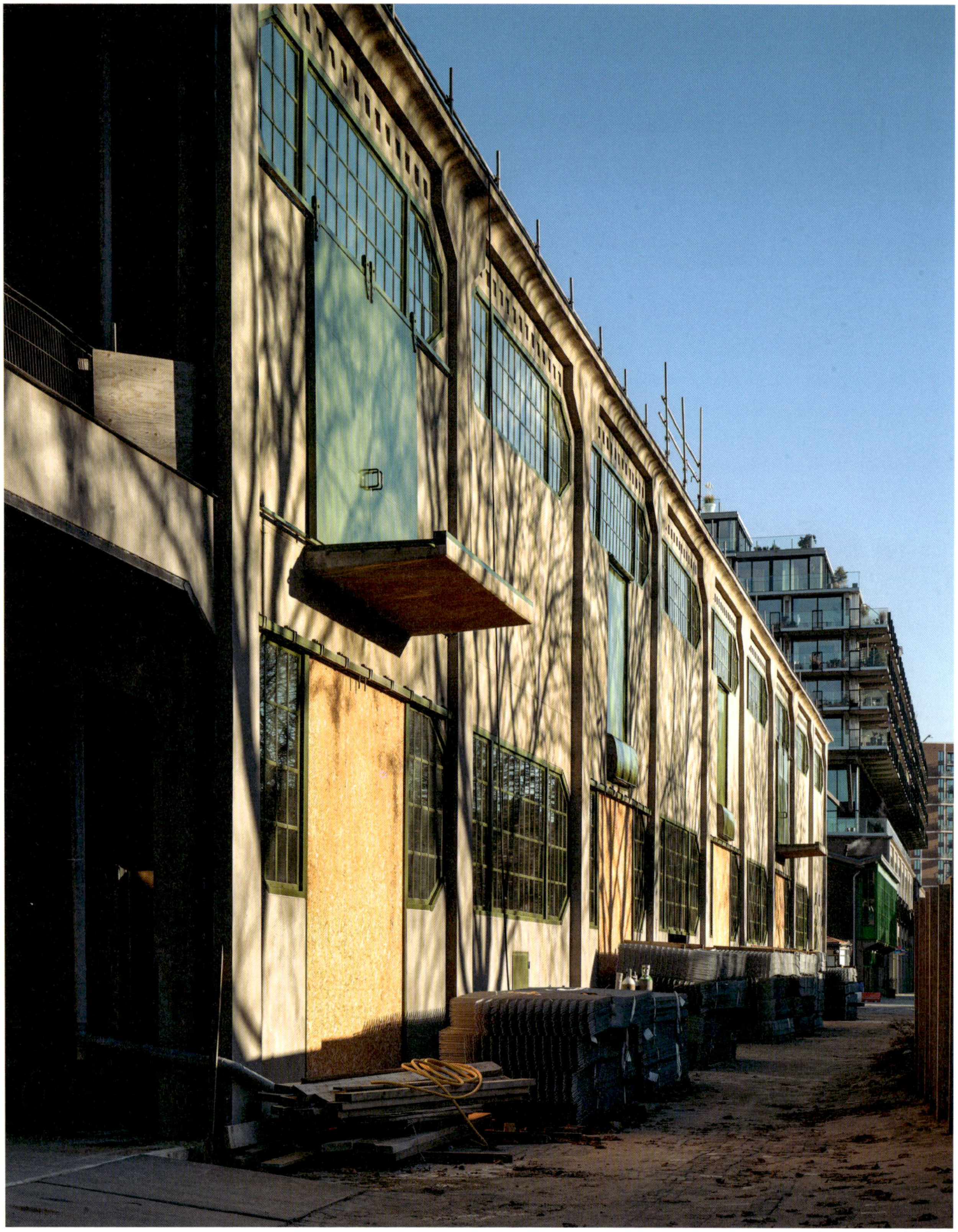

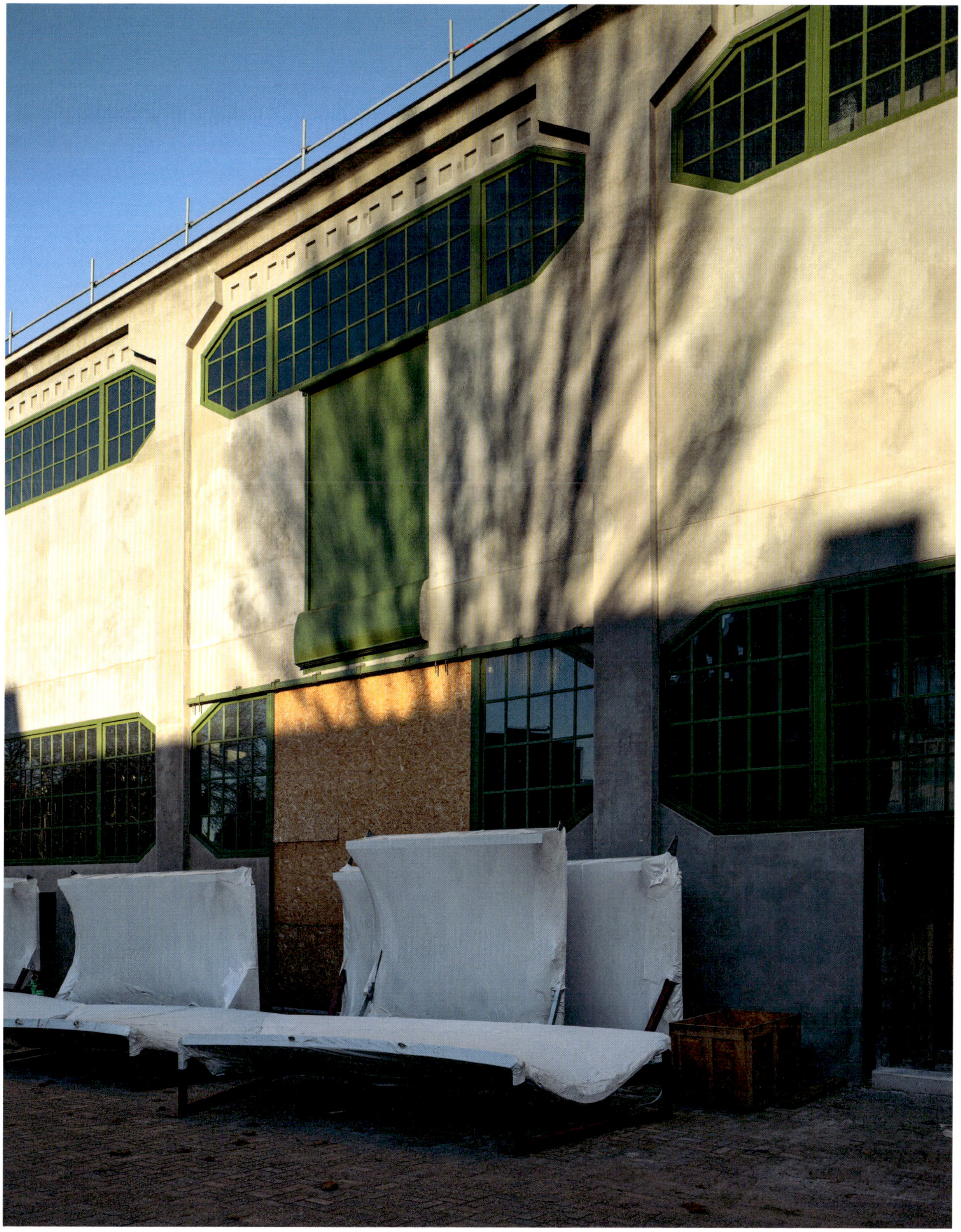

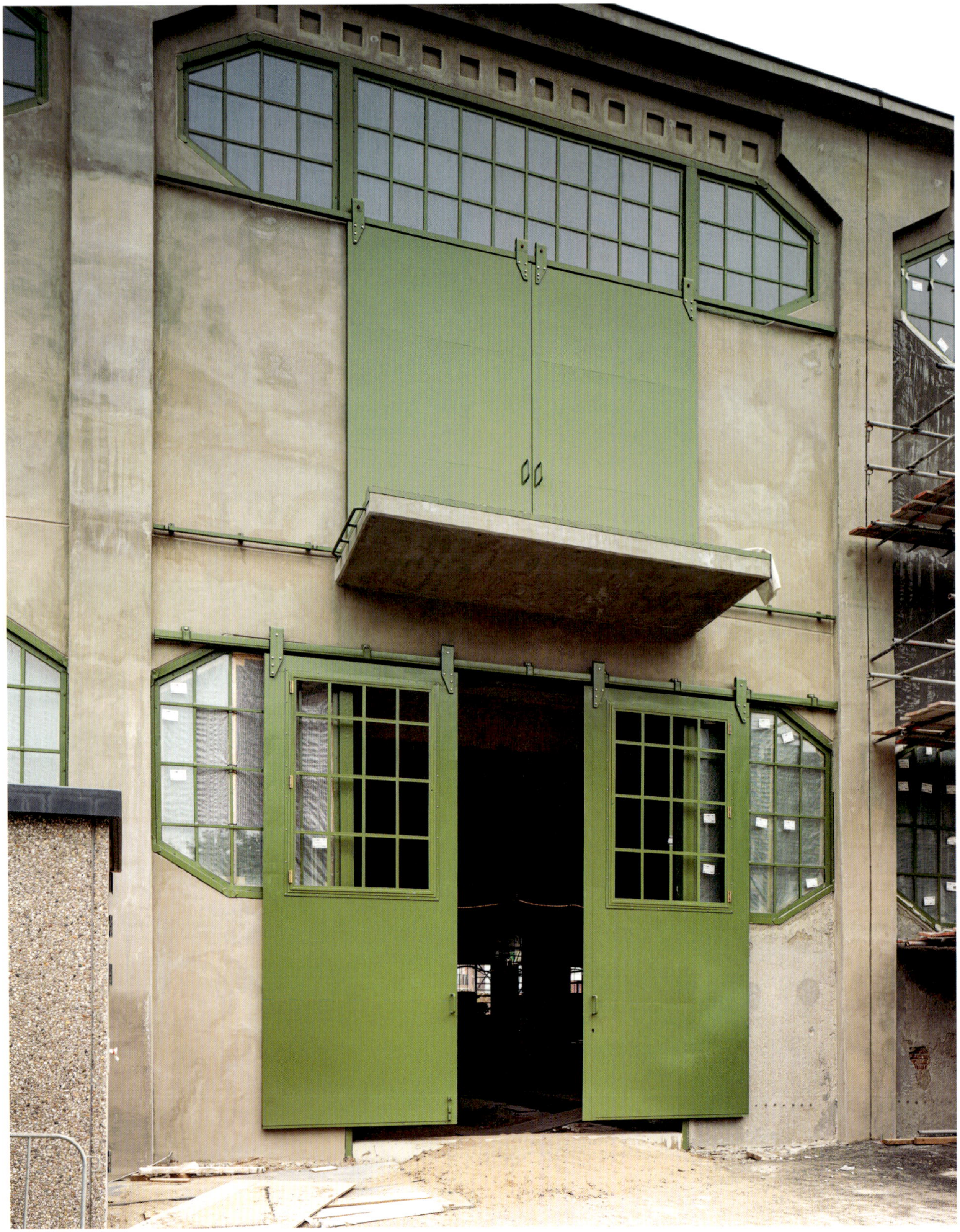

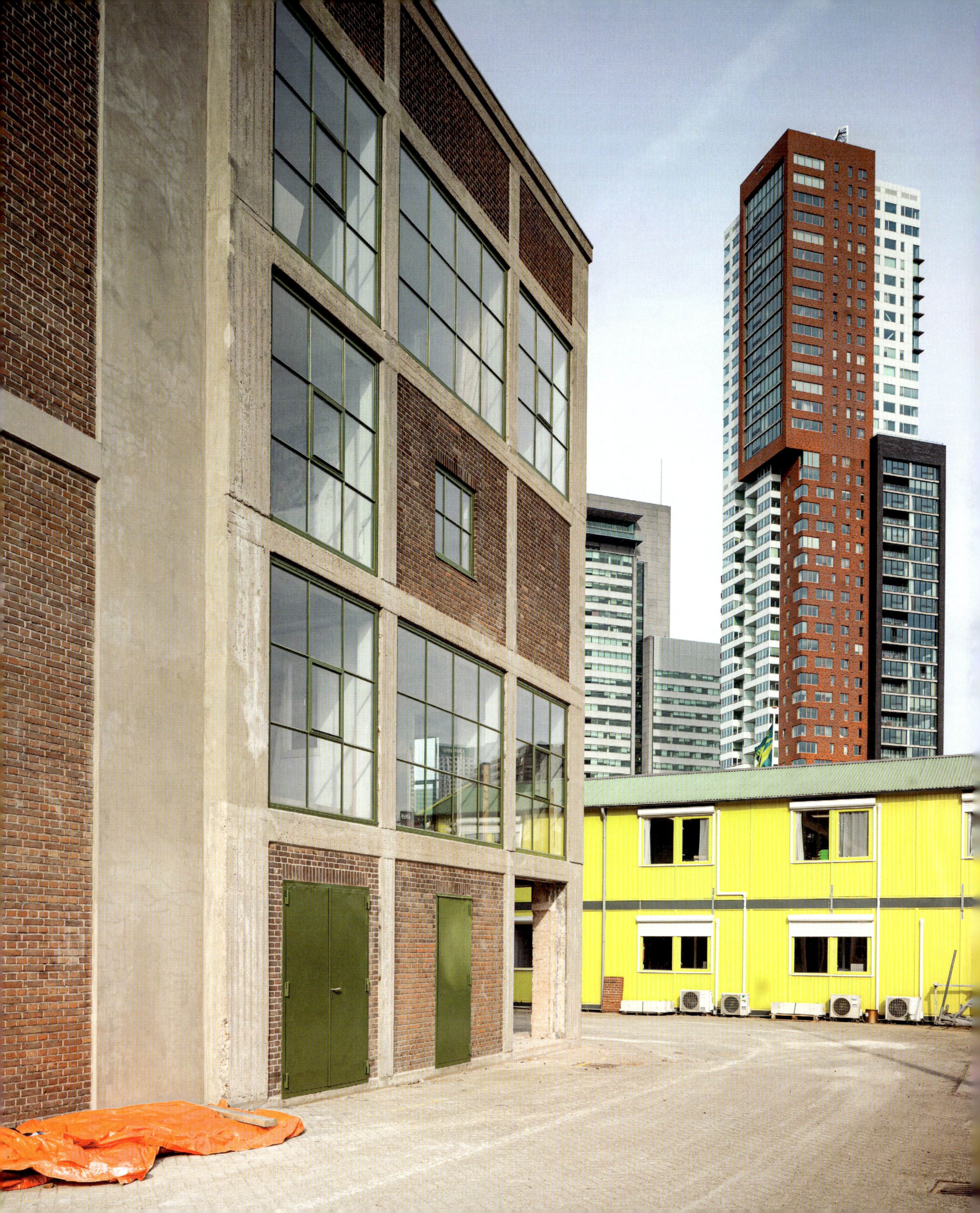

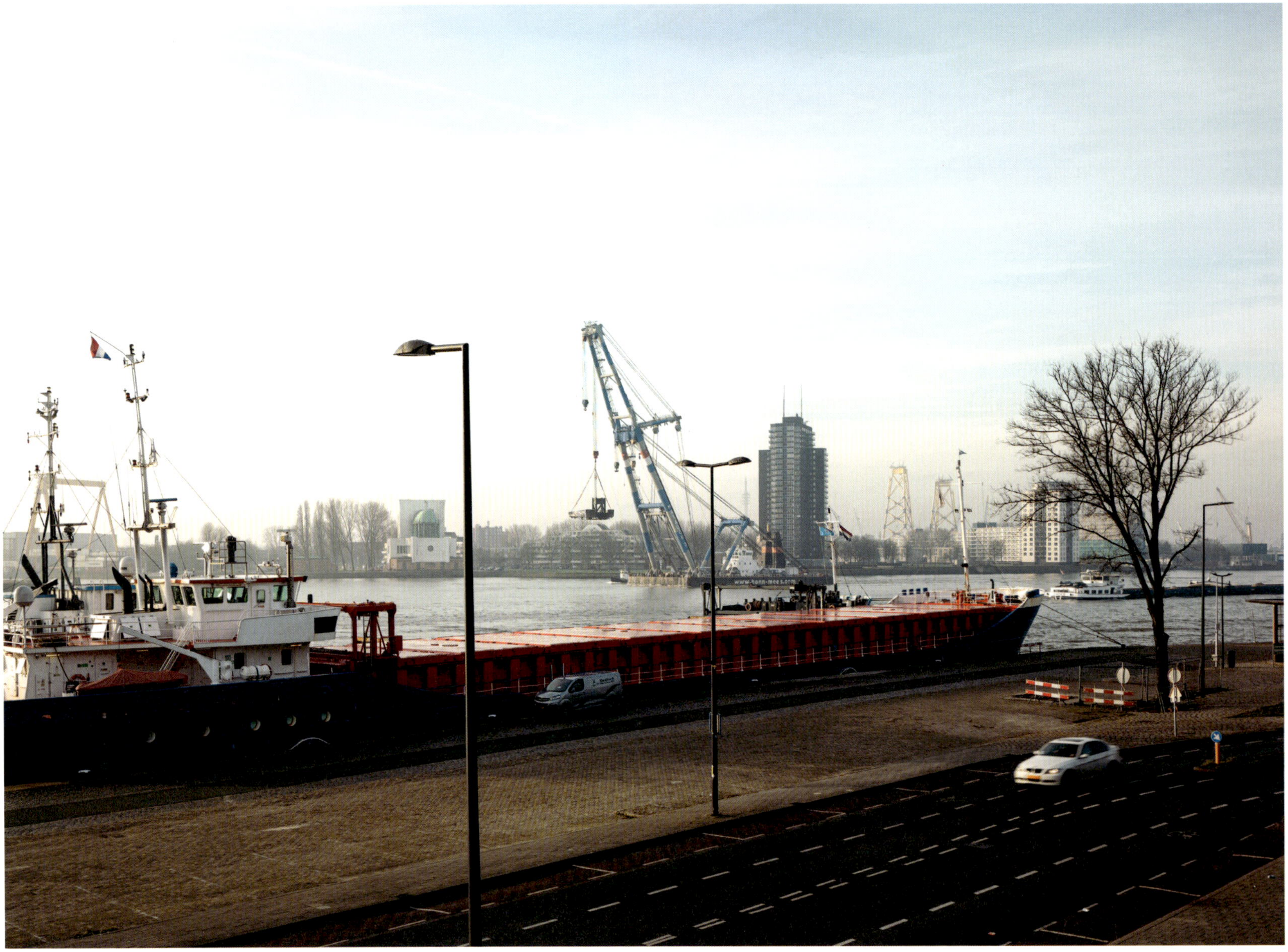

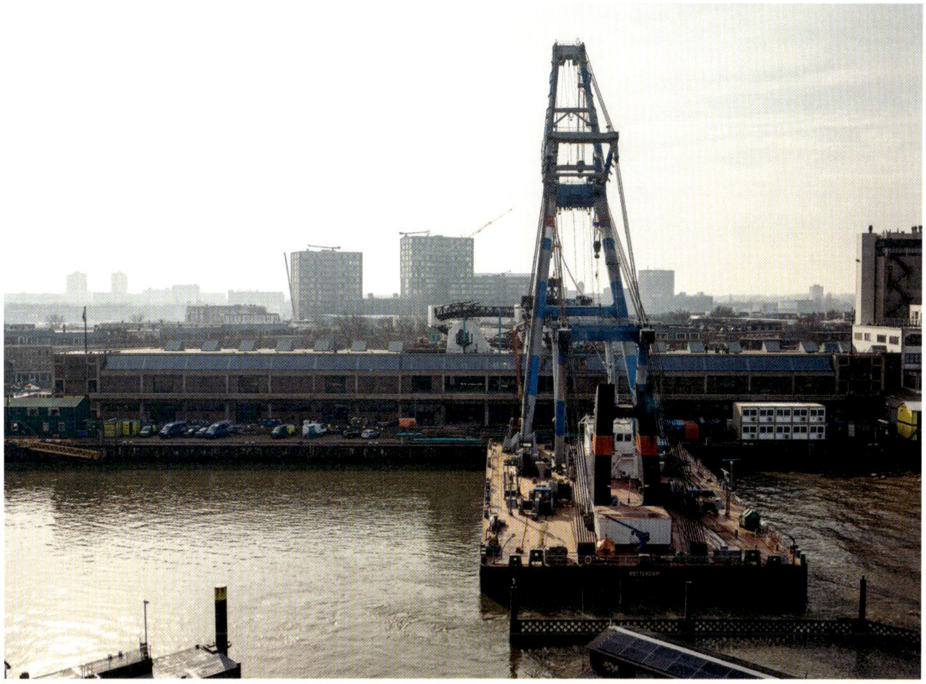

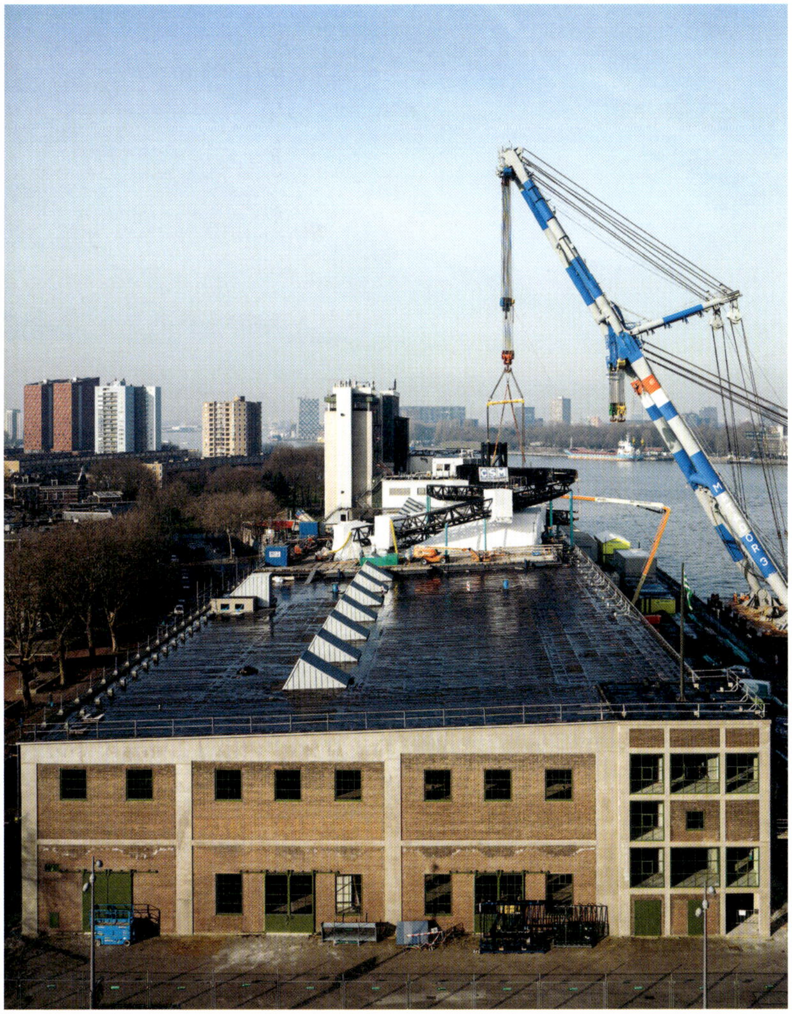

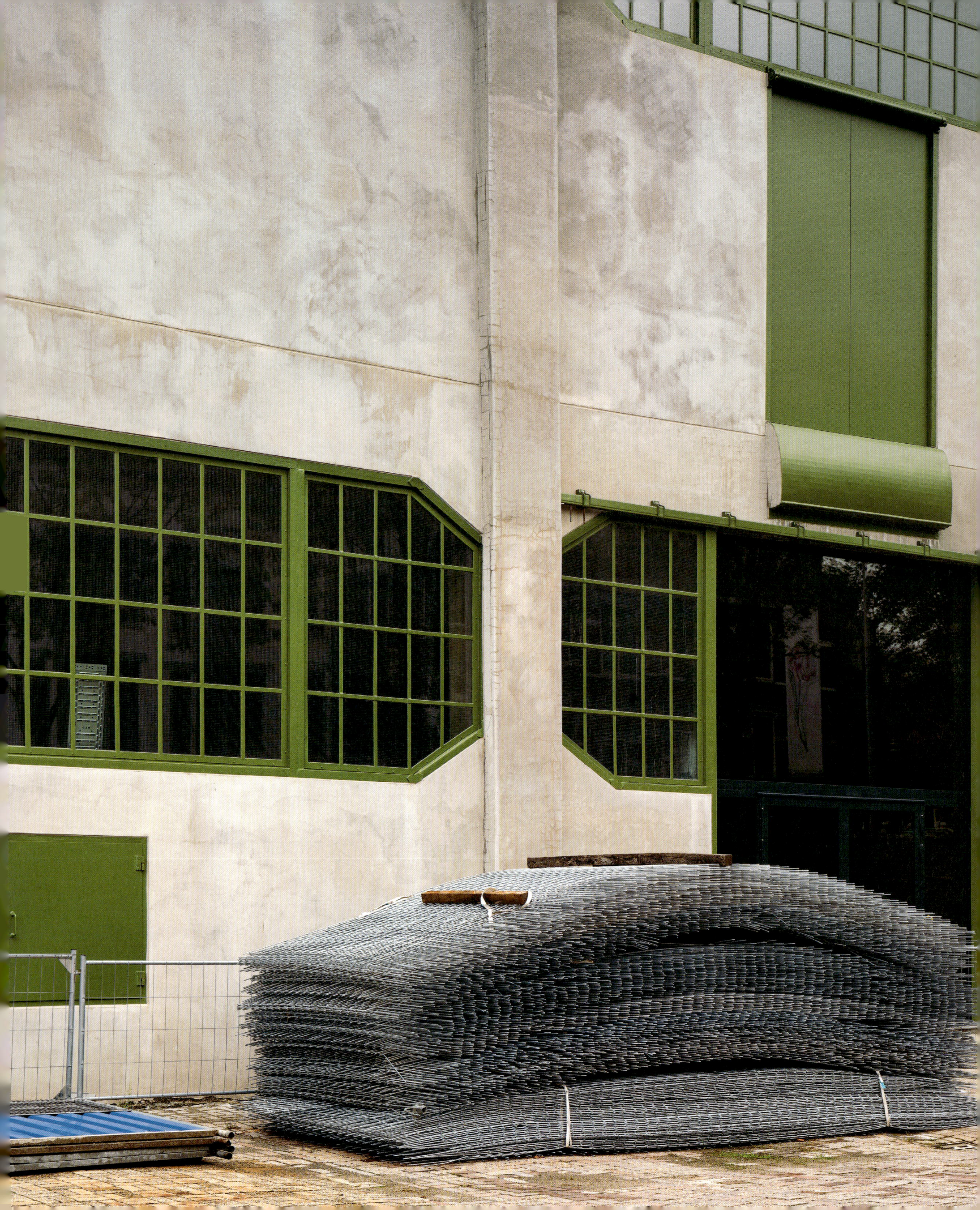

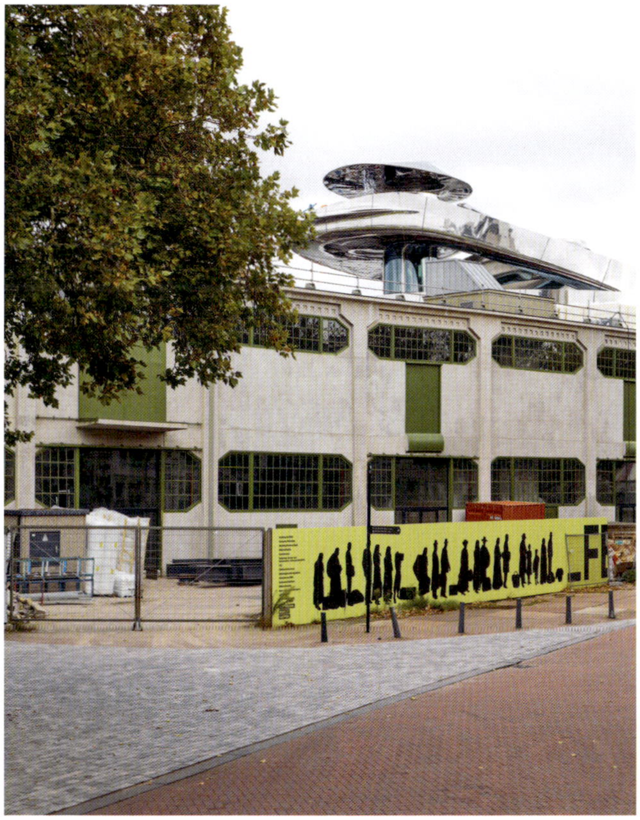

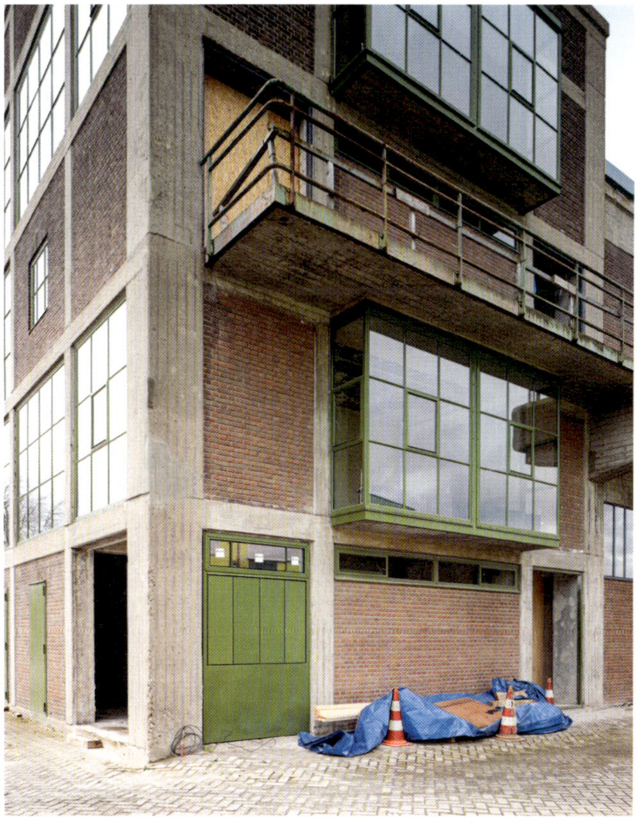

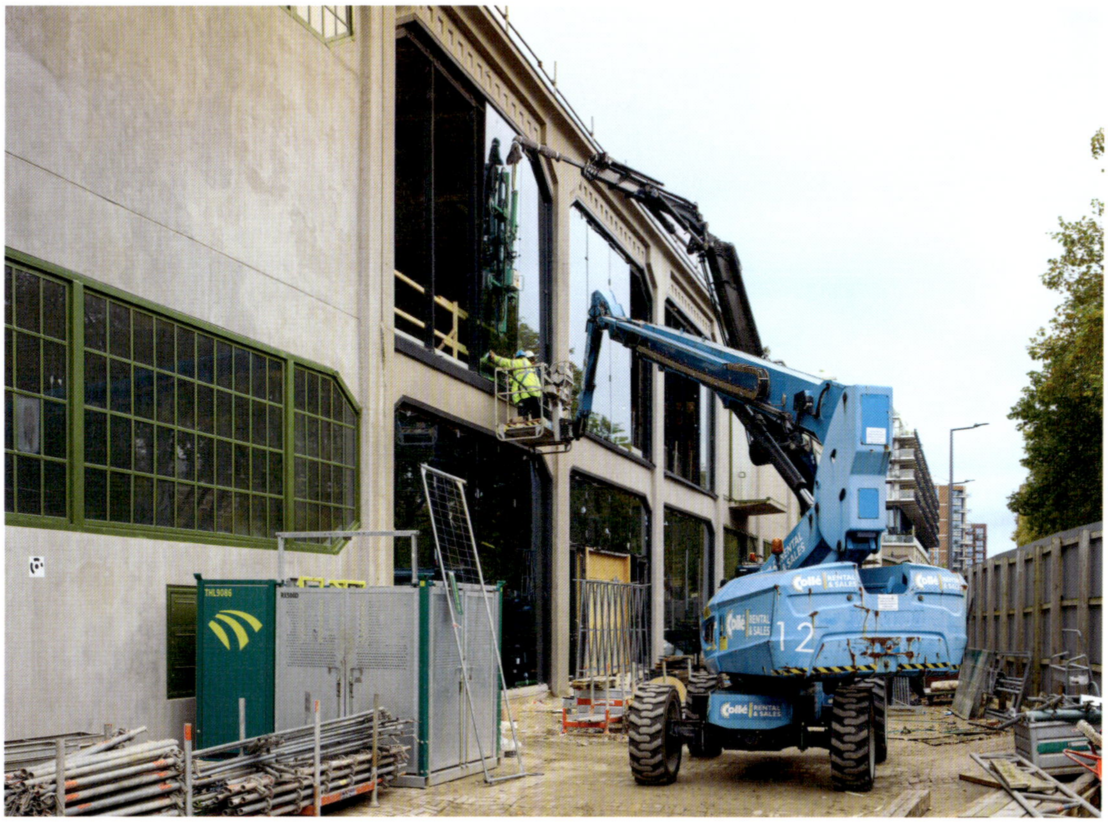

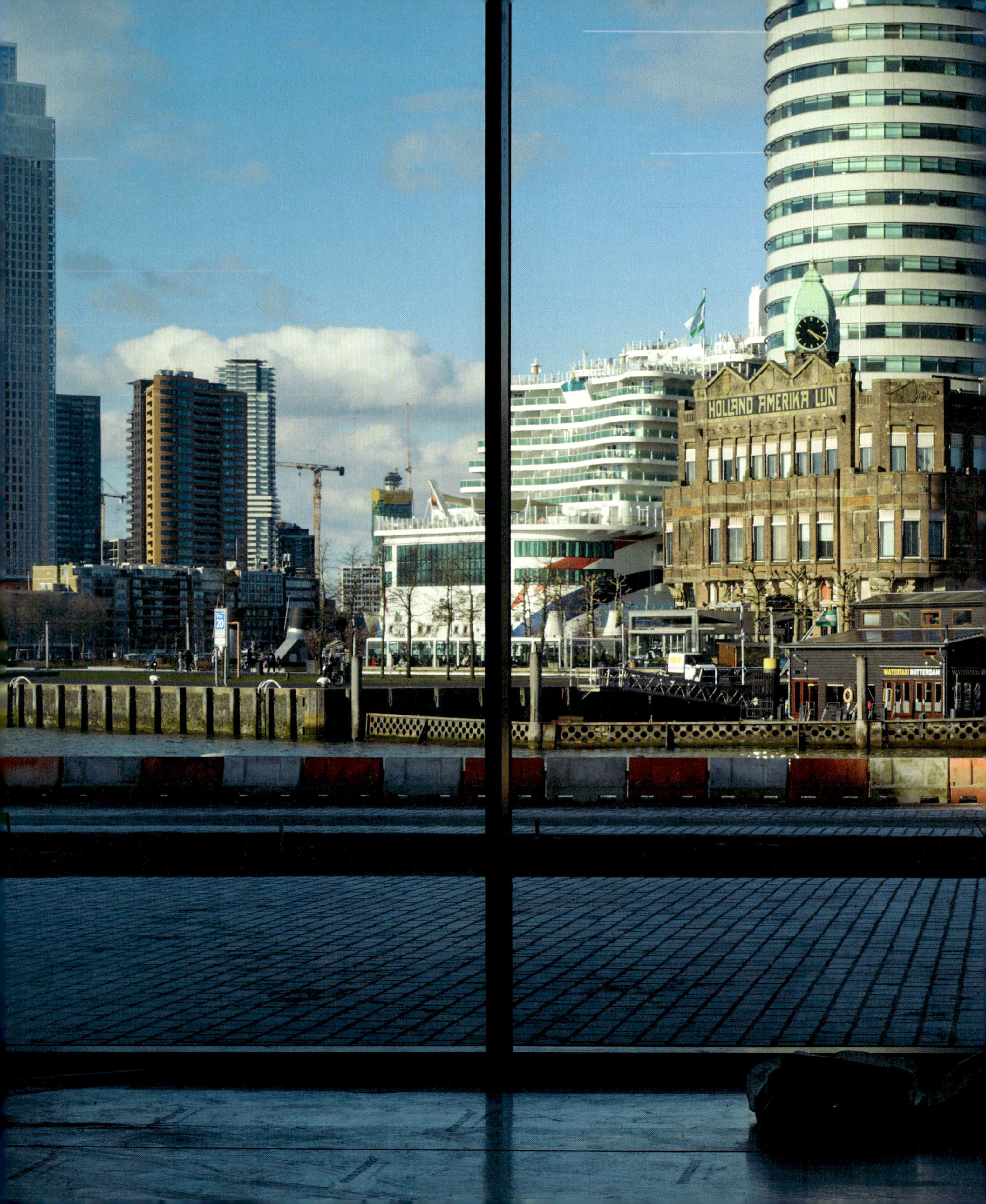

HOLLAND AMERIKA LIJN
WATERTAXI ROTTERDAM

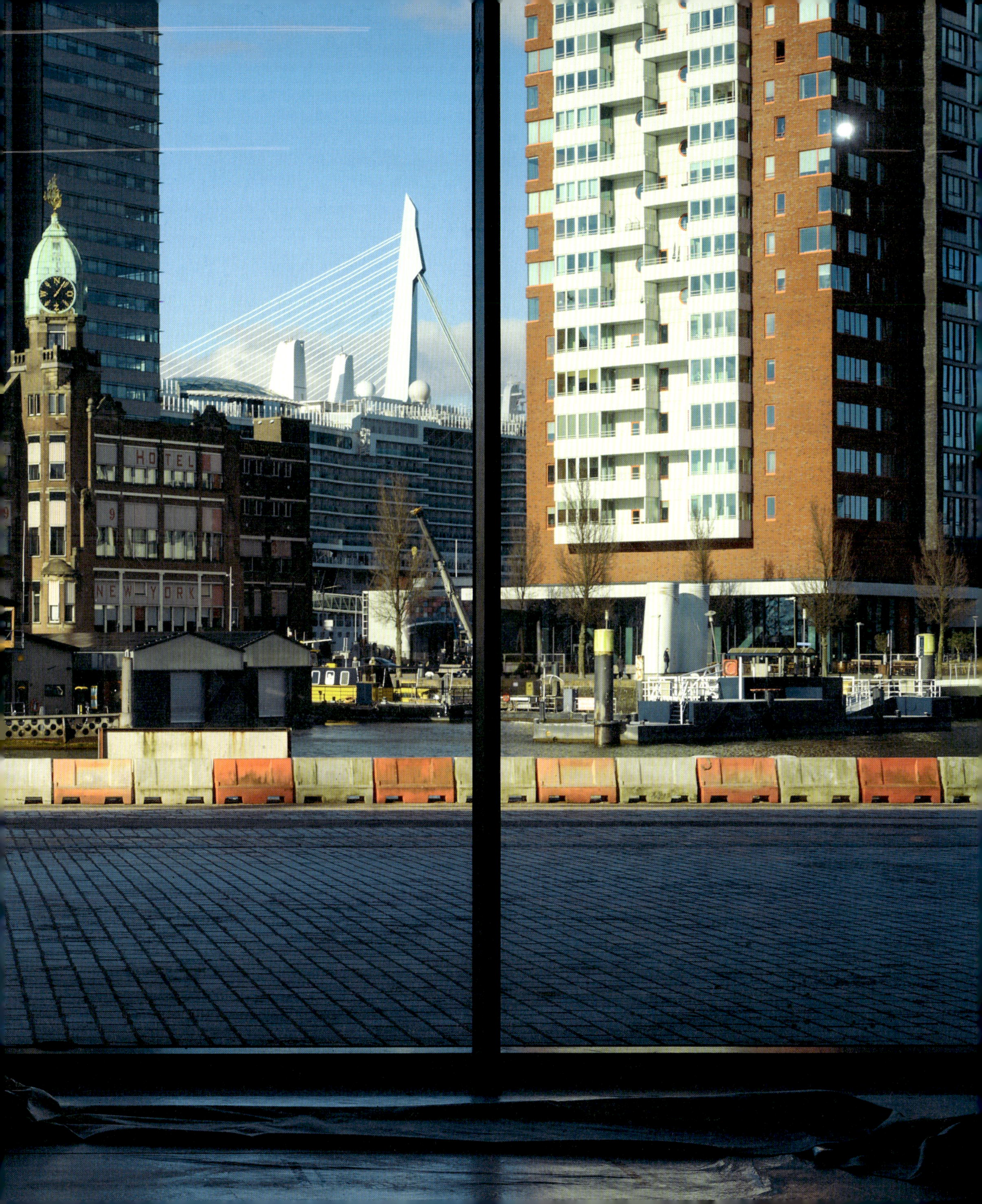
HOTEL
NEW YORK

“For the restoration plan of the warehouse, we did extensive historical research. The building reflects the history of the city of Rotterdam: the importance and growth of the port, the damage caused by the war and the contemporary redevelopment of the surrounding city district.”

Philip Mannaerts, Restoration Architect at Bureau Polderman

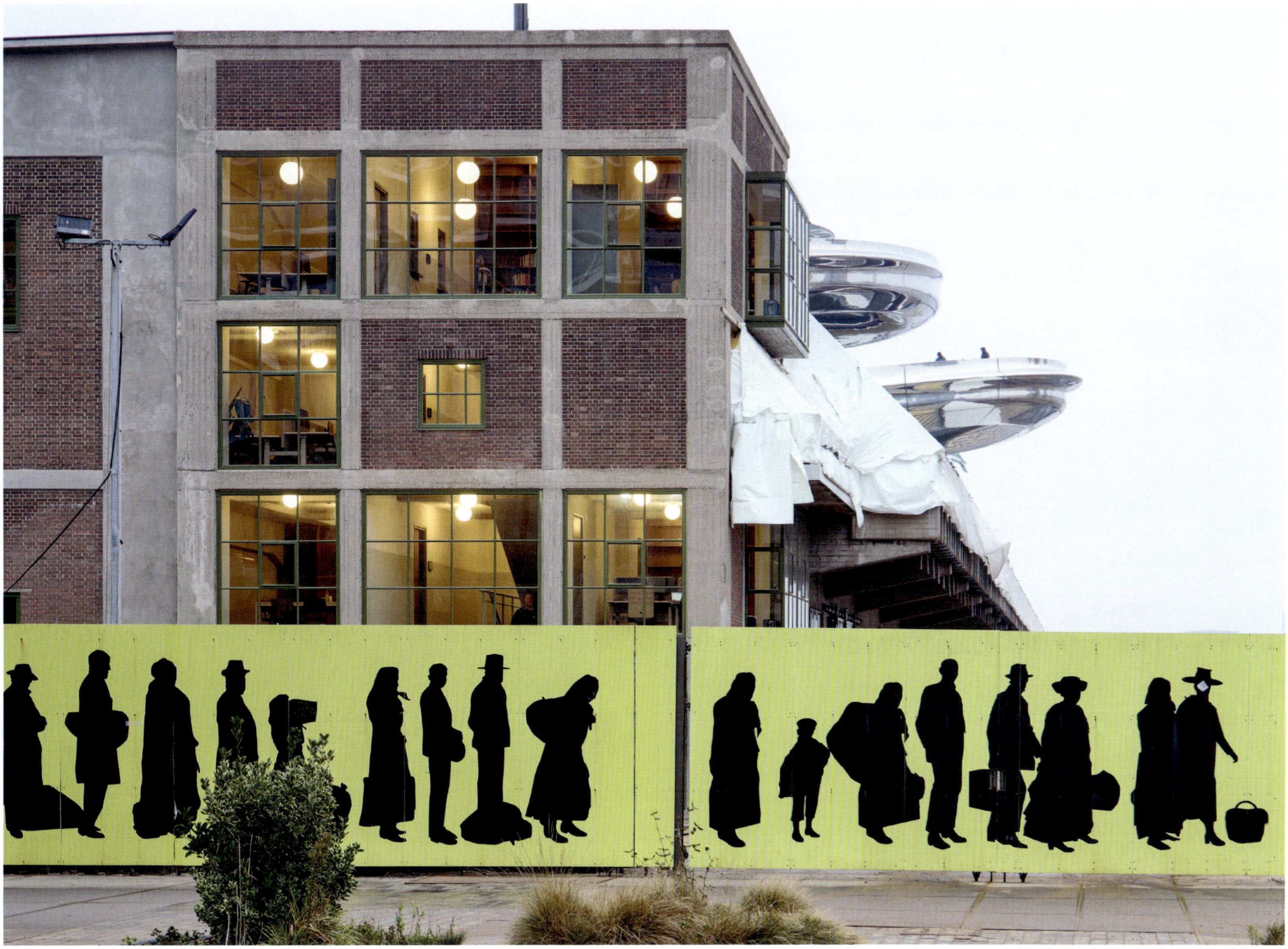

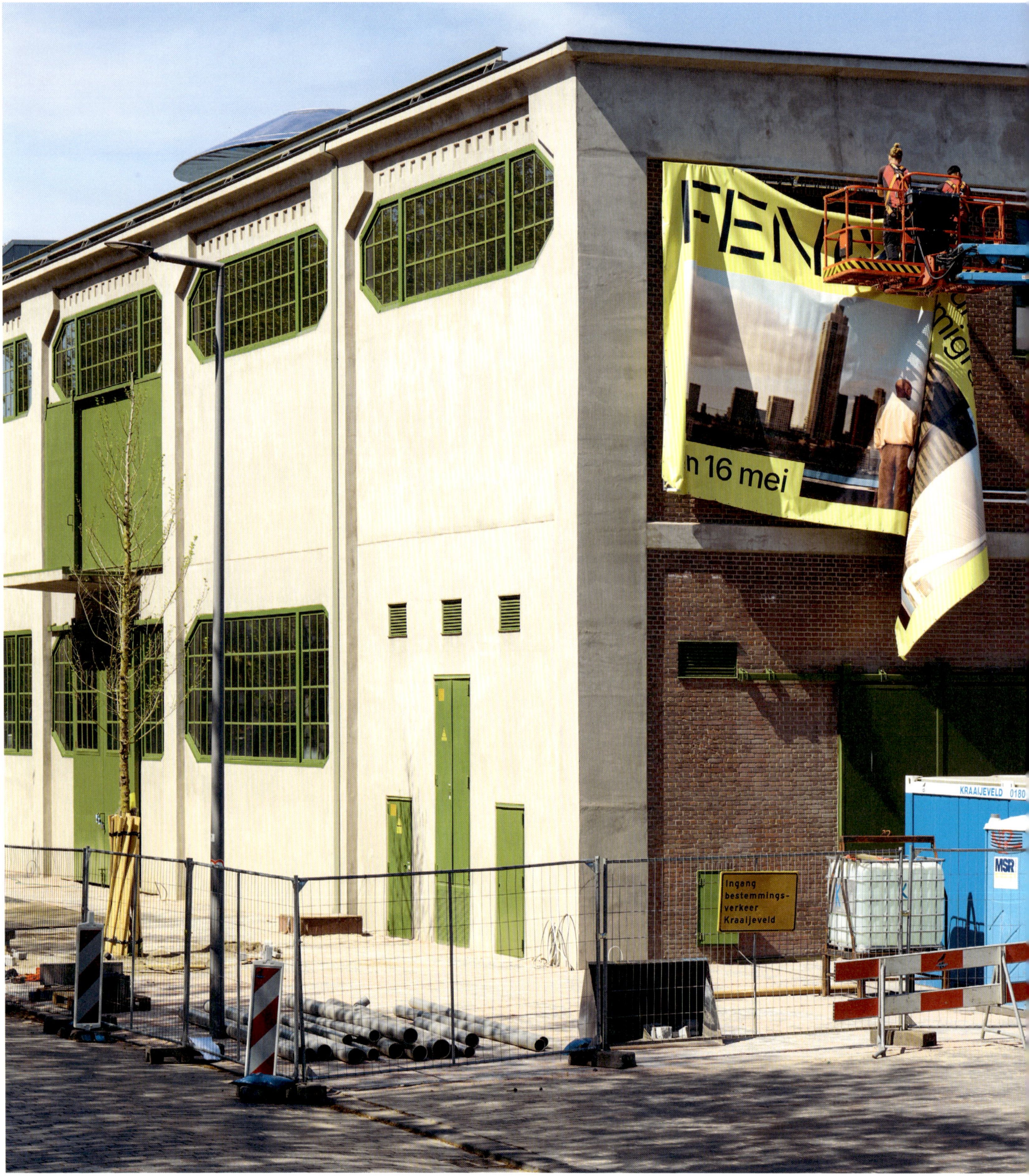
n 16 mei
Ingang
bestemmings-
verkeer
Kraaijeveld
KRAAIJEVELD 0180
MSR

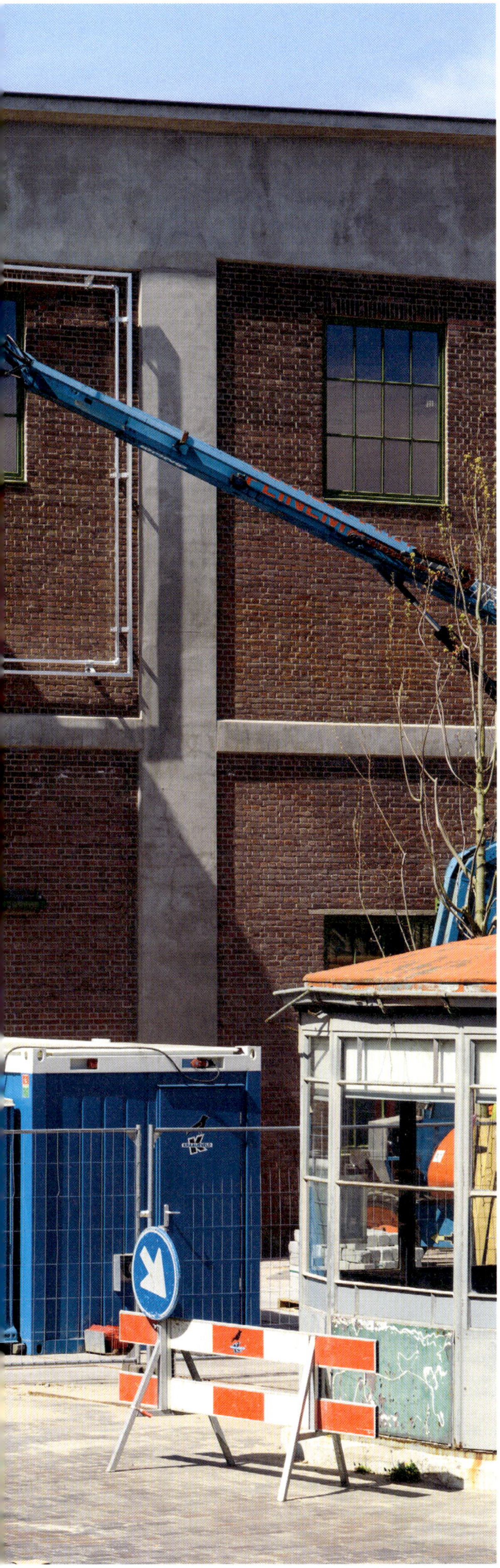

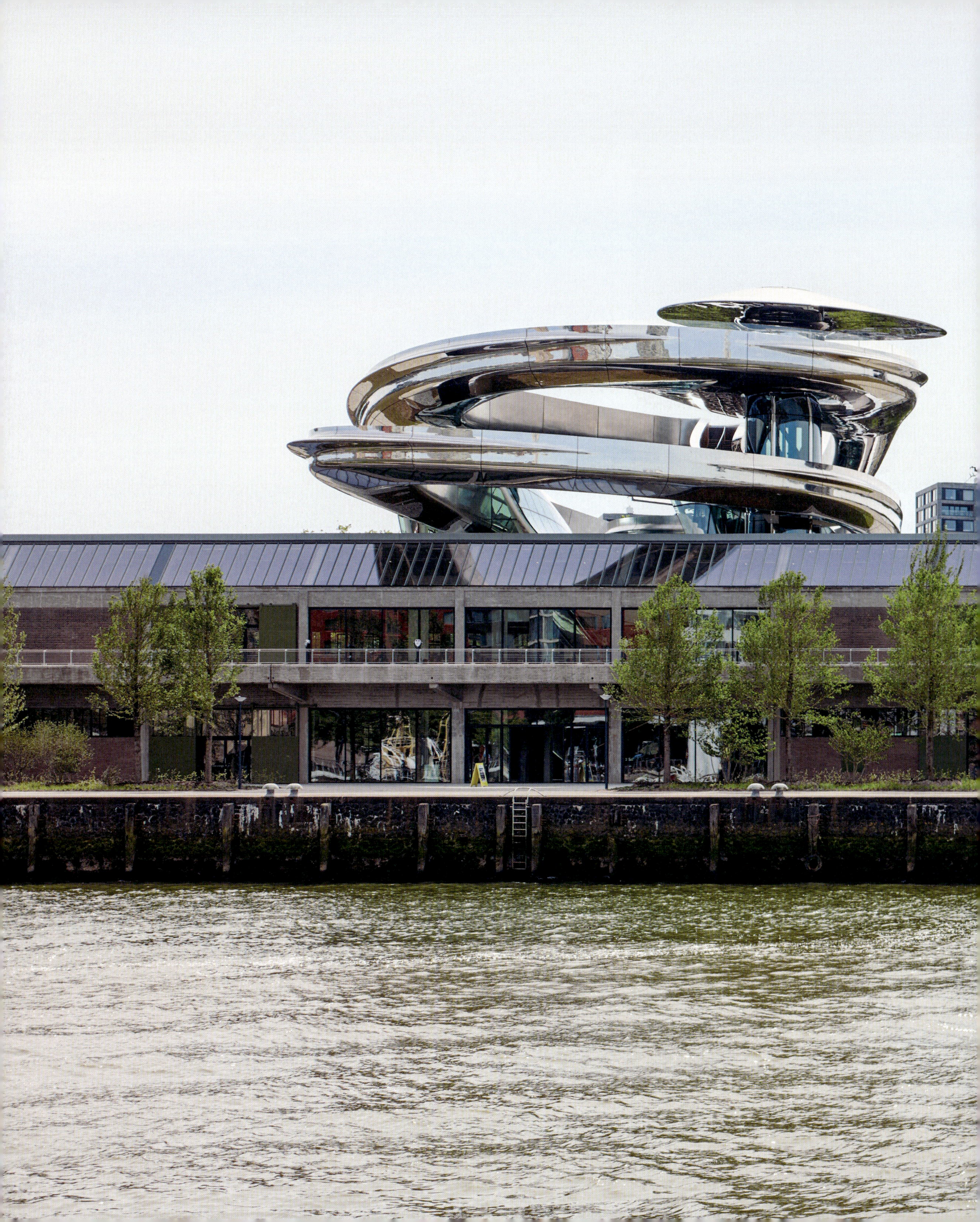

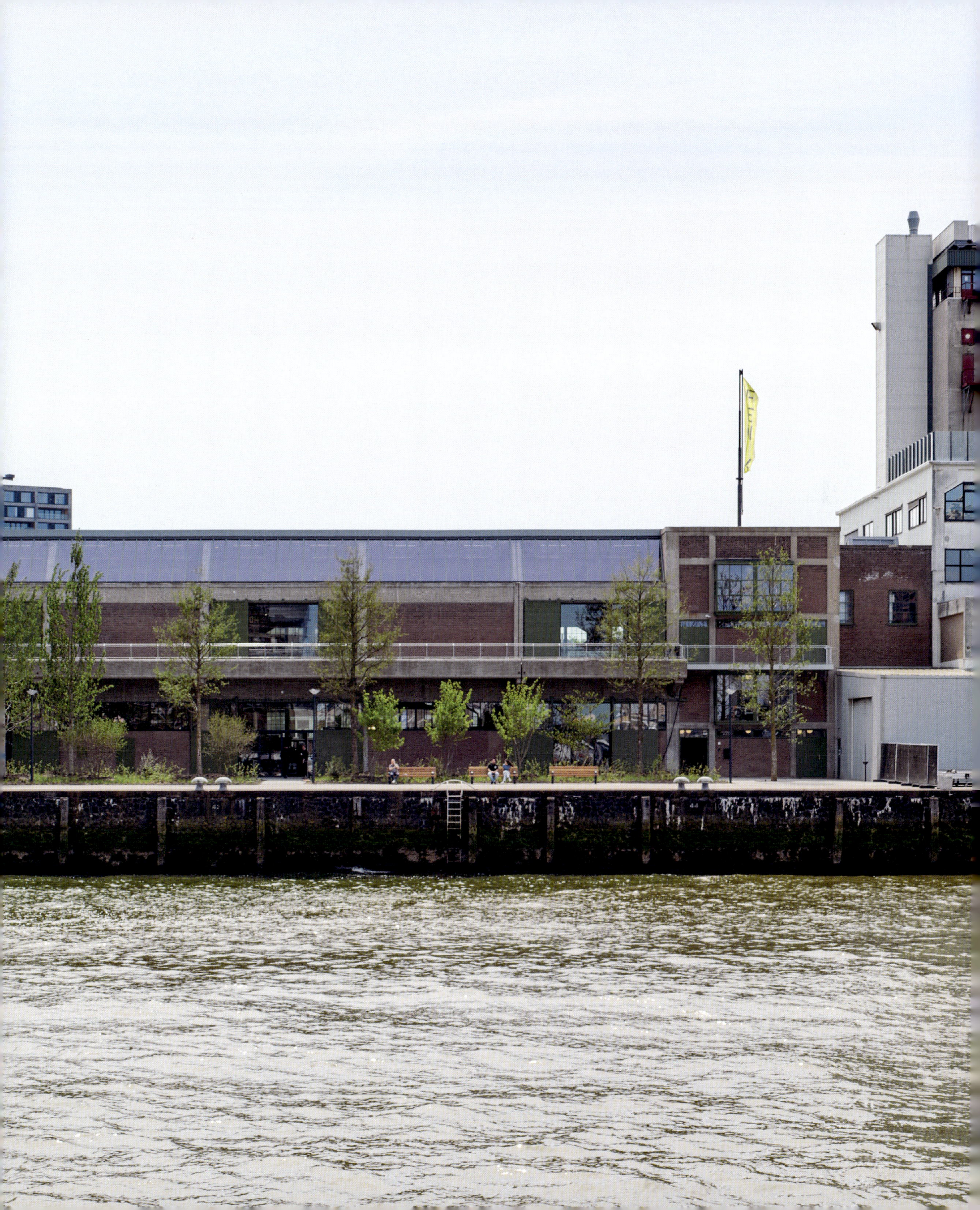

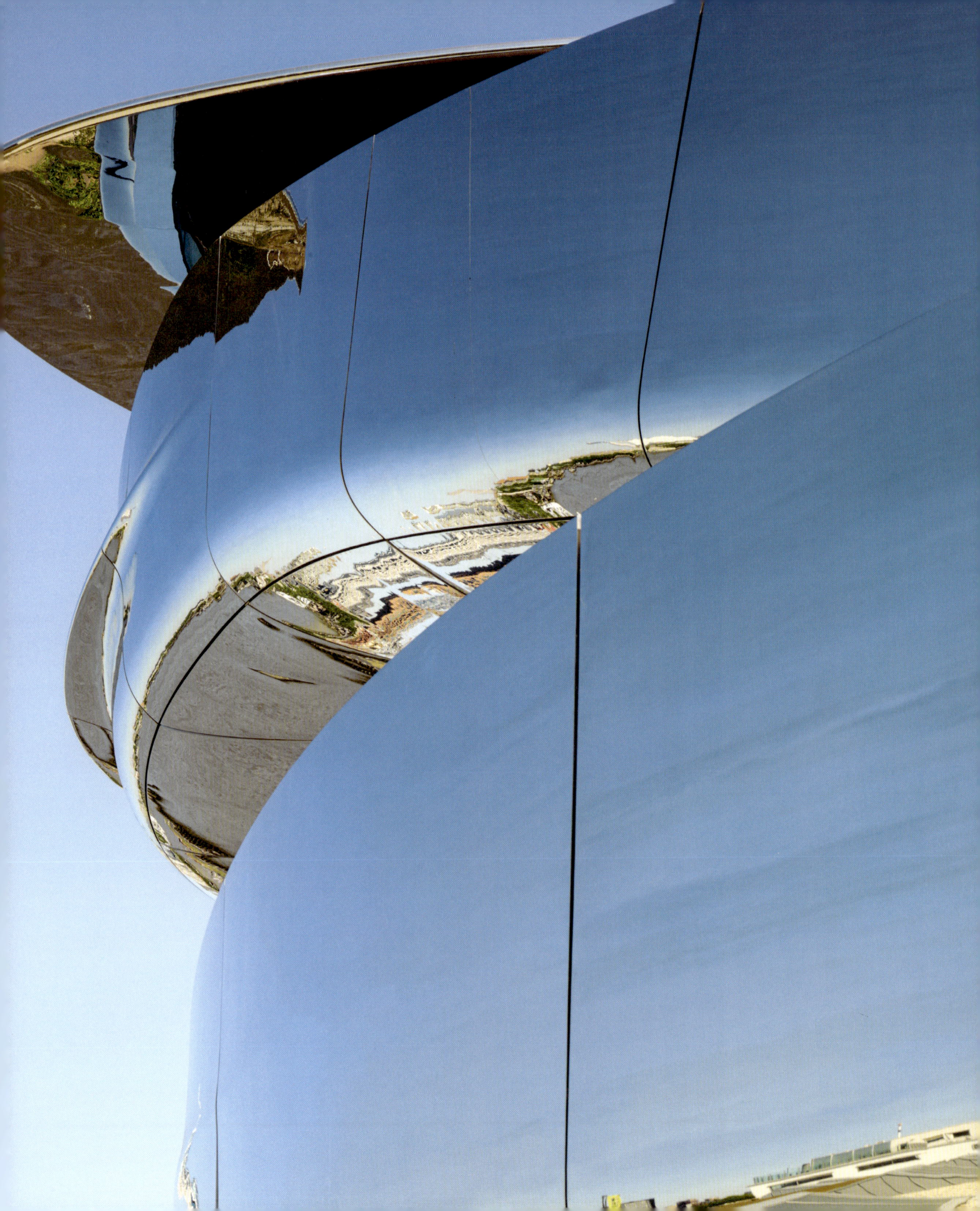

Tornado

The defining new feature of the building is the Tornado – a double helix staircase evocative of rising air that climbs from the ground floor and flows up and out of the rooftop onto an outdoor viewing platform. You can enter the stairs in two different ways, leading you on either a short or a long journey to the top. The Tornado offers a panoramic view across Rotterdam and the Maas River, 24 metres above ground level. The dynamic structure is clad in polished stainless-steel panels, made in Groningen, the Netherlands. The canopy that sits at the top of the structure is 17 metres long and was transported by boat from Groningen to Rotterdam before being assembled and lifted into place. The wooden staircase, which emerges onto the platform, is 550 metres long. The staircase is made out of 12,500 unique wooden planks. The wood evokes the feeling of stepping aboard a ship: your journey has begun.

Fenix: A Resonance Of Humanity And Time

Ma Yansong
Founder of MAD

Citizen. Man. Woman. Child. The new and the unknown. Fenix in Rotterdam embodies the universality of history, connecting us through the collective essence of human experience: the pursuit of understanding. Here, research is movement, a distortion that transforms past narratives into forward motion.

Architecture at Fenix becomes a reflection of time – a dynamic interplay of departure and arrival. While rooted in history, it advances, layering stories and perspectives. The creative process, like time, weaves a web of linearity and complexity, sometimes retreating momentarily, yet always progressing. The museum stands as an architectural metaphor for this perpetual evolution, a timeless dialogue between what was, what is and what could be.

Anchored by its deep connection to Rotterdam's past, Fenix transforms a historic warehouse into an immersive experience of memory and identity. It becomes a vessel for stories of migration and shared human resilience. The monumental Tornado serves as both a tangible artefact and a metaphorical journey, embodying the whirlwind of emotions, histories and futures that converge within the museum's walls. It propels visitors beyond boundaries, inviting them to ascend and expand their vision.

At the heart of the Tornado's design lies a double-spiral structure that interlocks into one, guiding visitors on two distinct yet interwoven journeys. As they ascend or descend, they encounter others at different heights, their paths converging in moments of reflection – both literal and metaphorical. The polished stainless-steel railings echo this dynamic, offering reflections of themselves and others in motion, emphasising the shared humanity of their unique experiences.

The Tornado, framed in stainless steel, reflects the city and the horizon, amplifying the journey with infinite visual and emotional depth. It mirrors humanity's aspirations while preserving the warehouse's legacy as a sanctuary of stories and dreams. This dynamic space encourages visitors to confront uncertainty, envision a better future and recognise the interwoven nature of their own stories with those of others.

Fenix is not just architecture but a living testament to motion, emotion and identity. It is a symphony of solid and void, echoing the organic flow of nature and human ingenuity. Together, the warehouse and the Tornado encapsulate a journey that resonates with the city and humanity – a bold manifesto of the contemporary spirit.

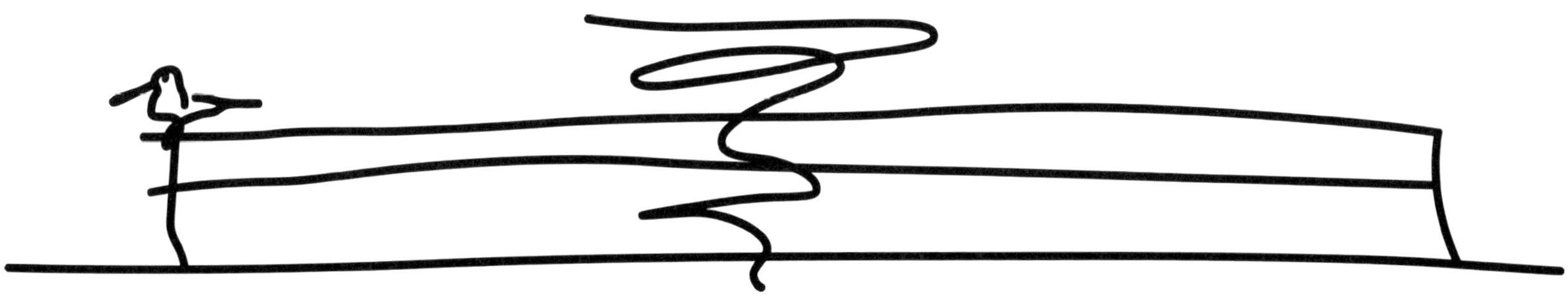

First sketch design by Ma Yansong of Fenix and the Tornado, 2018

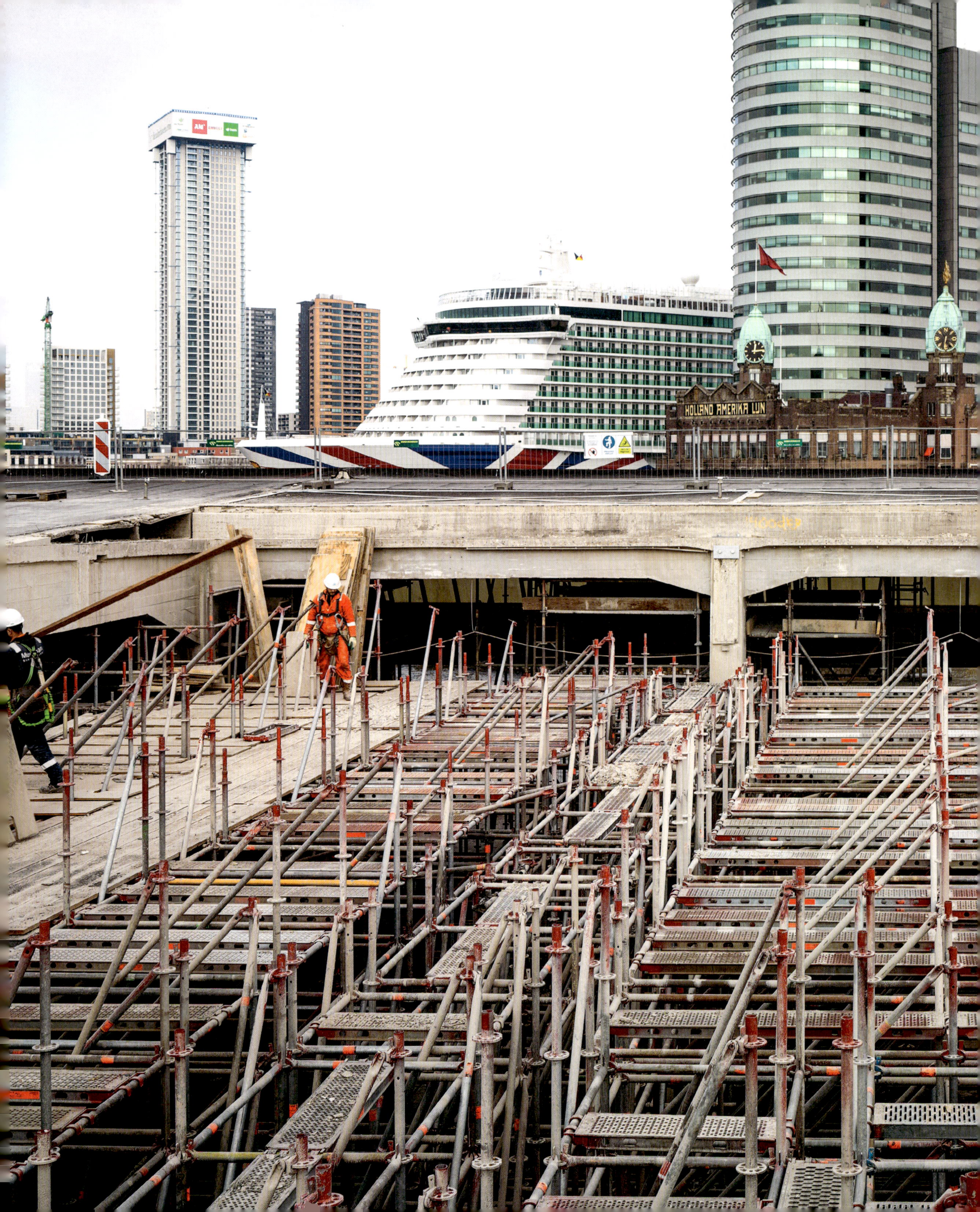
HOLLAND AMERIKA LIJN

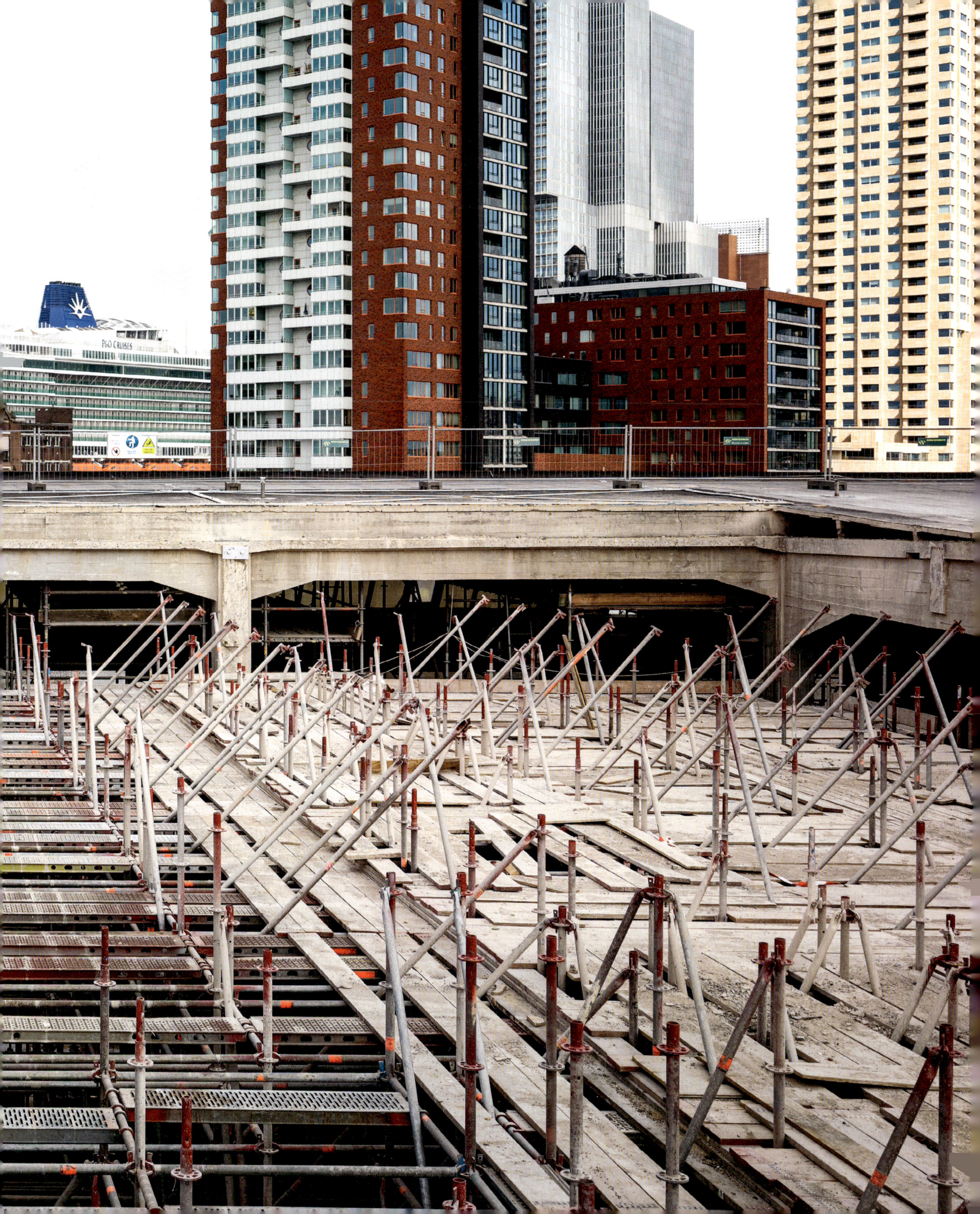
P&O CRUISES

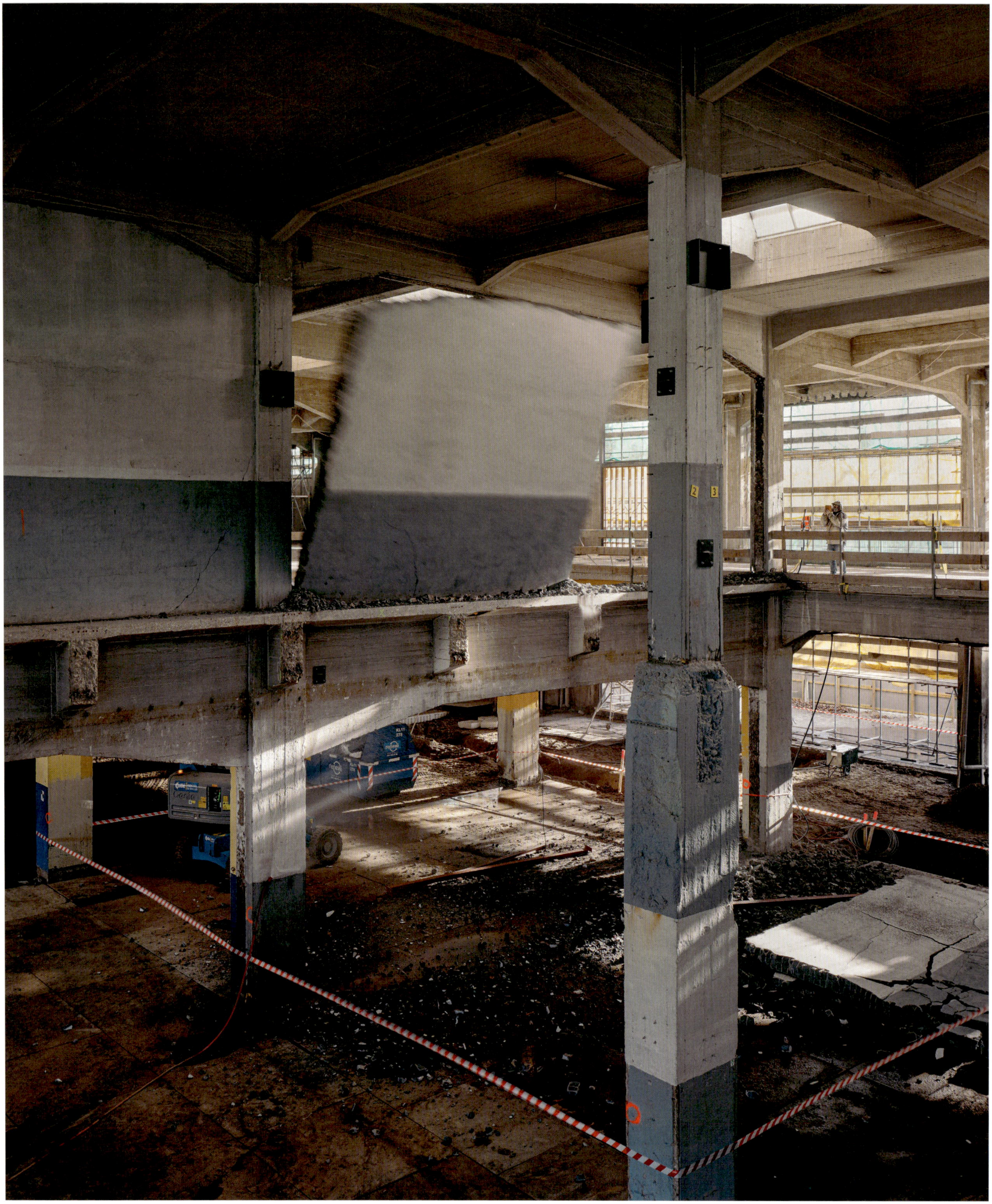

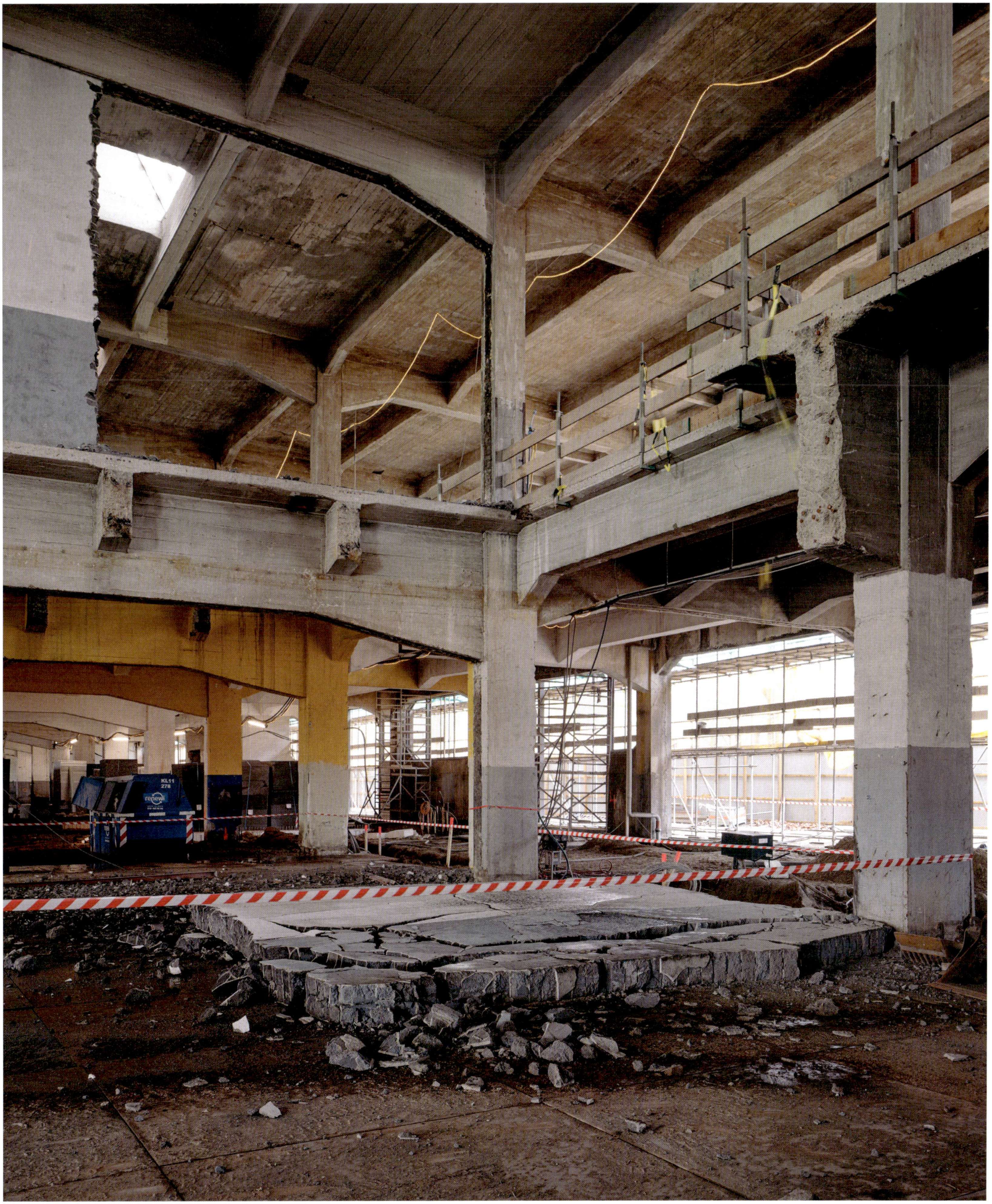
KL11
278
renewi

“As welders, we unite the metal section of the Tornado at Fenix. Singapore, Bangladesh, and now Rotterdam. We travel all over the world.”

Mezanur Rahaman, Imran Hossain,
Mohammed Ali, Mamum Mia and Tofazzal, Welders at CSM

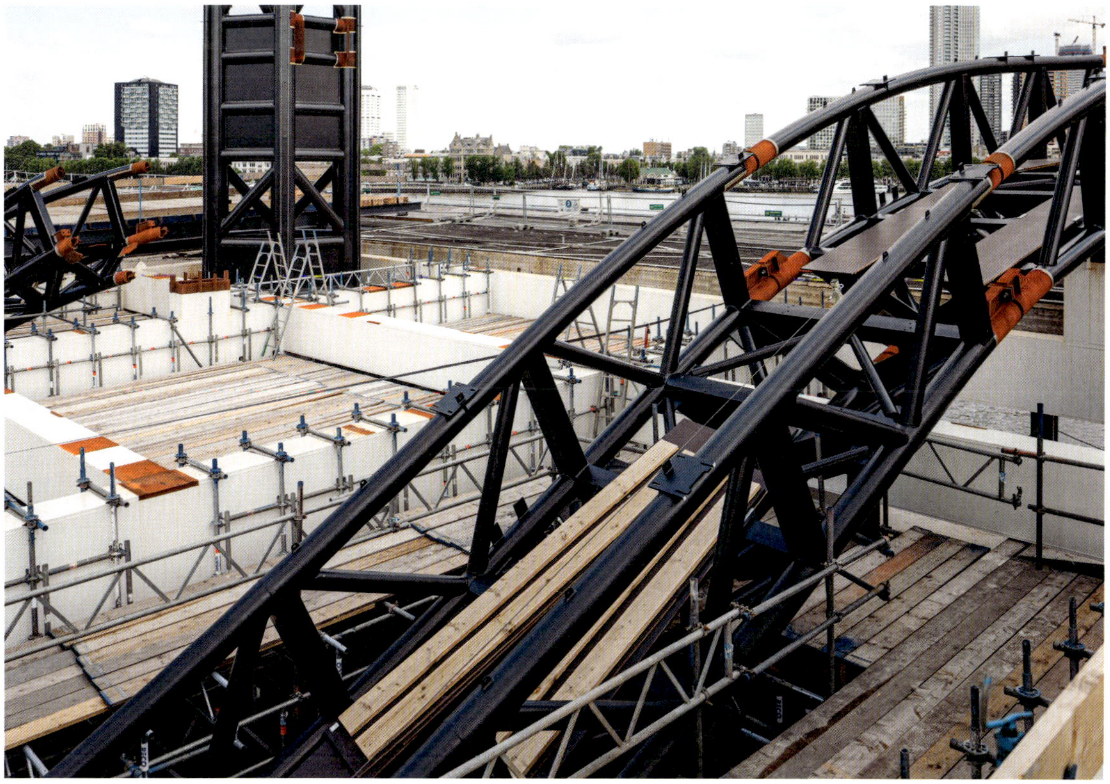

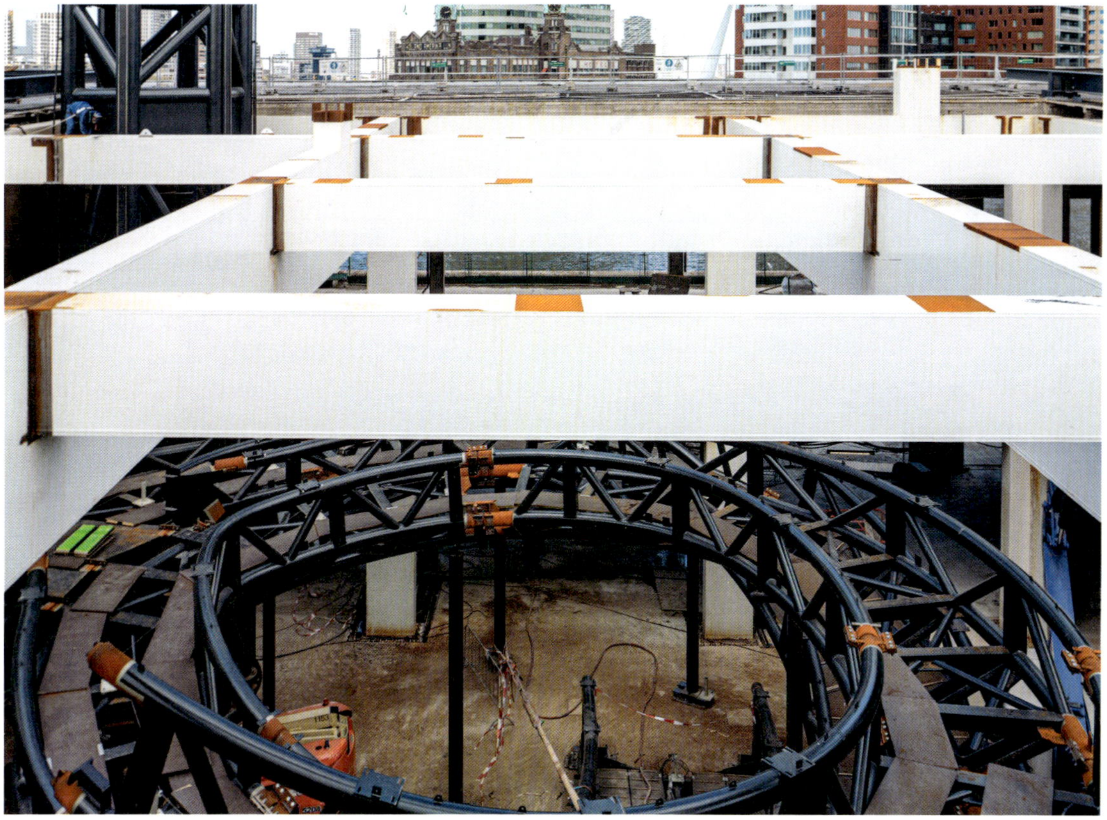

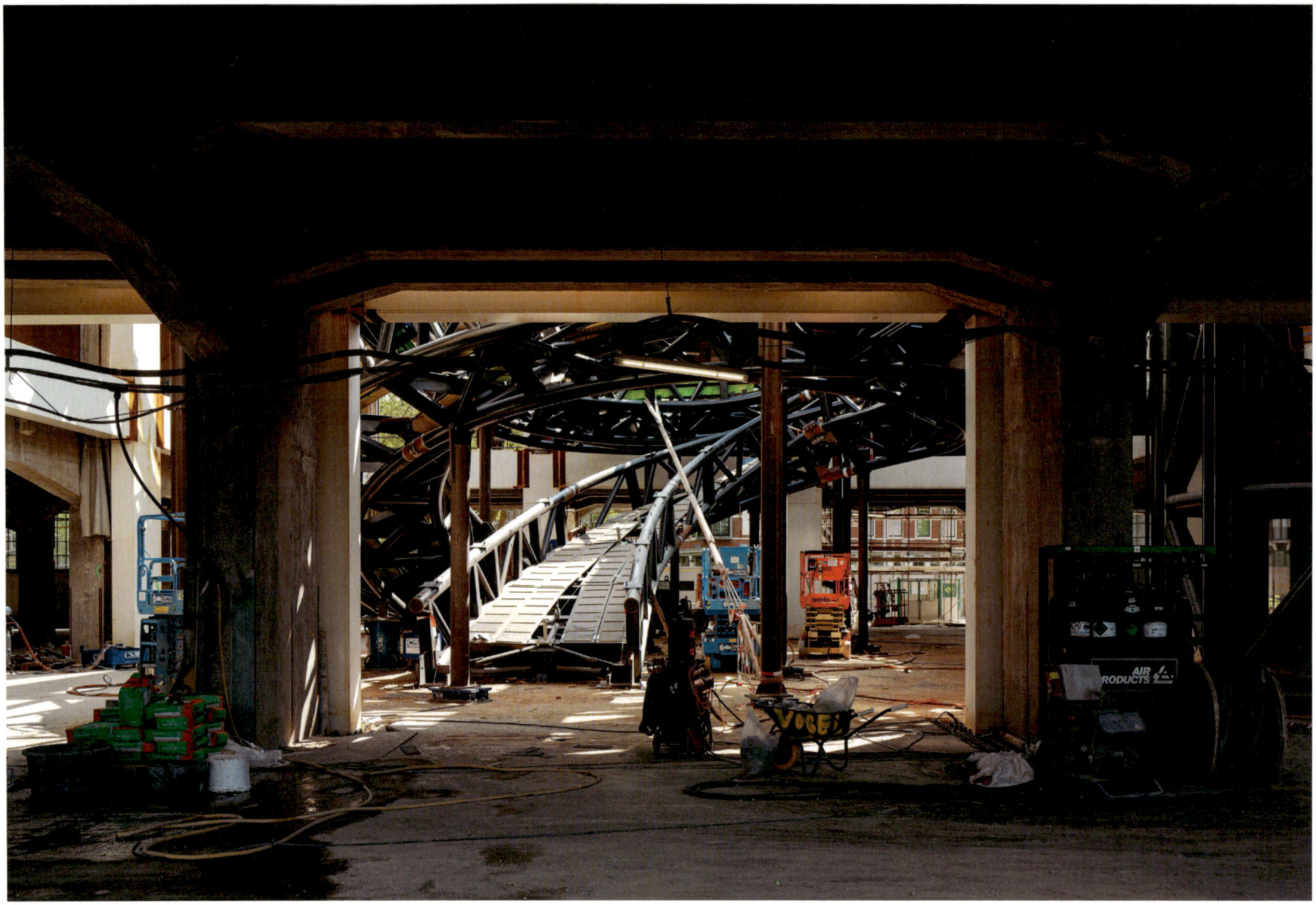

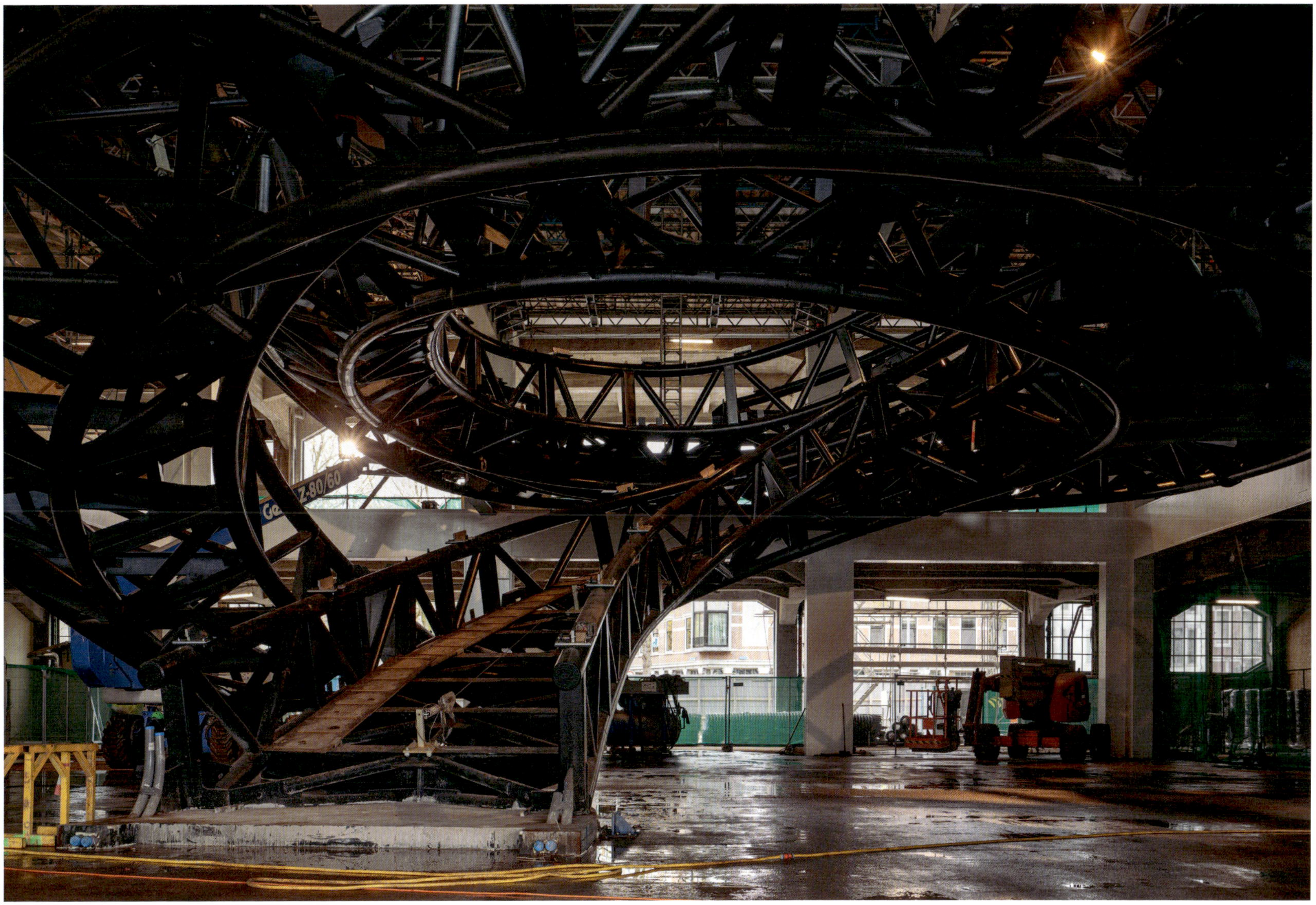

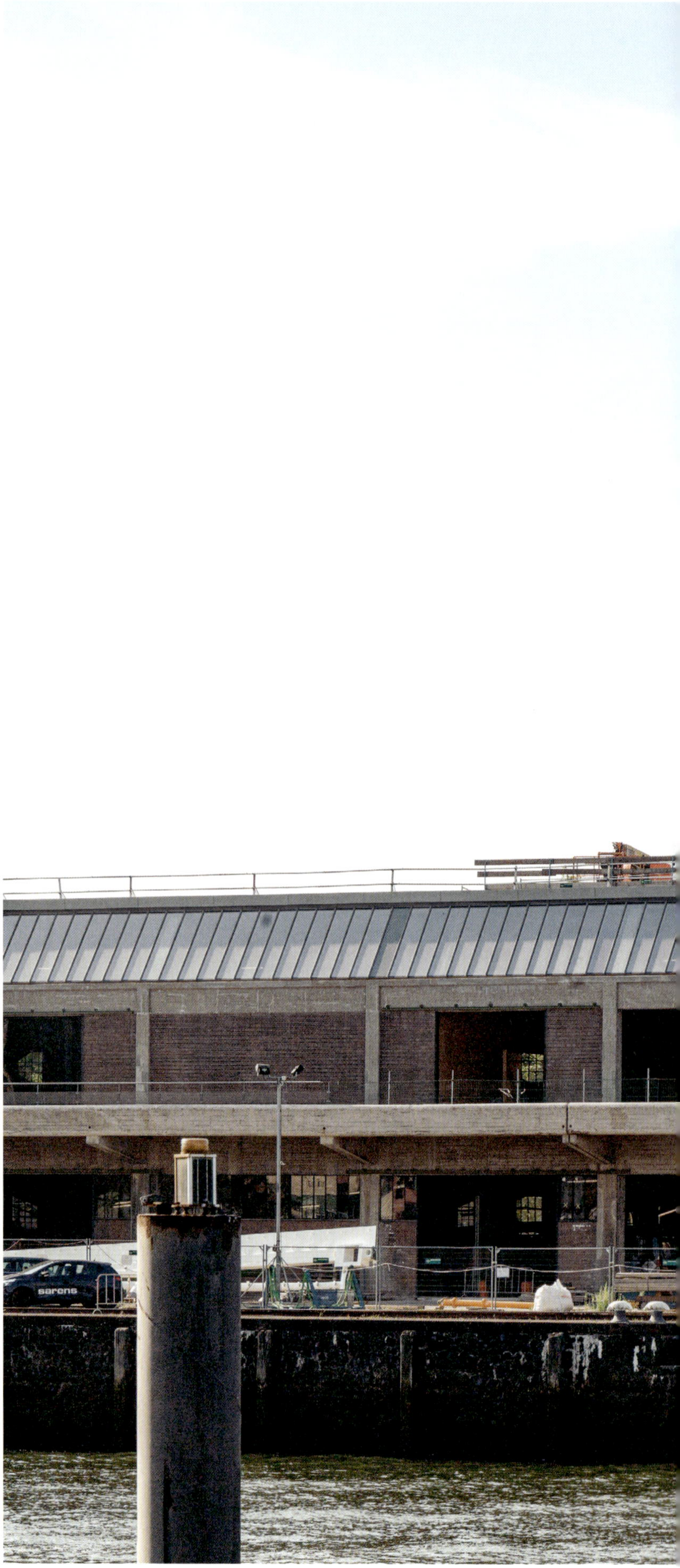

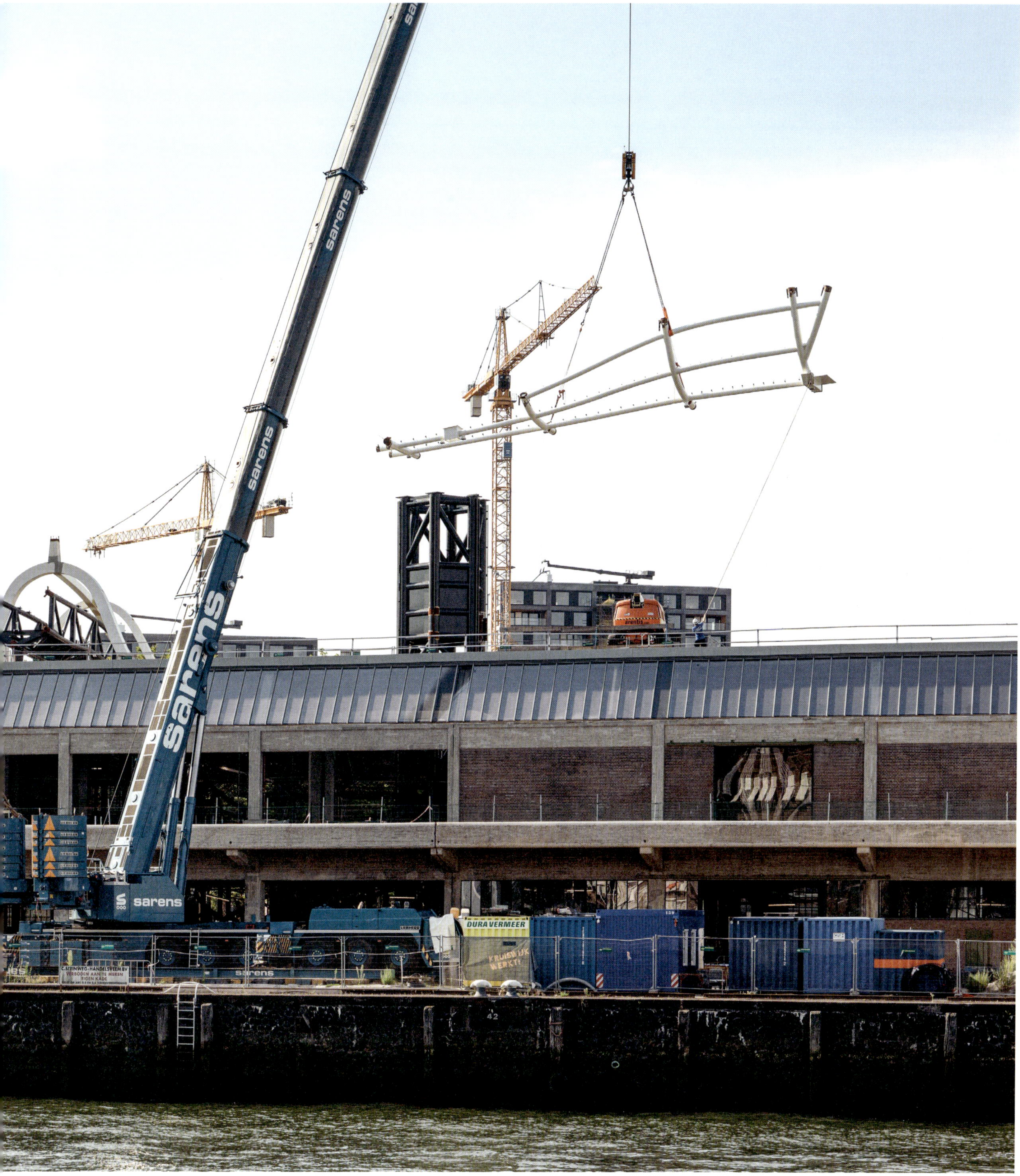

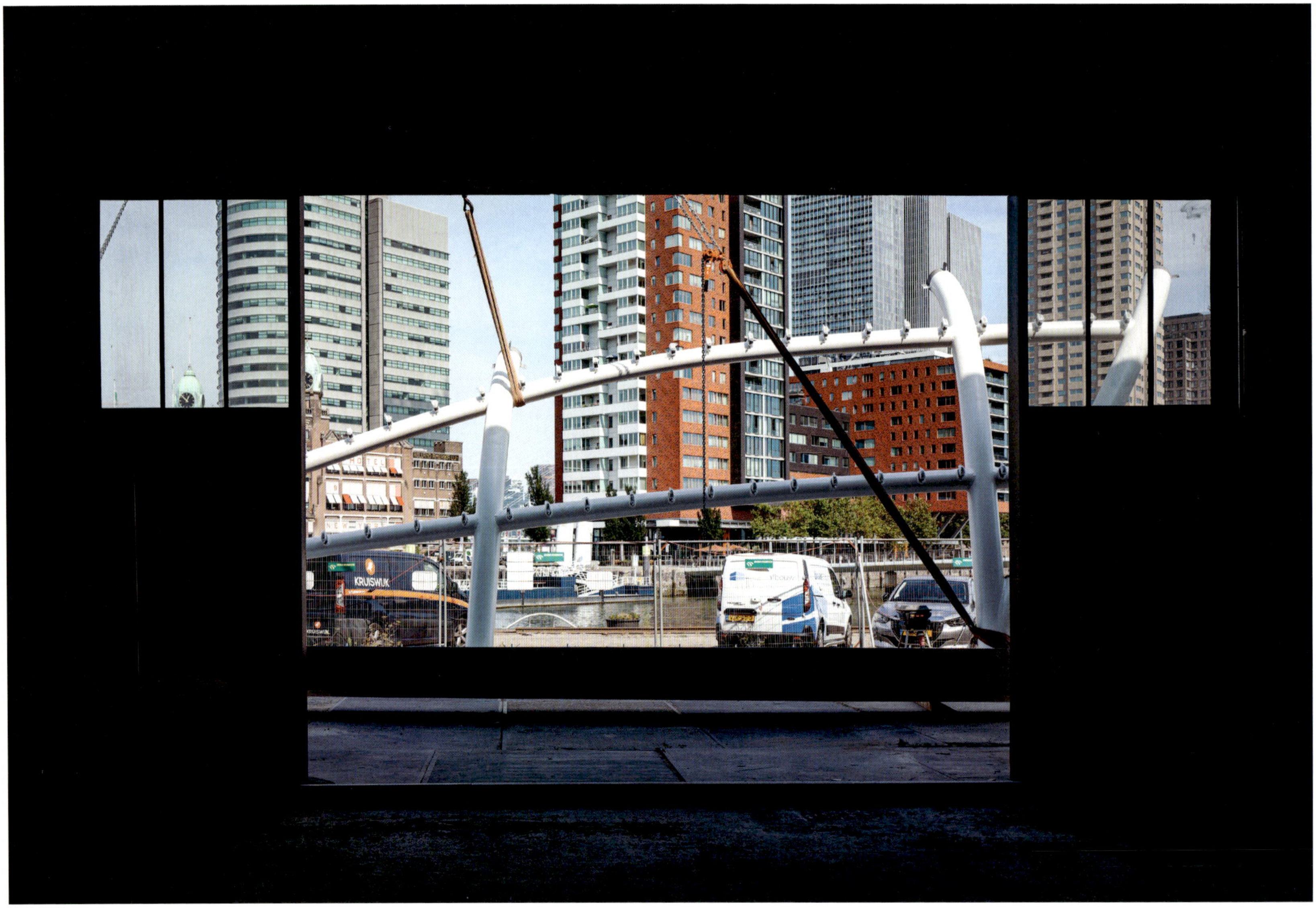
KRUISWIJK

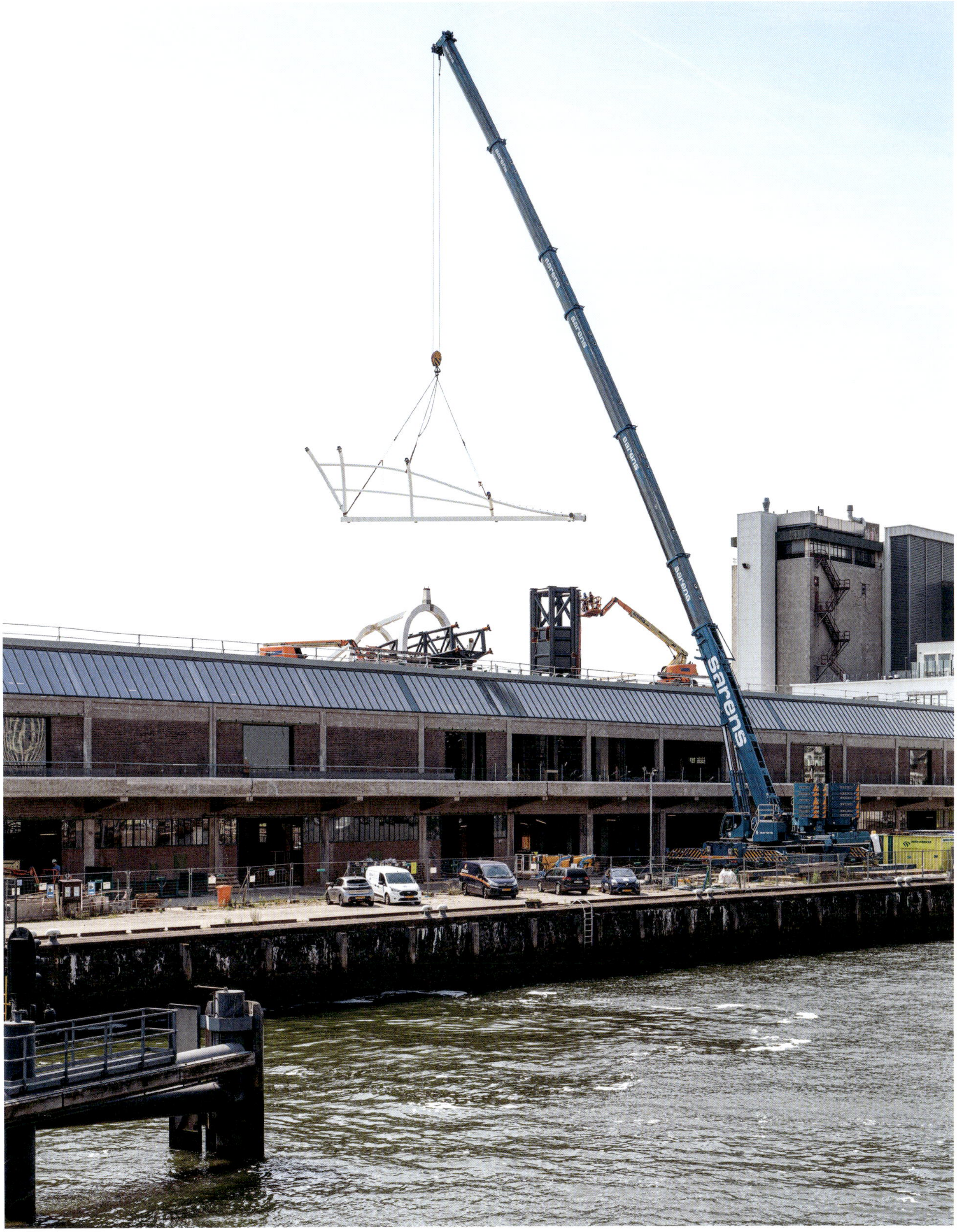
sarens

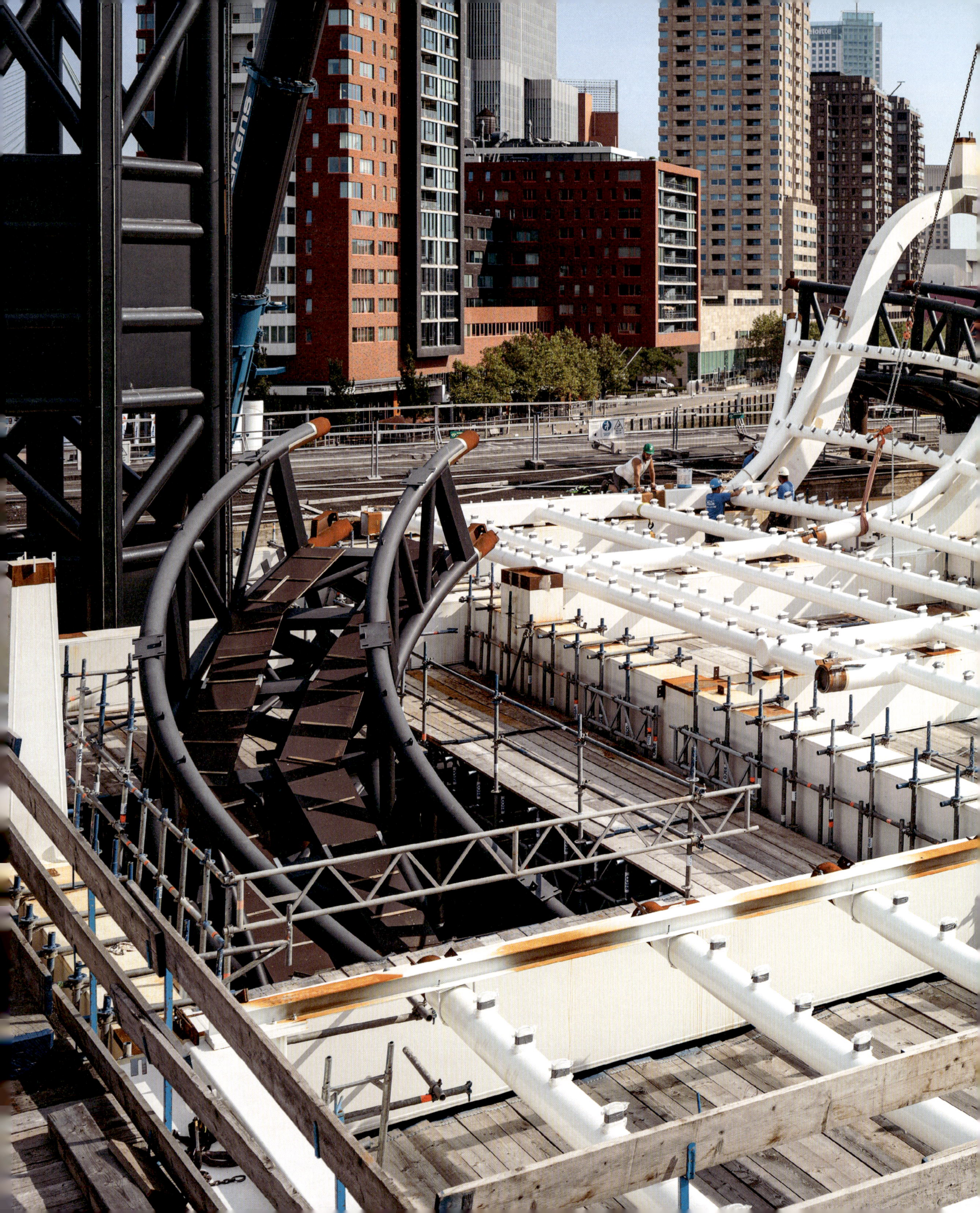

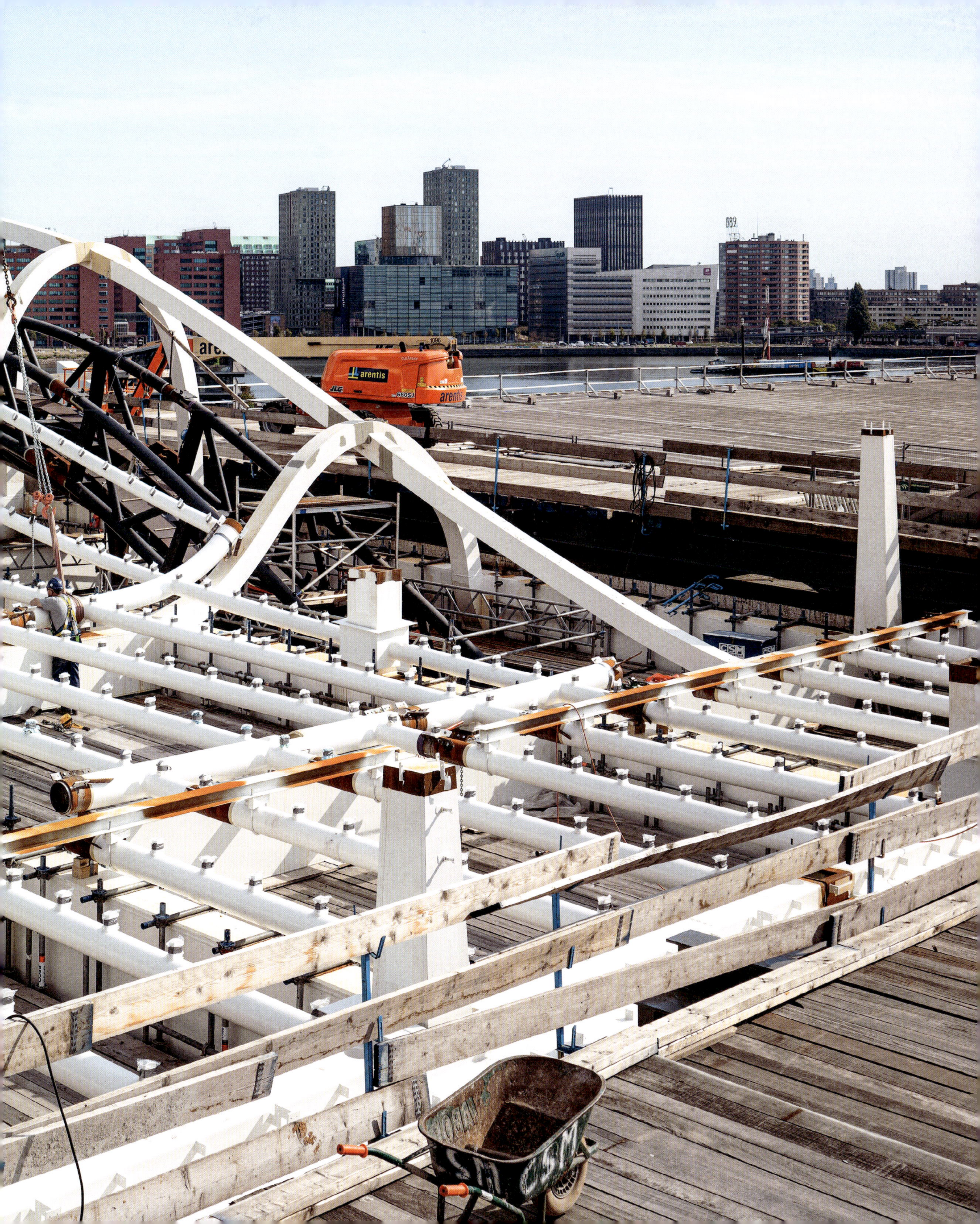
arentis
JLG
arentis
CSM

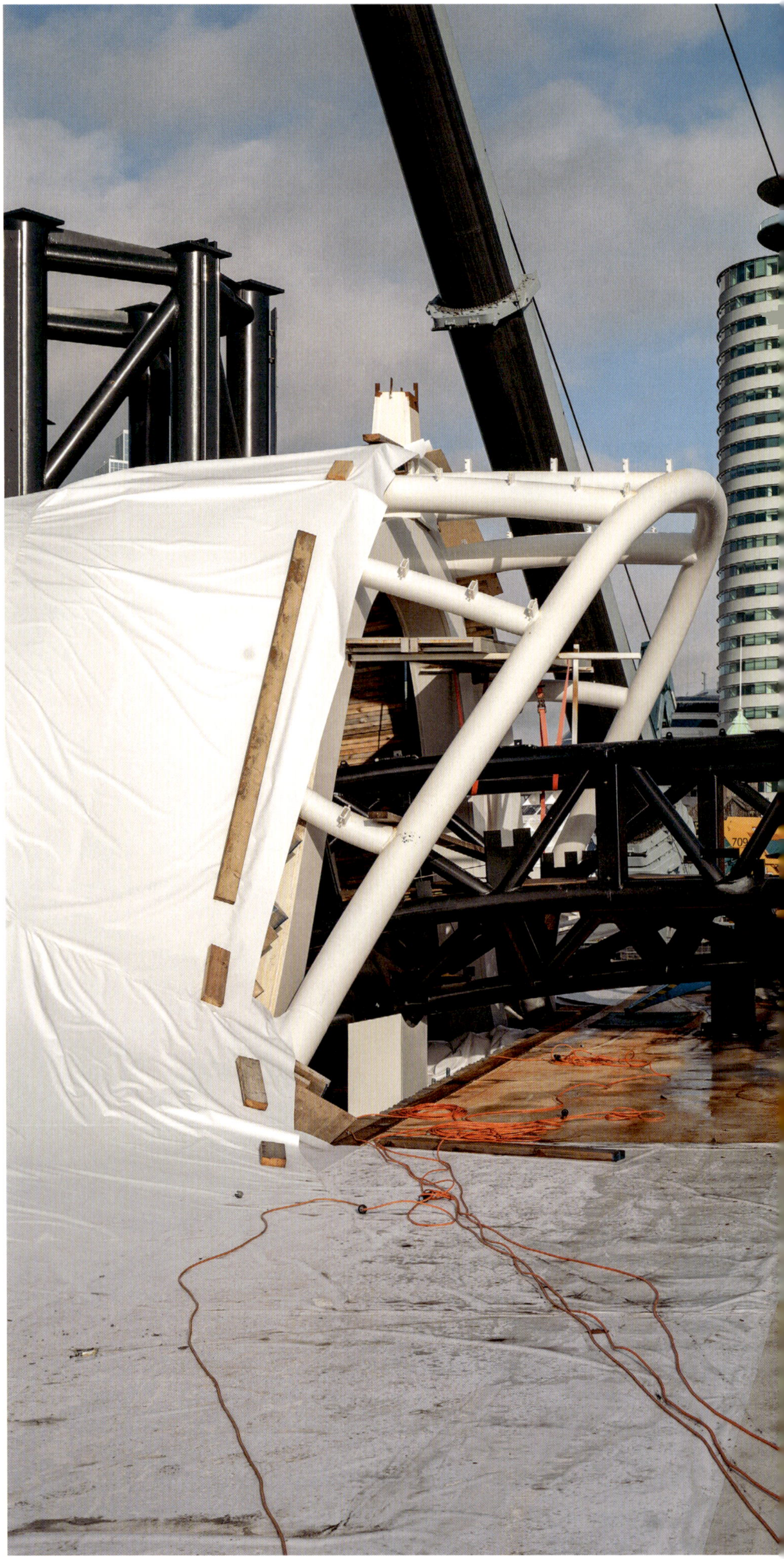

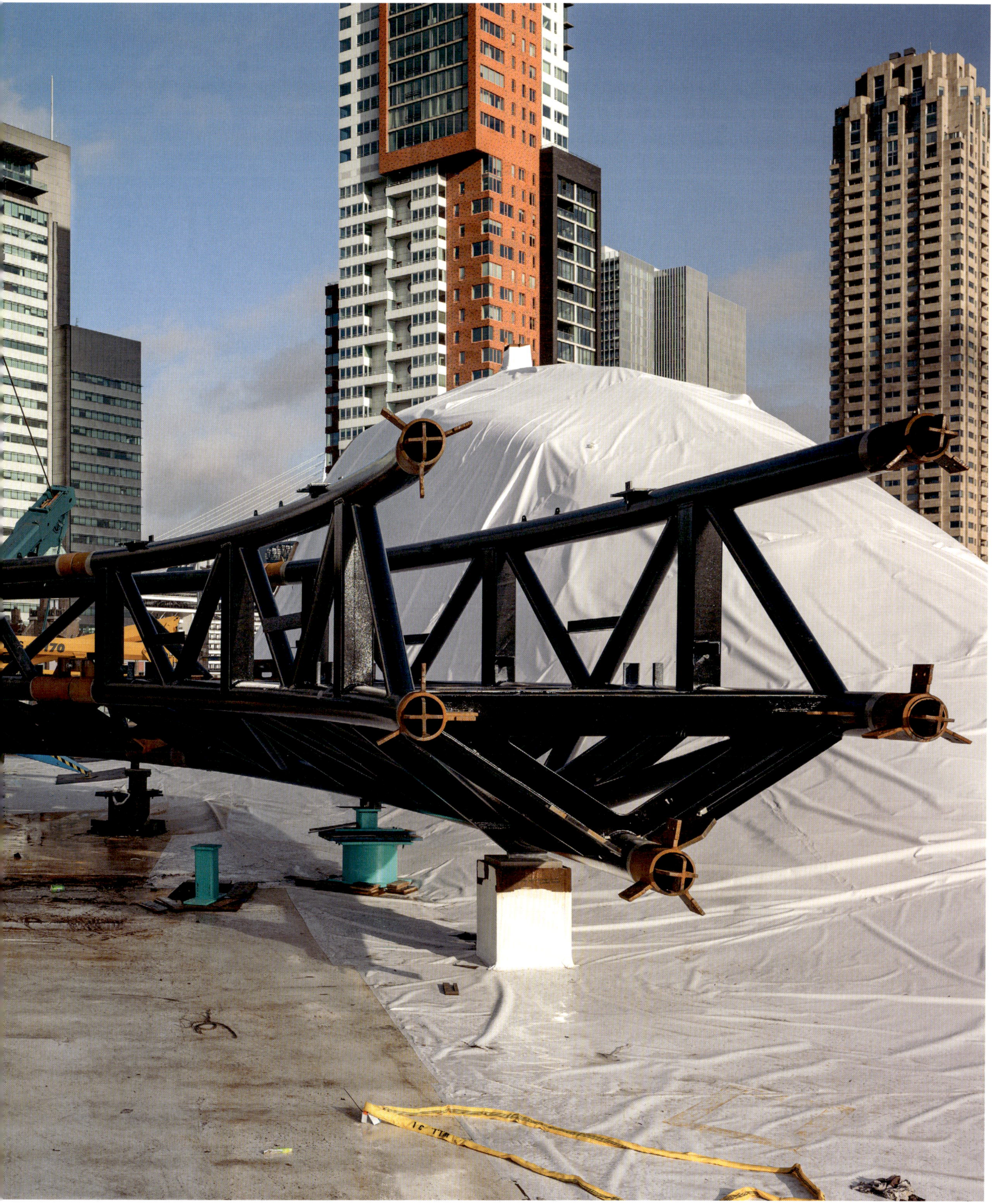

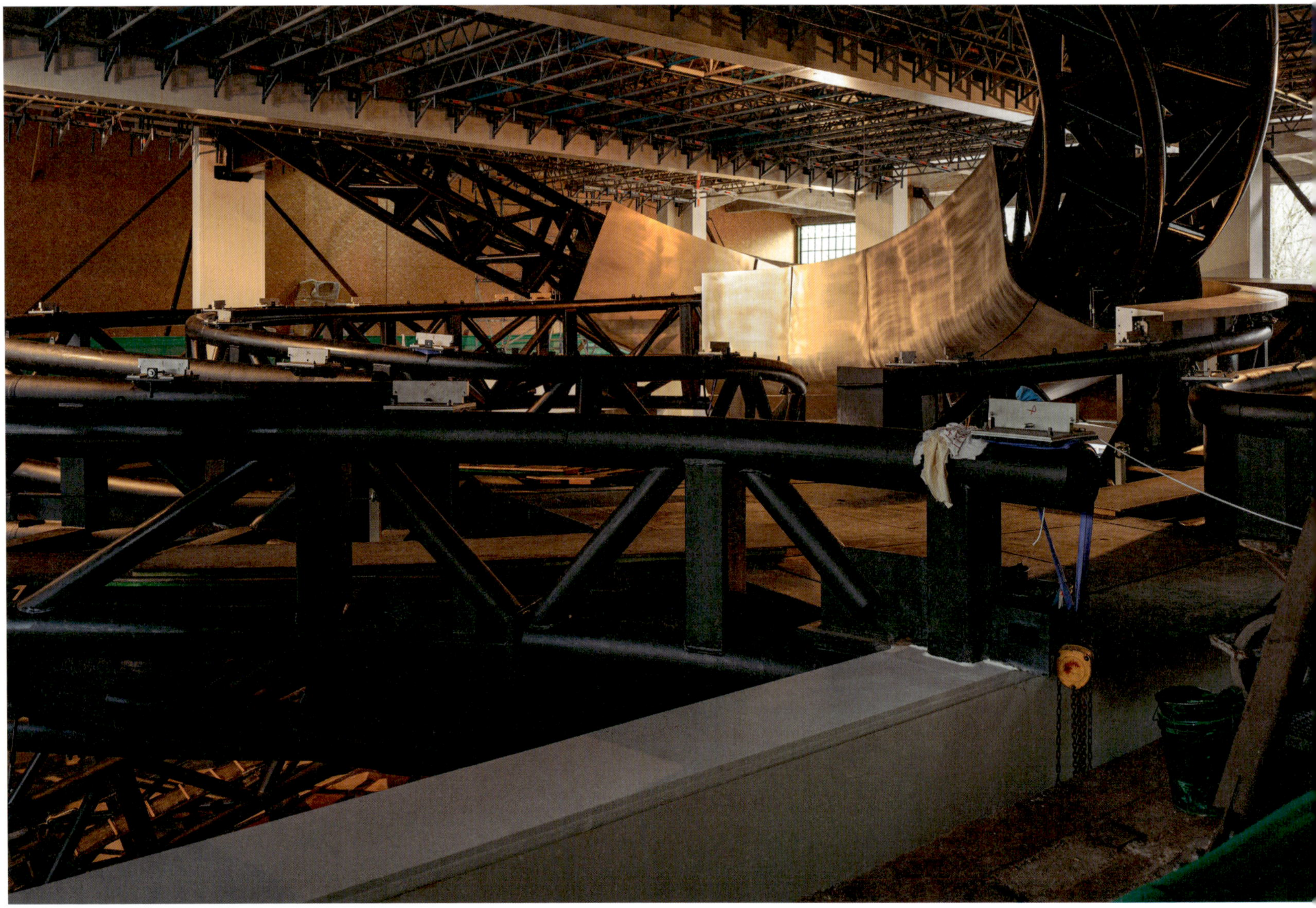

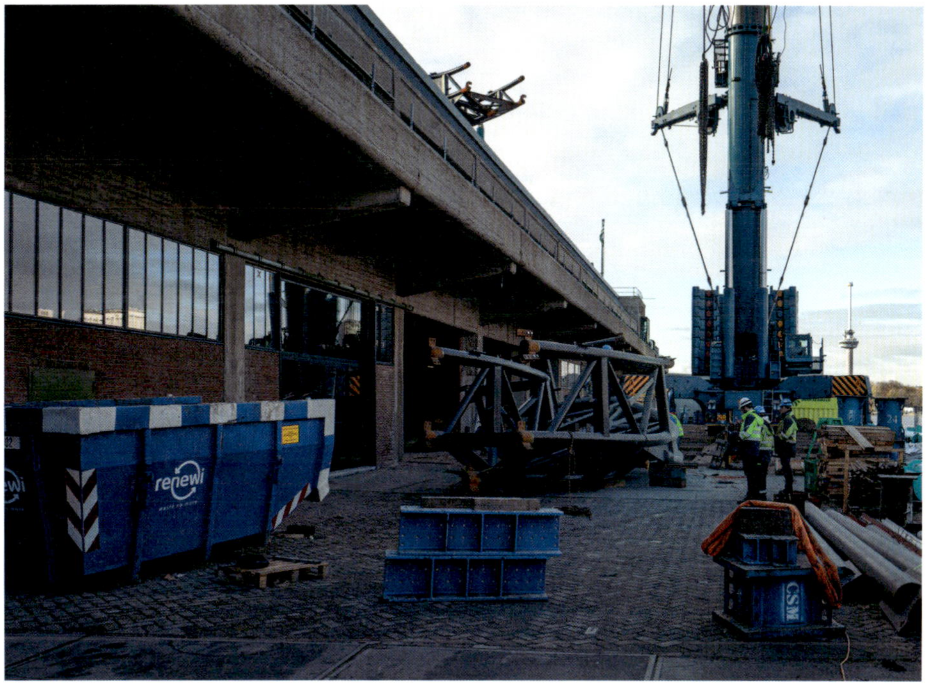
renewi
CSM

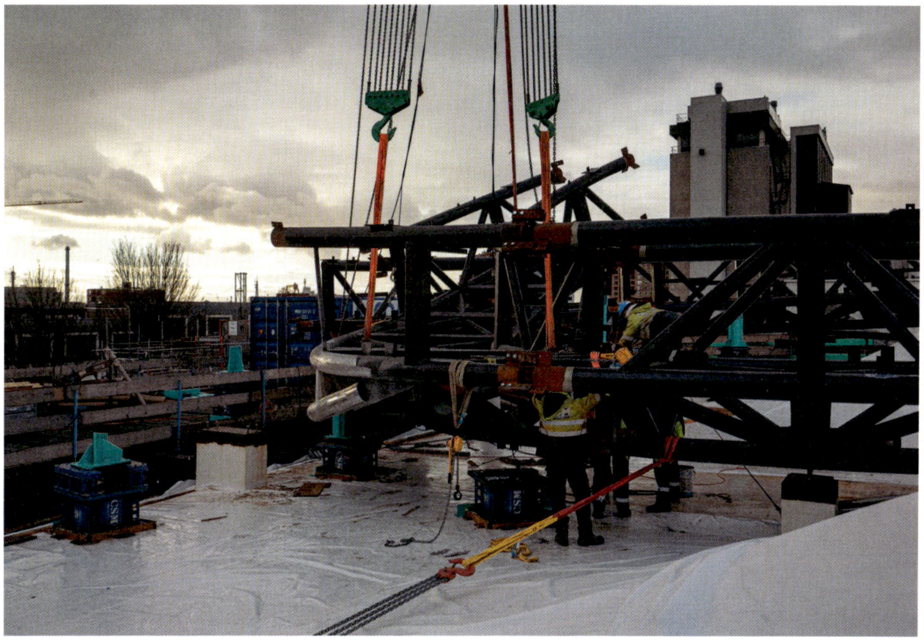

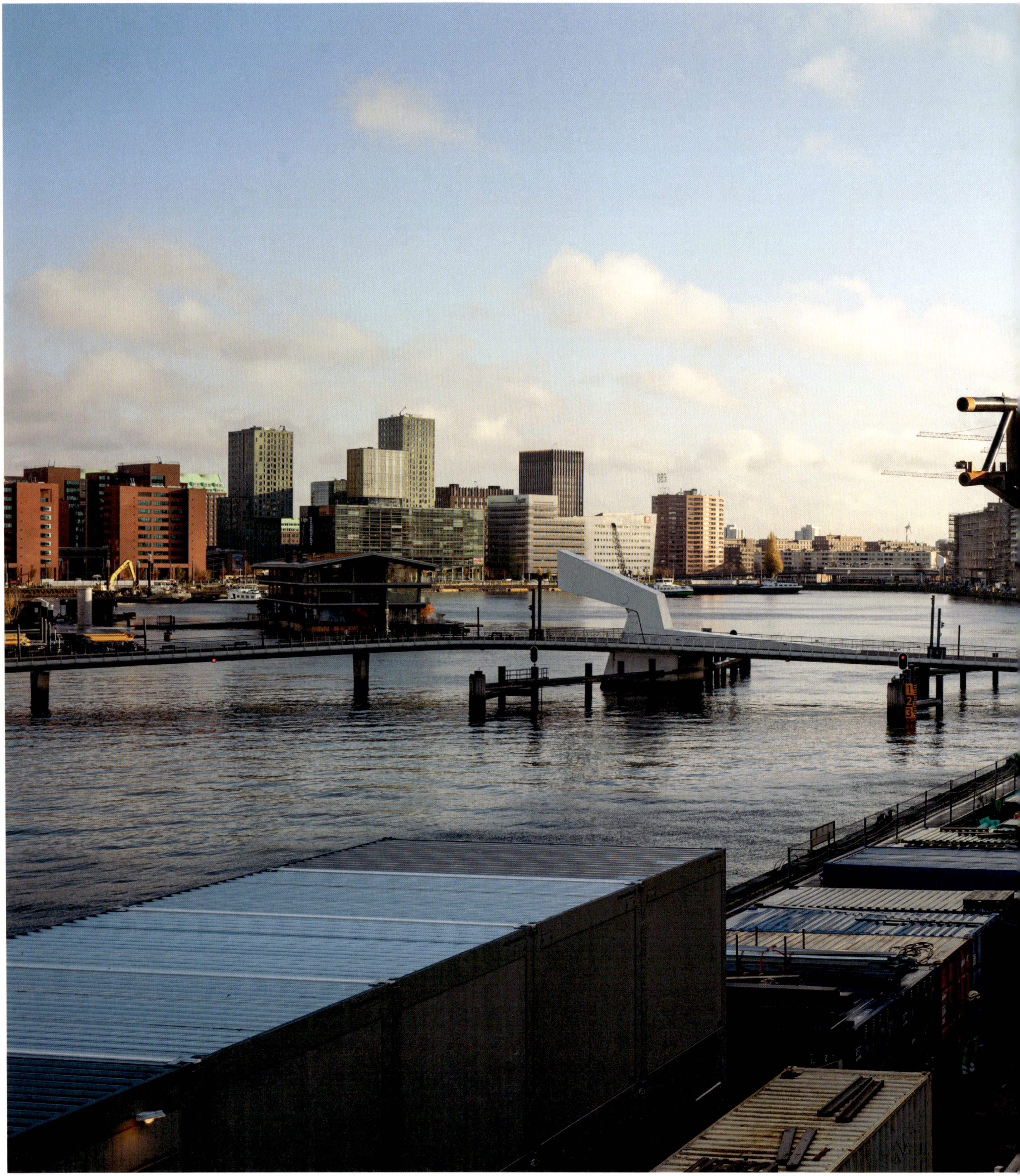

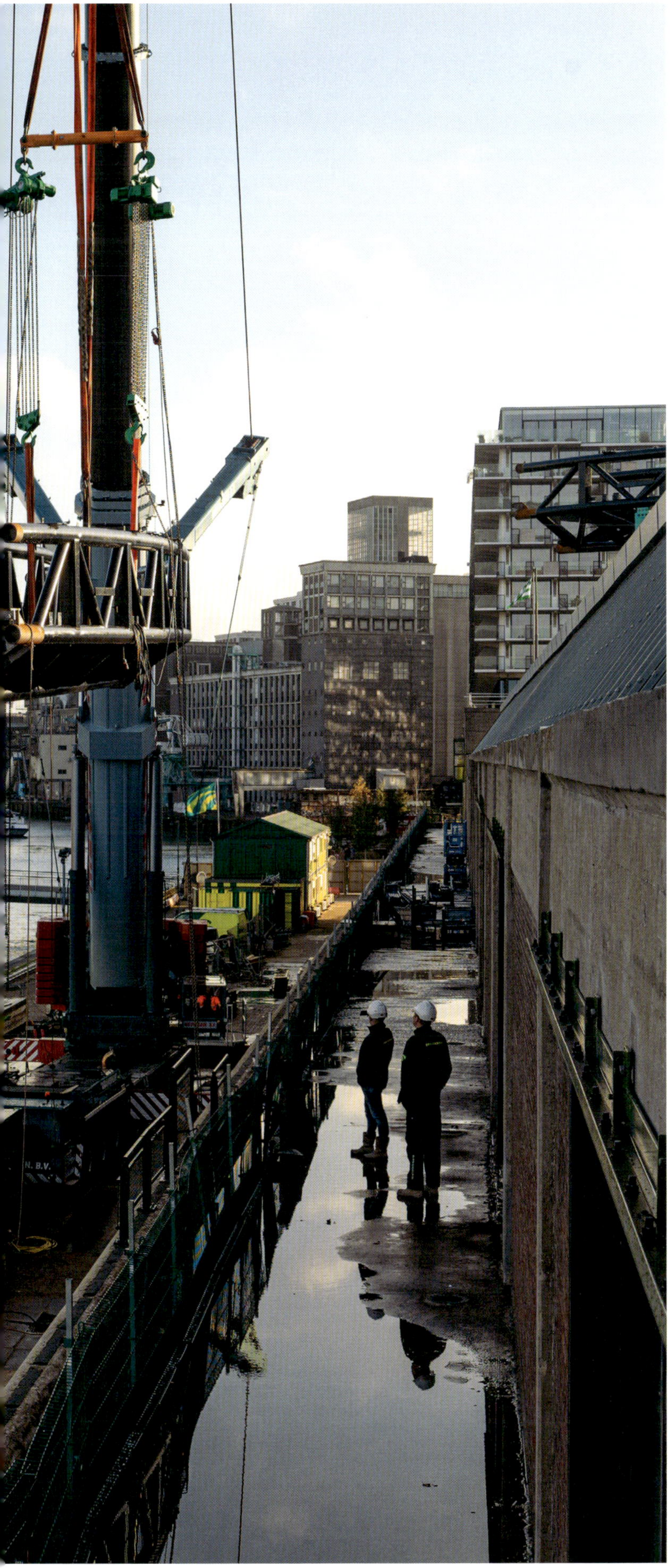

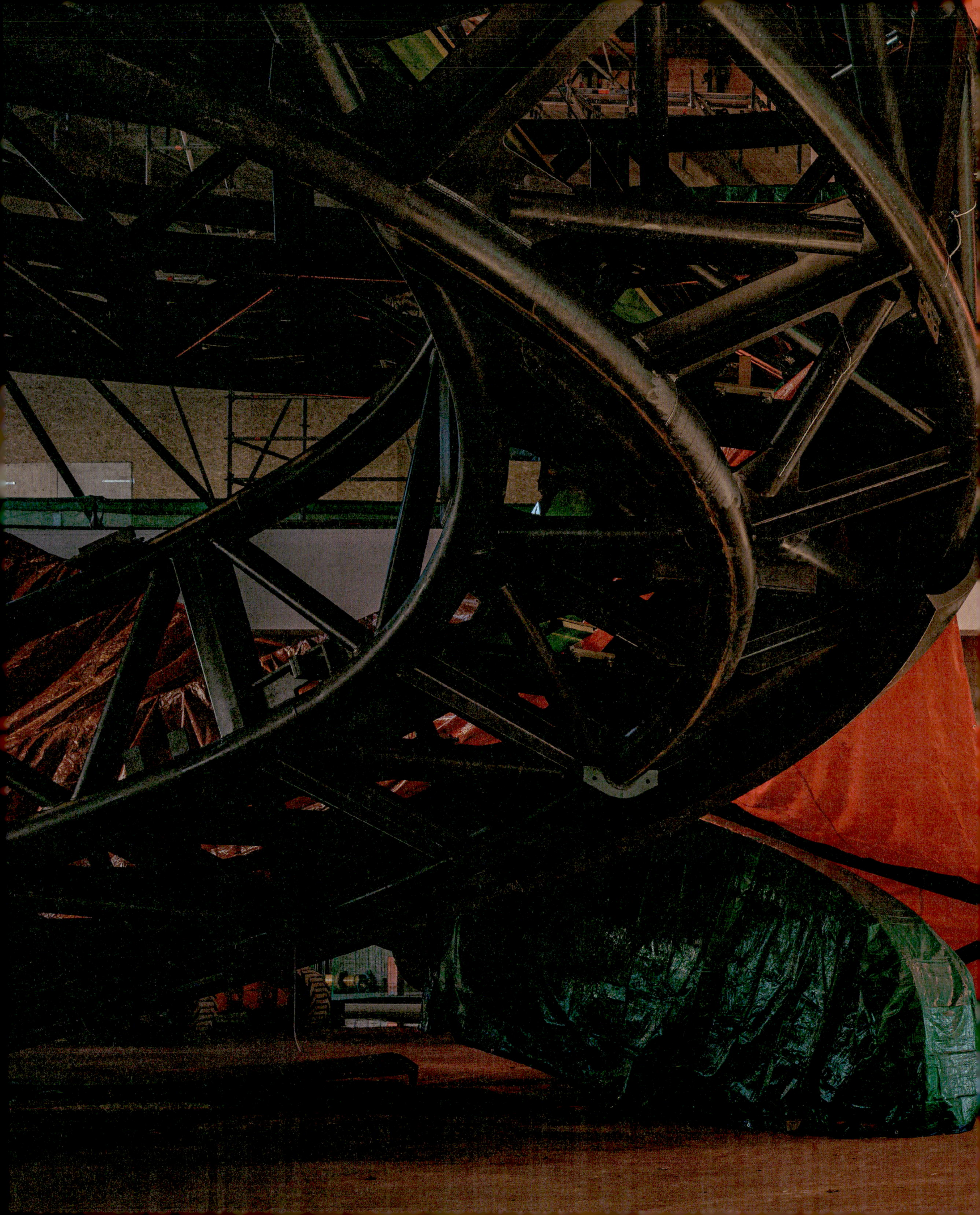

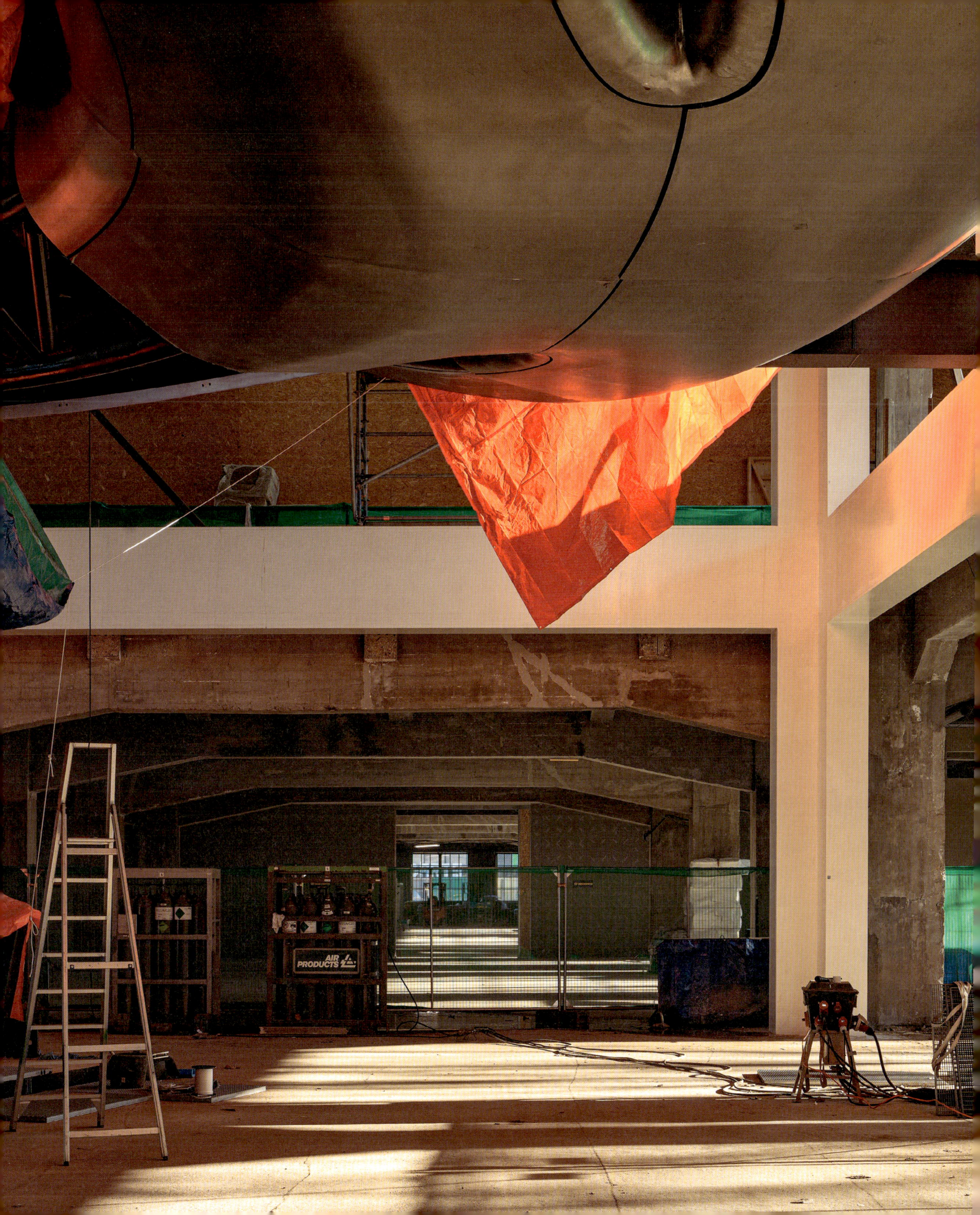
AIR PRODUCTS

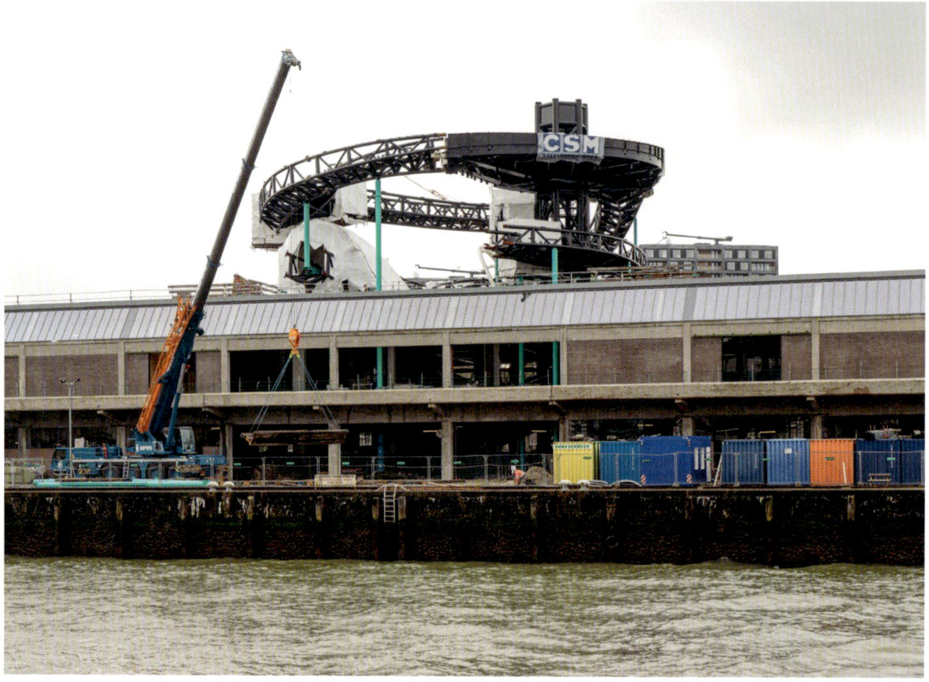
CSM

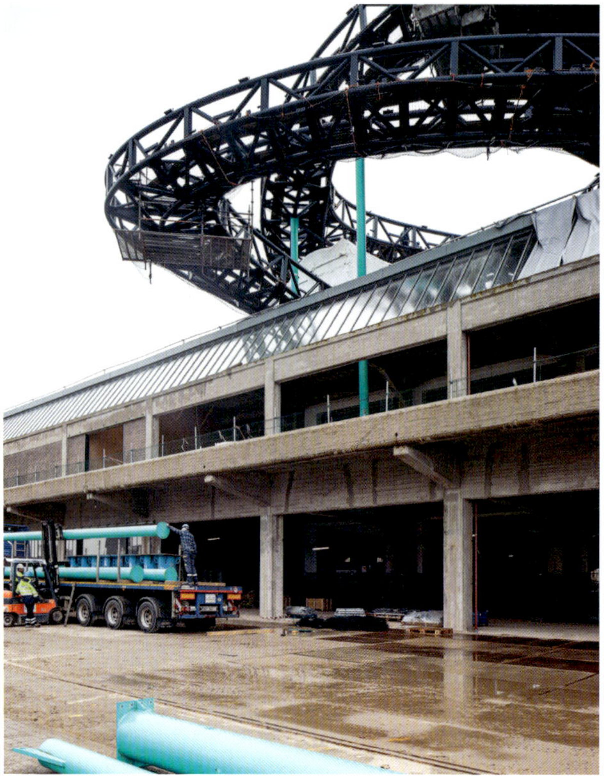

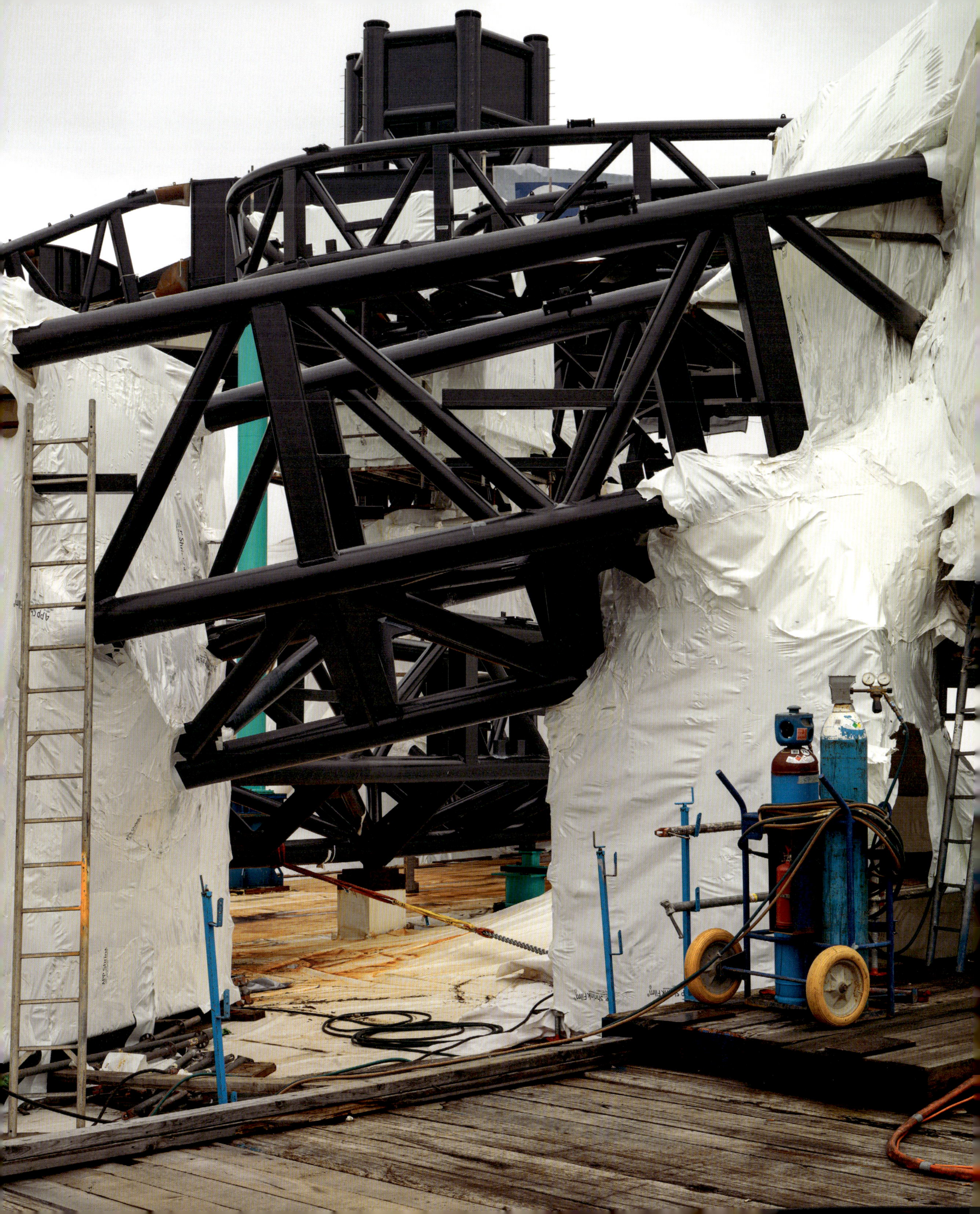

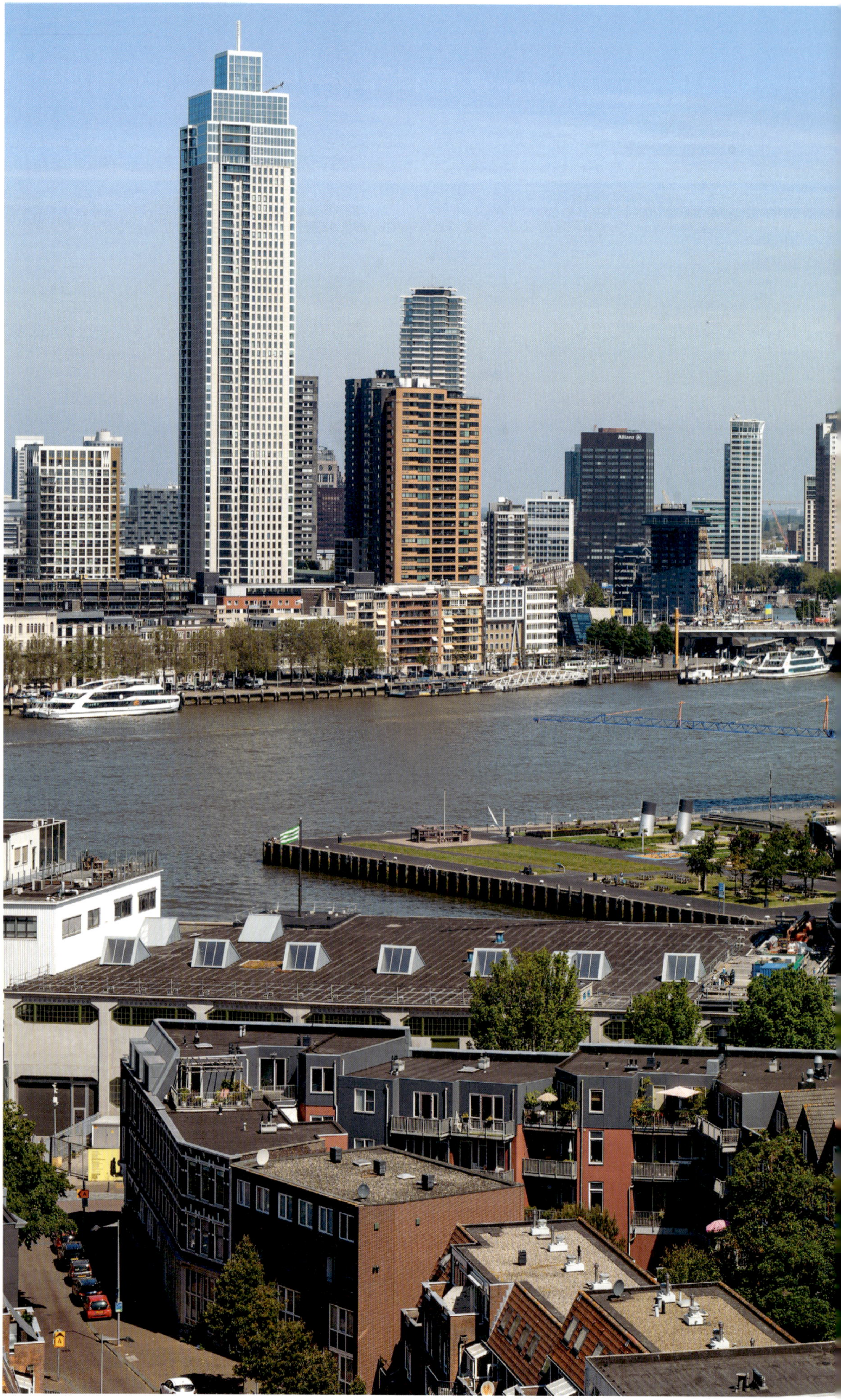

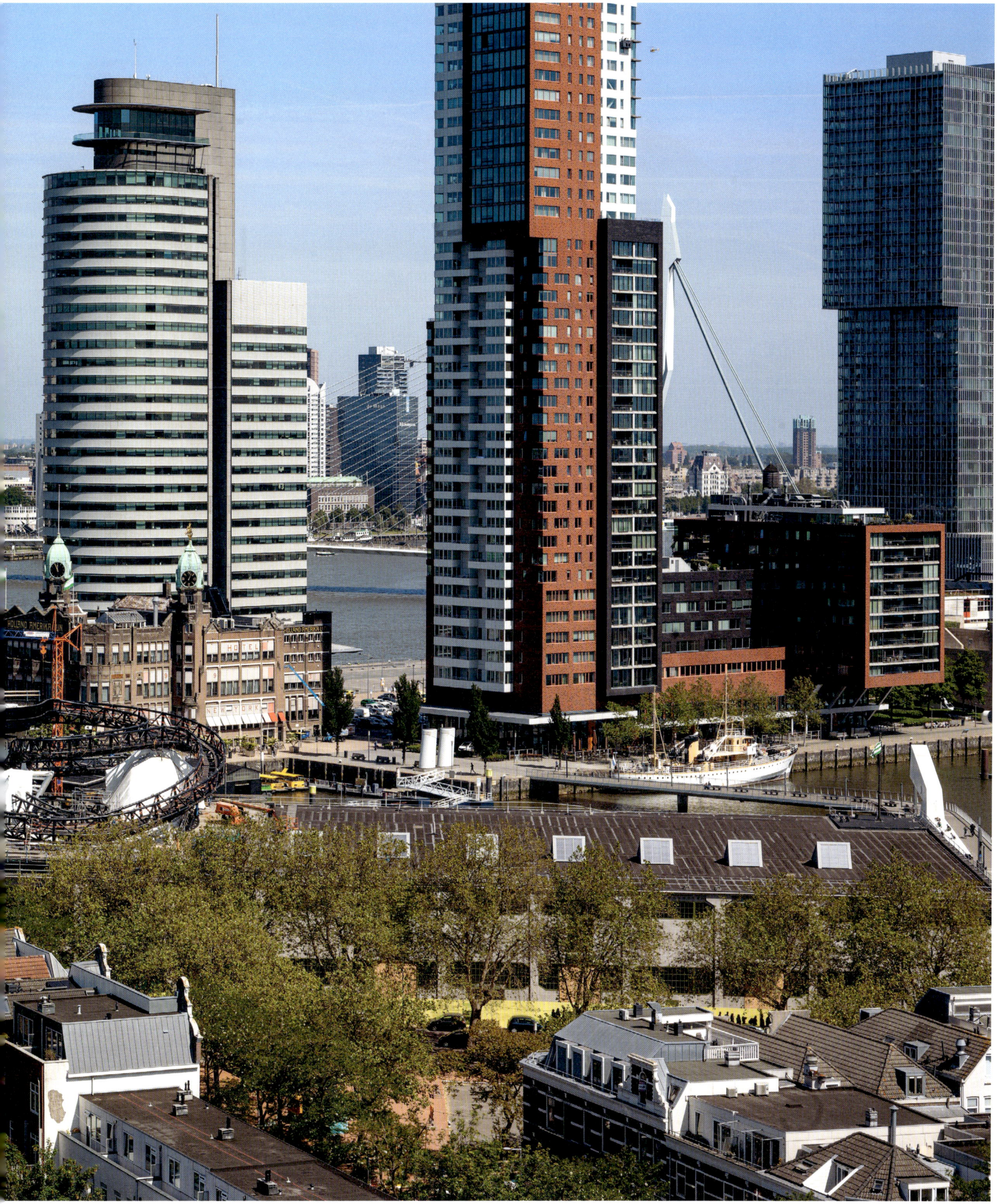

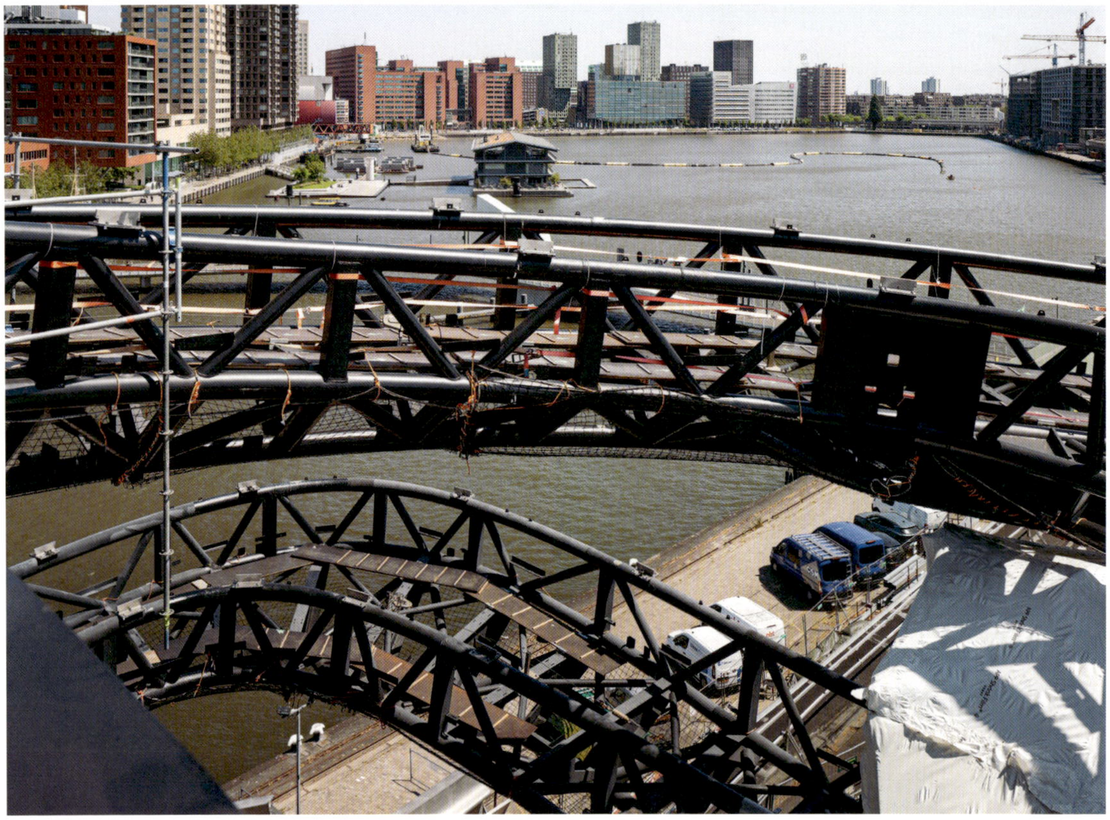

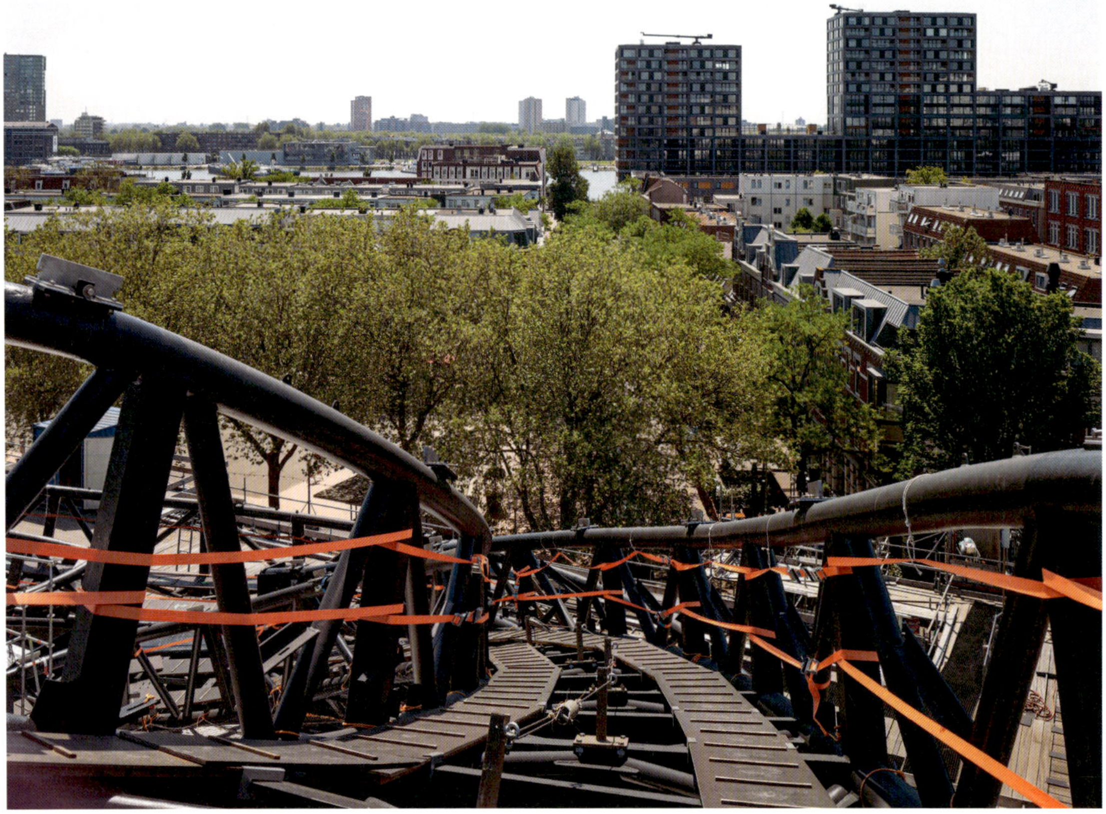

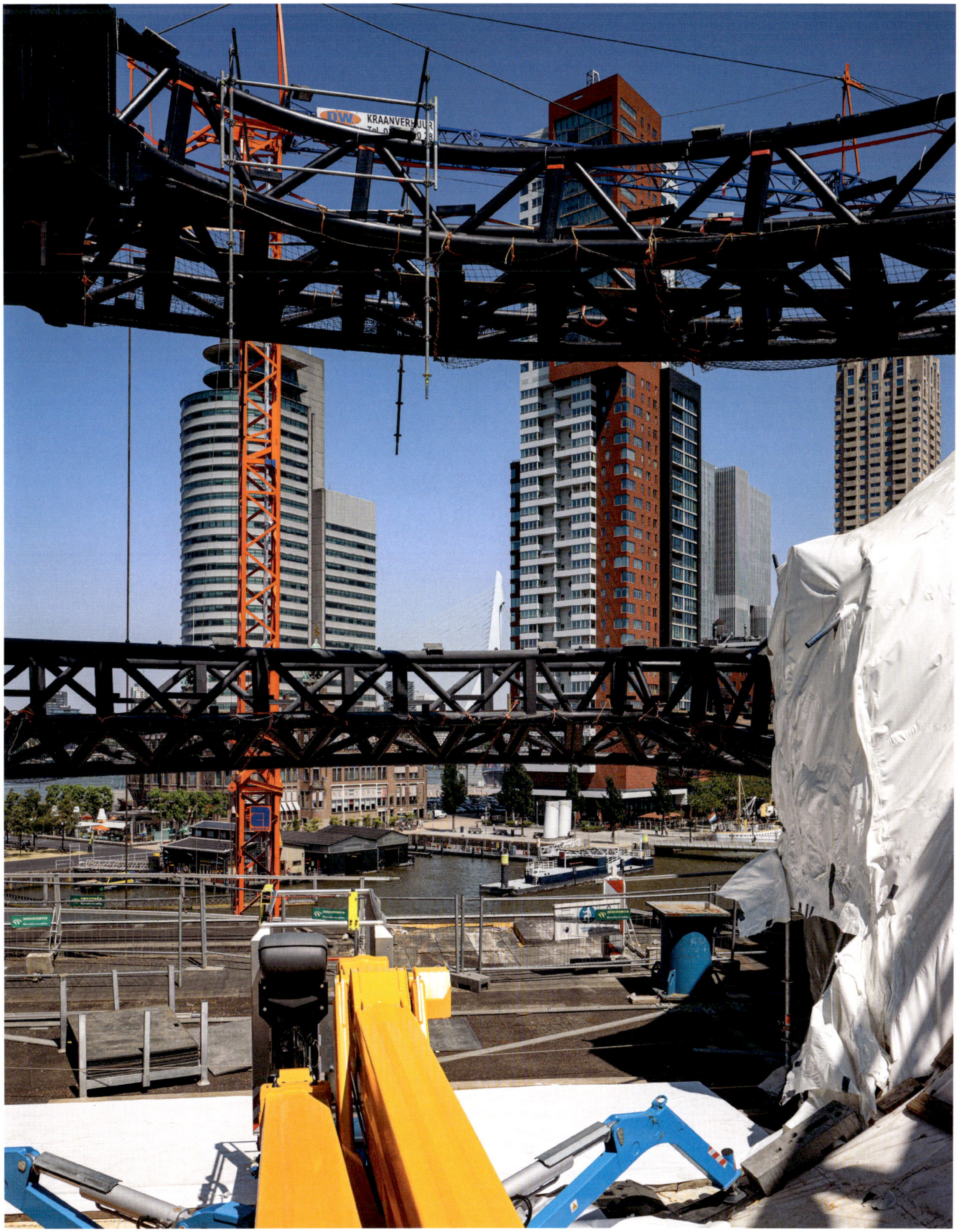
KRAANVERHUUR

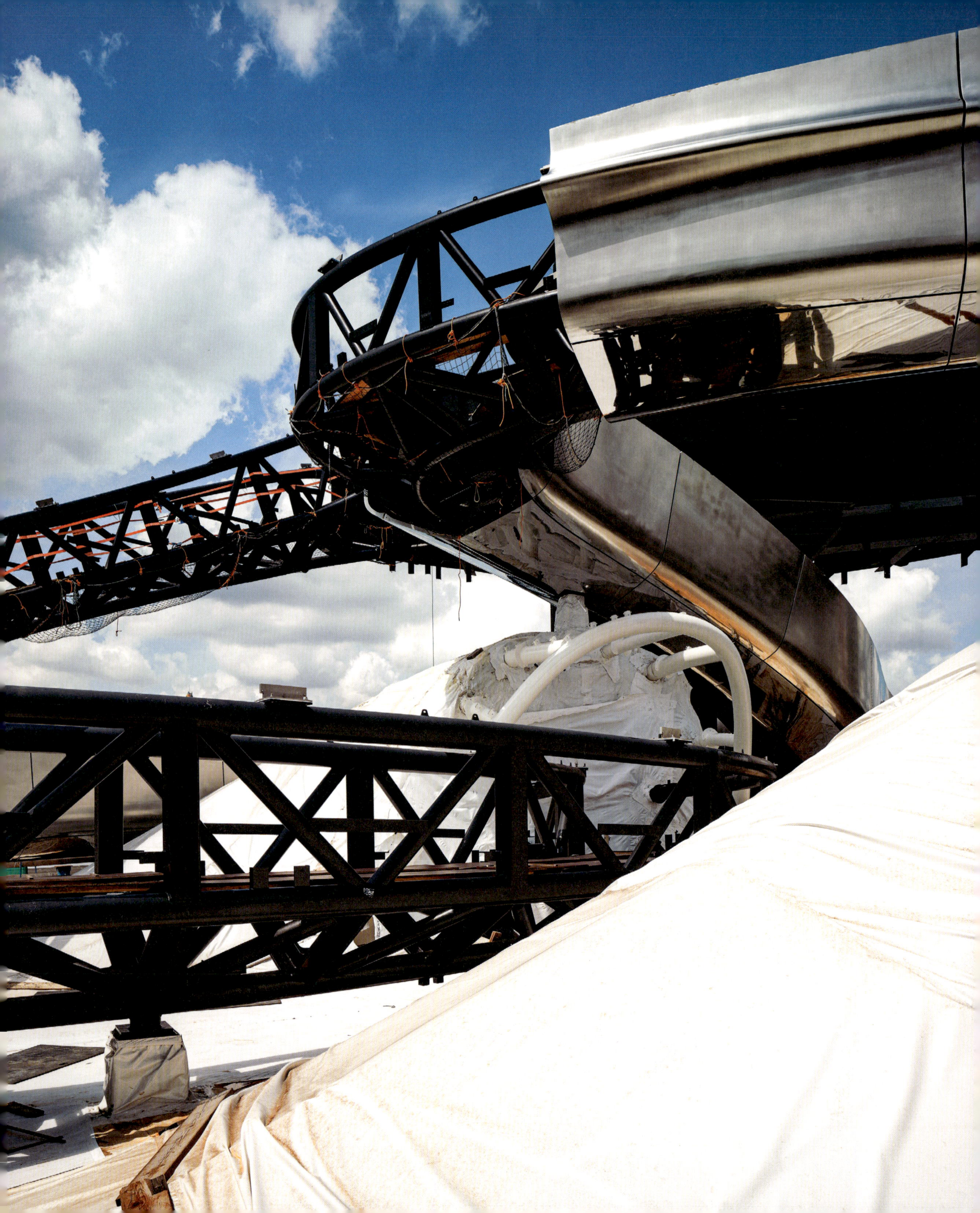

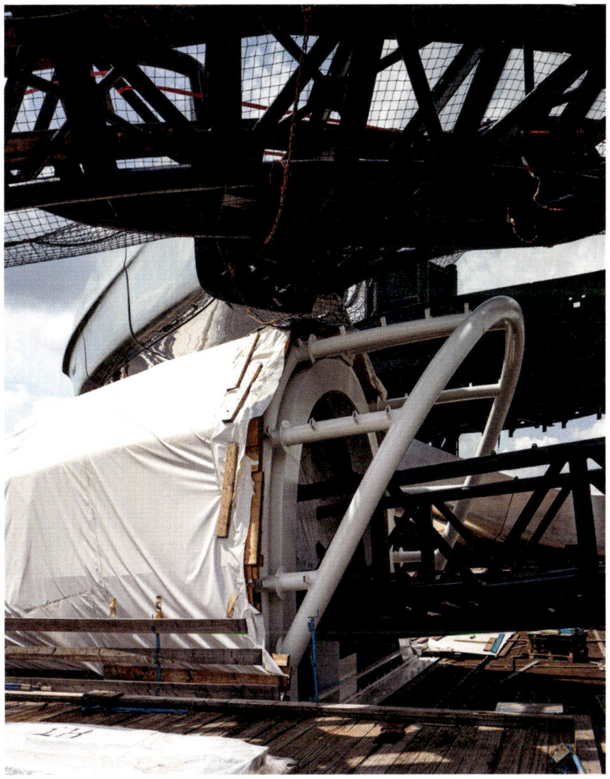
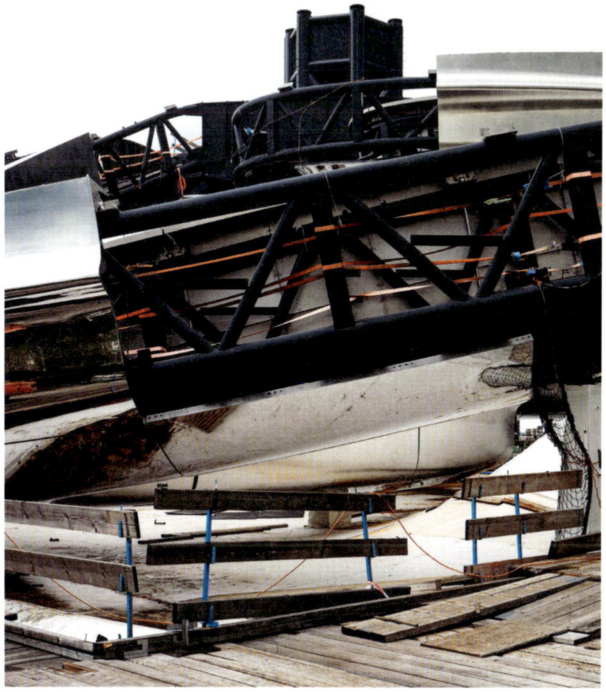
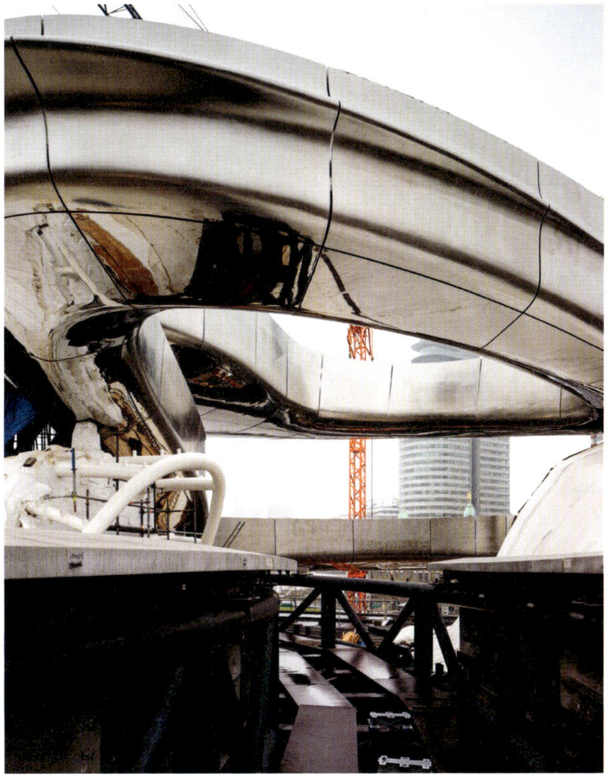
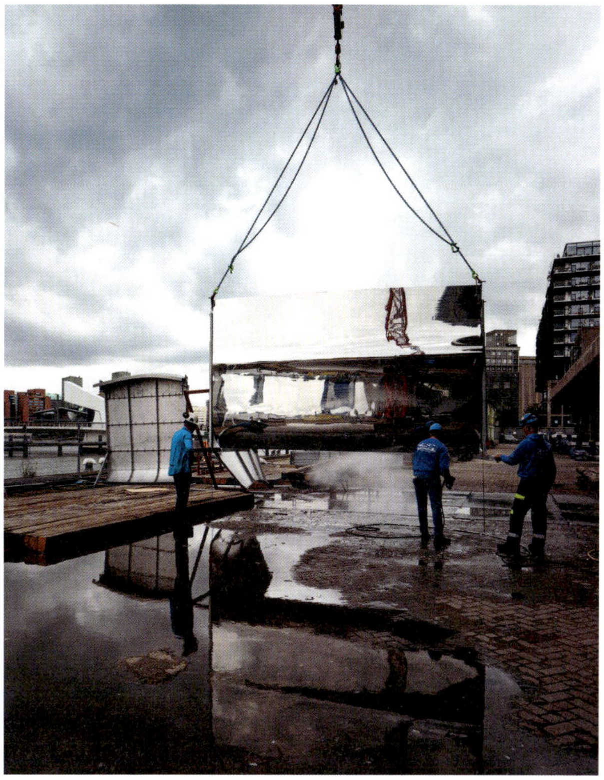

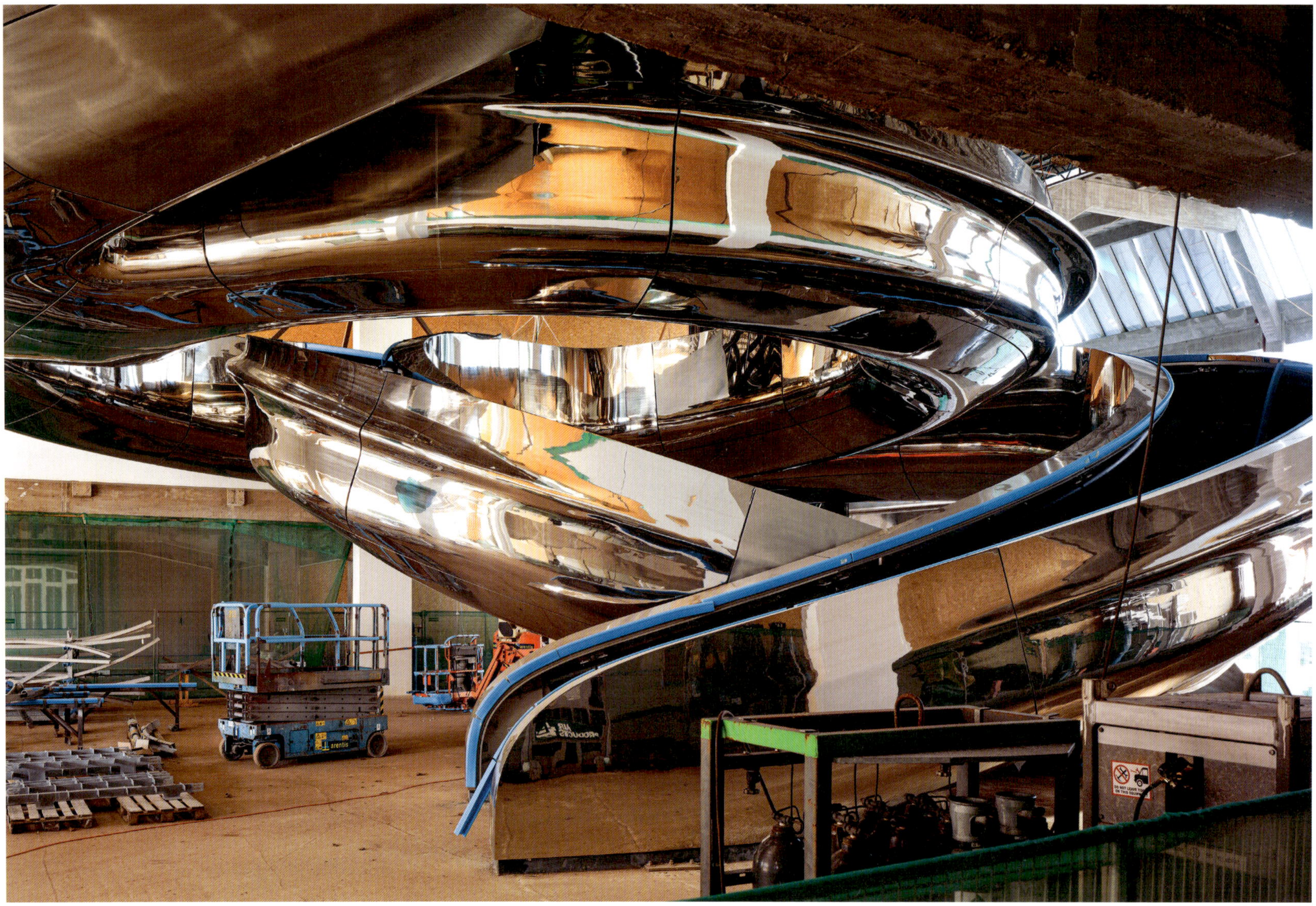

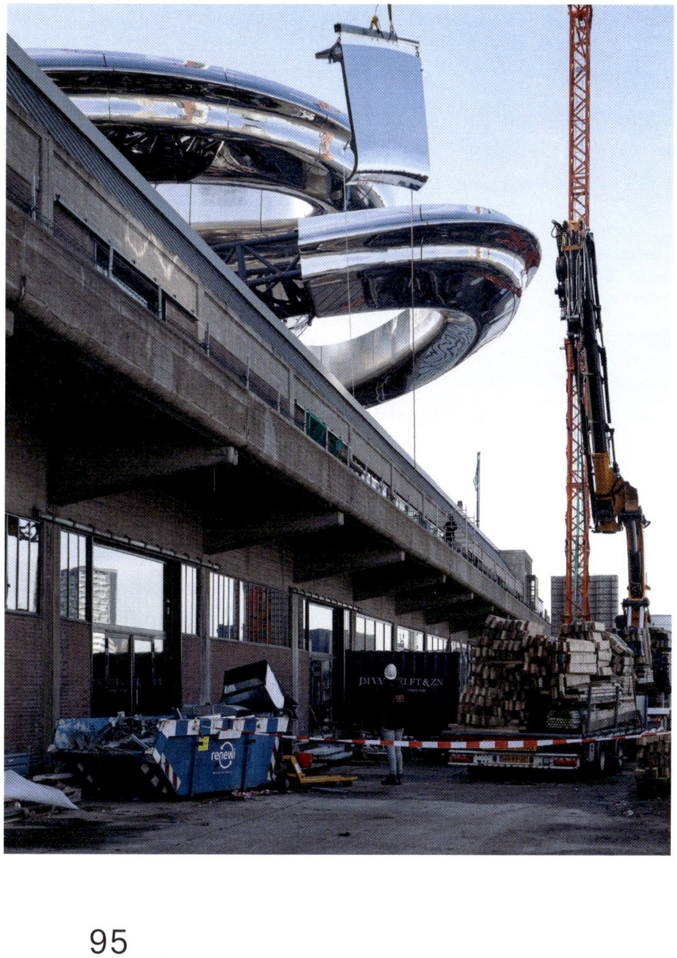

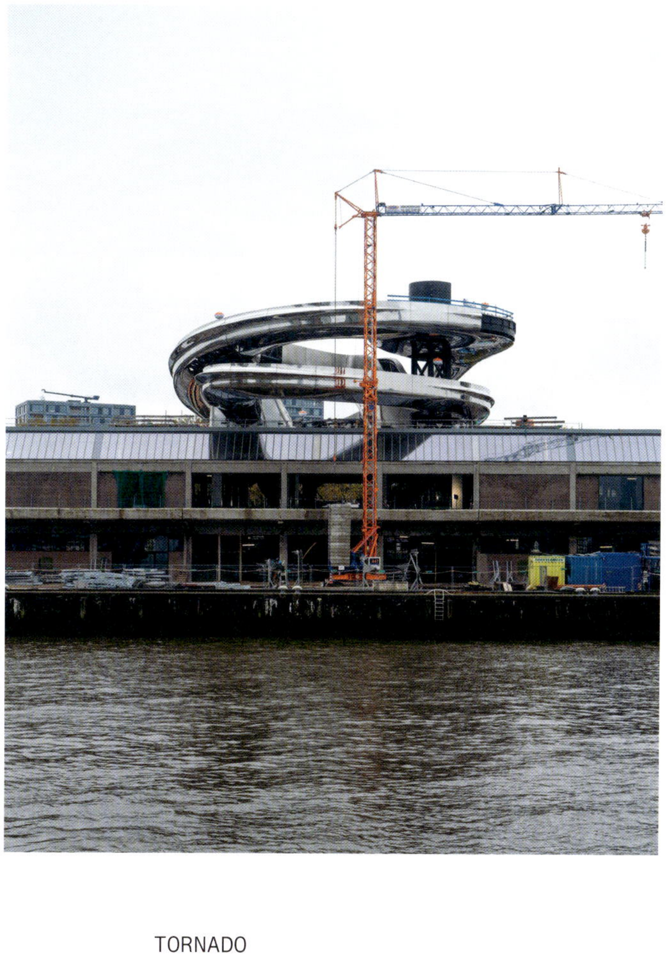

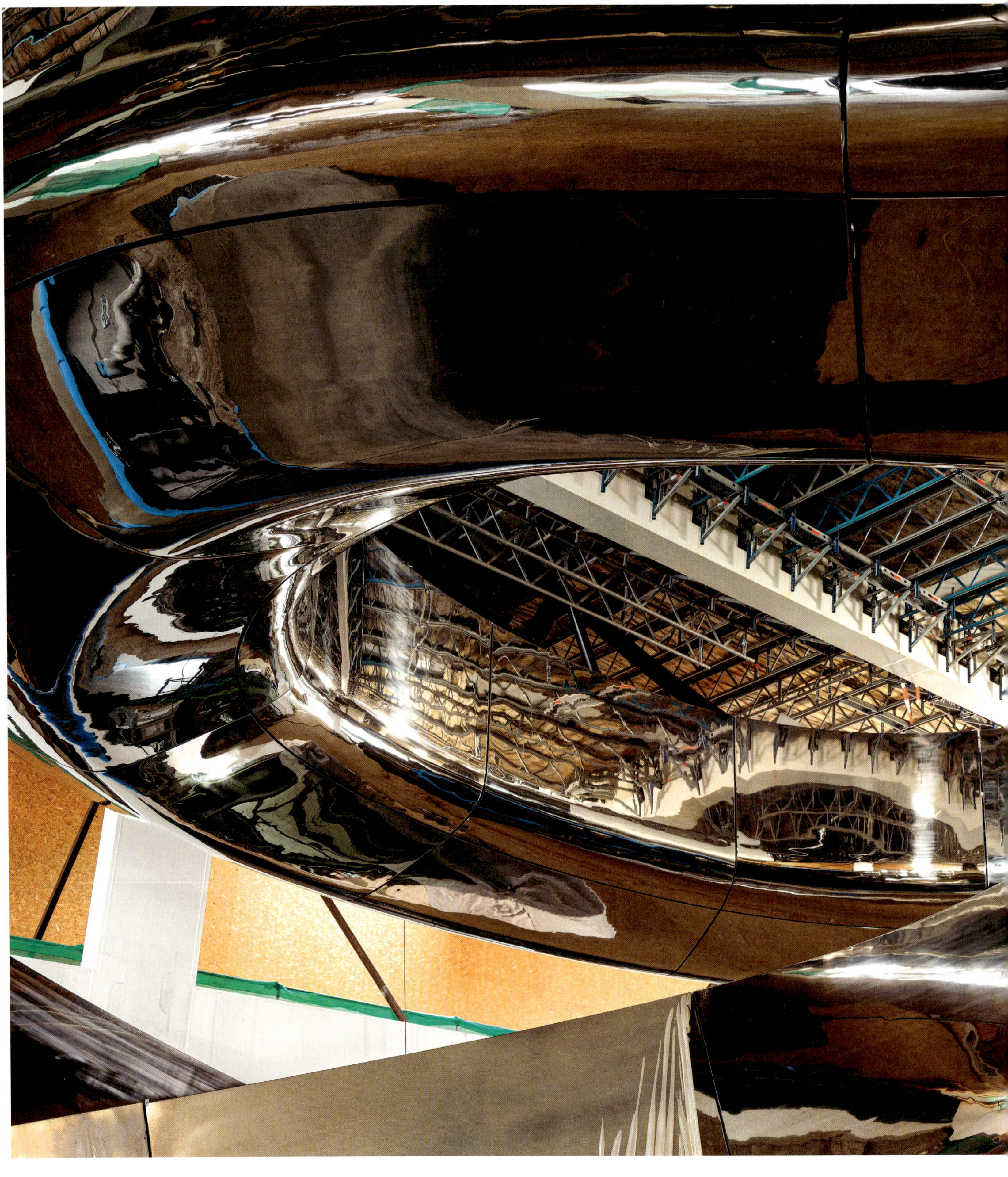

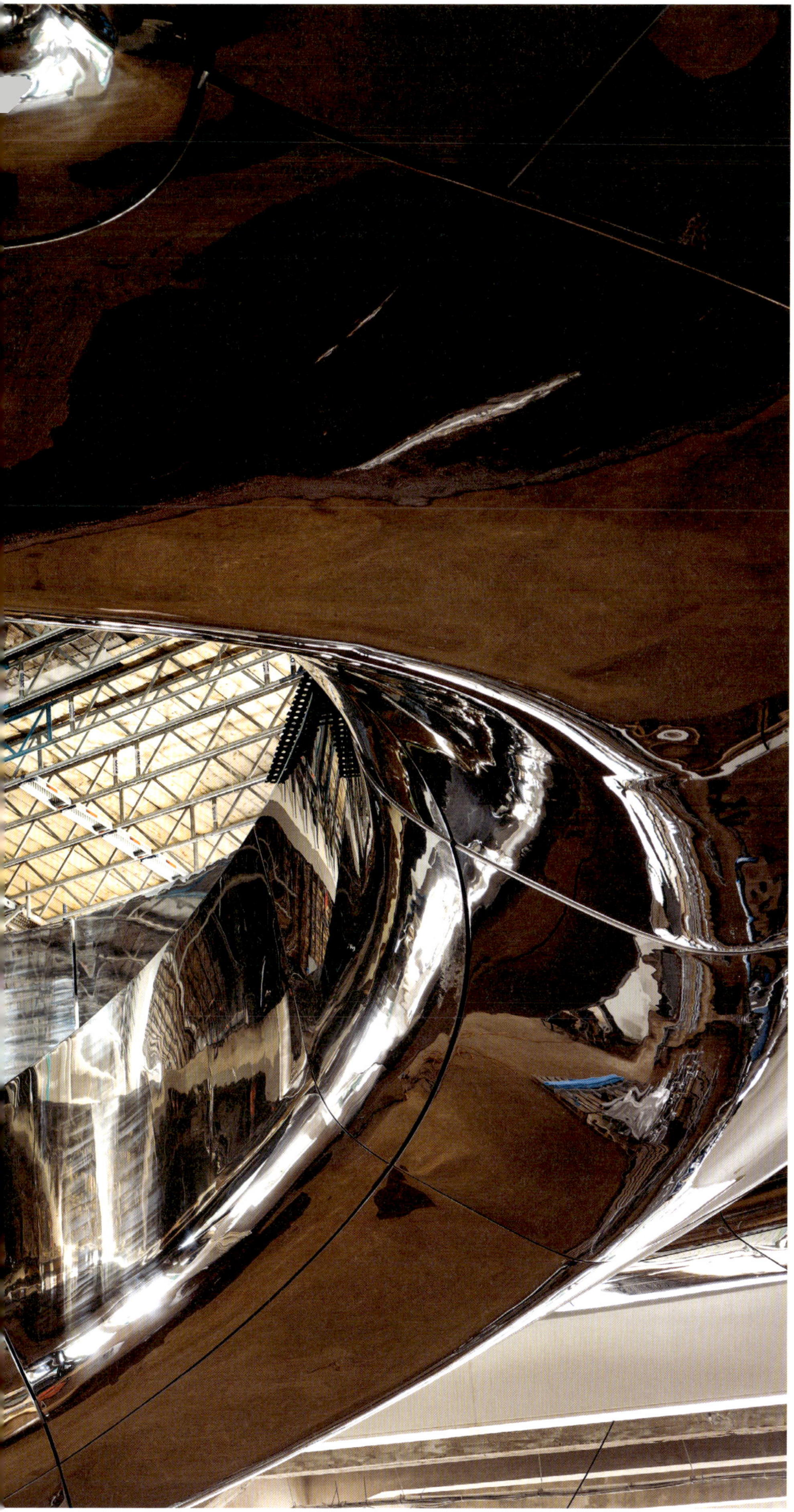

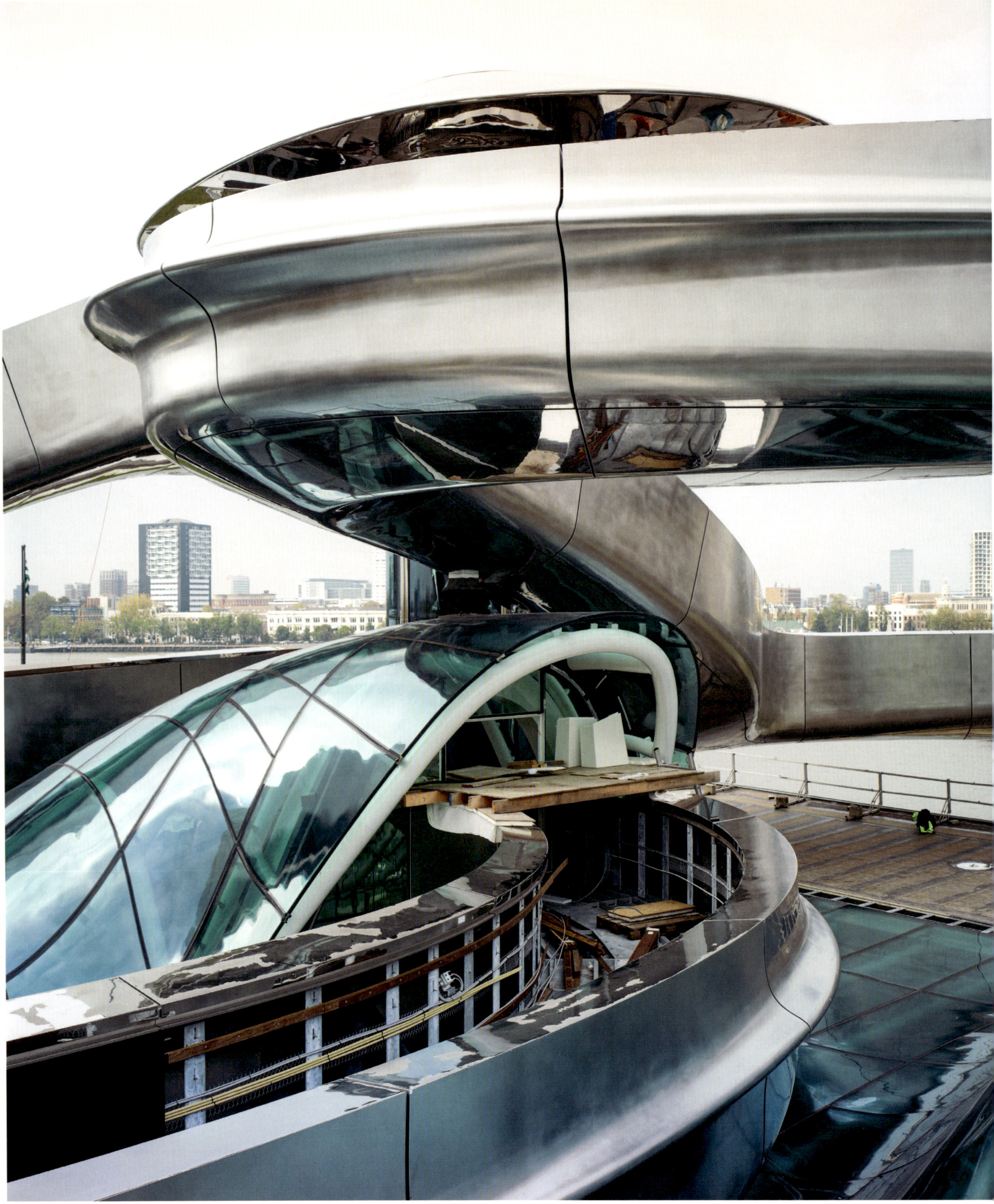

"I made the dynamic calculations for the Tornado. I analysed movements and translated the architectural design of the Tornado into concrete structural support. So that visitors can walk on the Tornado safely and comfortably."

Ikram Talib, Structural Engineer at IMd Consulting Engineers

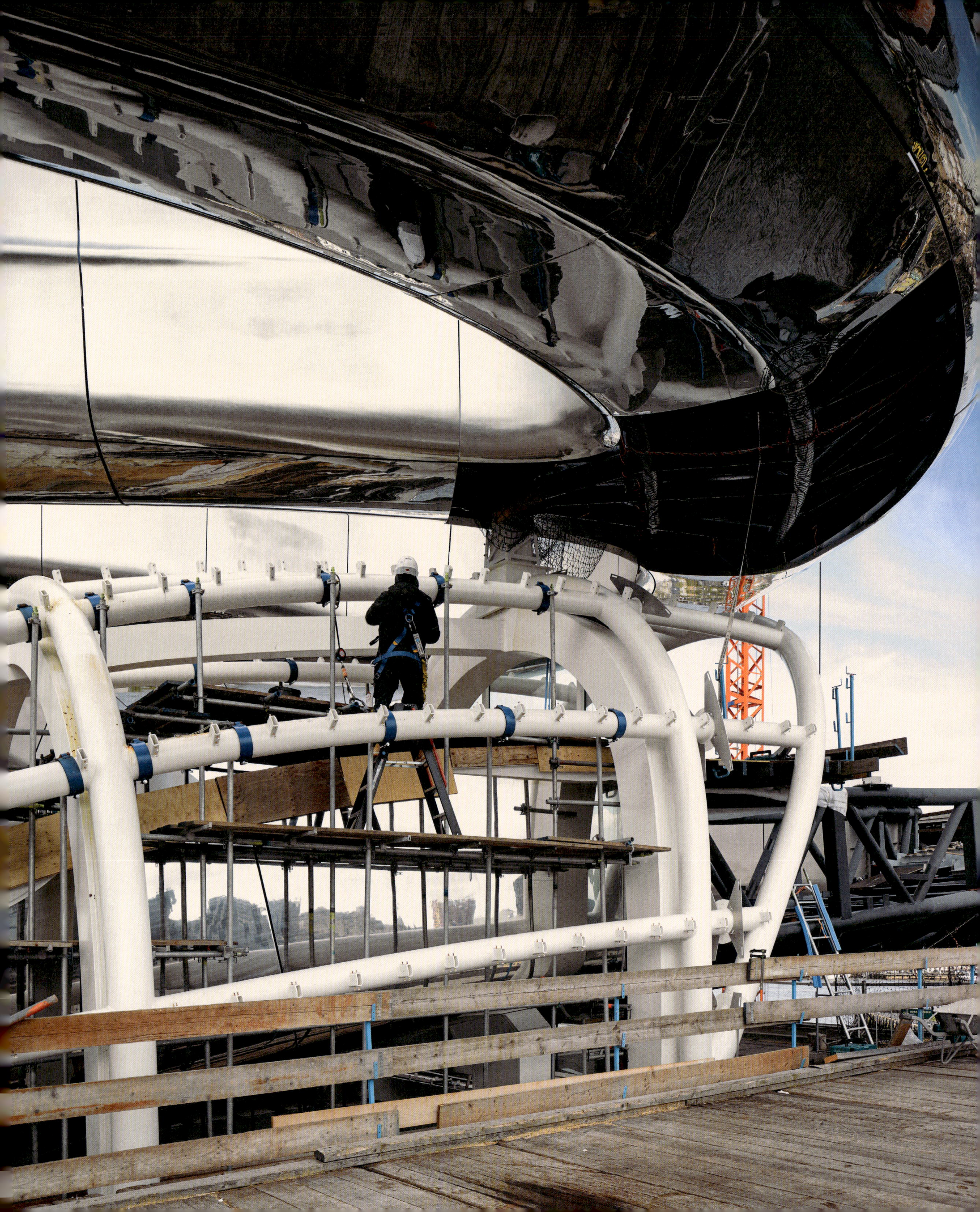

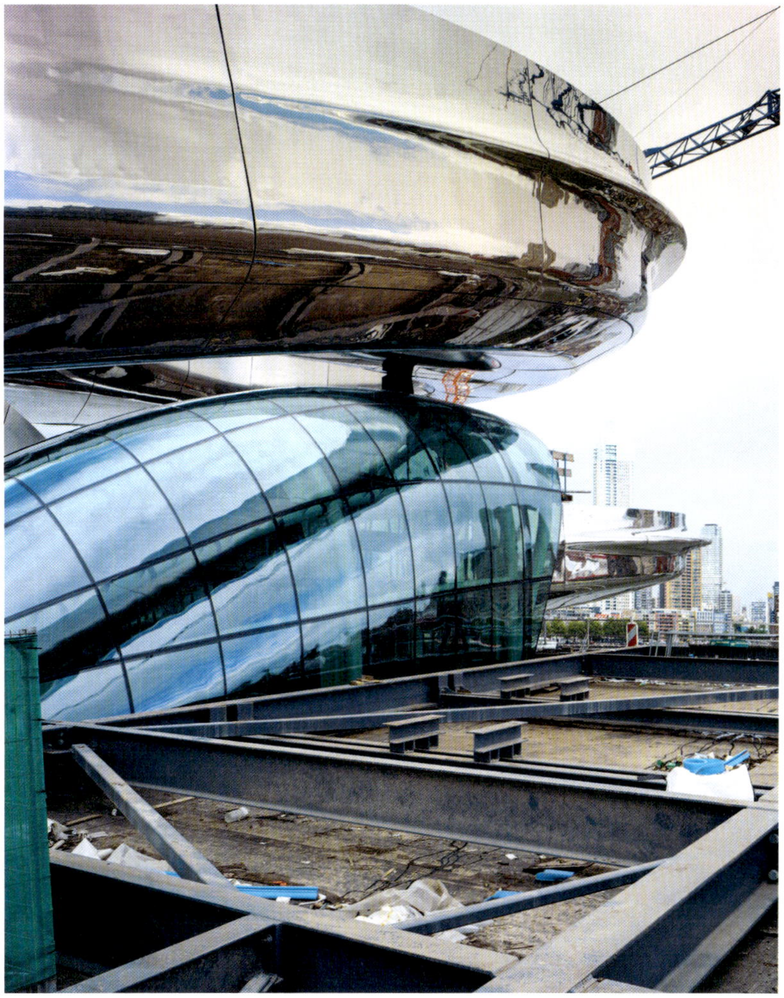

“Every plank of wood we use is different. We have installed around 12,500 planks. Most of them are handled by machines, but some of them can only be crafted by hand.”

Alex Hofrichter, Director of Woodwave

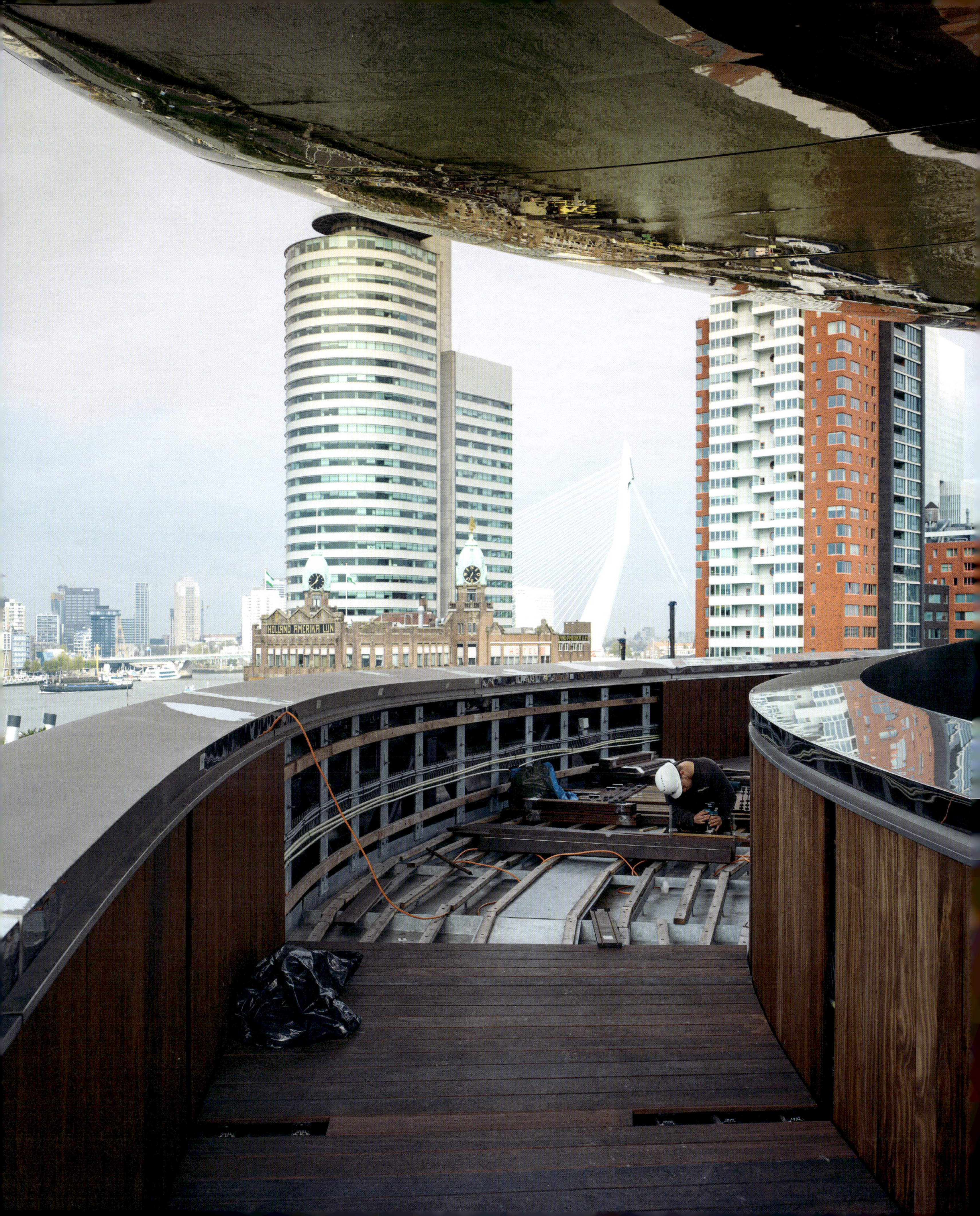
HOLLAND AMERIKA LIJN

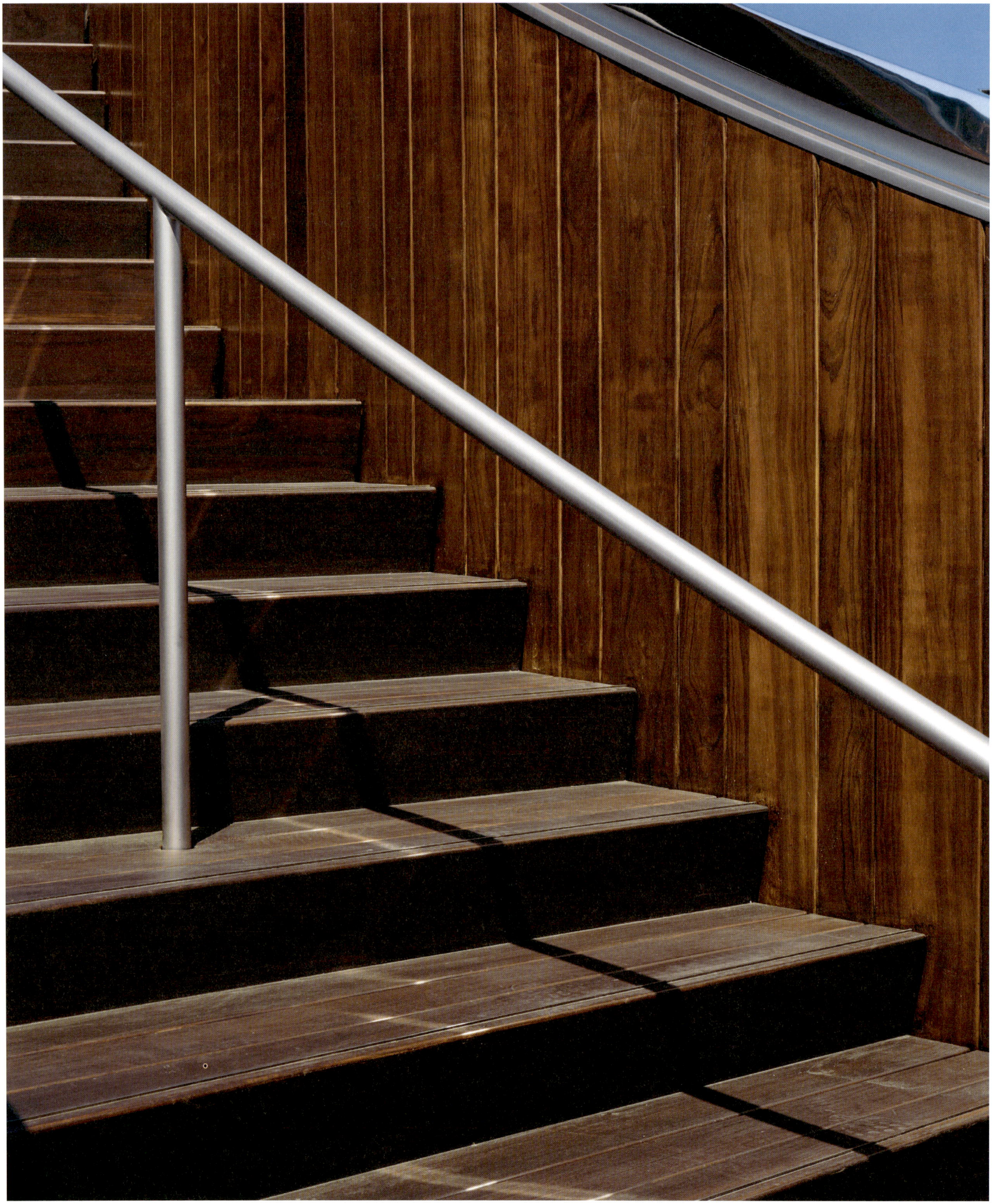

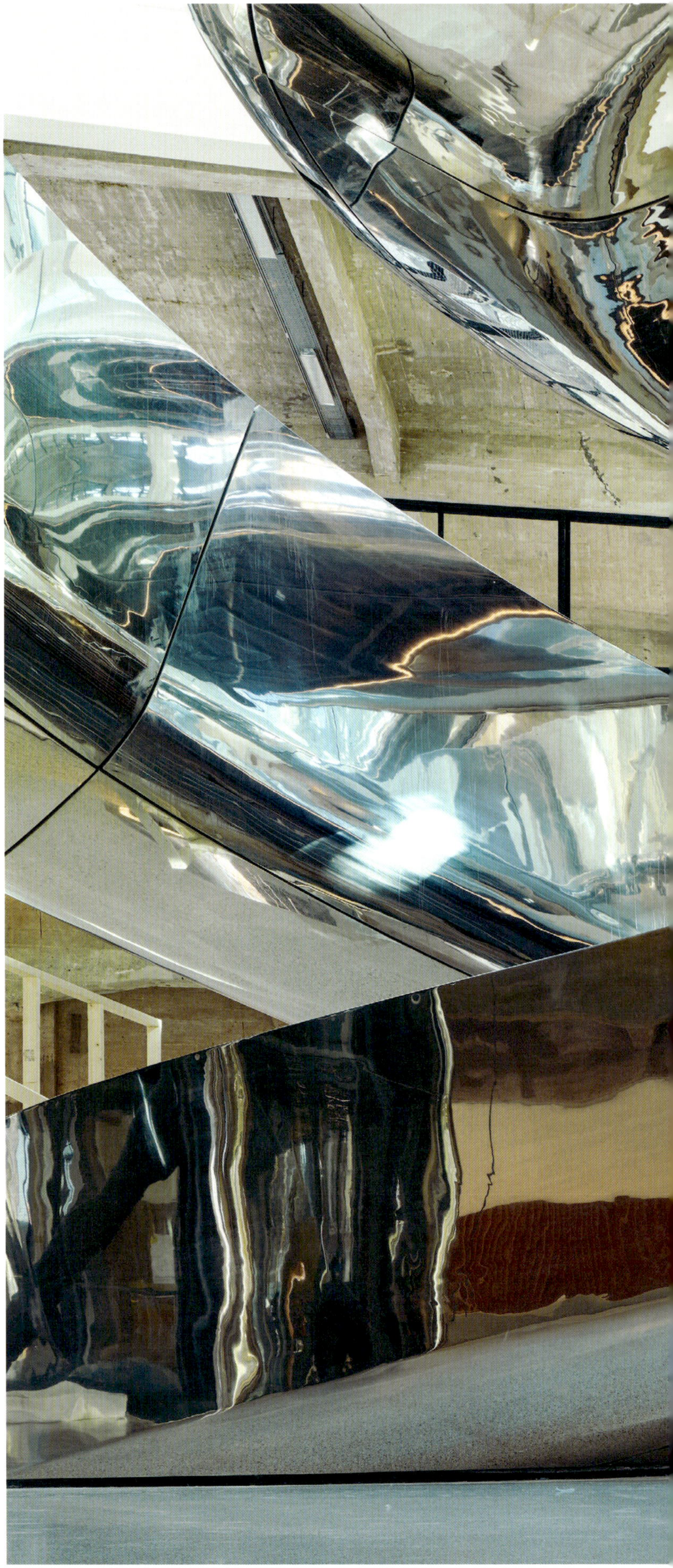

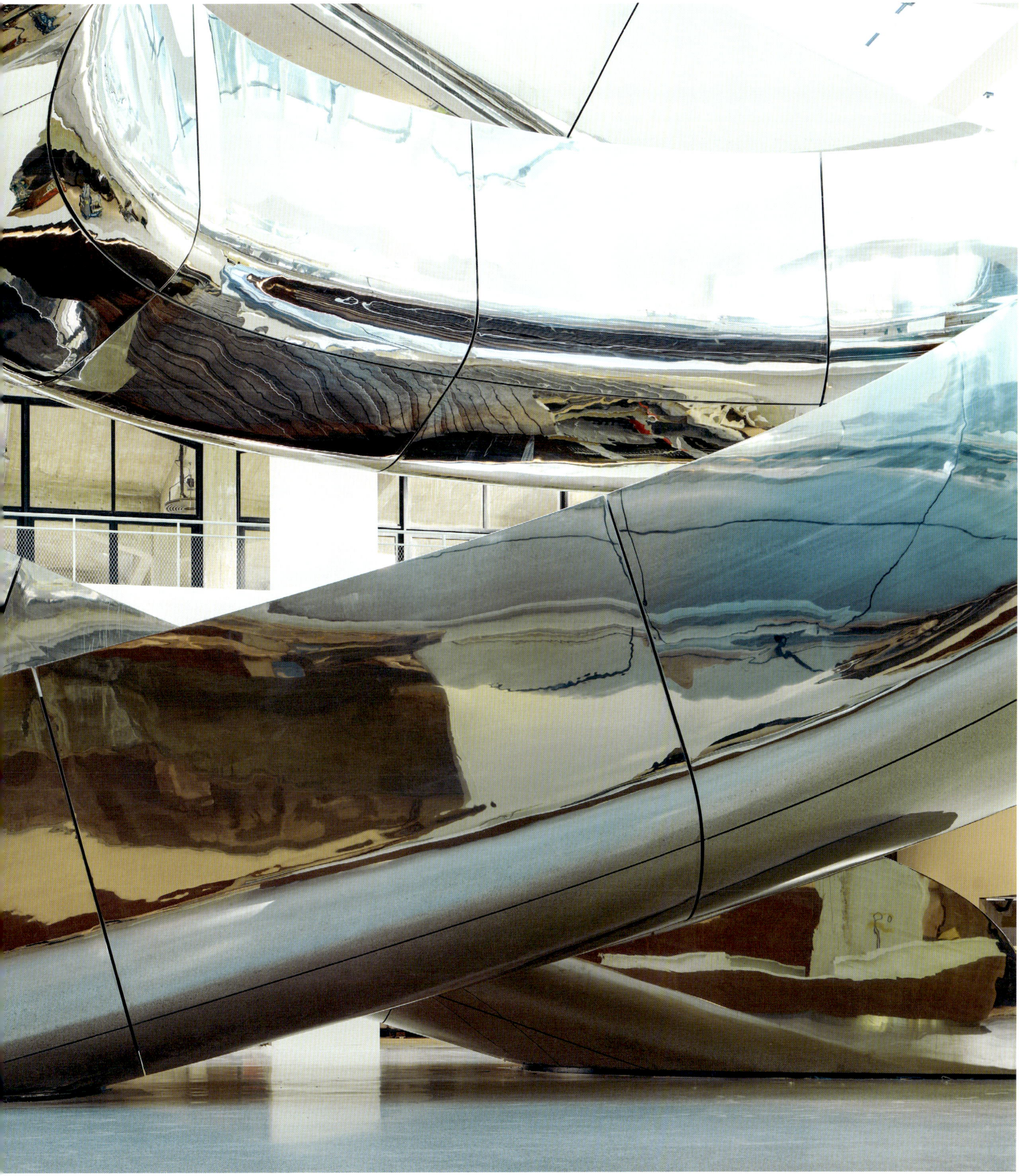

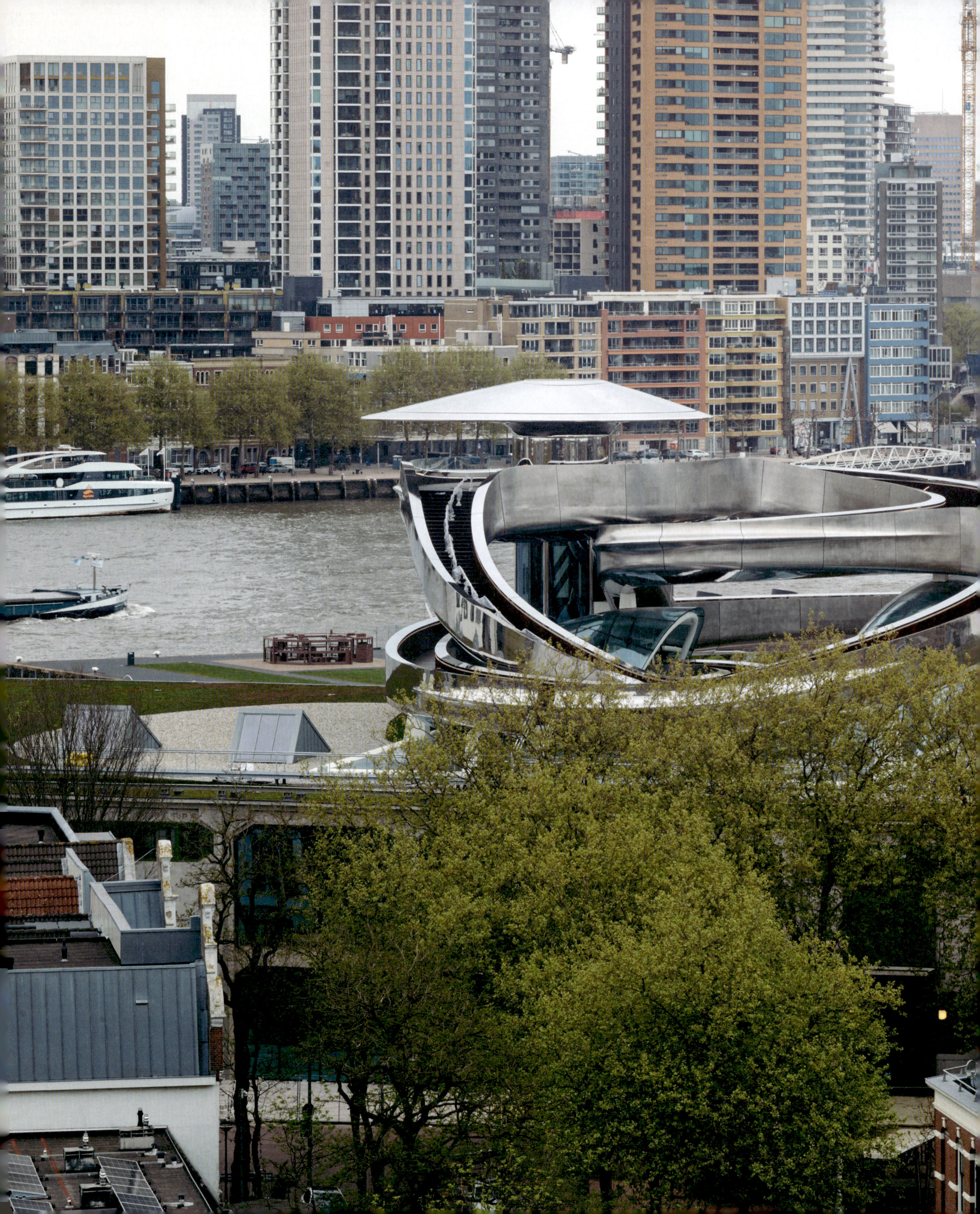

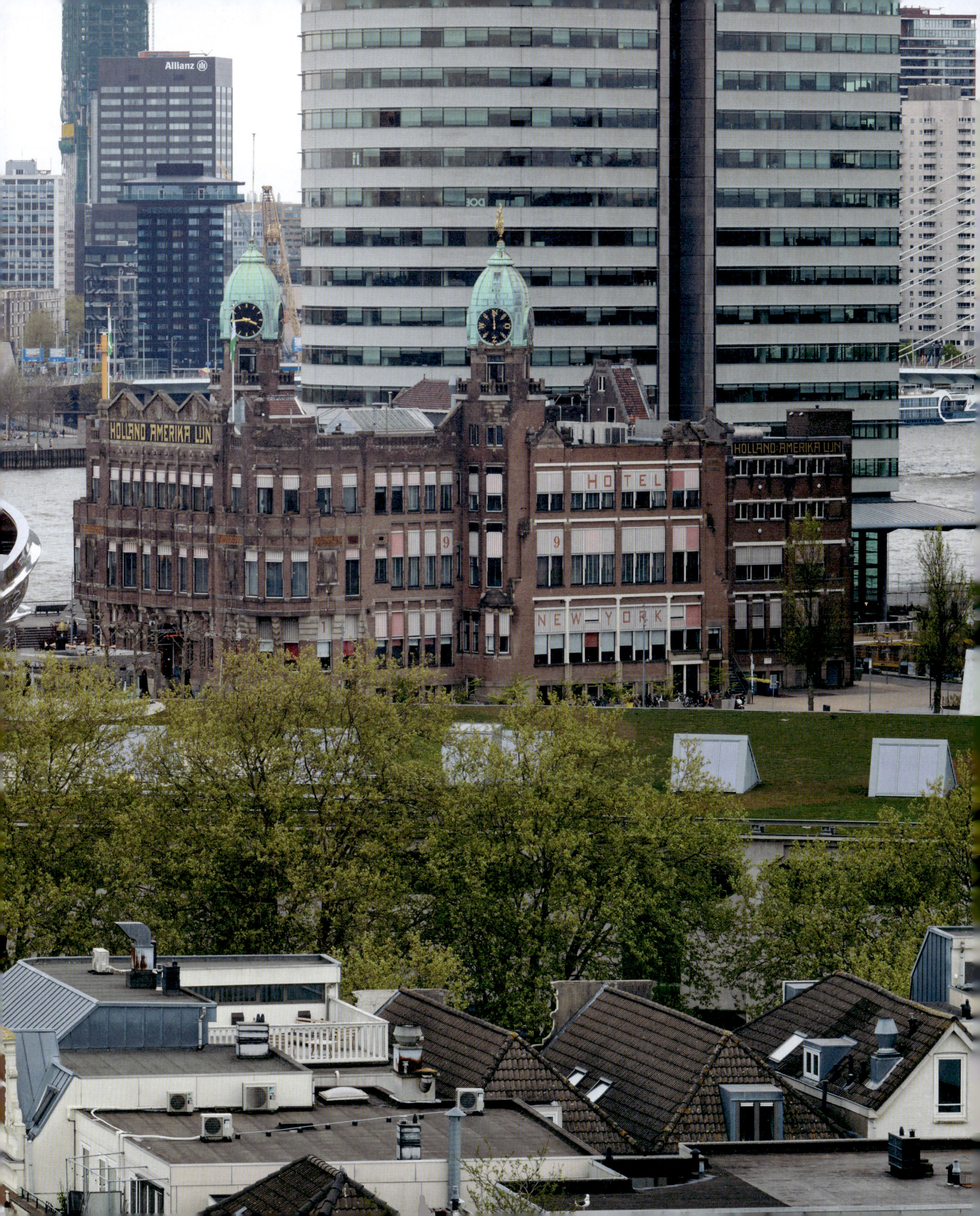
Allianz
HOLLAND AMERIKA LIJN
HOTEL
NEW—YORK
HOLLAND-AMERIKA LIJN

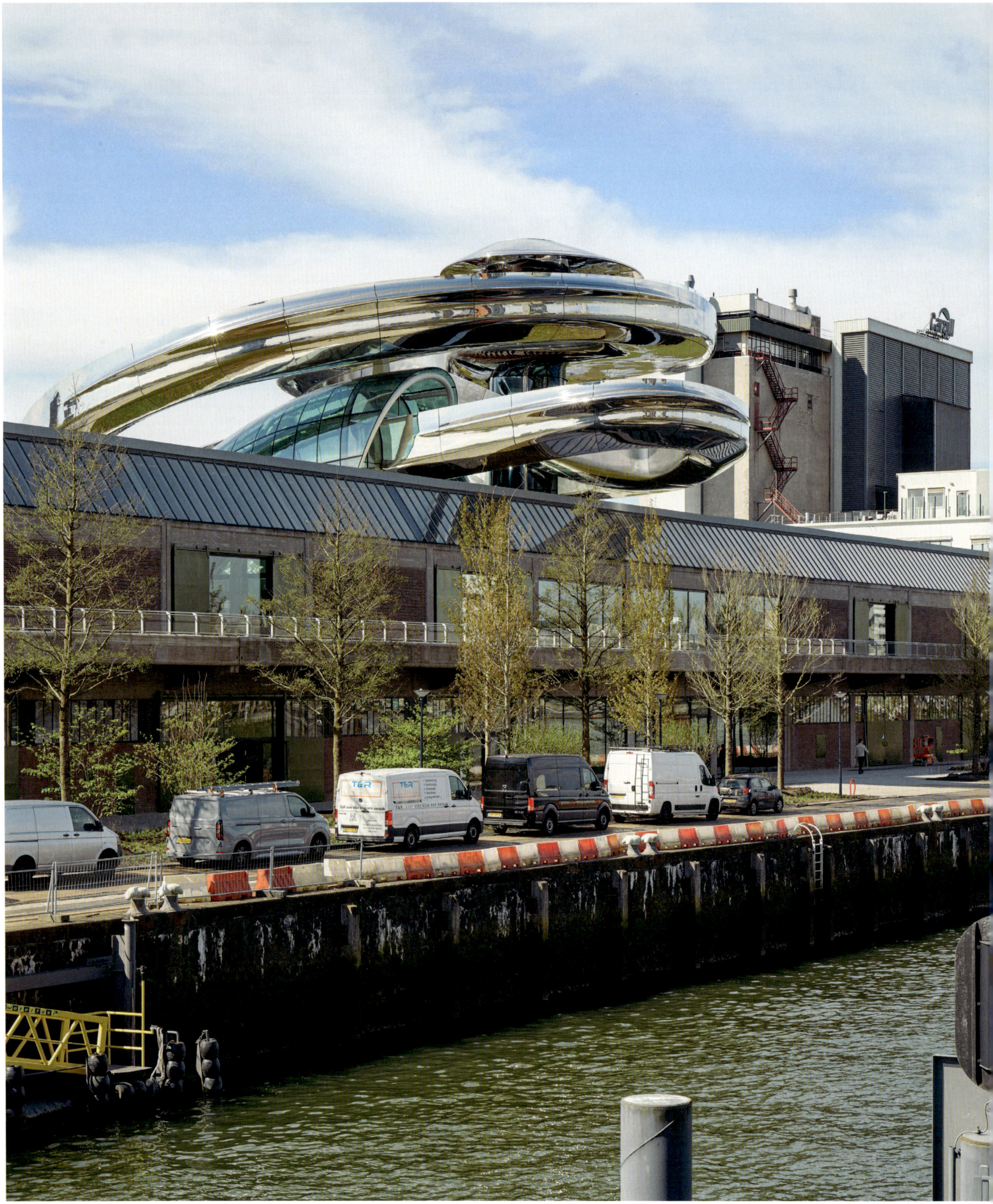

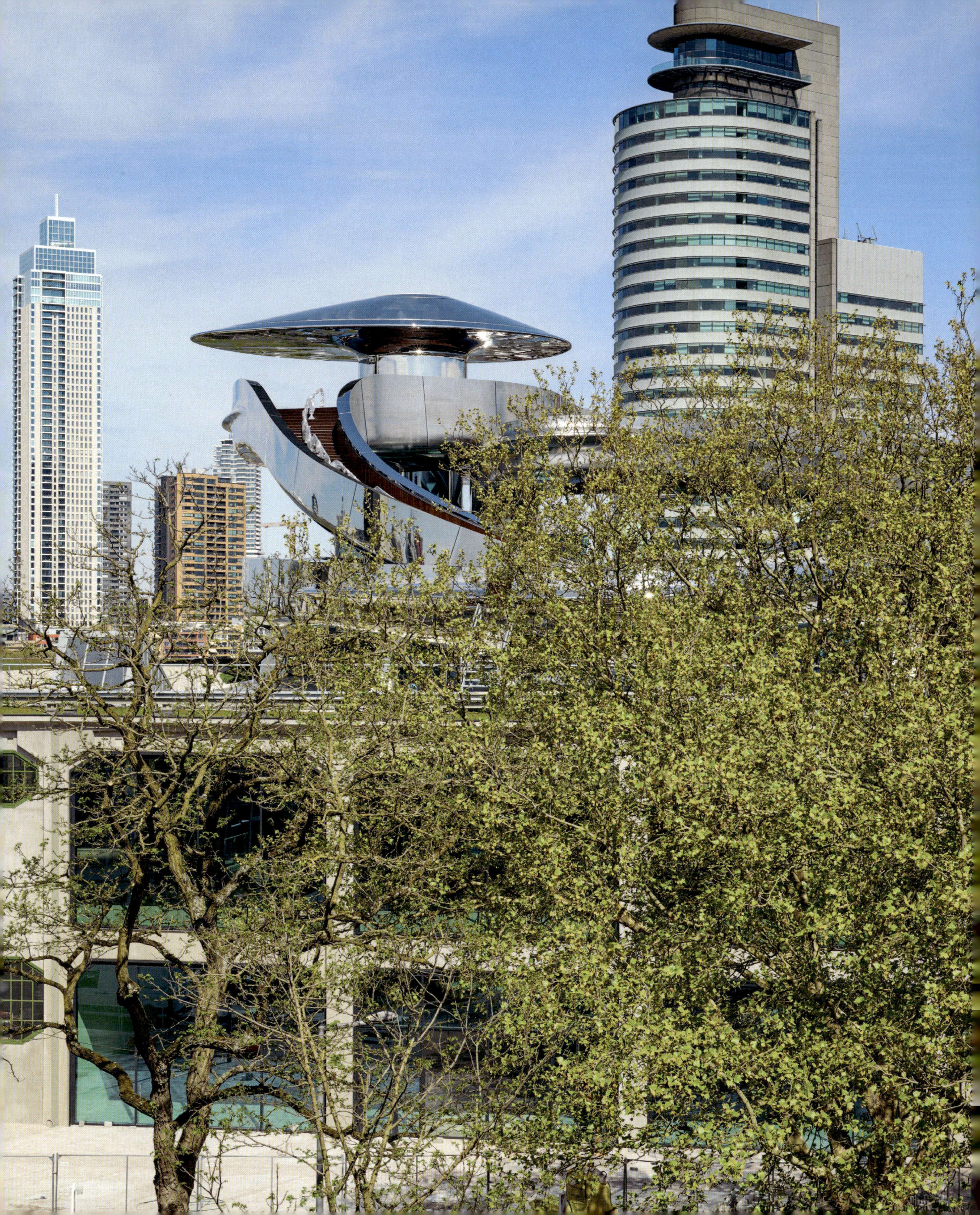

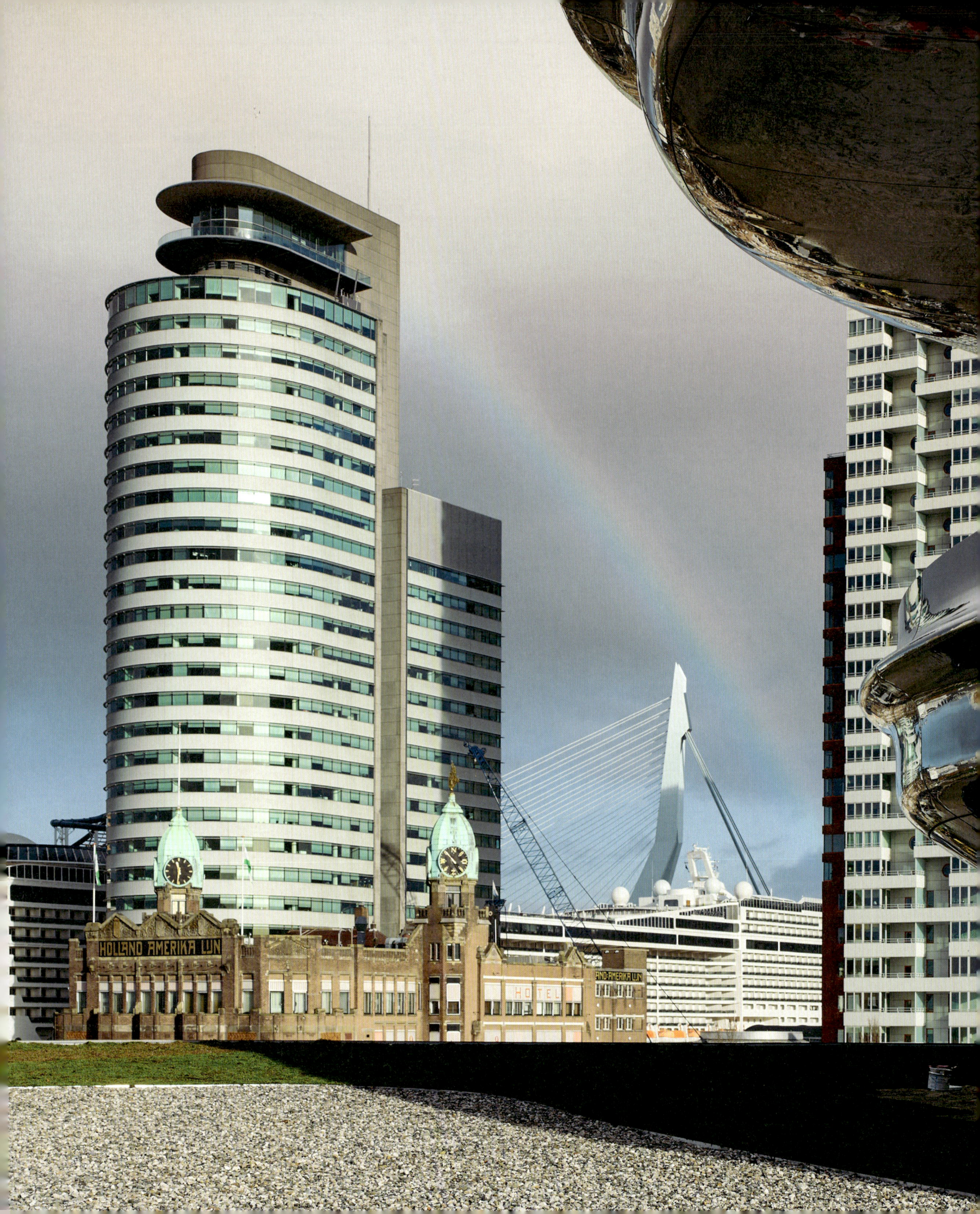
HOLLAND AMERIKA LIJN
HOTEL

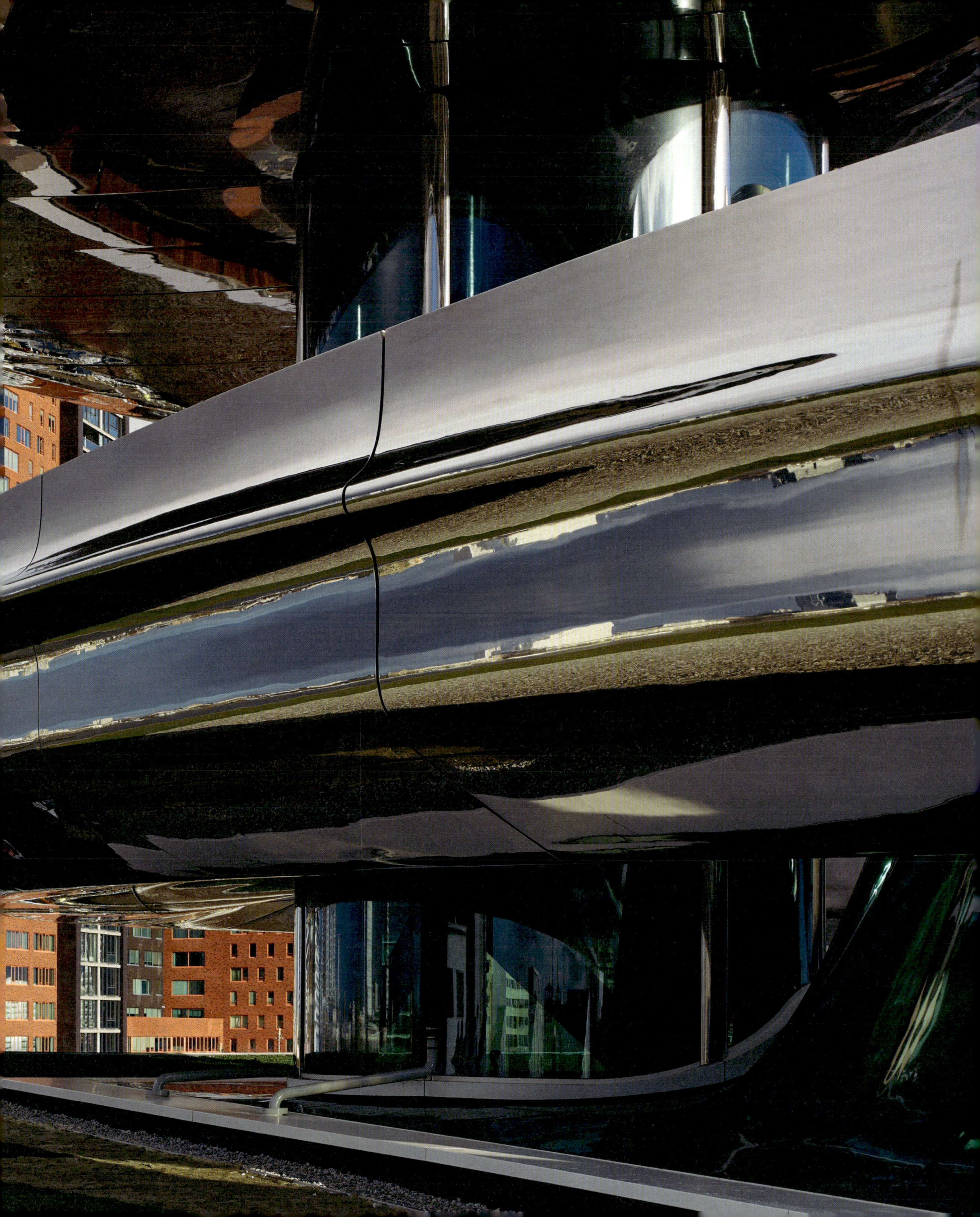

Weaving Life

Andrea D'Antrassi
Associate Partner at MAD

I worked on the project of Fenix from the very beginning. From the start, I sensed... its intrinsic universality: a polyphonic dialogue between past and present. The decision to preserve the original warehouse structure, with its austerity and well-defined lines, reflects this dialogue. The pre-existing building has its own language and a strong legacy closely tied to the history of Rotterdam, yet it is from the foundation of the warehouse that the Tornado emerges. This, in my opinion, is what defines the identity of the project.

A simple, industrial structure crowned by the unexpected – a double-helix weave of stainless steel extending beyond the building and opening up to the city. It is a tumultuous movement, yet at the same time, gentle. You feel embraced as you climb the steps of the Tornado to reach the top. It is a progression that has its own rhythm, its own tempo, but obviously the resulting impression – because that is what it is all about – is deeply intimate and personal.

The monumental staircase holds both a physical and an evocative value. In its magnificence, the Tornado can be seen from afar, the highly polished steel reflecting the light and its shine rendering the structure almost transparent. The contrast between materials is a choice favoured by Droom en Daad, that MAD also embraced: the solidity of the concrete represents memory, while the Tornado and the steel embodies a projection into the future.

The staircase features two spiral ramps that offer two different ways to experience the space: a slow lane that extends the tour, creating the large overhang above the Maas river, and a fast lane that leads more directly to the panoramic viewpoint, where a 360-degree vista allows visitors to reconnect with the city. As the ramps ascend, they intersect to form landings before parting again in a continuous game of pursuit and separation. It is a dance: starting from the lobby atrium, it moves beyond the sinuous glass surface of the roof to join up again, merging at the uppermost point of the staircase.

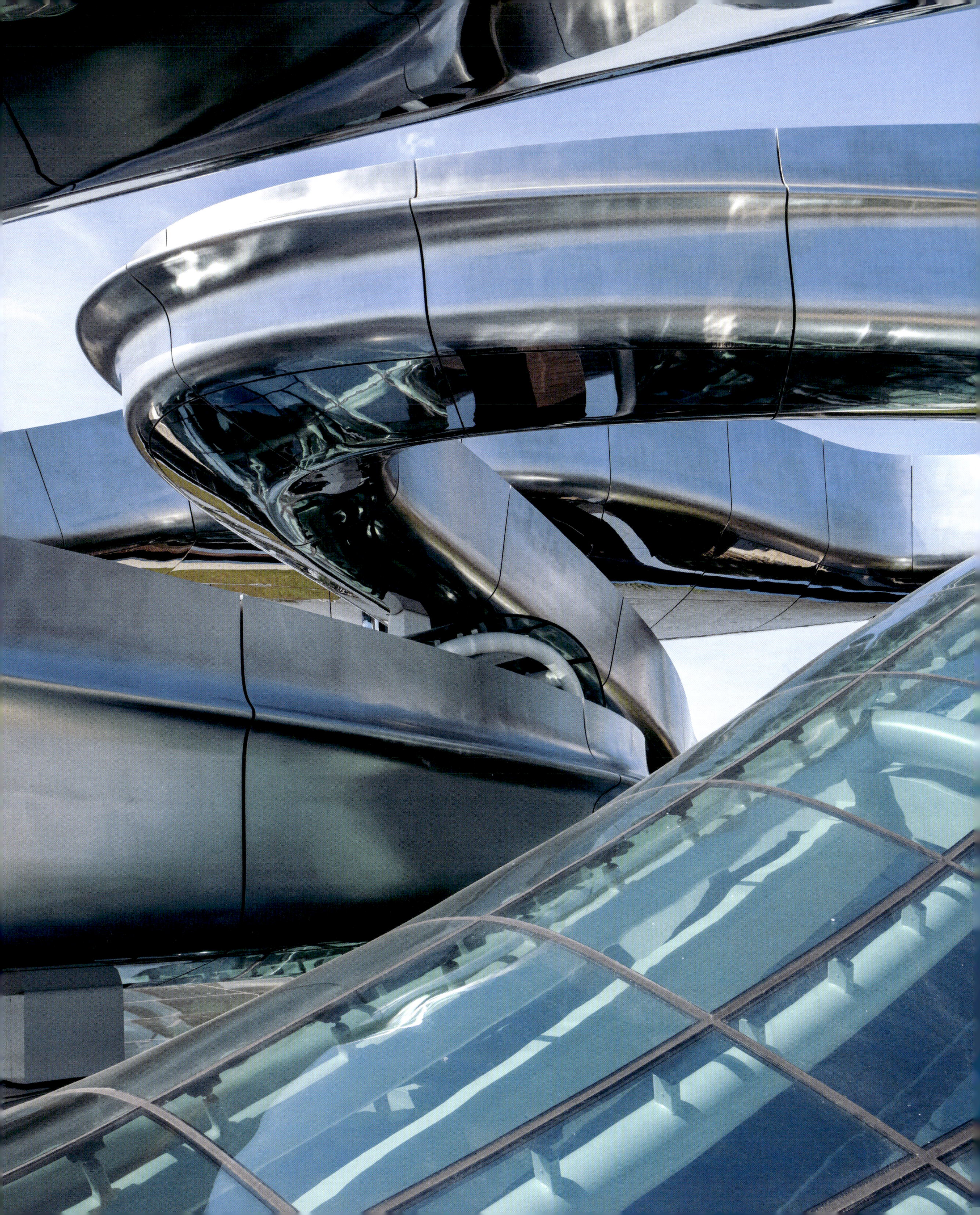

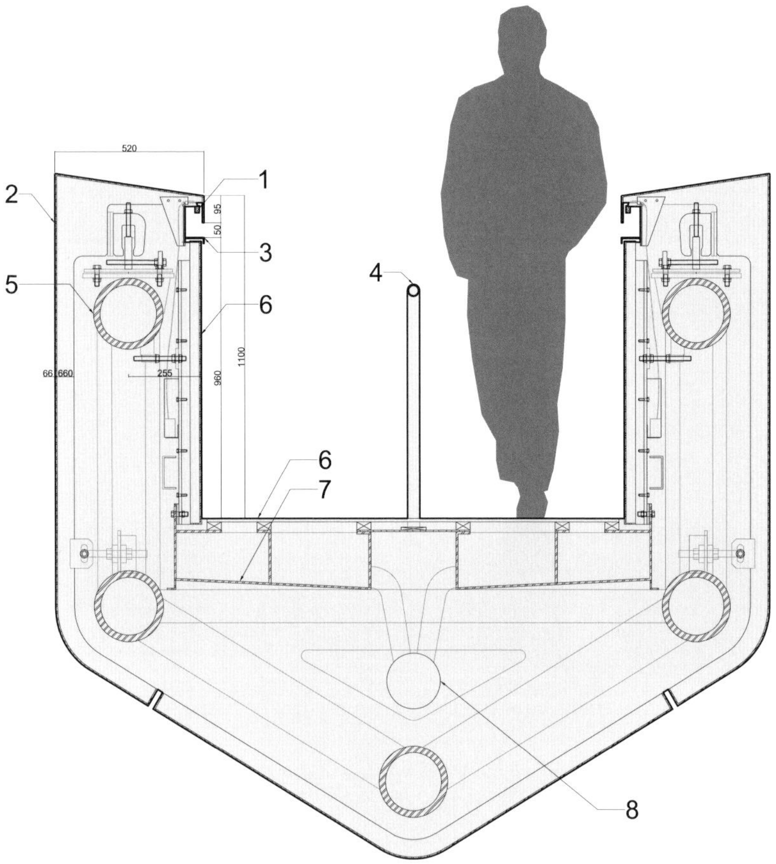

1. LED Strip
2. 6mm Stainless Steel
3. Cove Lighting
4. Handrail
5. Steel Space Frame Profile
6. Wood floor
7. Drainage Channel
8. Drainage Pipe

Section on the Fast Lane Exit

The Tornado's space frame has a truss-like structure recalling that of a roller coaster, composed of some 297 mirror-polished stainless steel panels.

The curves and sinuous lines culminate at the top, where the glass roof forms a double-curved surface permitting natural light to flood the lobby, and thus creating an ongoing dialogue with the outside. Two wave-like openings are formed in the glass surface to allow the two ramps of the Tornado to emerge. These openings have been dubbed cockpits for their resemblance to the similar space in airplanes.

In the lightness of its form, the Tornado seems to rise up weightlessly from theatrium, as if there were no pillars to support it. This was made possible by the meticulous structural design that pushed the materials' properties to their limits and made it possible to reduce to a minimum the points of contact between the Tornado and the lobby volume. Even the glass cylinder of the elevator, in addition to ensuring accessibility, provides structural support to the Tornado.

Kebony wood, chosen for its high performance and sustainability, forms the internal structure of the staircase, bringing warmth to the entire Tornado experience. Together with the steel of the outer cladding, it evokes the idea of a ship guiding visitors towards discovery.

Taking on the Fenix project was no easy task, though the vision for its future purpose certainly helped guide the way. The decision by Droom en Daad, and its president Wim Pijbes, to entrust the project to a firm like MAD was both courageous and forward-thinking. Architecture often straddles the lines between being anachronistic, bold, and futuristic – where the future feels more like an expanded present than a dramatic leap forward. Yet the Tornado's movement represents both momentum and thought, progress and pause.

Observing Fenix, I began to see how it weaves together life experiences, stories, expectations that we then shaped – not by abandoning the pre-existing, but by embracing it all and making it brighter both for the community and the citizens of Rotterdam, as well as for all the visitors who will connect with the museum on a deeper level.

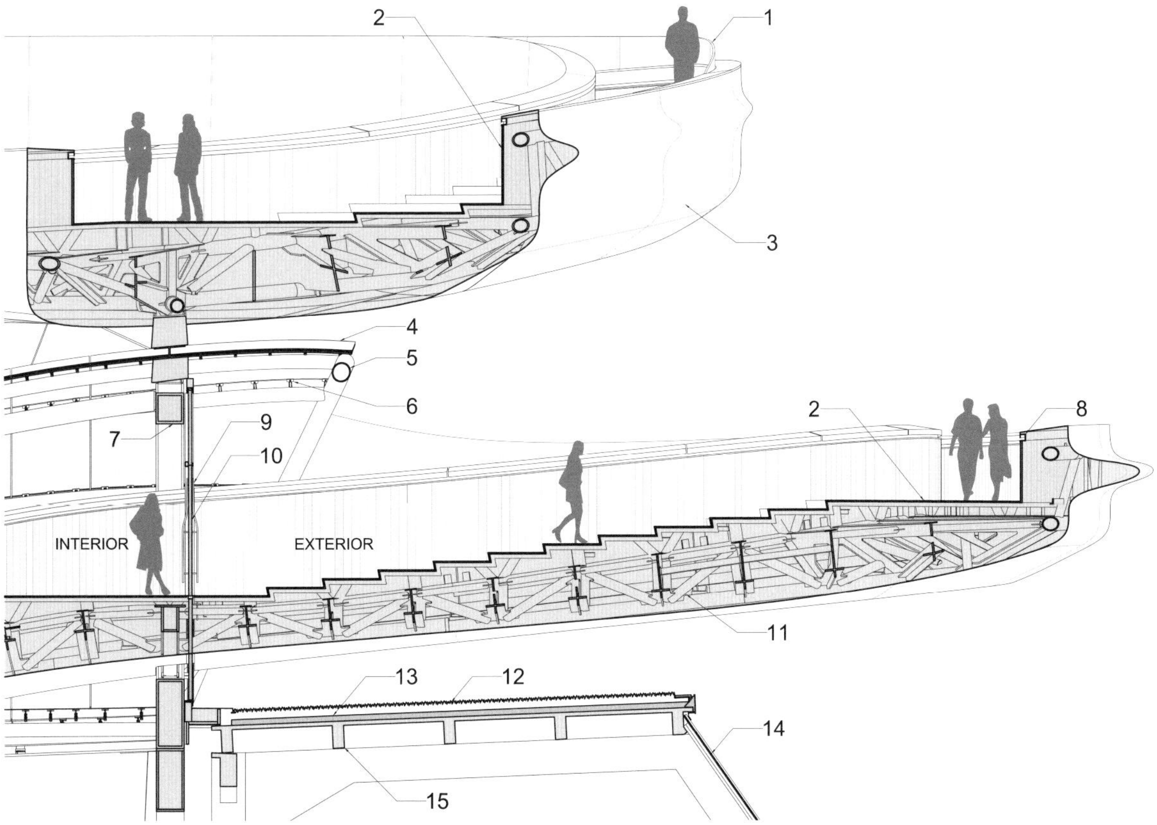

1. Glass Railing
2. Wood Floor
3. Stainless Steel Cladding
4. Glass Roof
5. Glass Roof Structure
6. Glass Connector
7. Structural Arch Frame
8. Cove Lighting
9. Door Handle
10. Glass Door
11. Structural Framing
12. Green Roof
13. Insulation
14. Existing Warehouse Skylight
15. Existing Warehouse Roof Structure

Section on the Fast Lane Cockpit

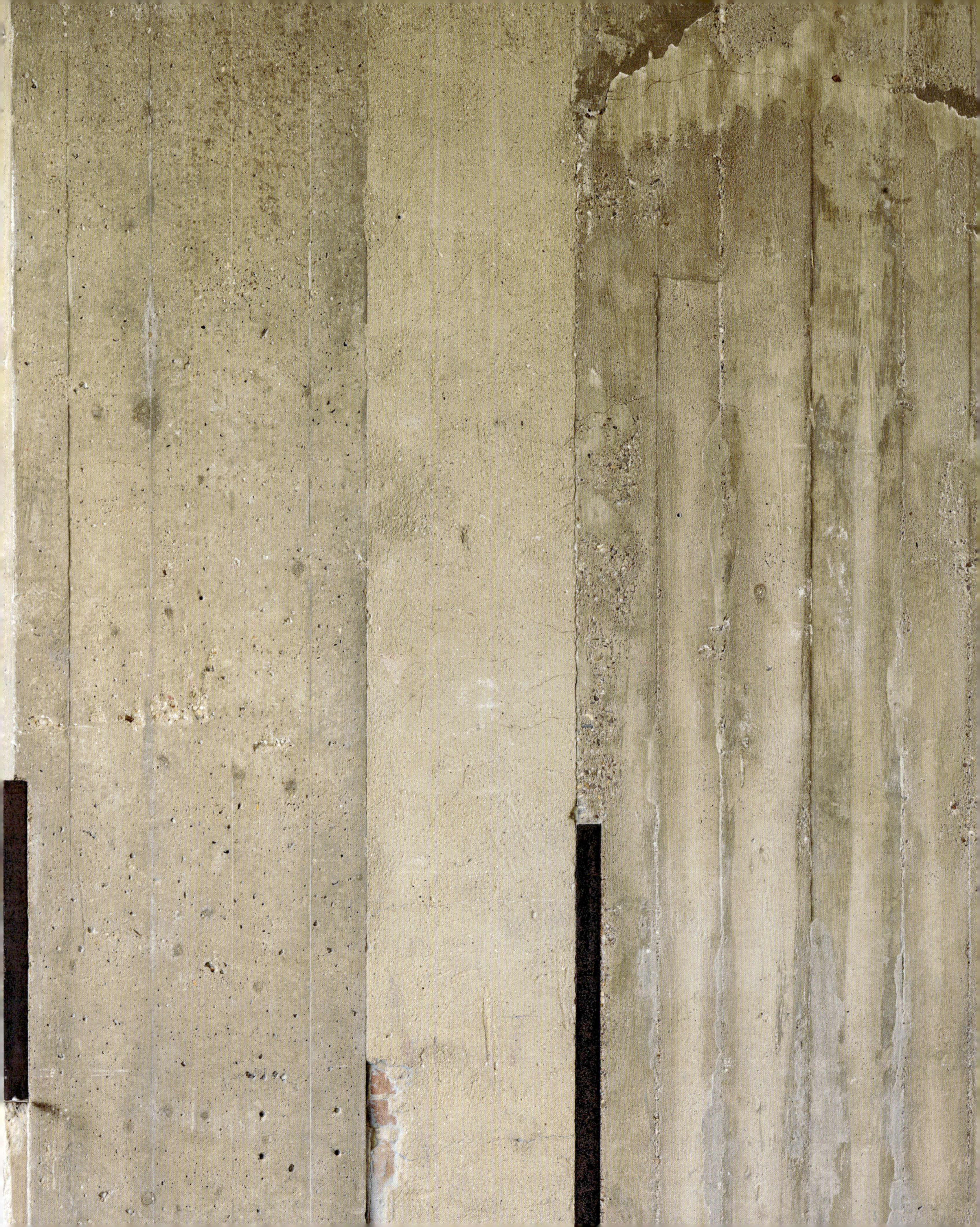

Ground Floor

Through revolving doors on both sides, you can now enter Fenix's atrium, in the heart of warehouse. The museum is accessed via entrances in the centre of the north façade on the riverfront and south façade. On arrival, you see the base of the Tornado, whose dynamic, twisting form is lit through the glass roof above the central atrium that allows natural light to filter into the lobby. Located on the ground floor are two exhibition spaces, the museum shop, restaurant, café, bakery and an Italian gelateria, and Plein. At 2,275 square metres, Plein is an indoor public square – a place for connection and exchange. It features three doors on each side, which can be opened out to create a welcoming covered public space which is freely accessible and open to all.

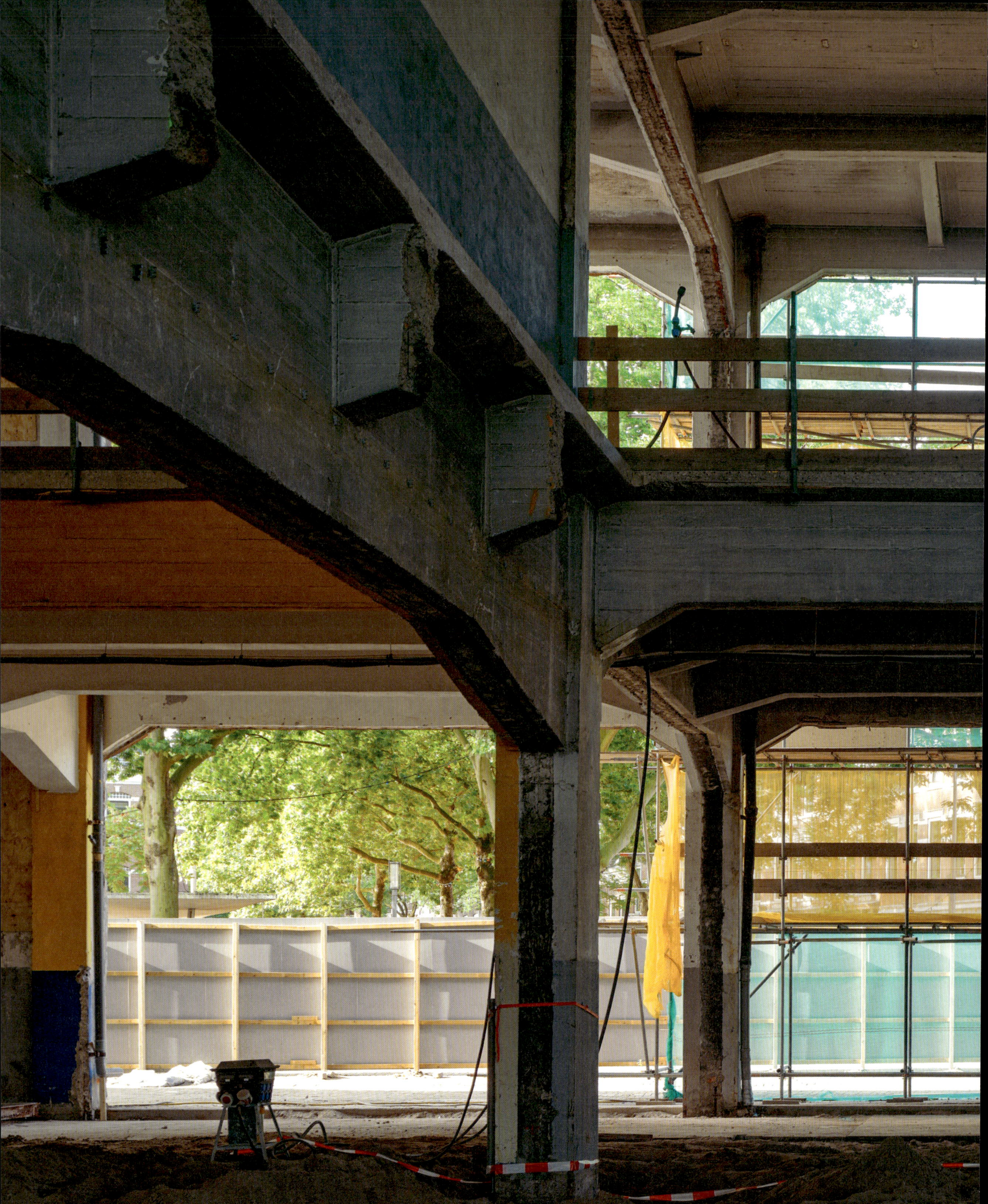

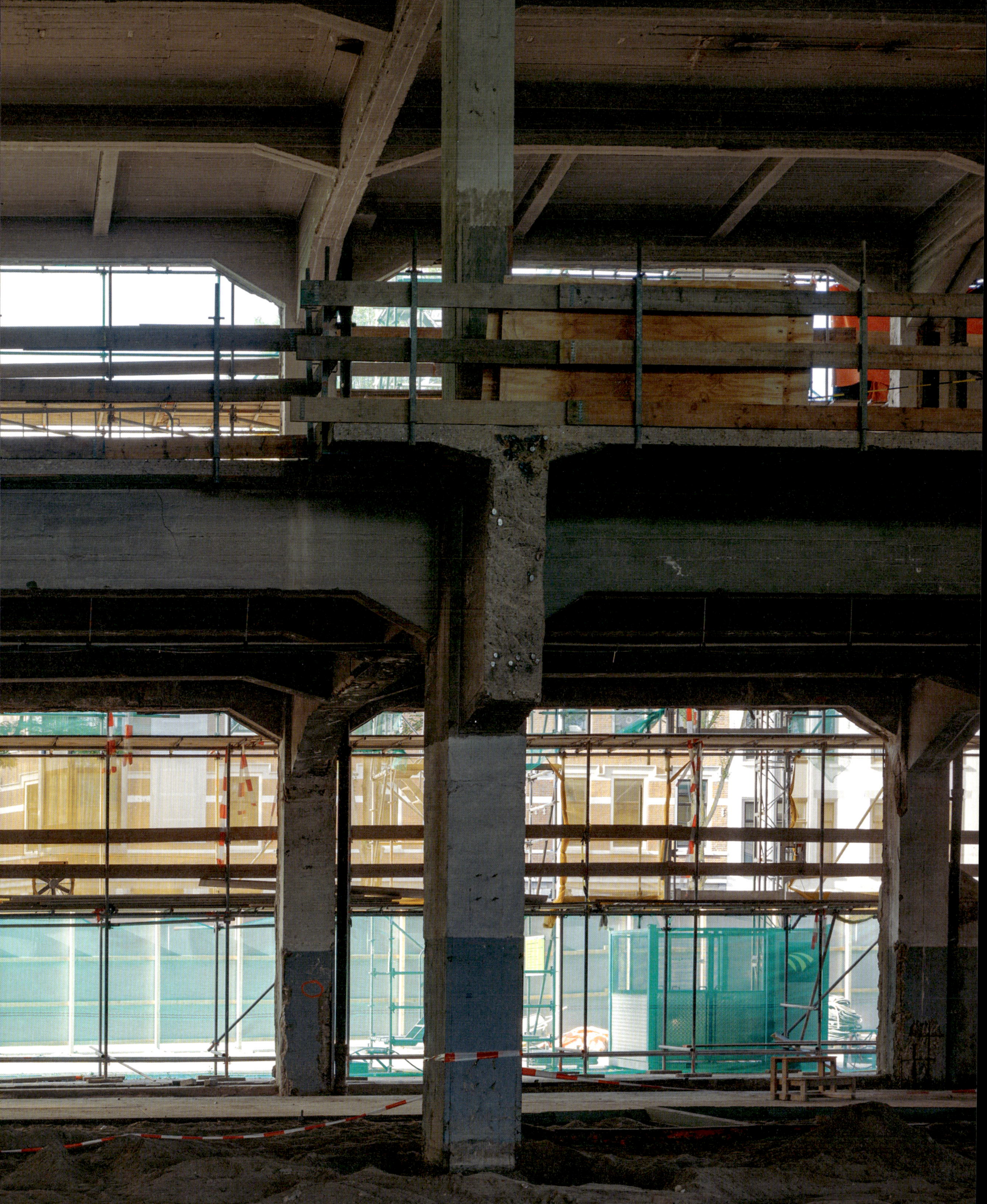

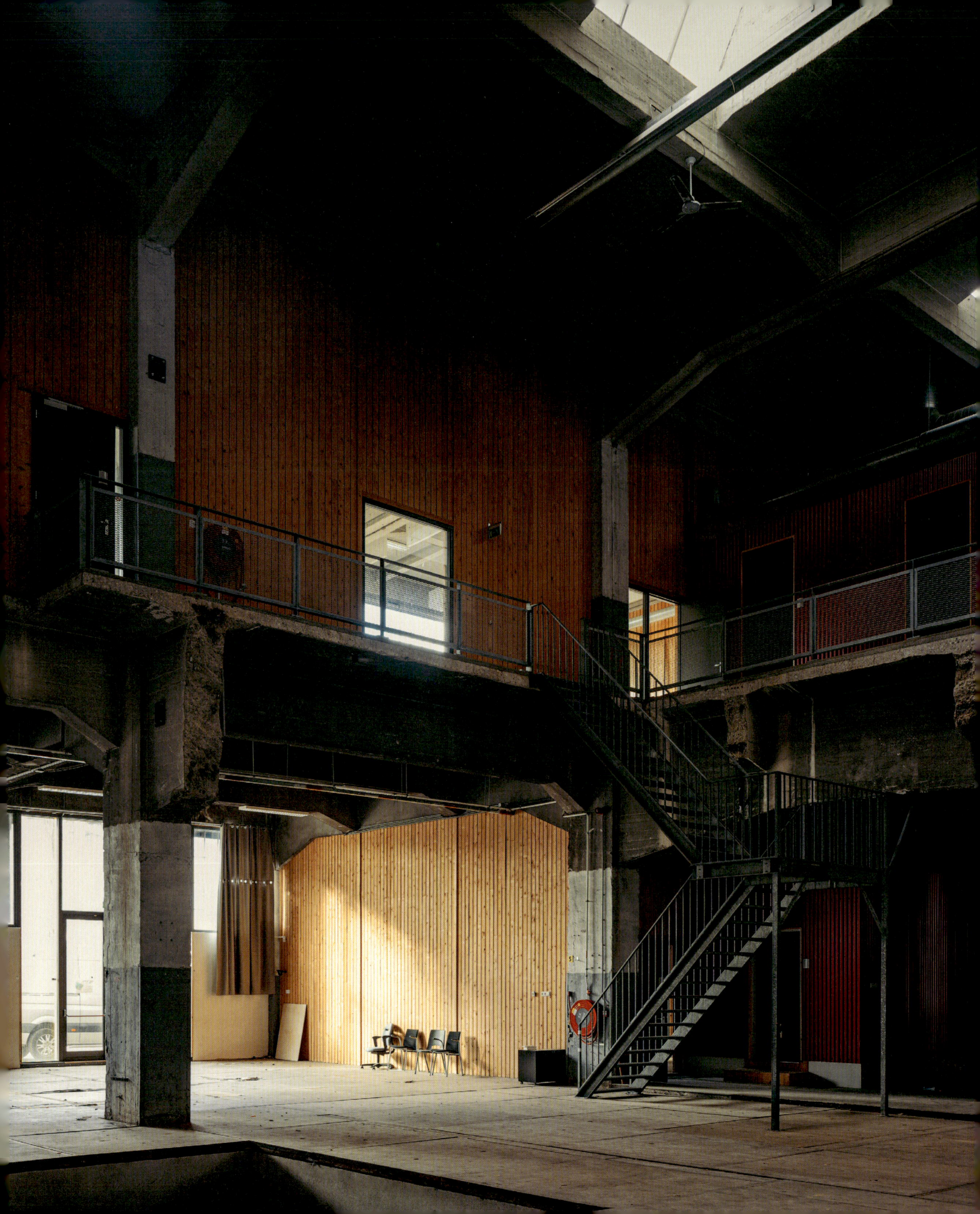

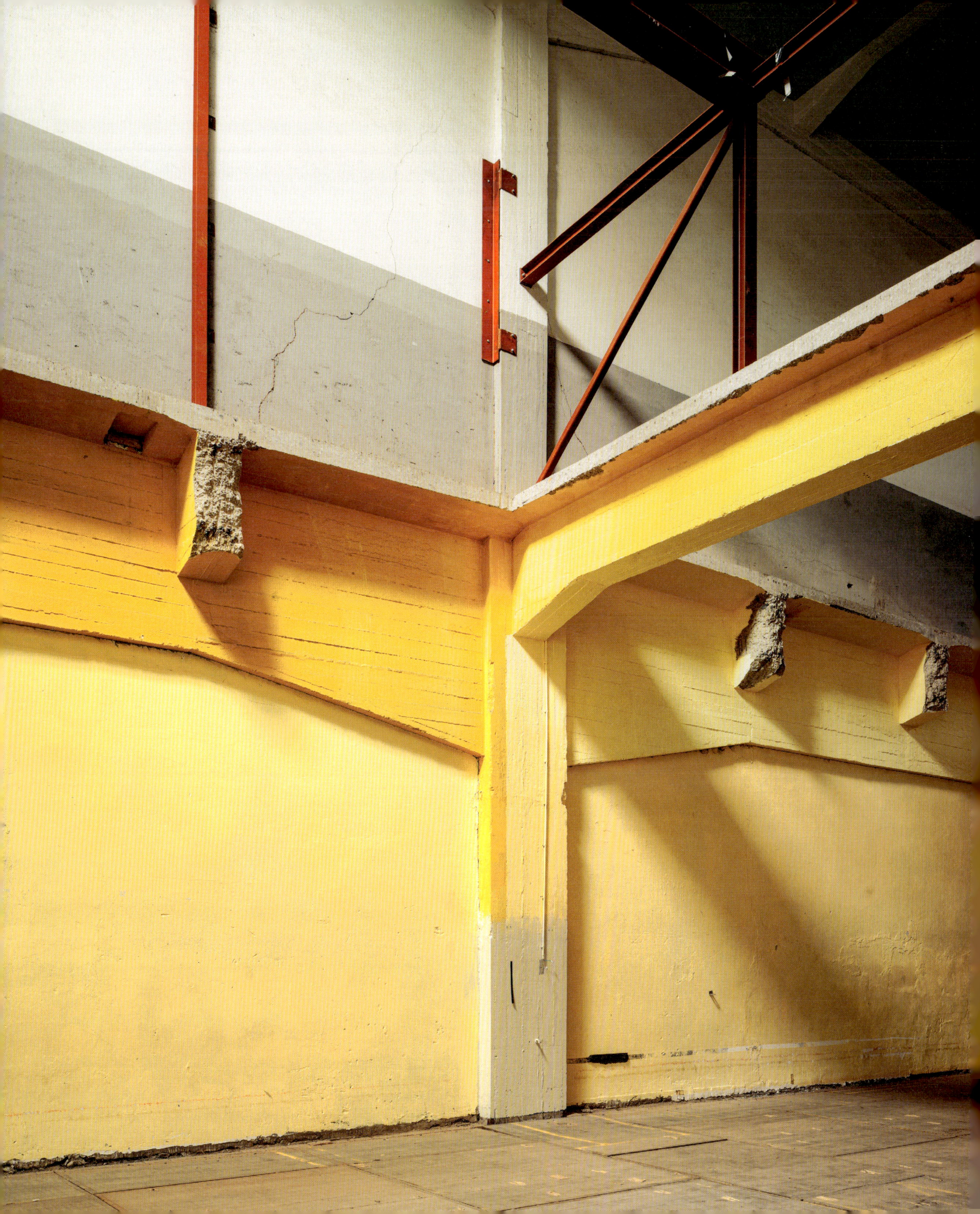

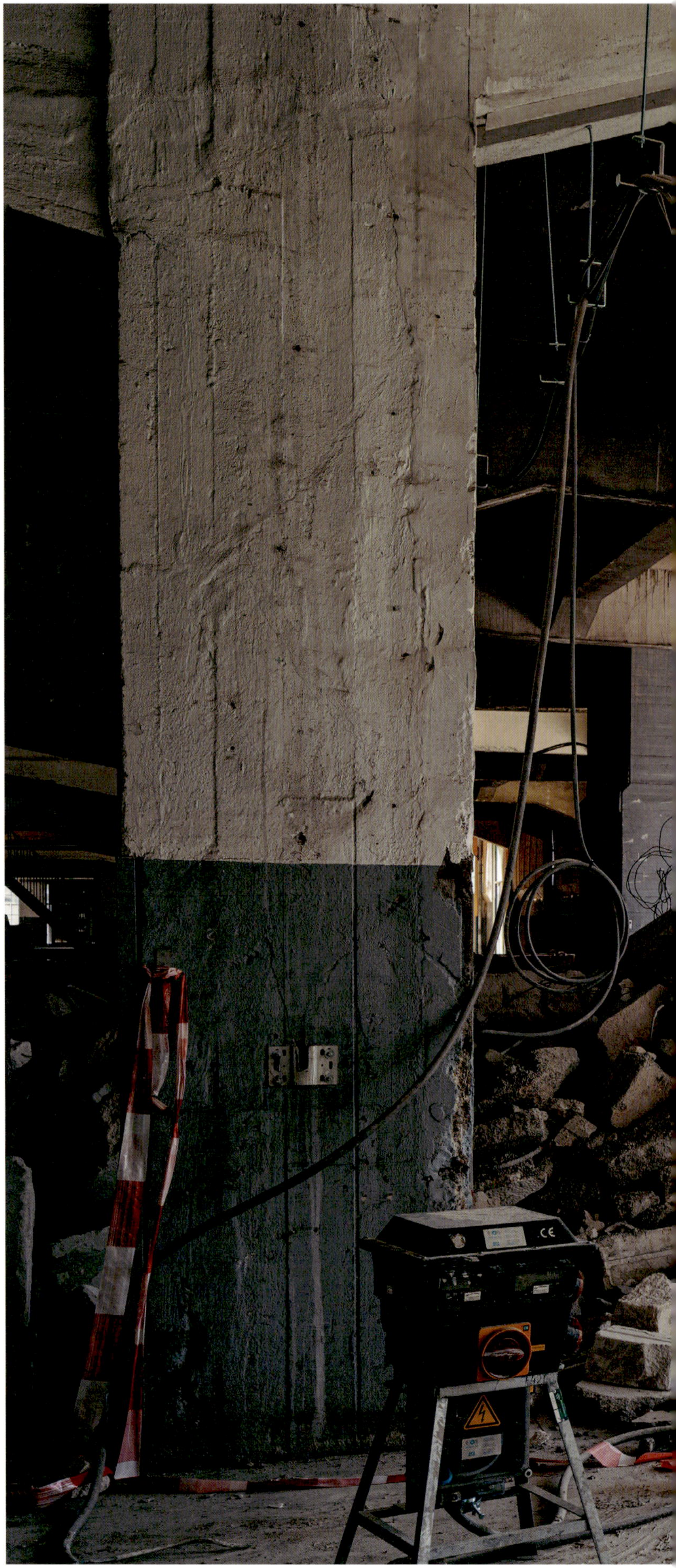

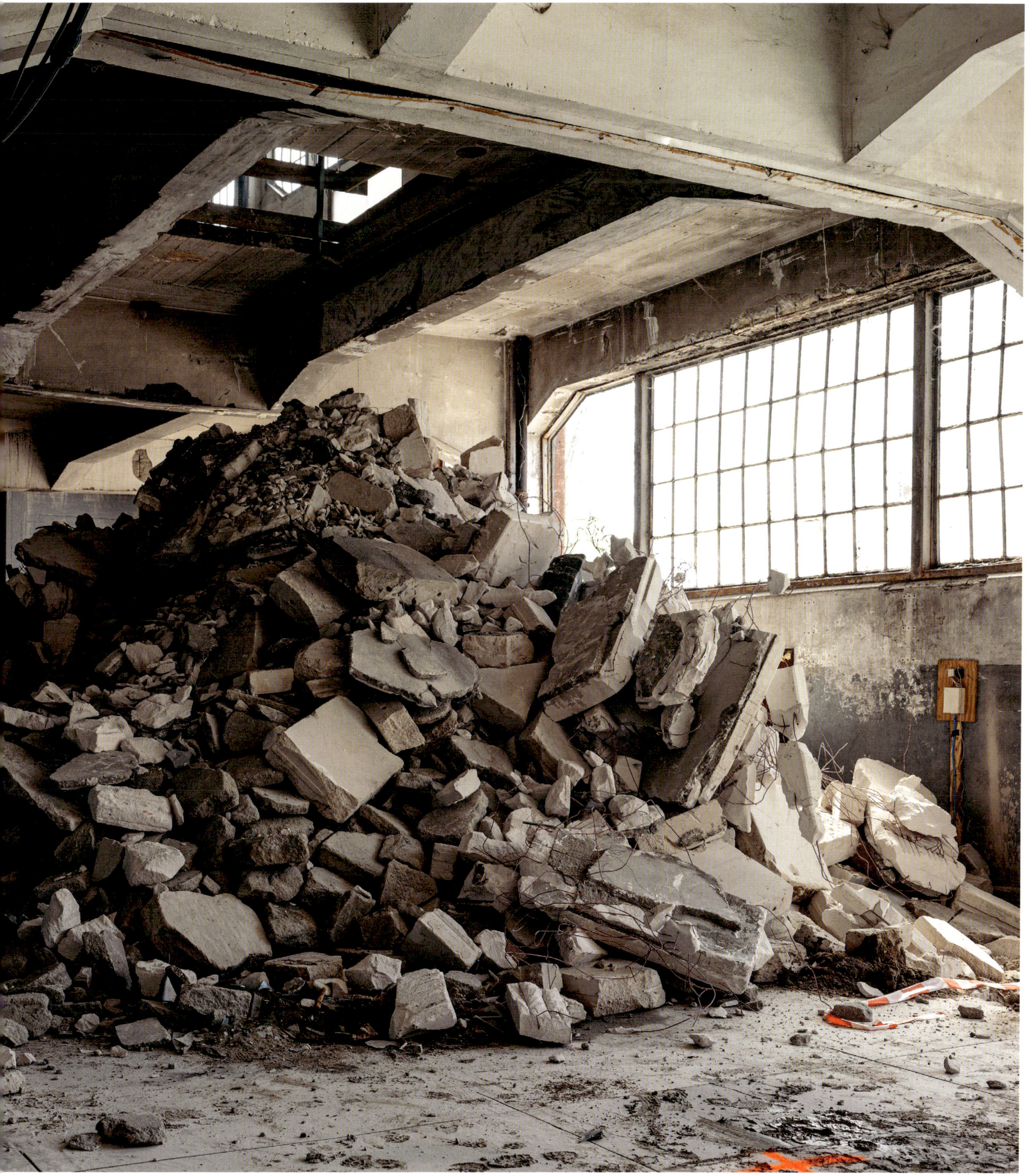

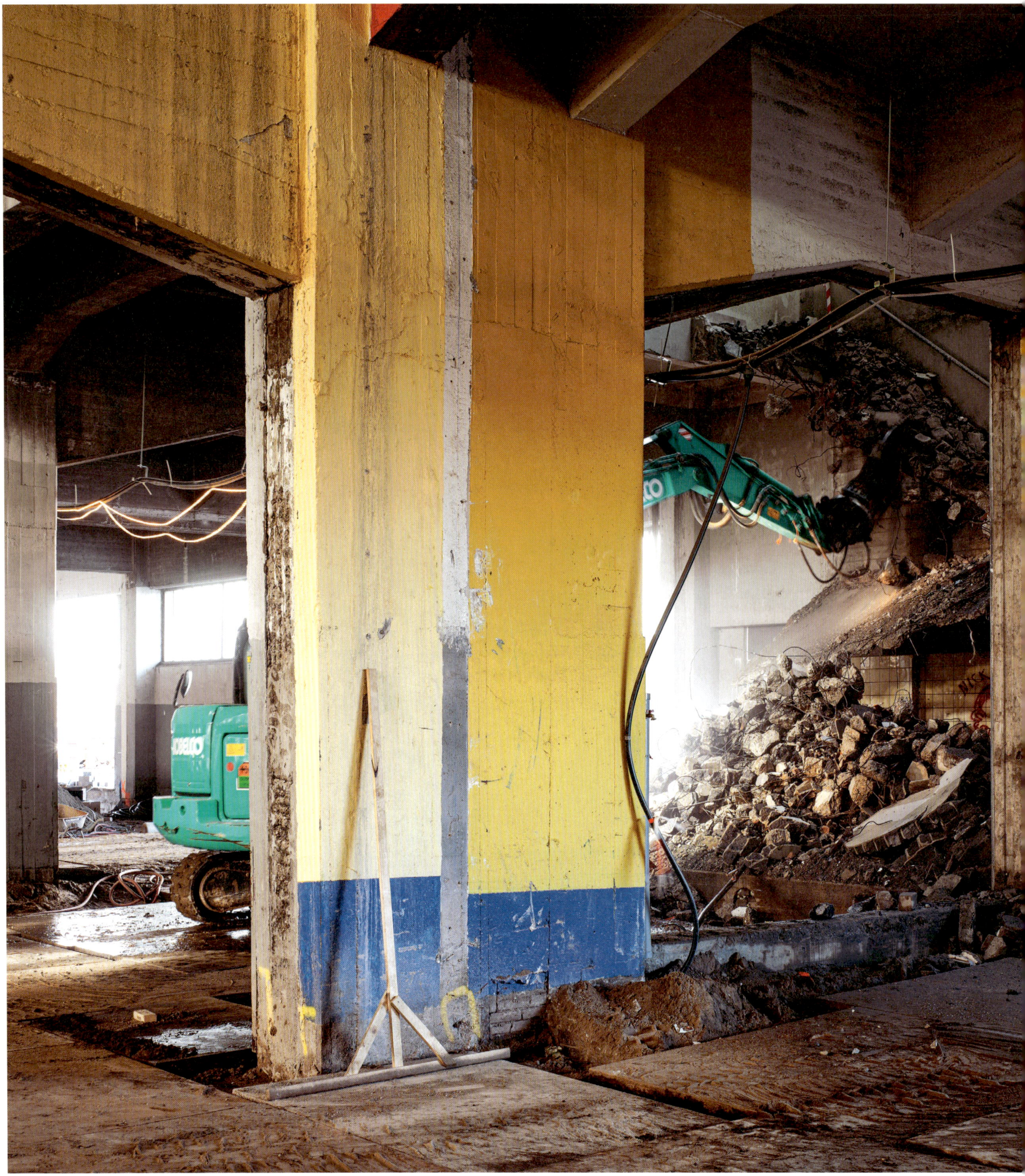

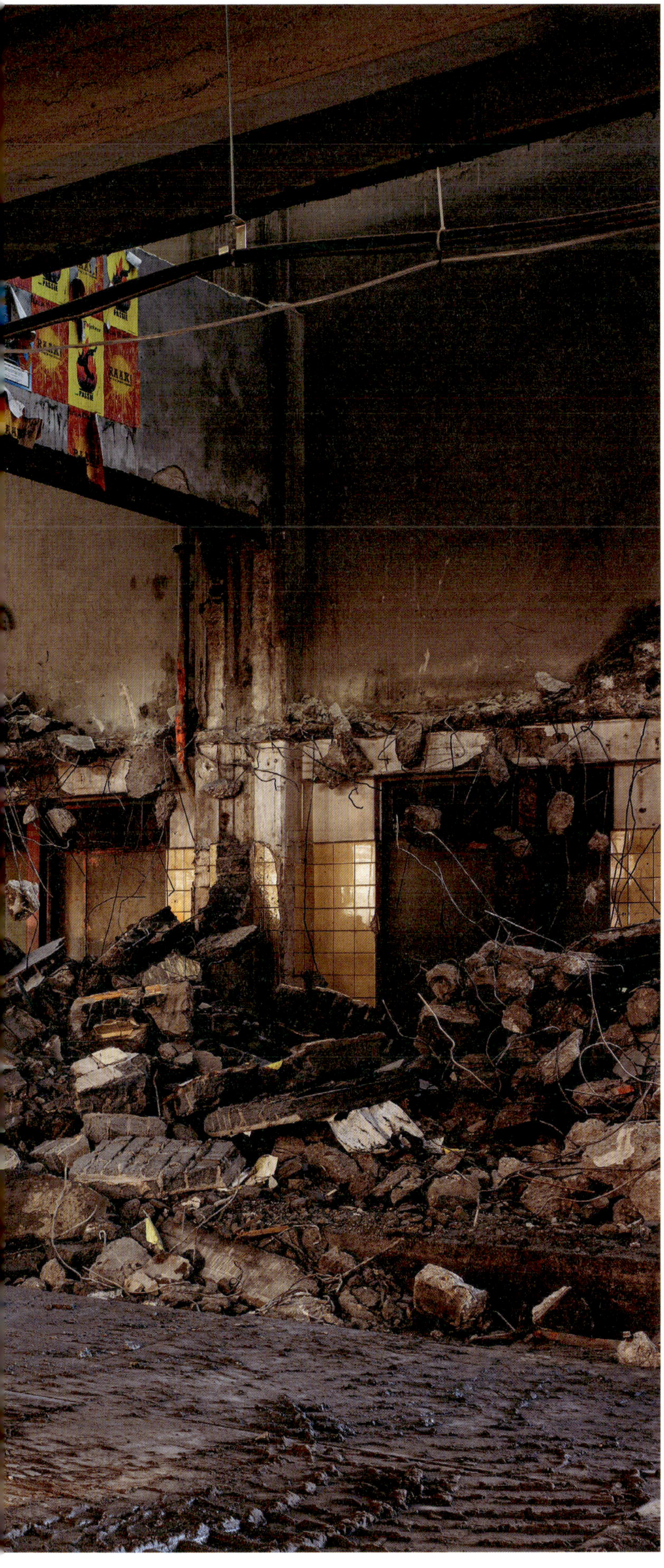

“The foundation of the building is a huge part that we will no longer see later on, but is an essential part that carries everything.”

Loes de Jong, Intern at Dura Vermeer

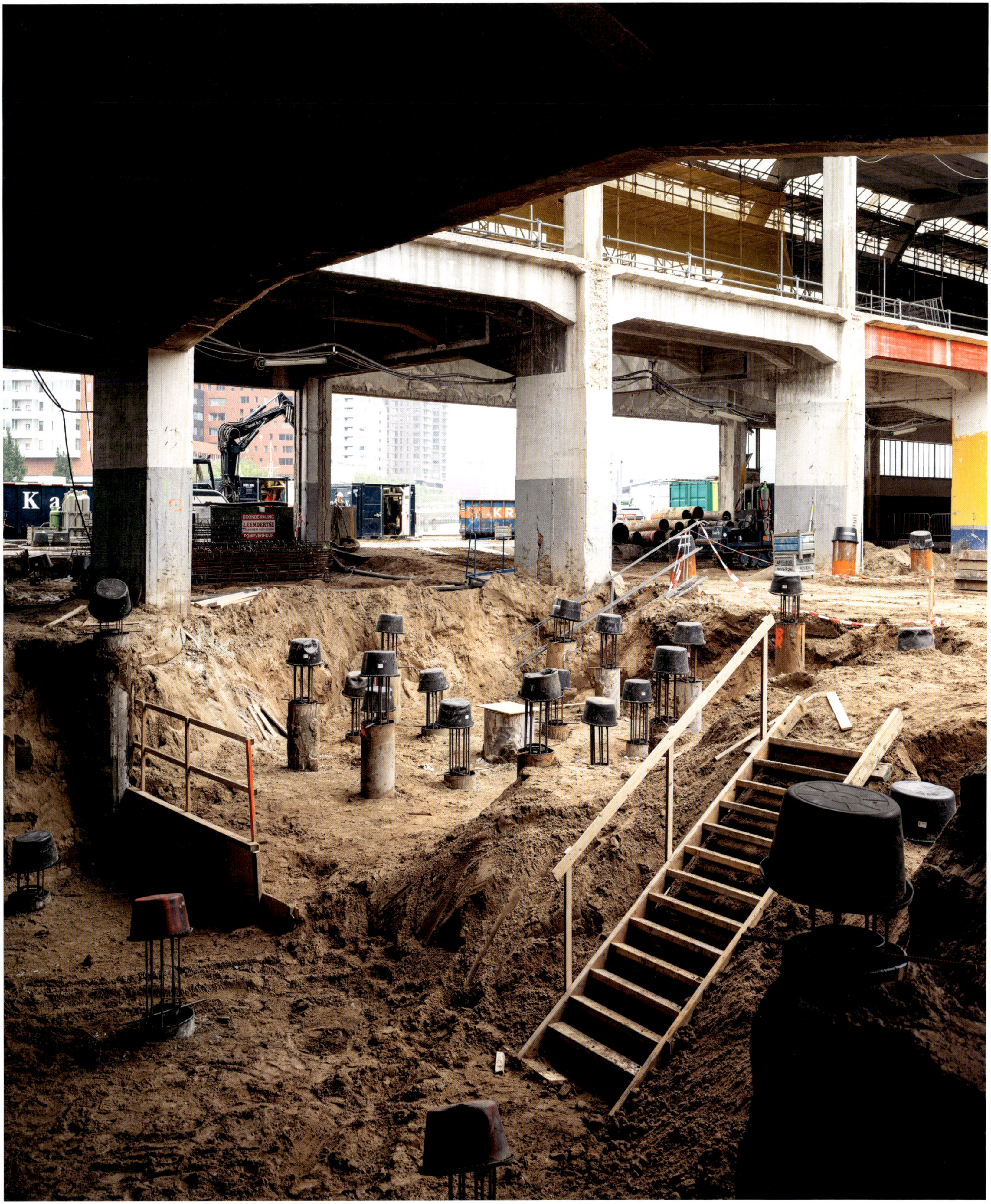
BRONBEMALING
LEENDERTSE
POMPVERHUUR

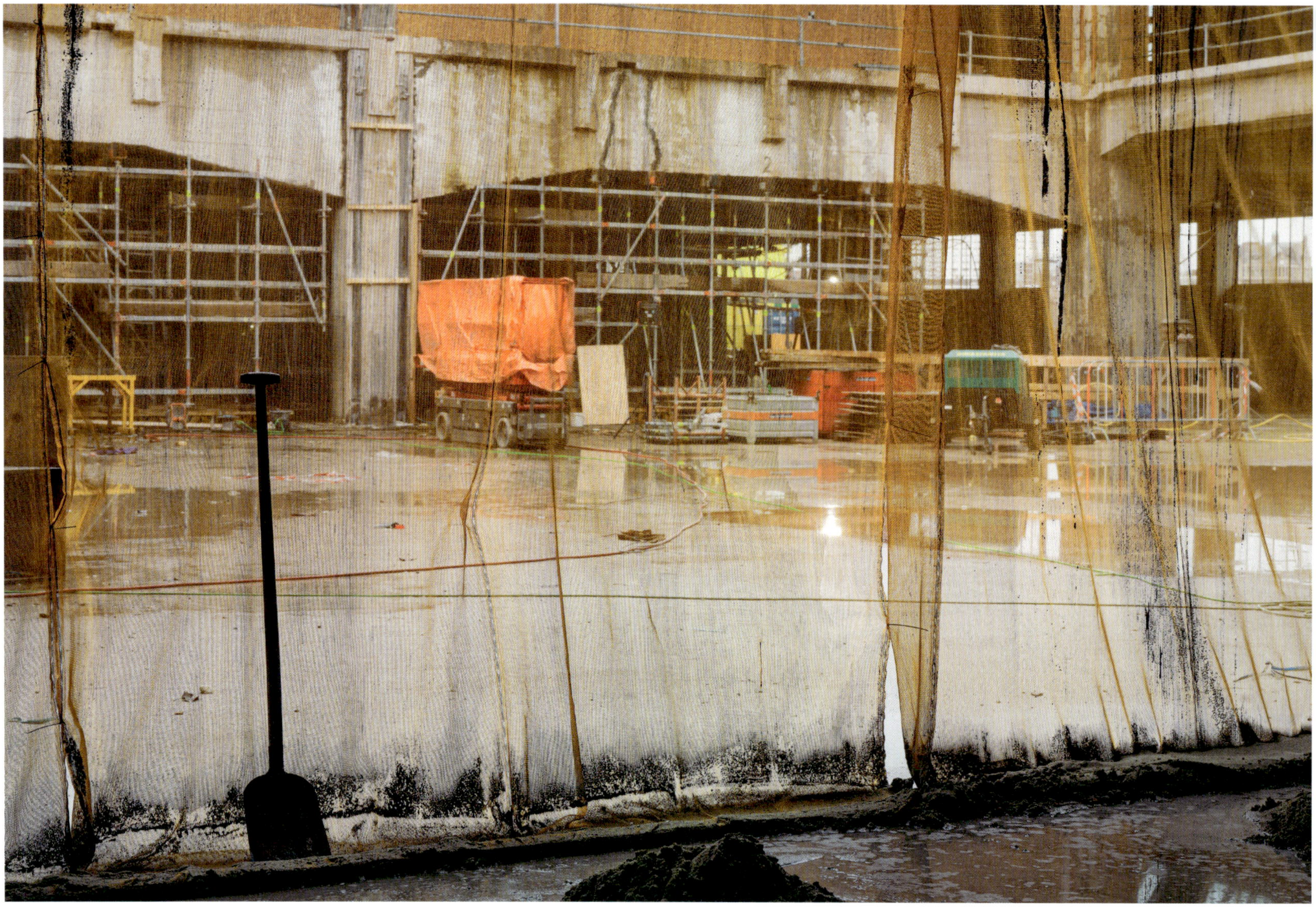

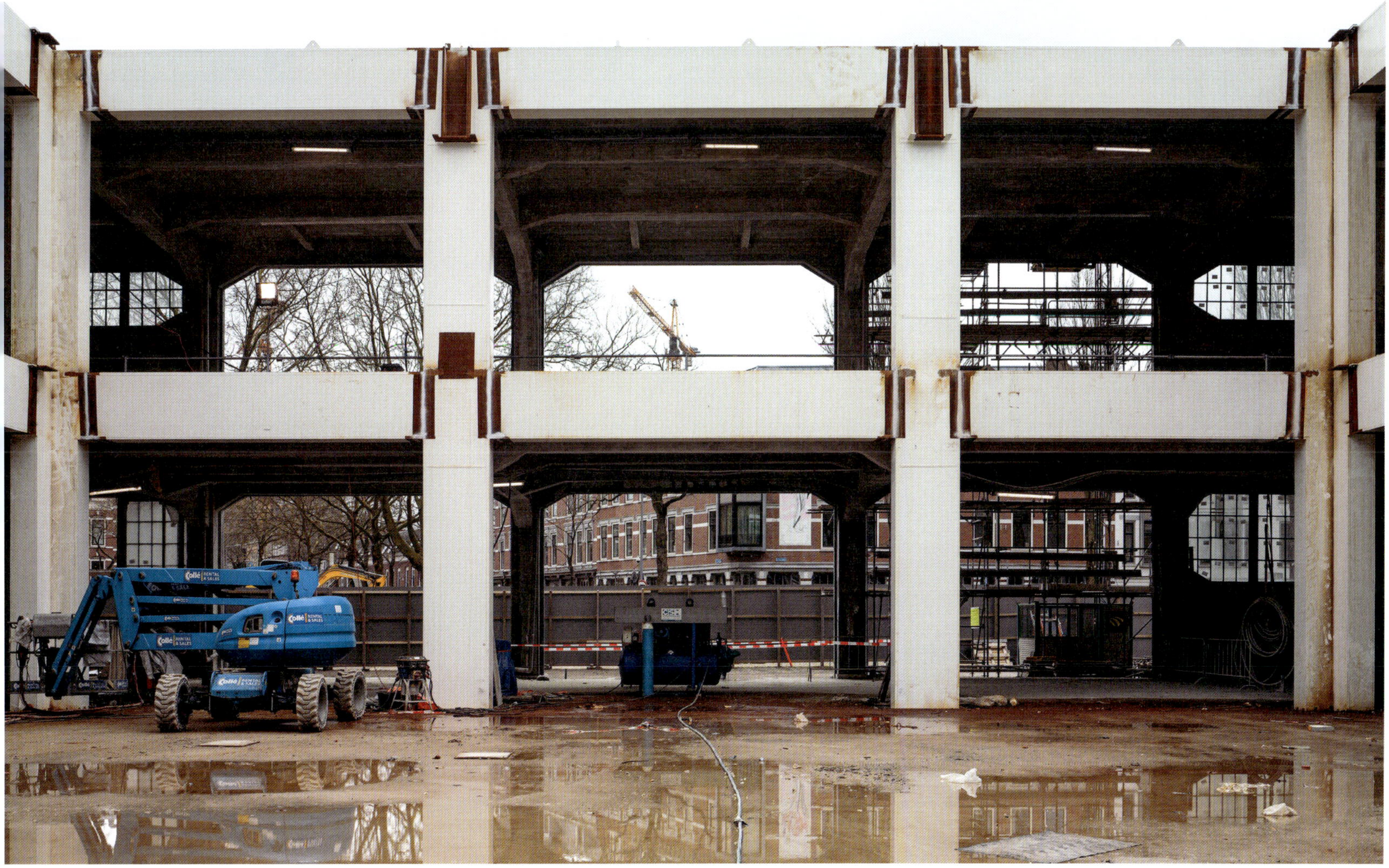

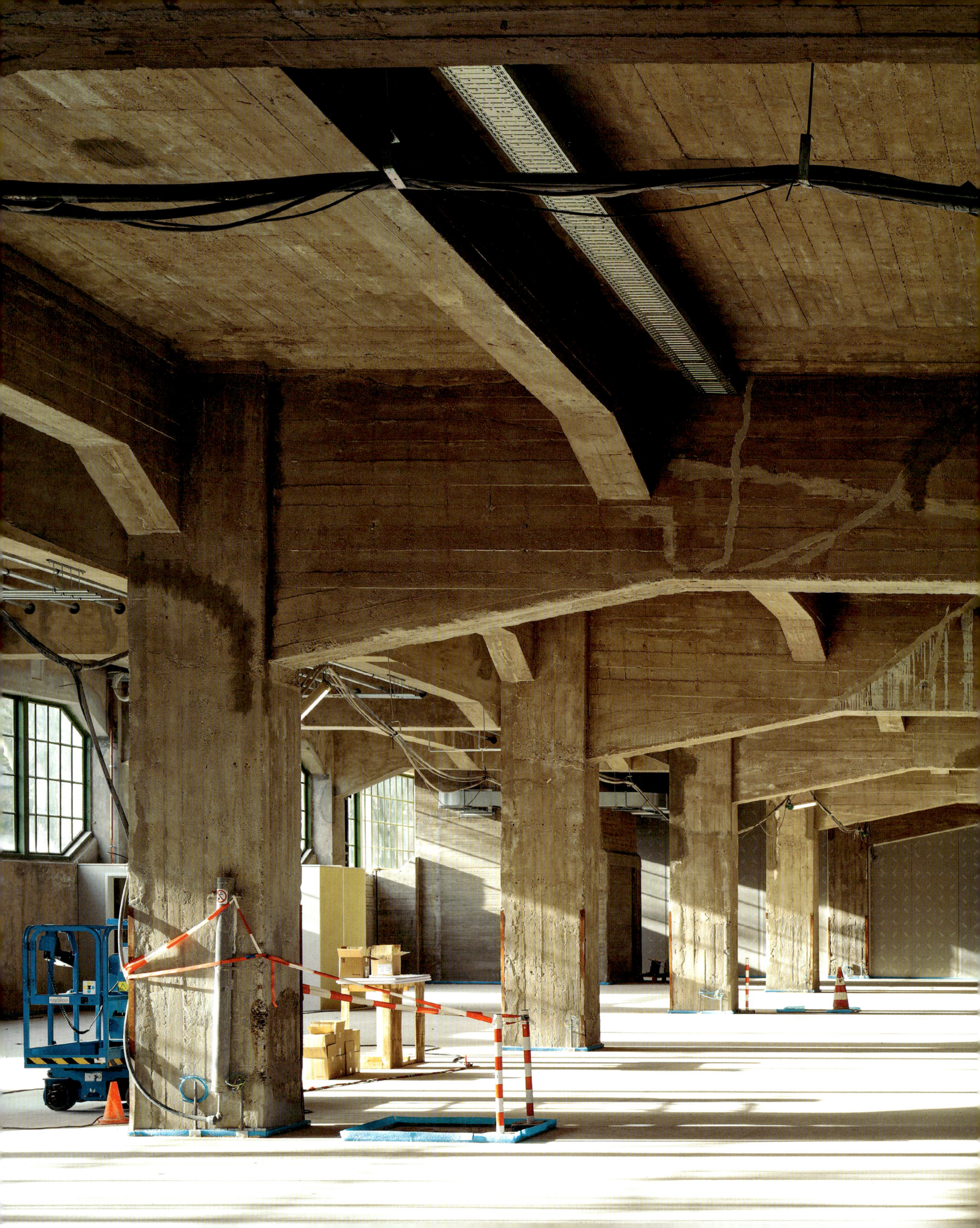

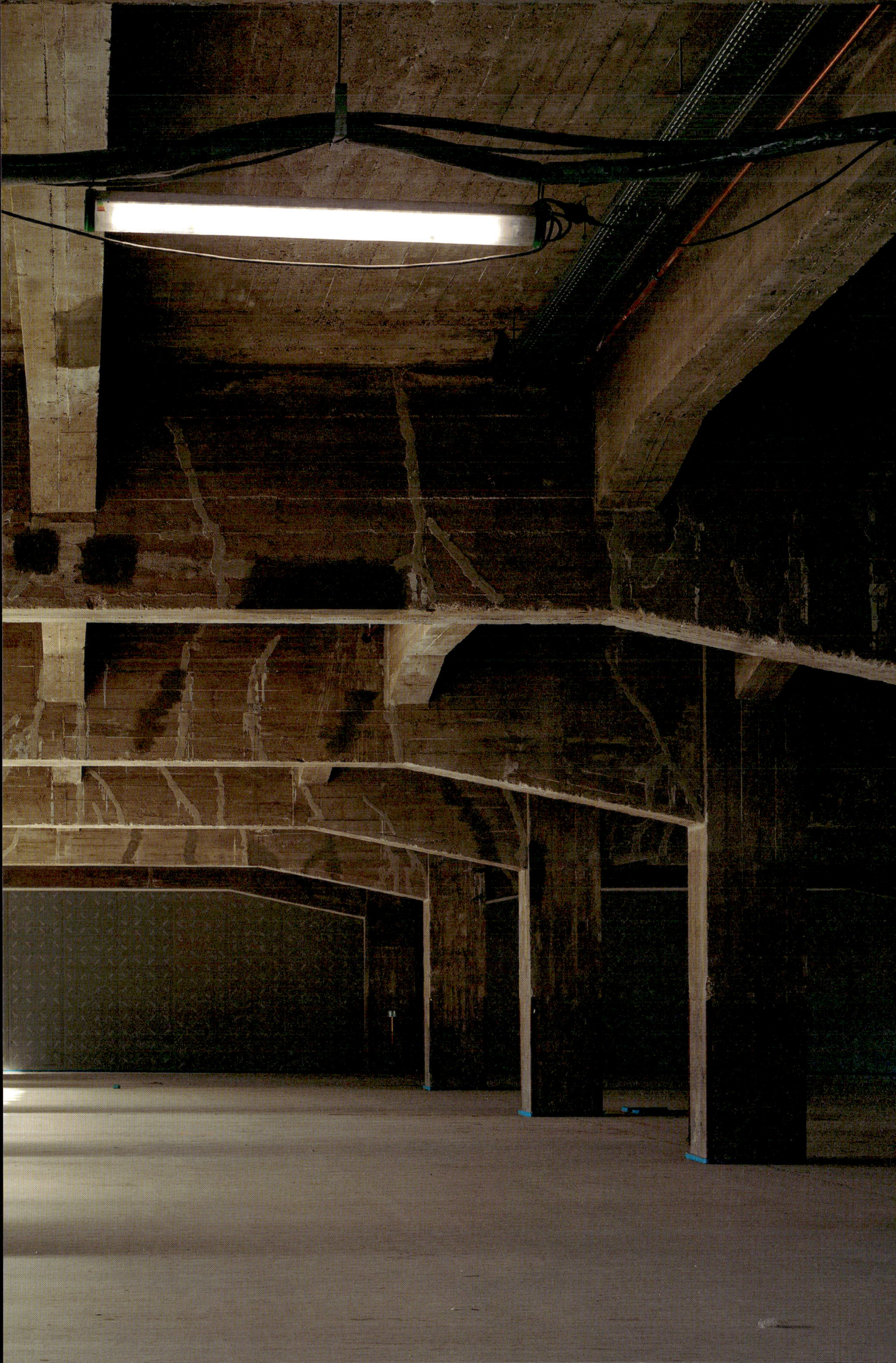

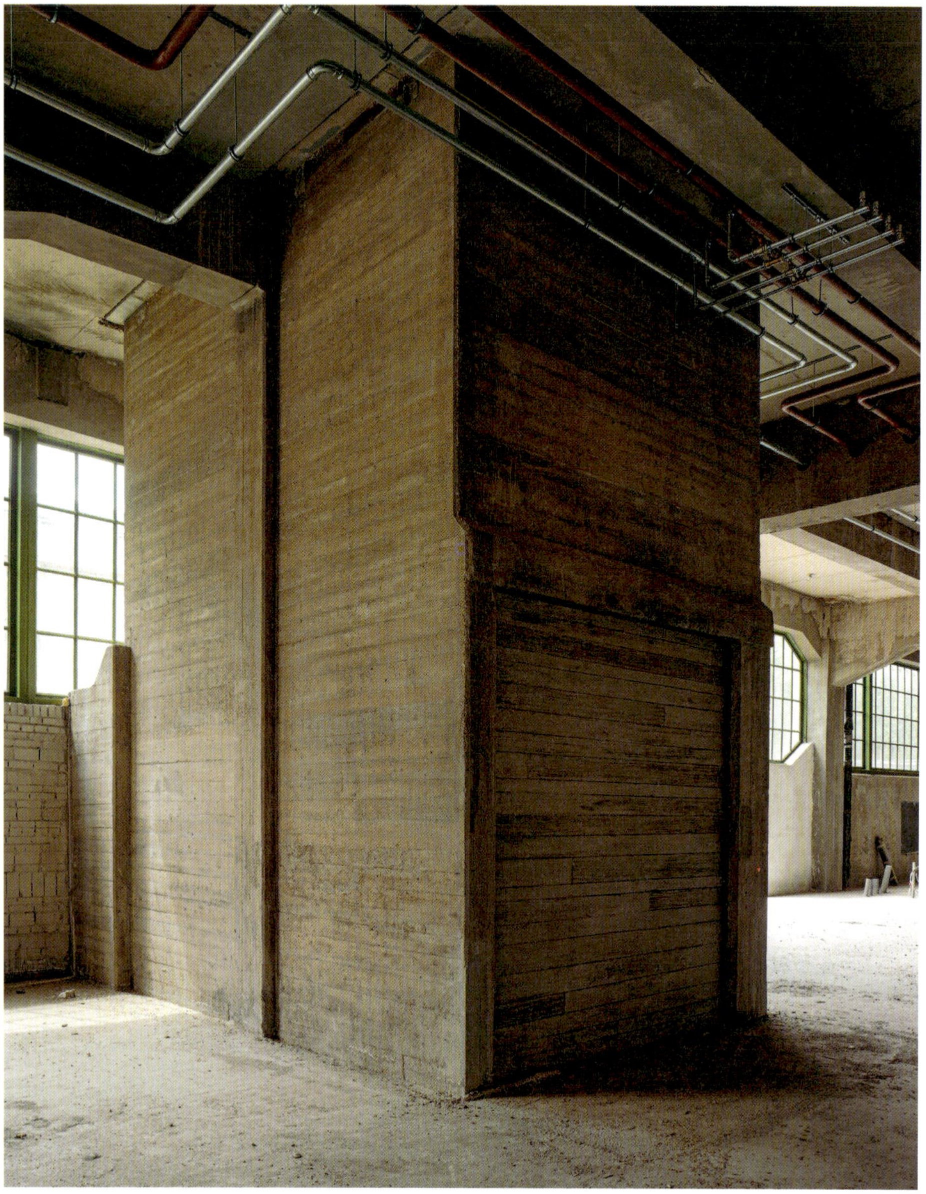

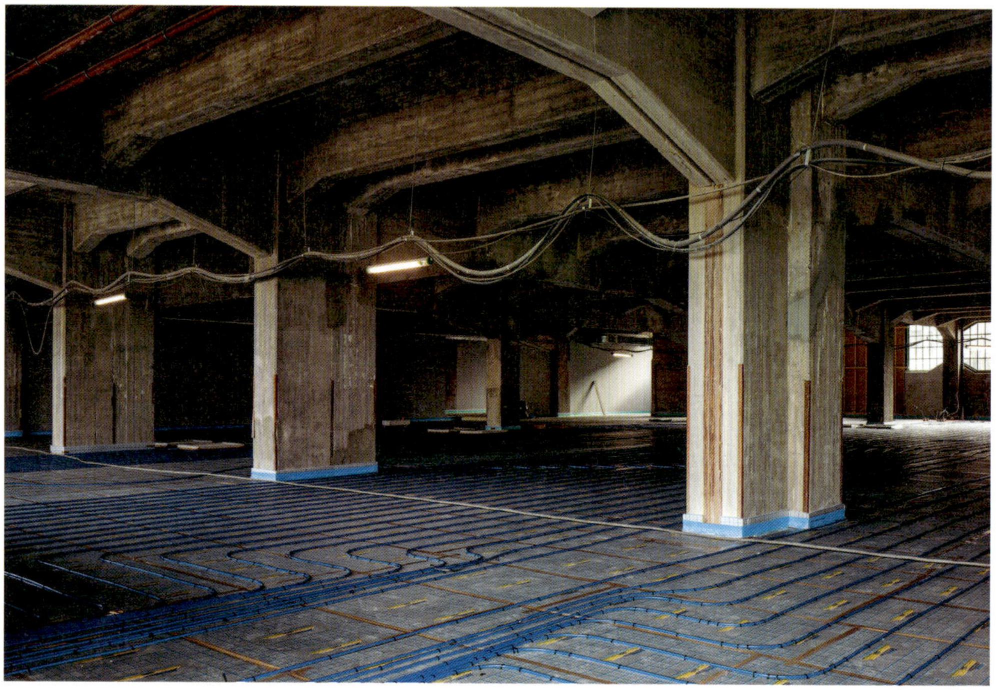

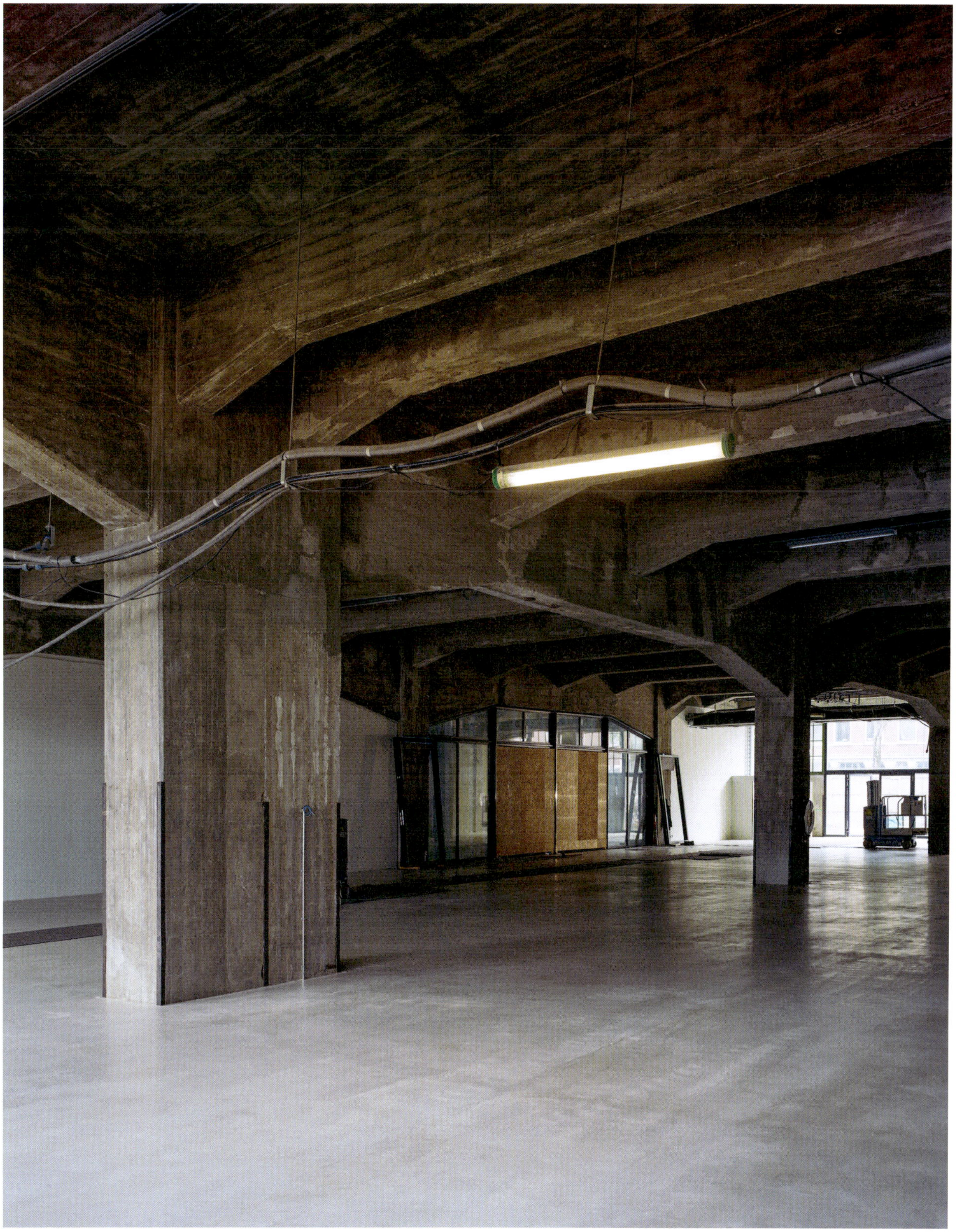

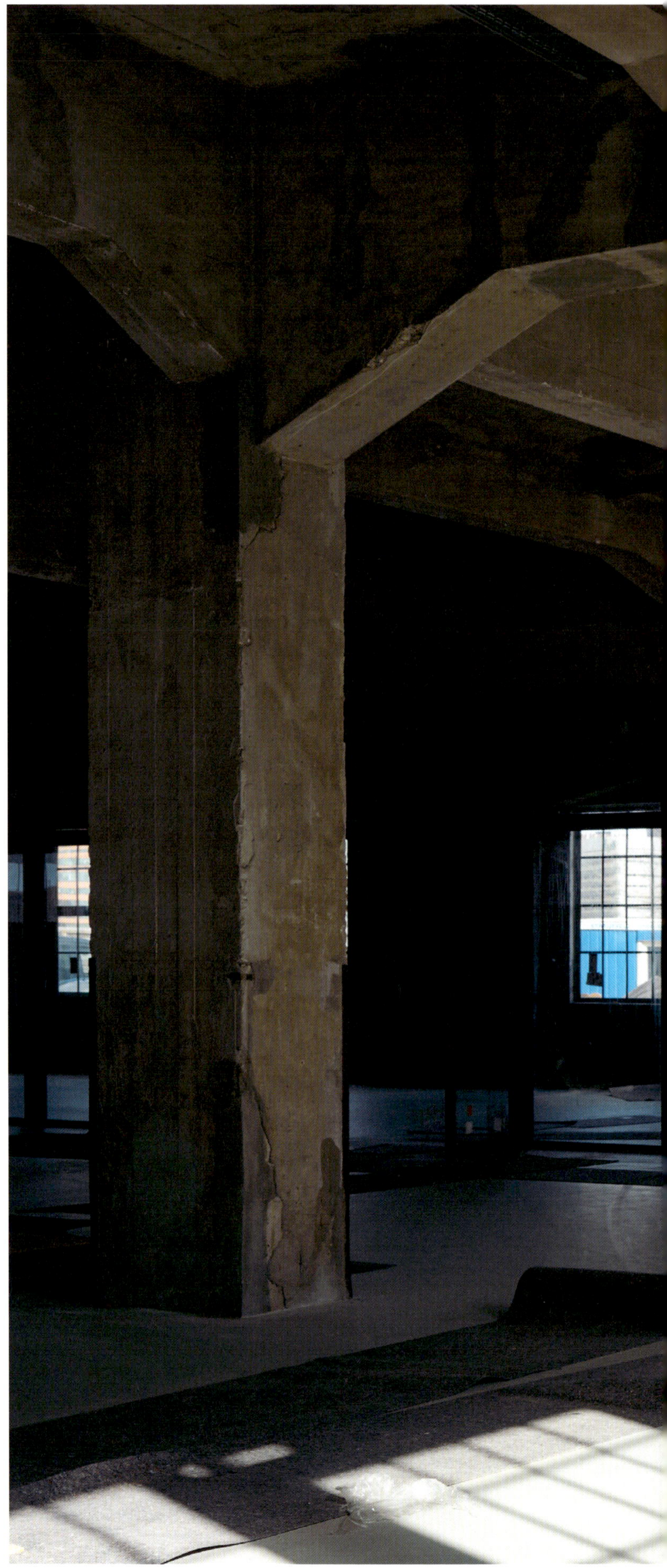

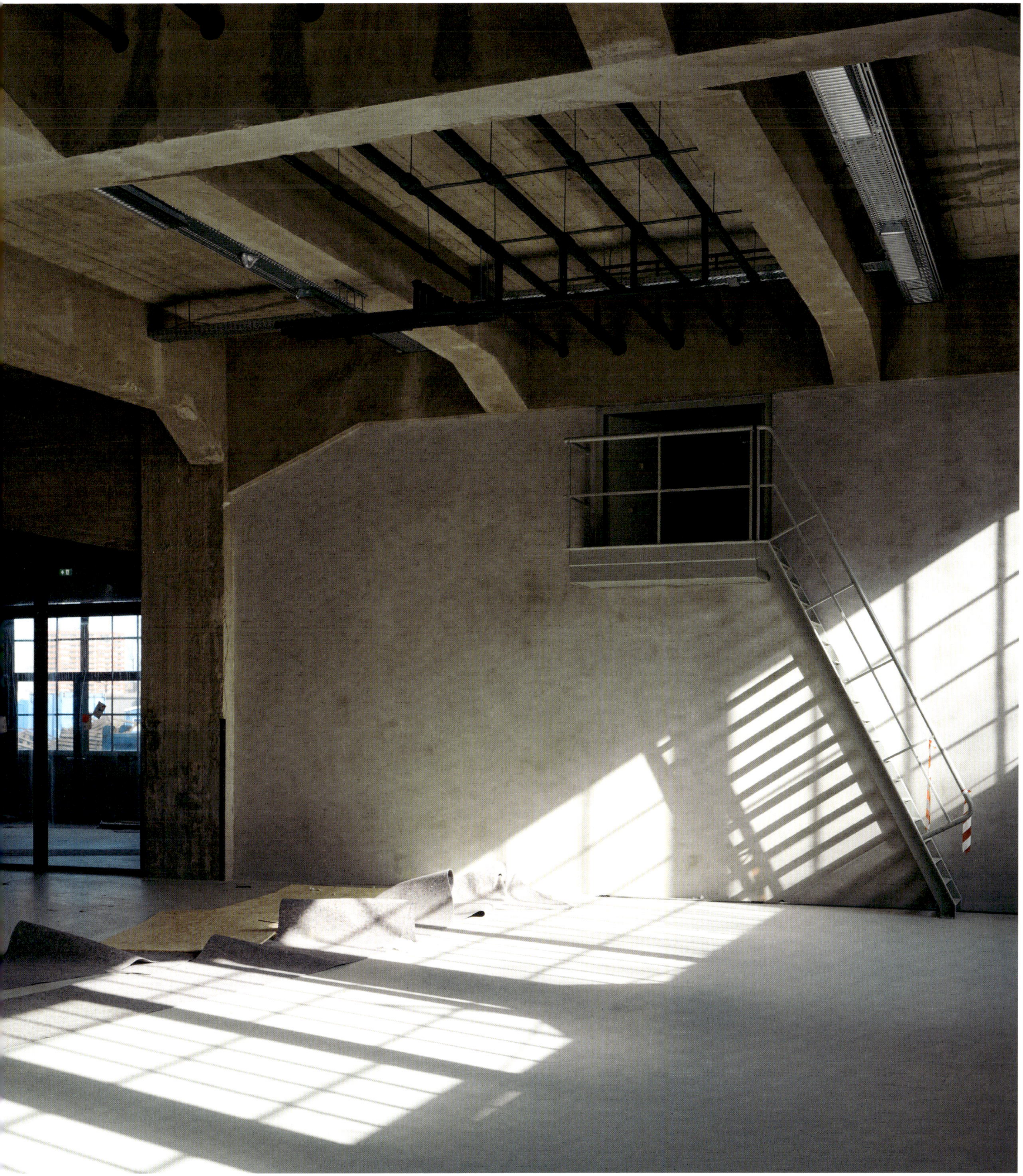

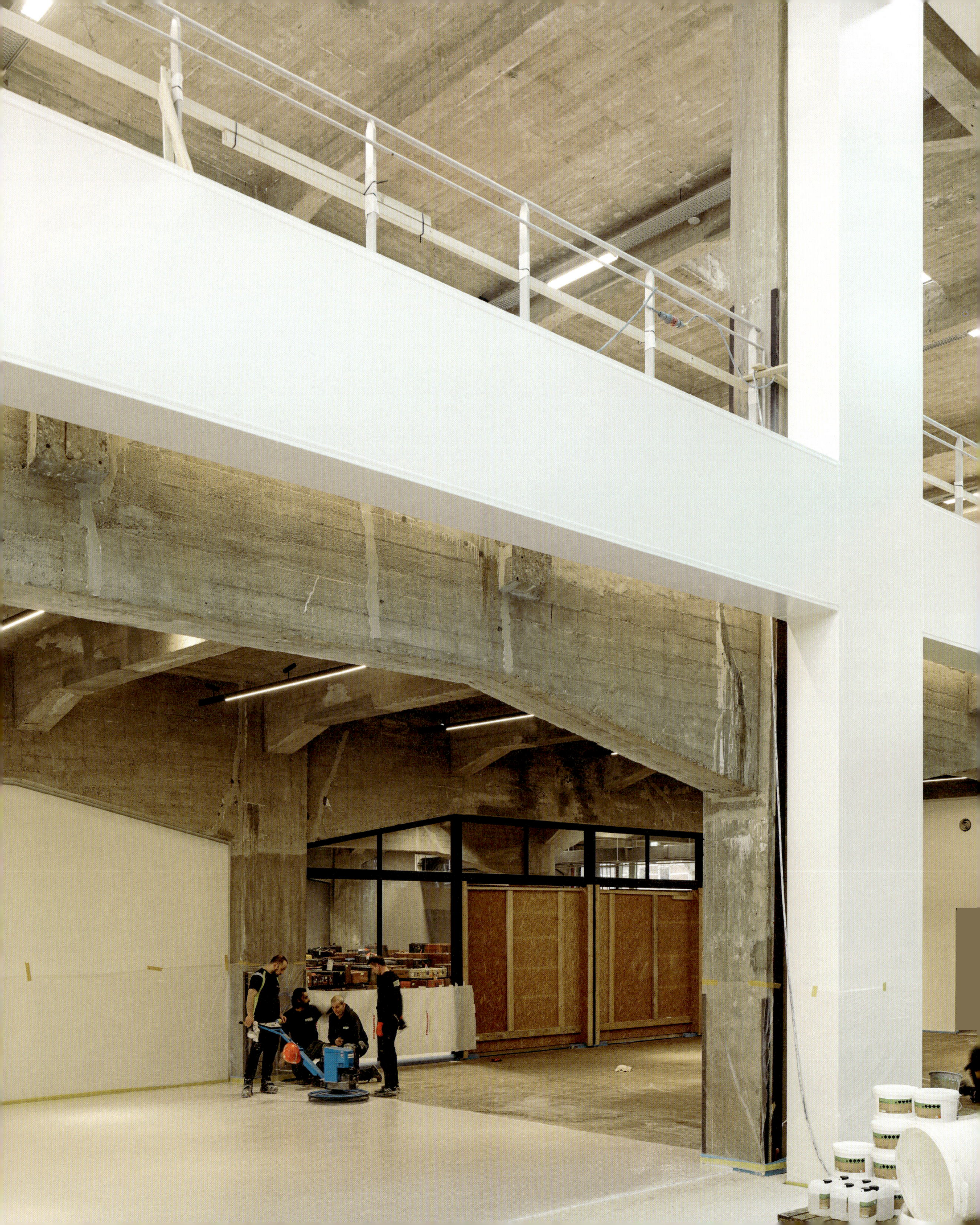

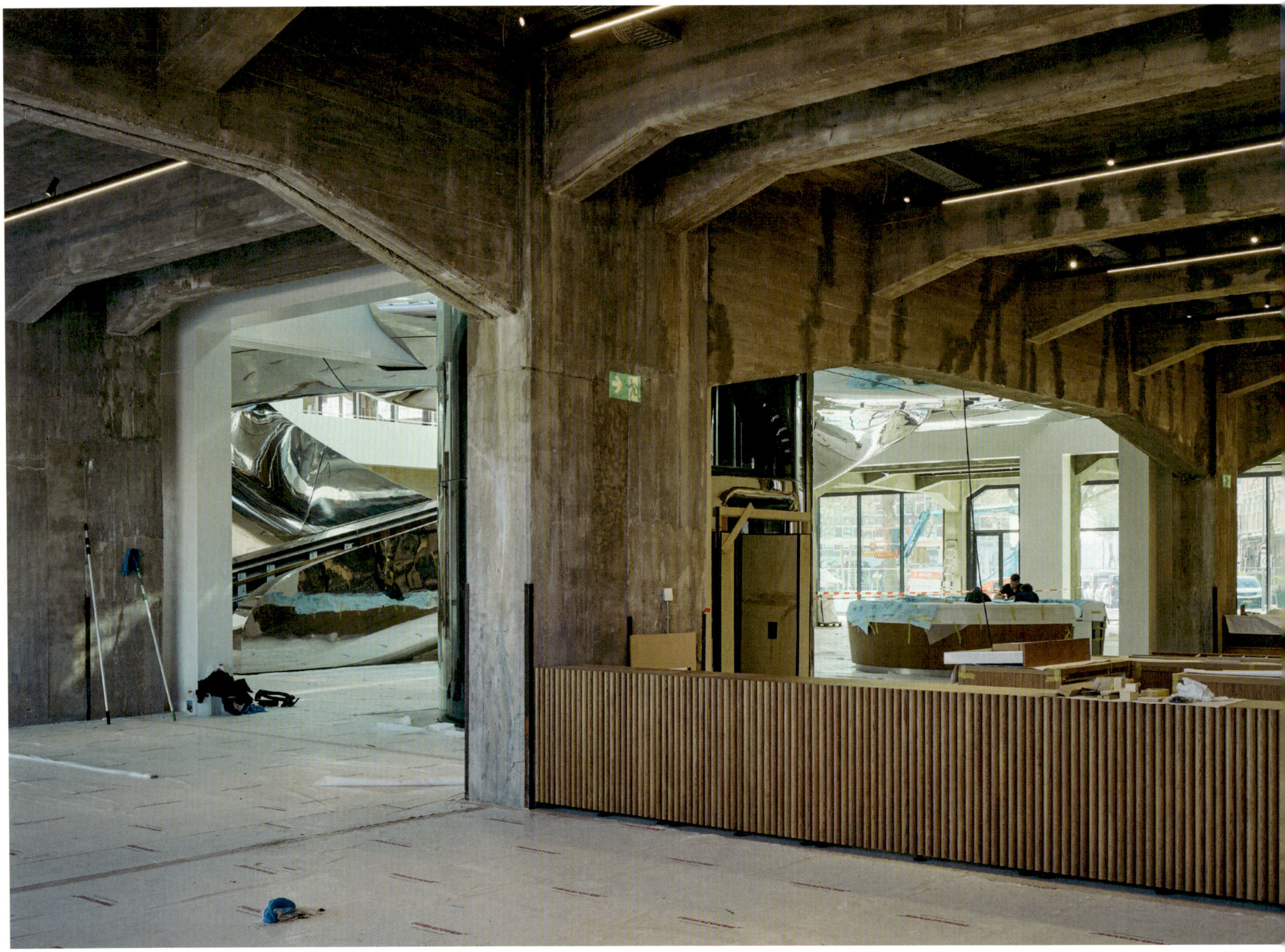

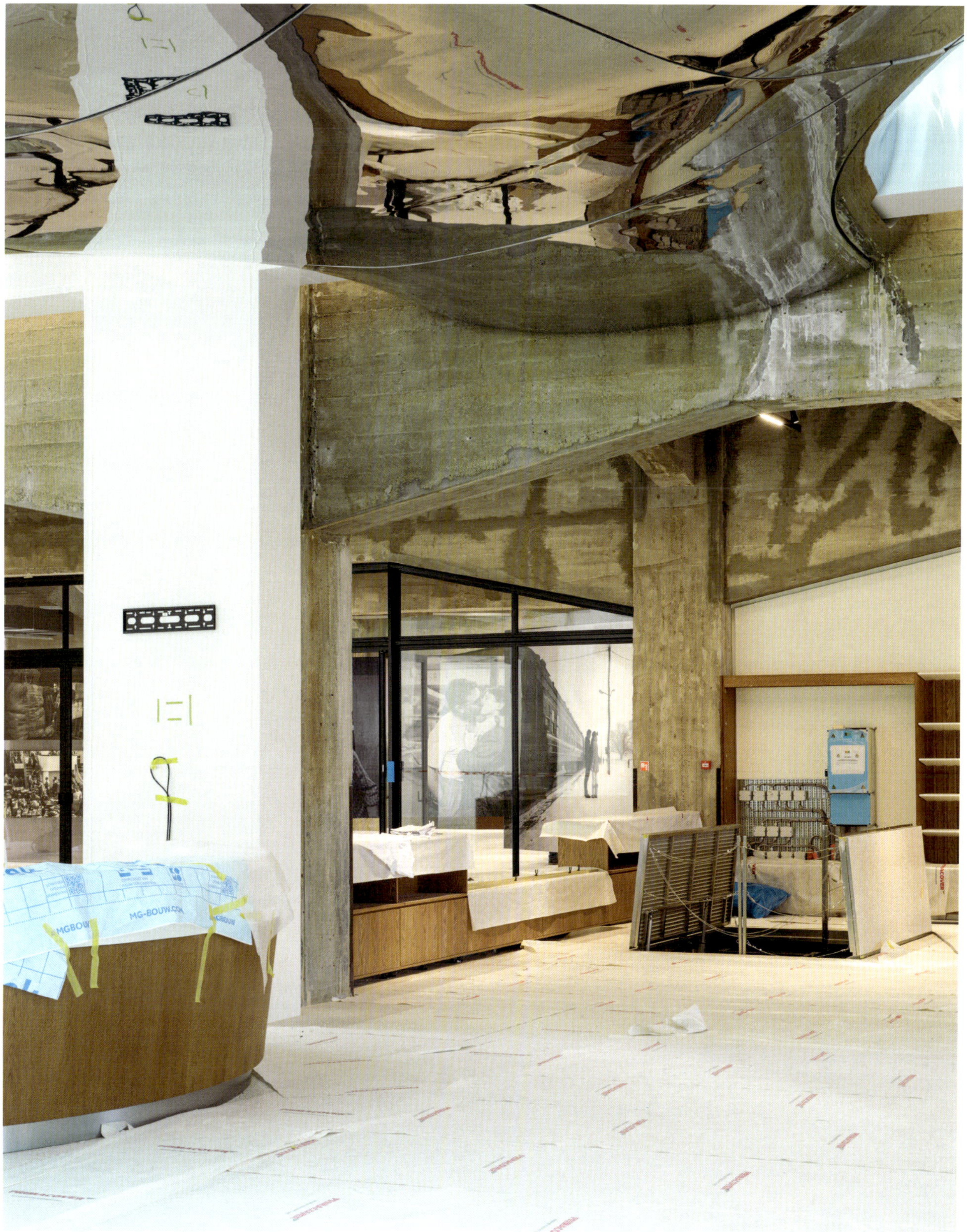
MG-BOUW.COM

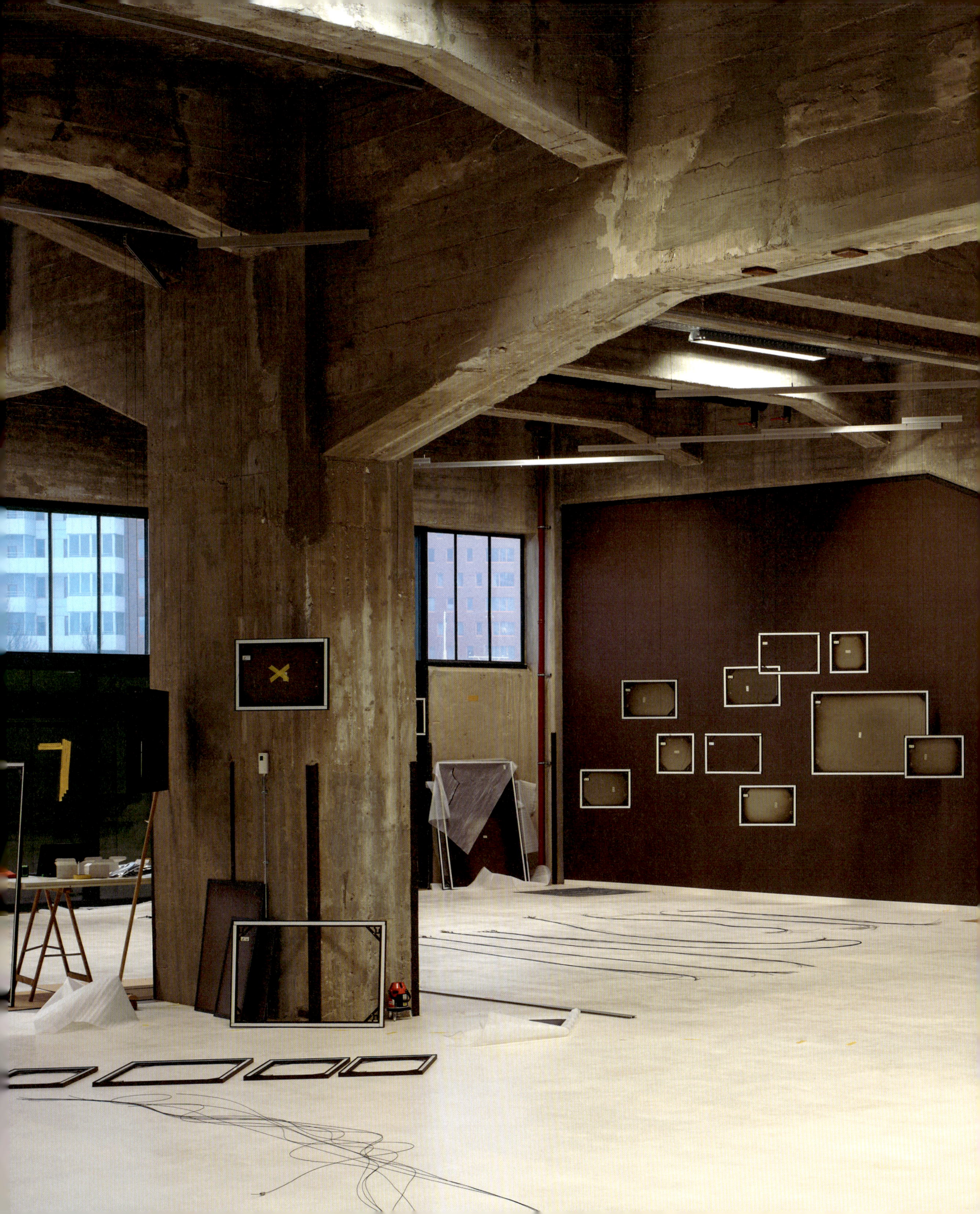

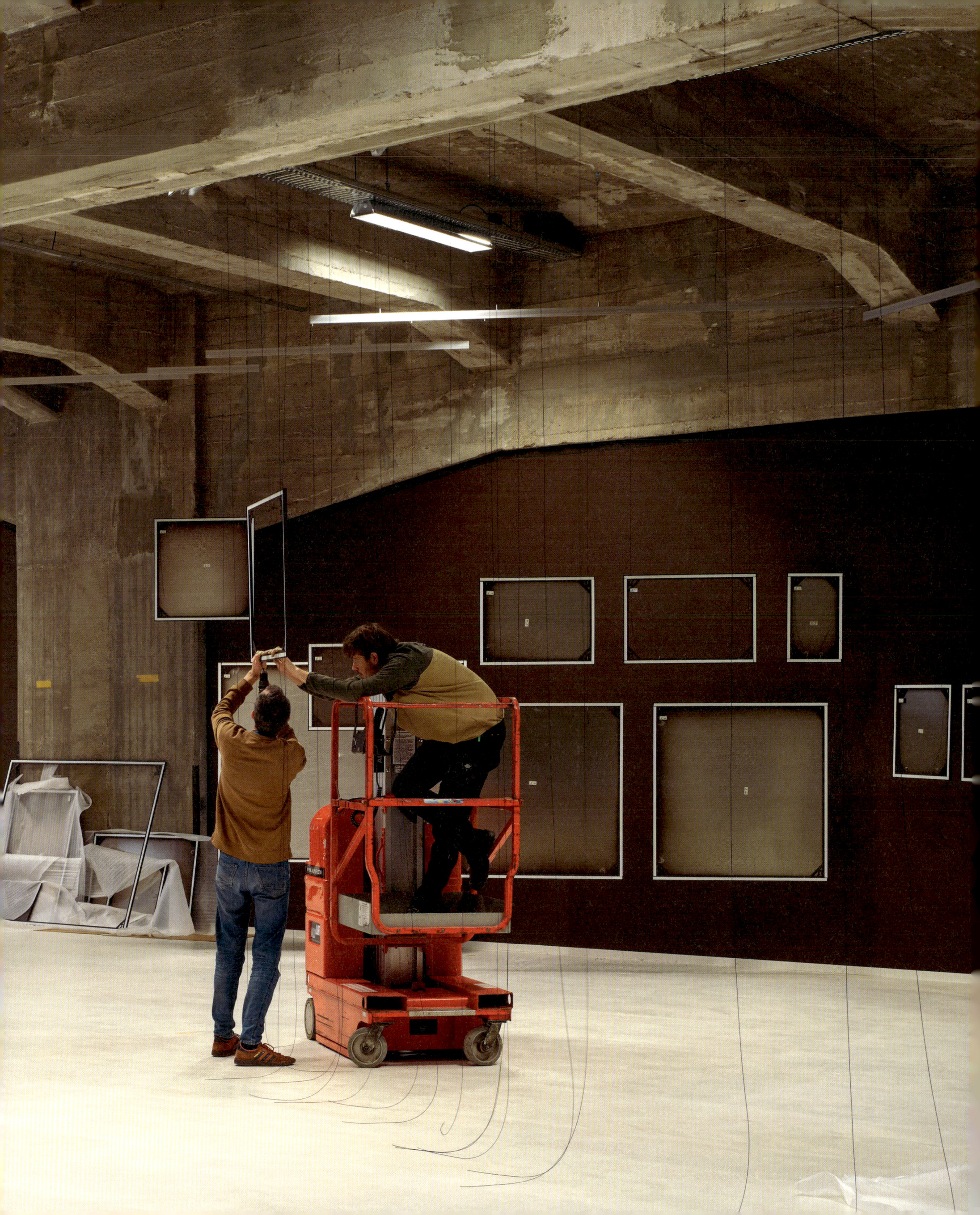

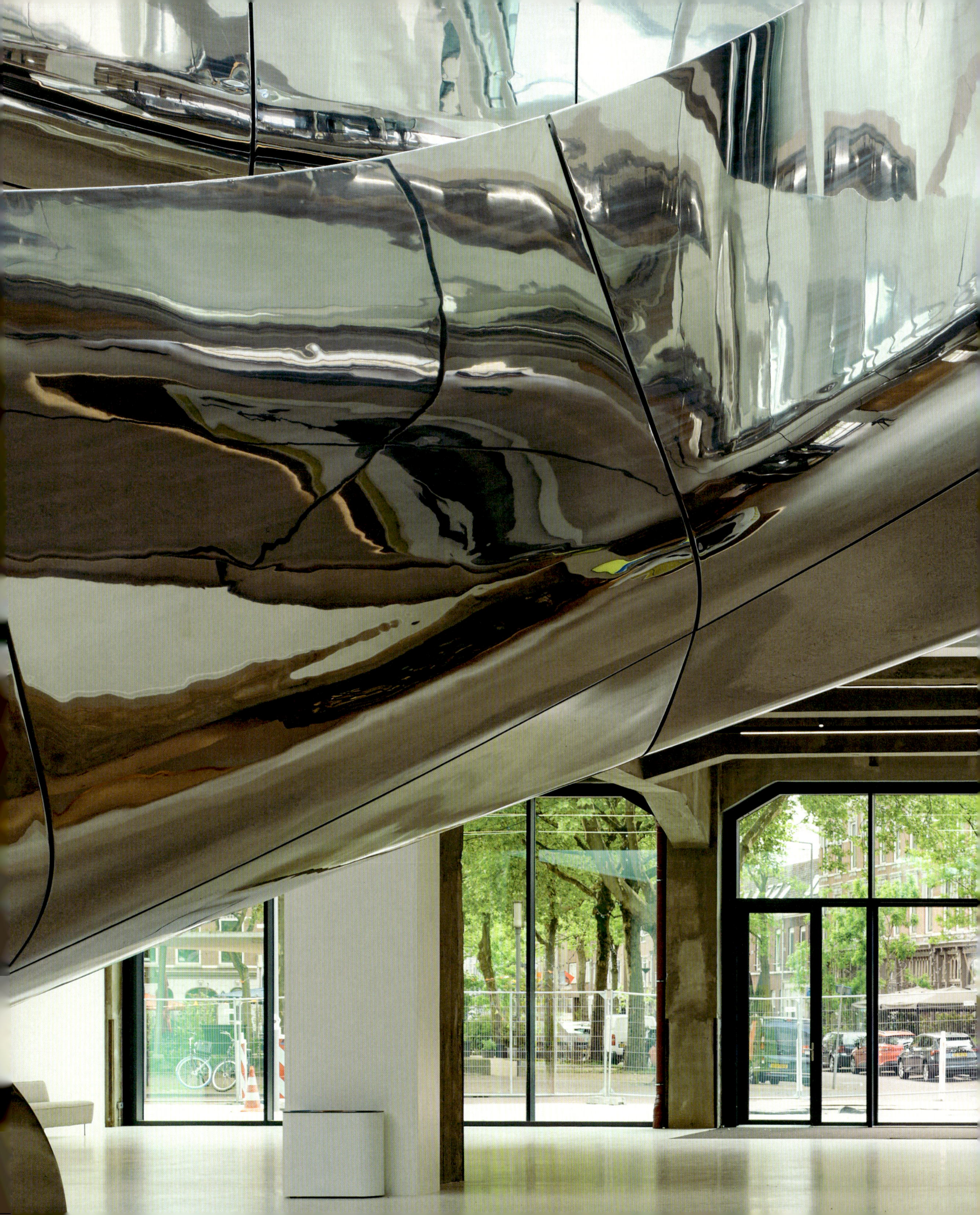

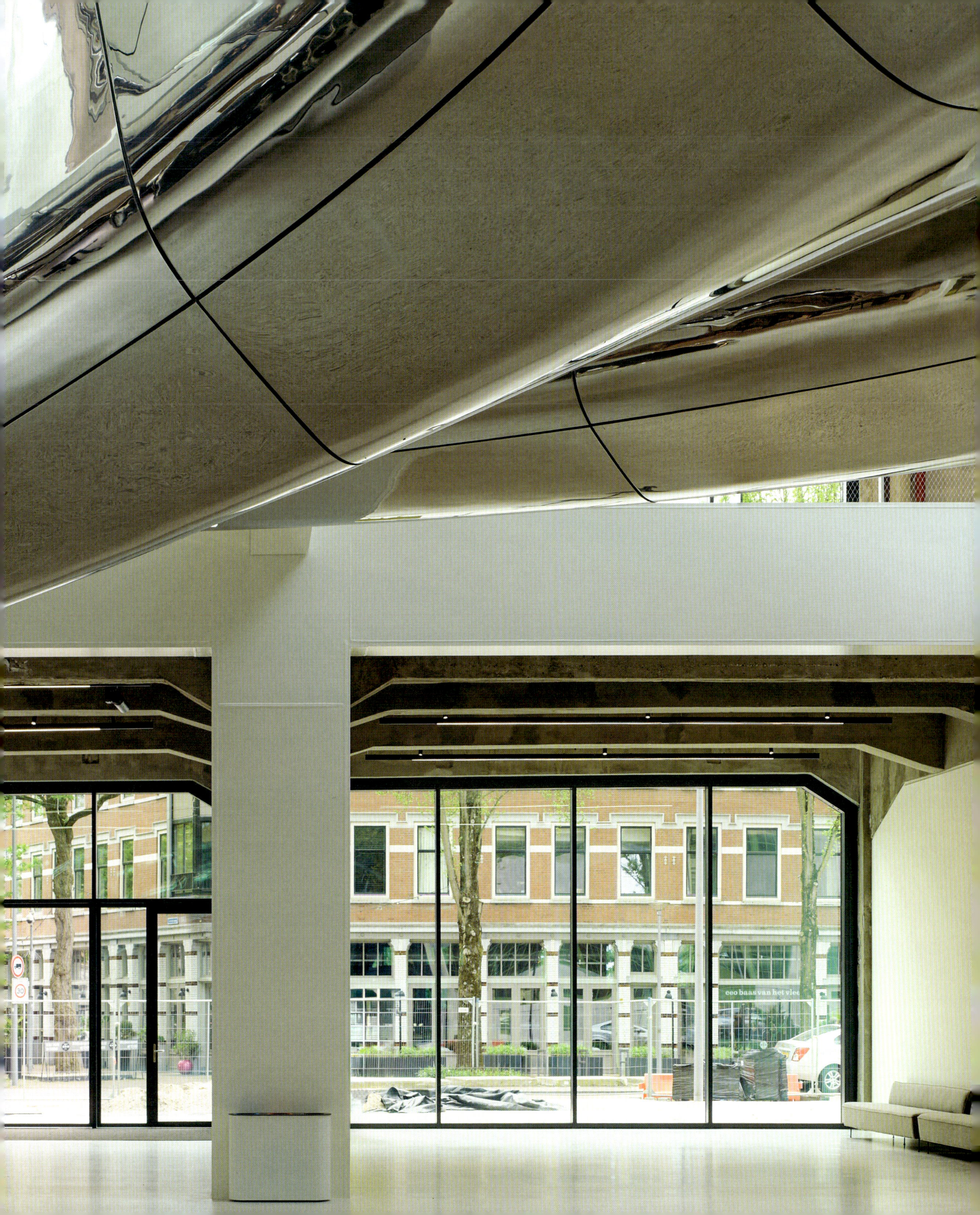

First Floor

On the first floor, there is a vast gallery space dedicated to the Fenix collection. The original layout of the floor has been kept. The warehouse was once used for the storage of as many goods as possible; it is incredibly spacious and straight forward. It is very functional and designed in conjunction with its purpose, largely constructed from one material: concrete. The concrete supporting structure covers all the structural parts of the building: columns, beams, floors, and roof light casings. These structures date from the original construction period (1917–1921) and are therefore an example of relatively early concrete use, certainly on this scale. Rotterdam was ahead of its time in its usage of concrete on large-scale buildings, such as the Van Nellefabriek (1925–1931) and the City Hall (1914–1920). Some of the reinforced concrete in Fenix was rusted and therefore had to be replaced. Visible cracks were repaired using epoxy. You can still see where reparations have been done: a way to show the journey of the warehouse.

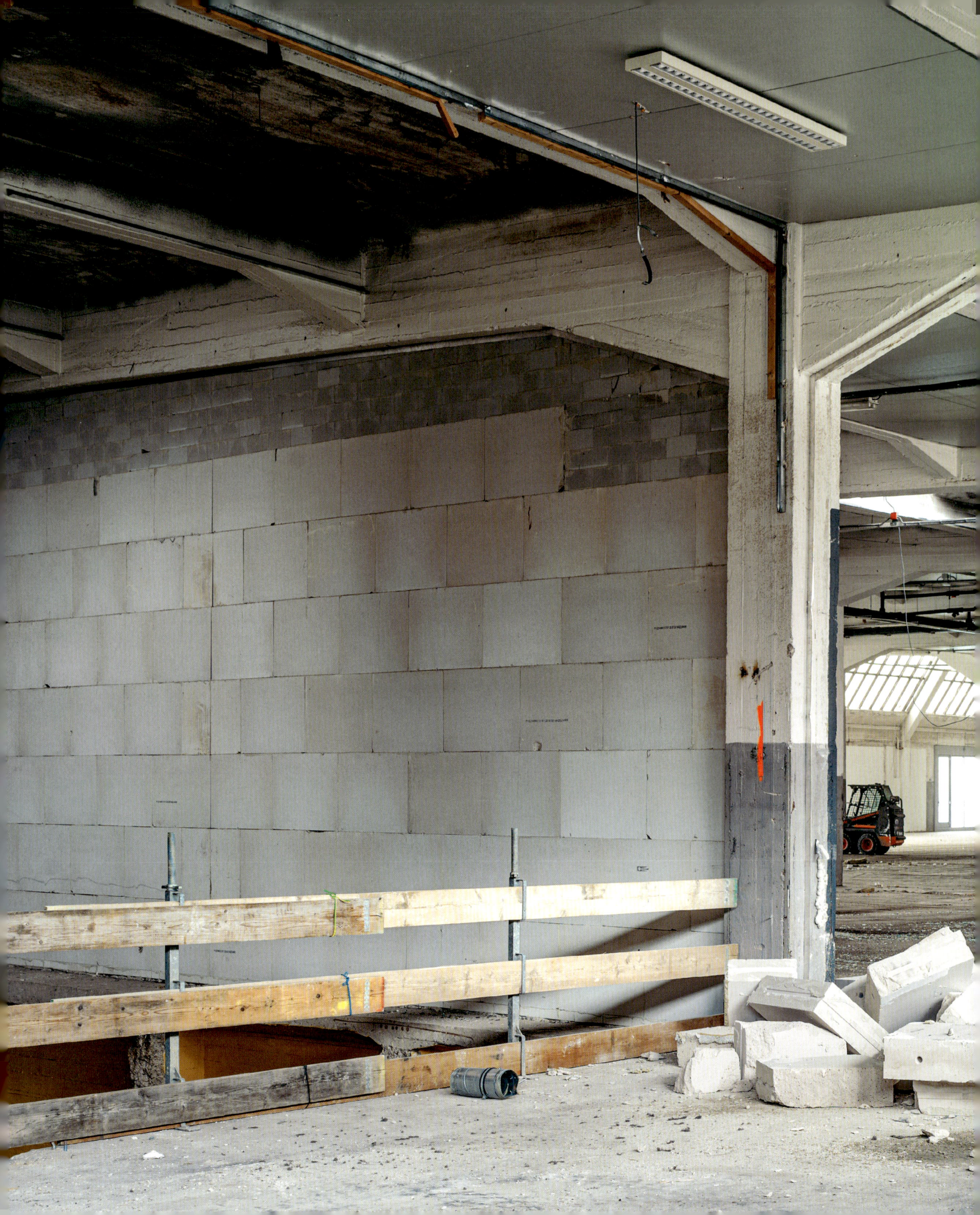

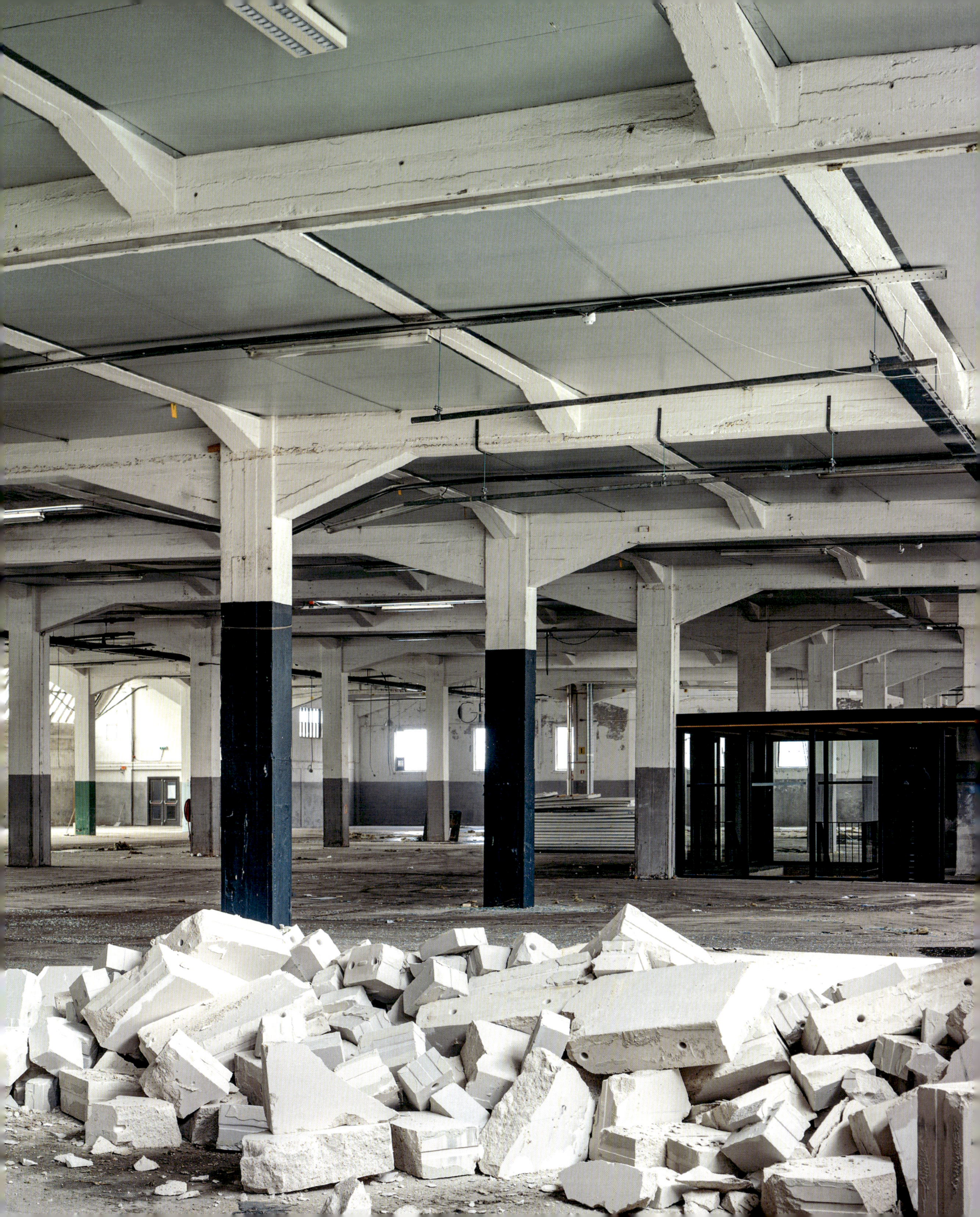

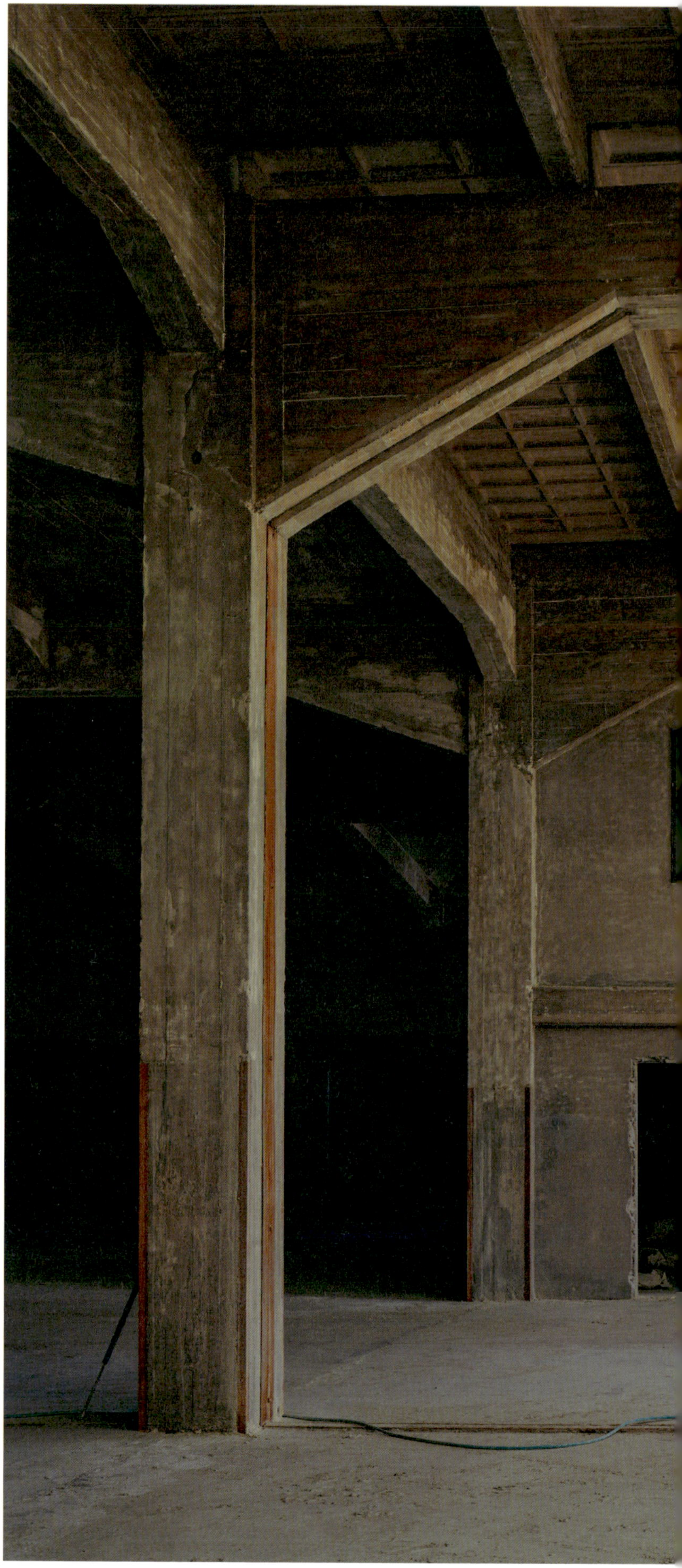

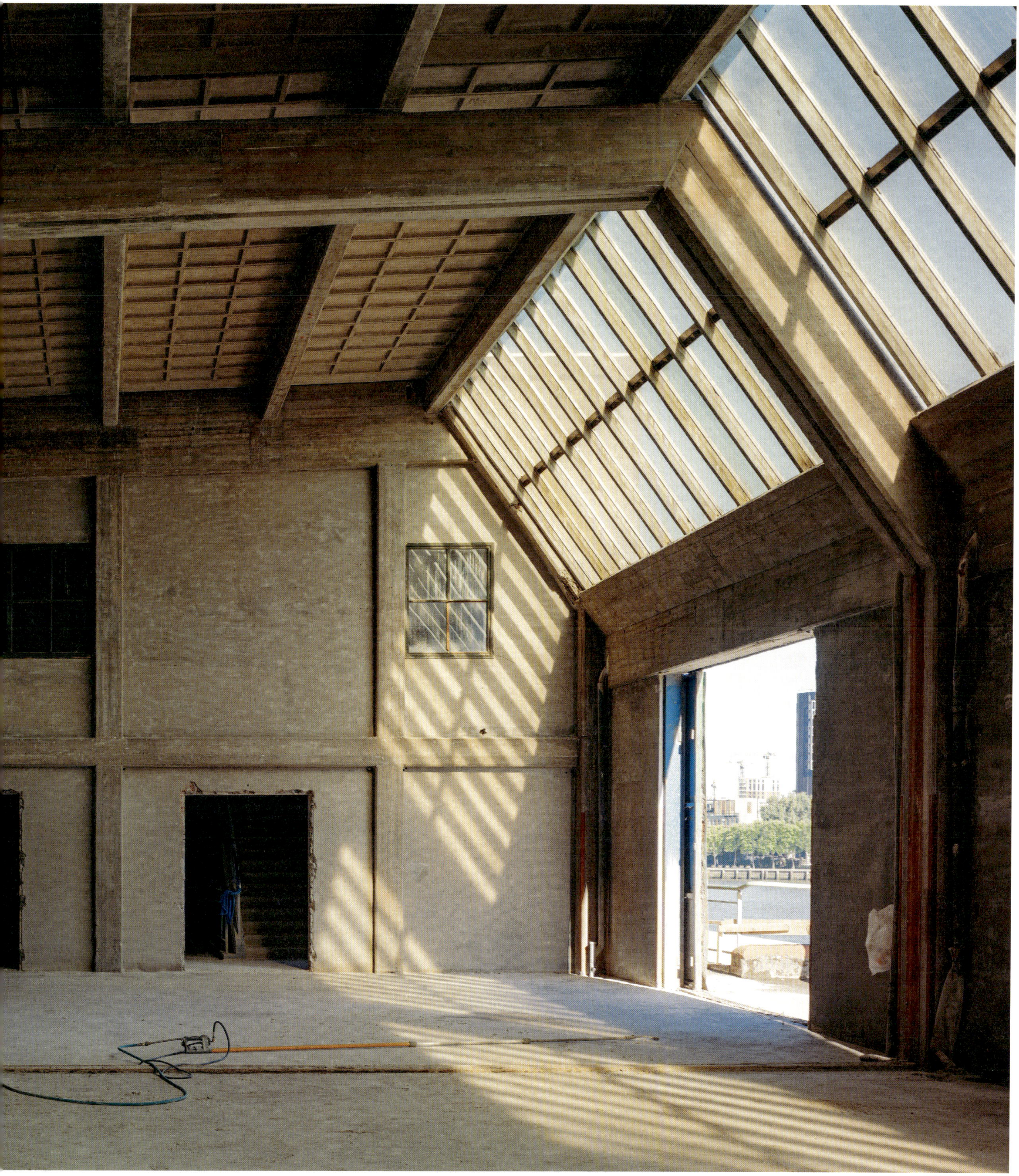

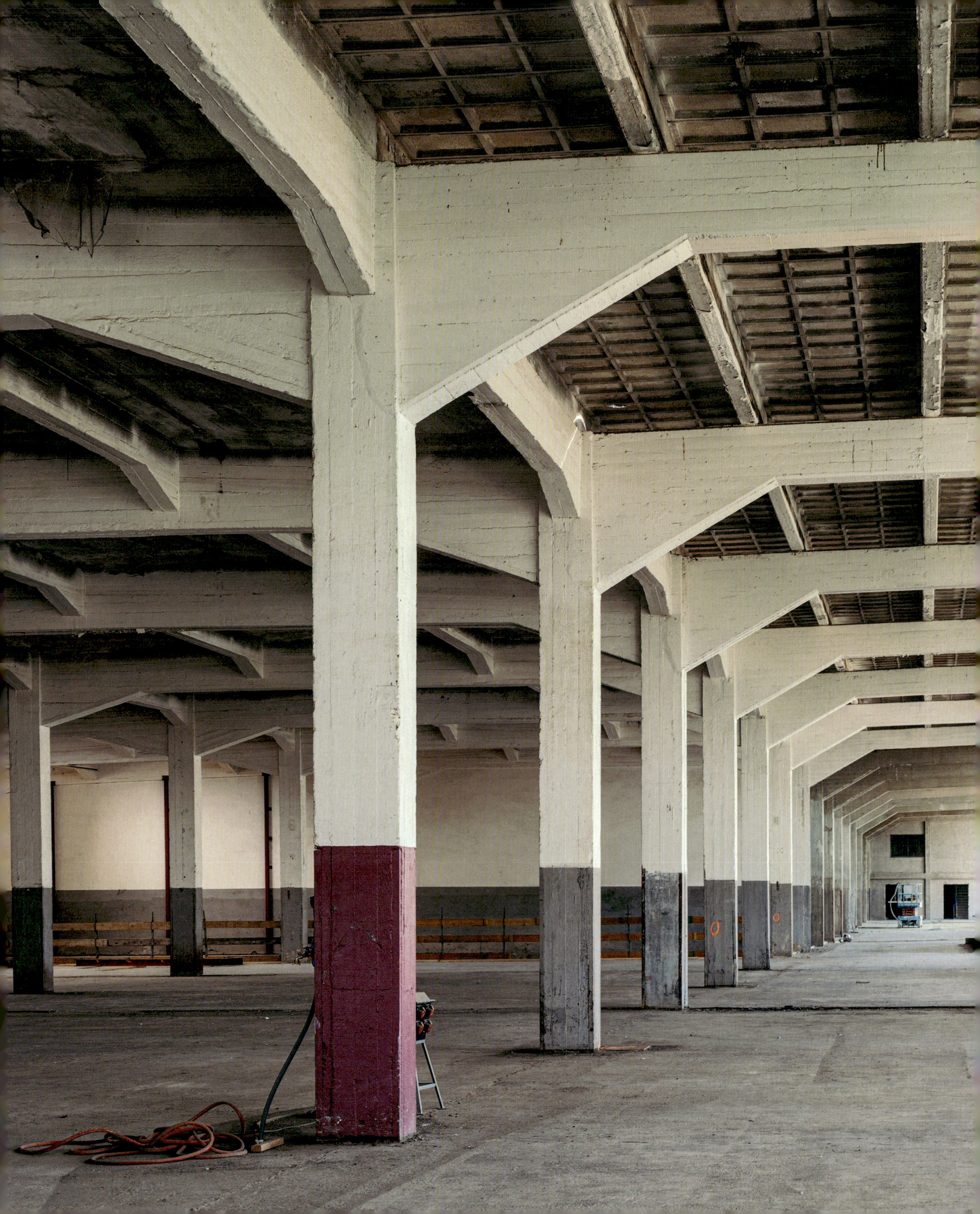

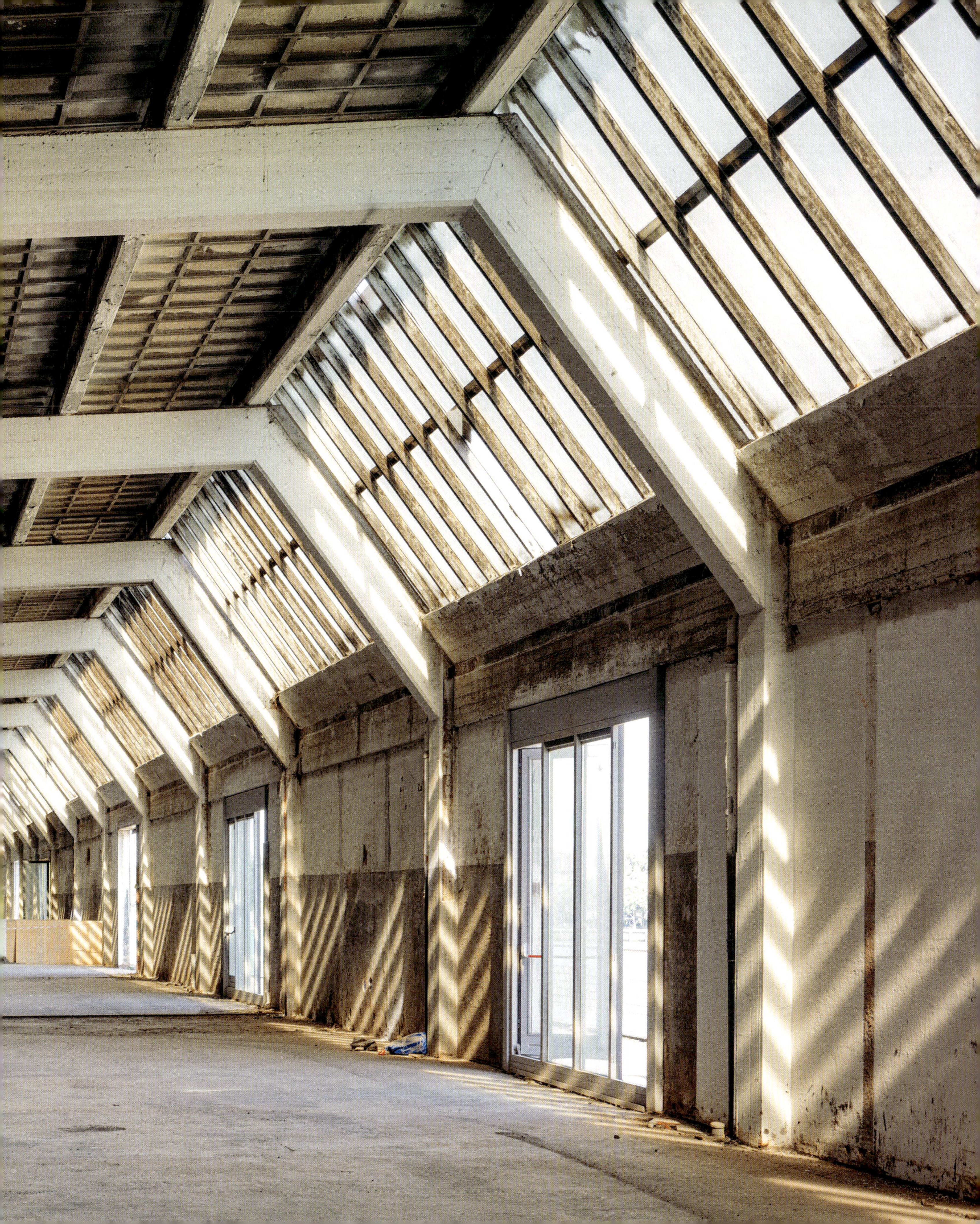

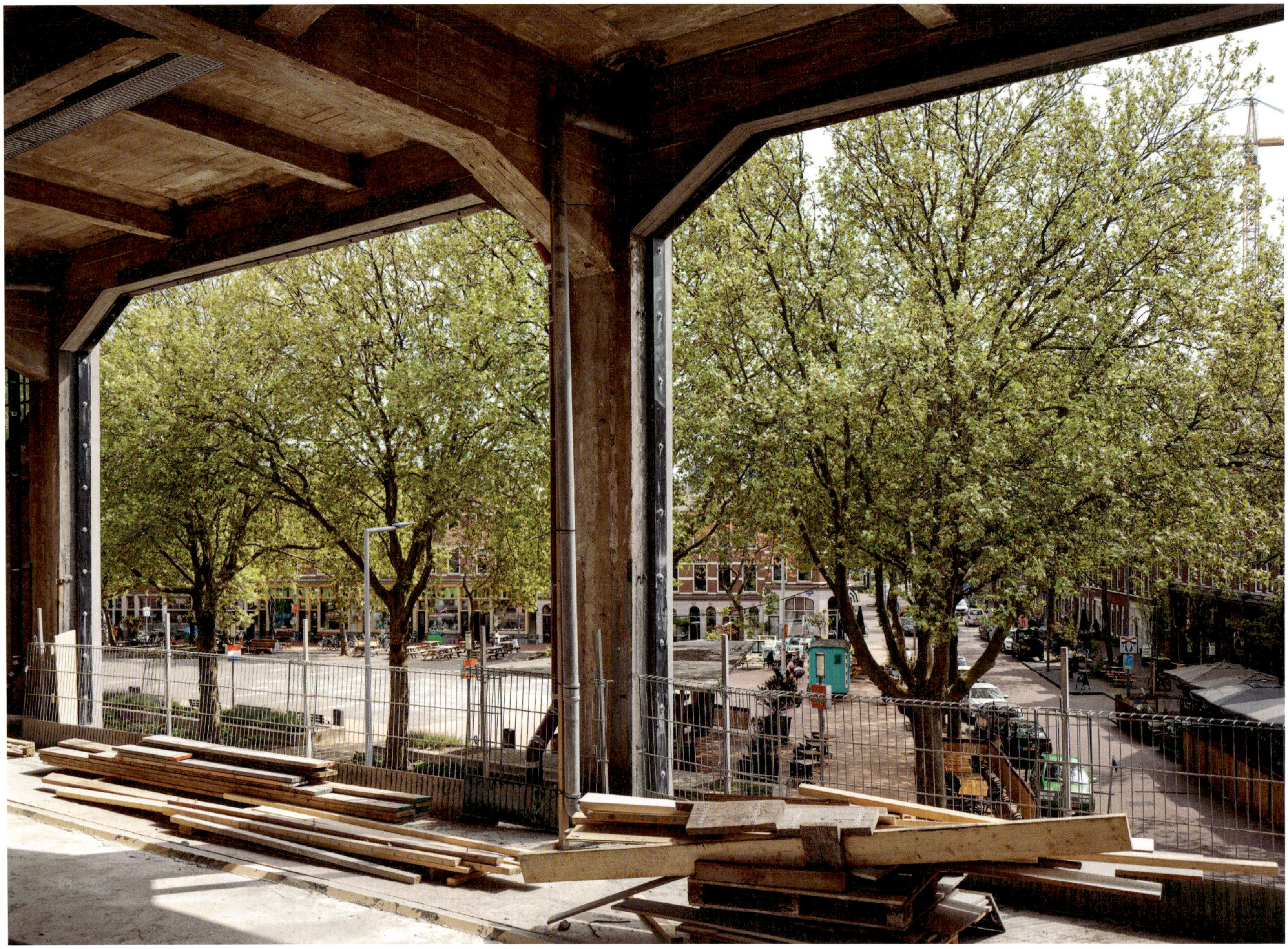

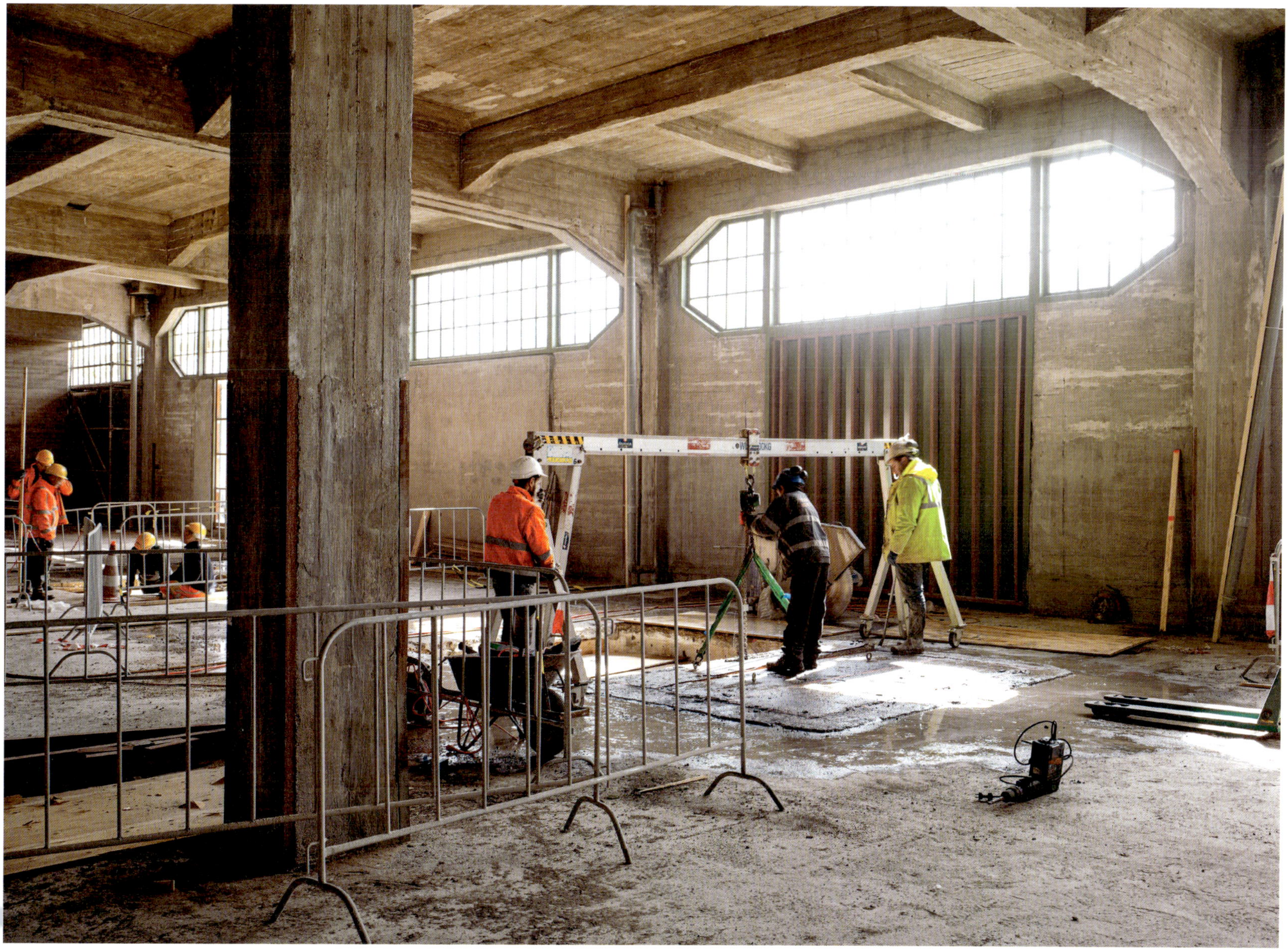

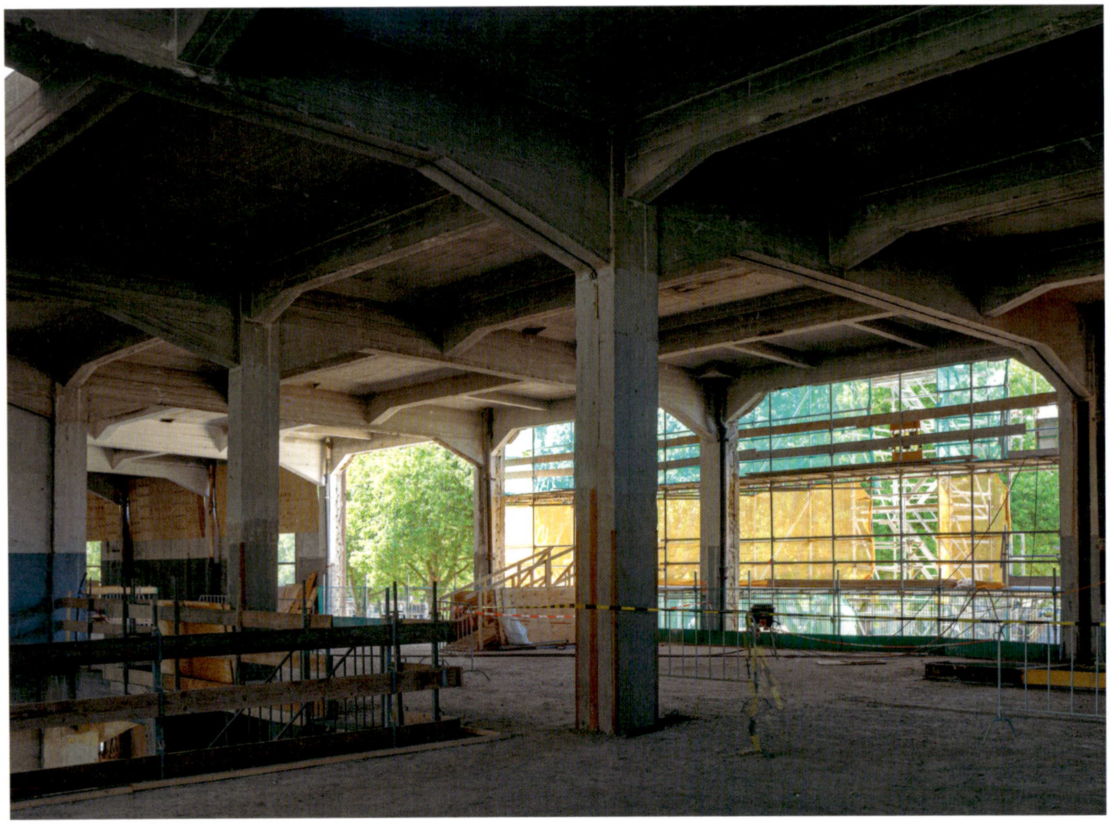

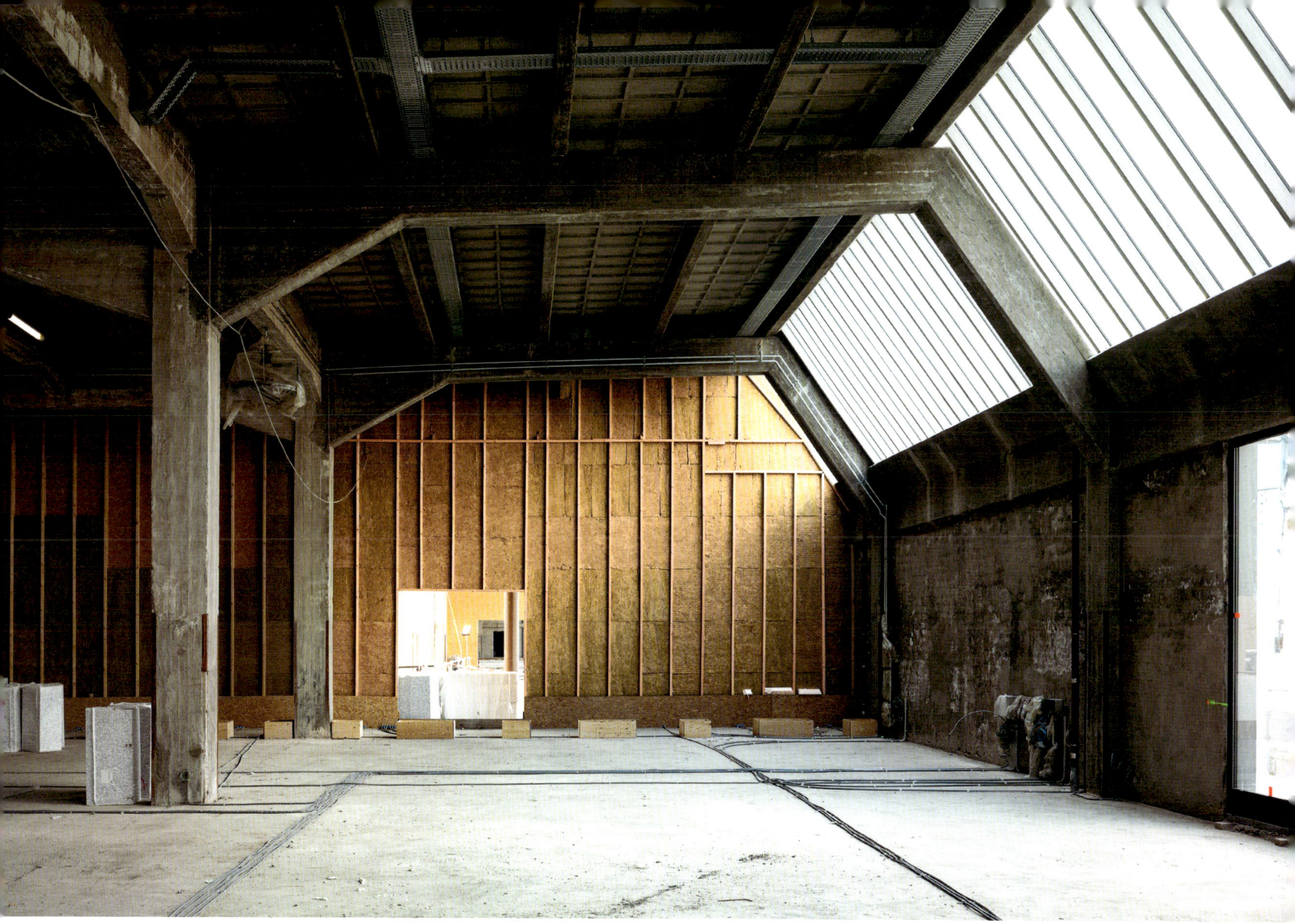

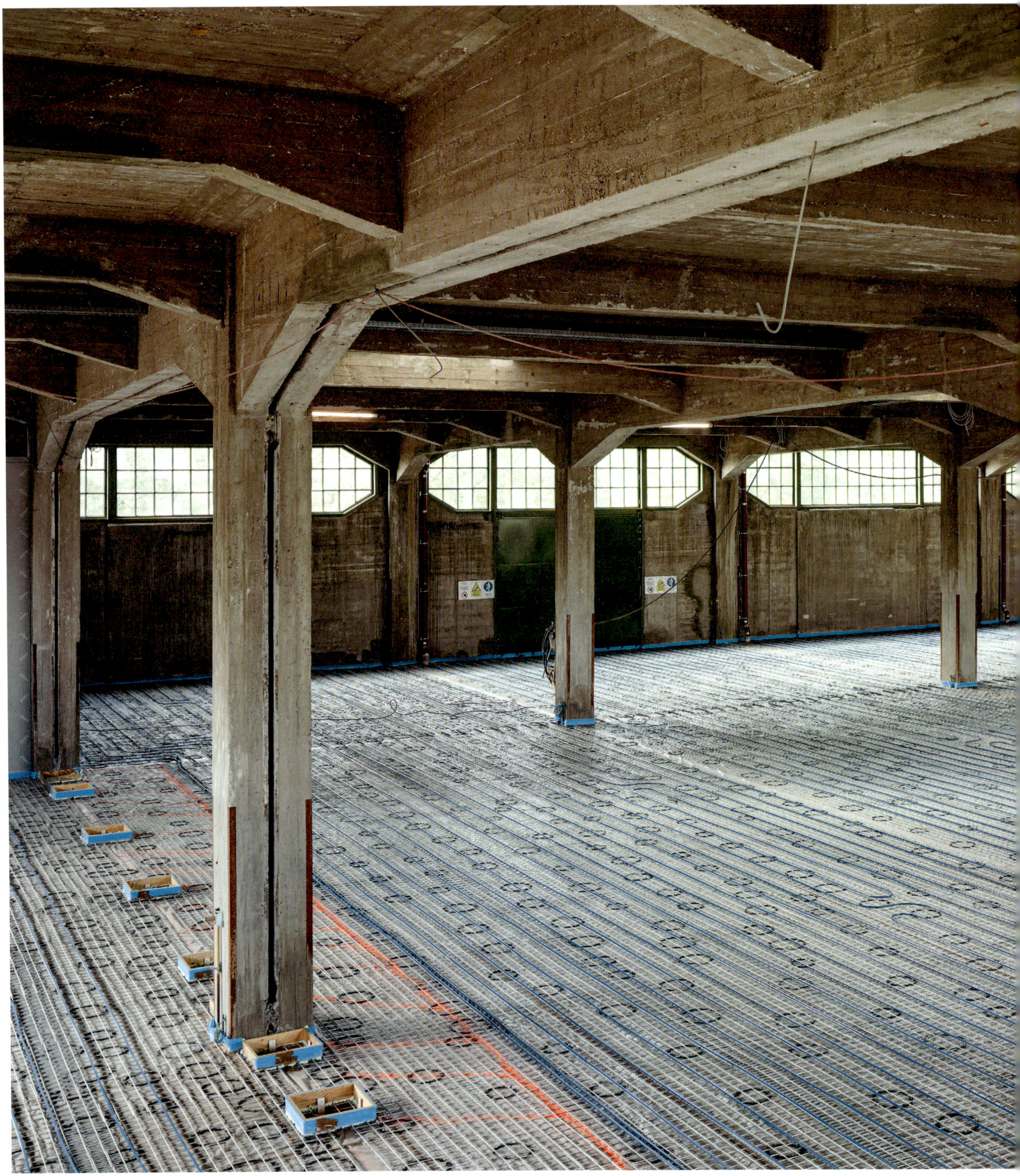

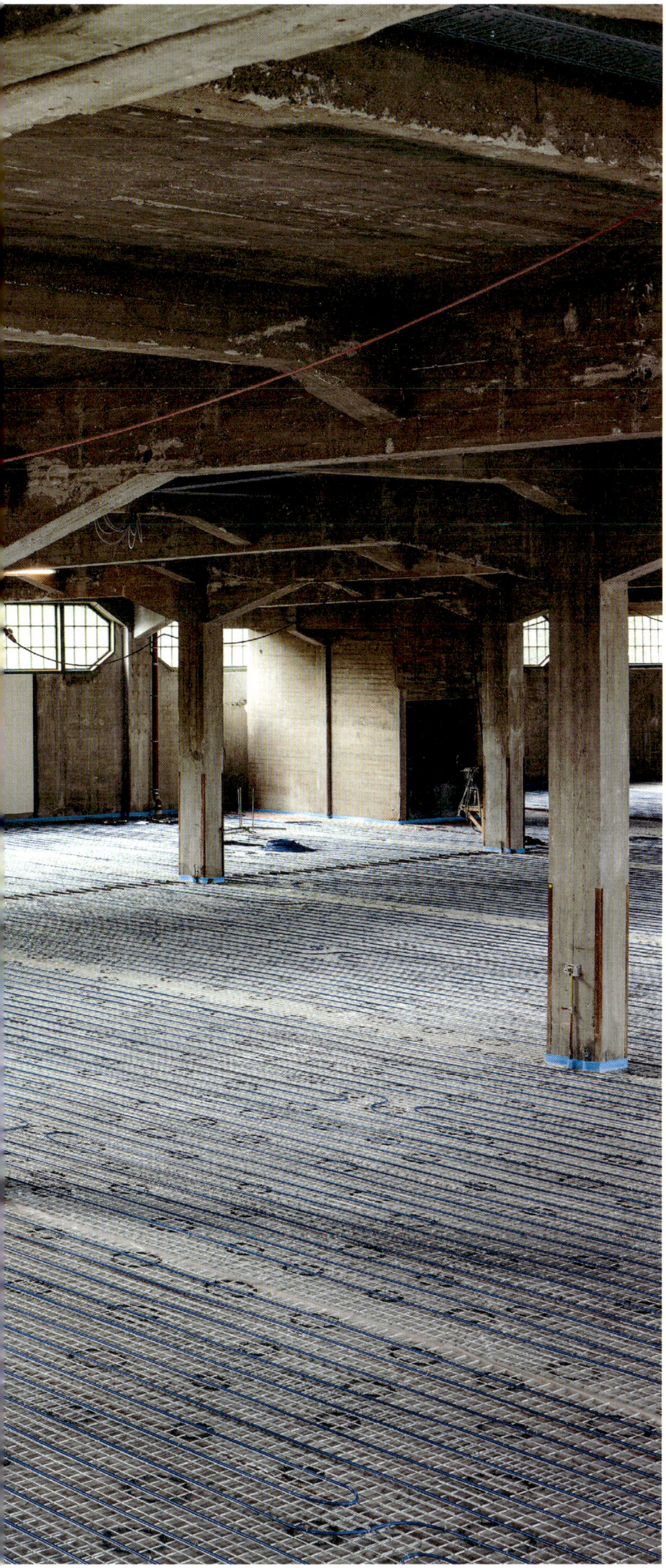

“It is the most time consuming and hard thing I have ever done in my life. The spaces are enormous. We blasted 30,000 square metres of concrete. These are the walls that everyone is able to see. So, it is extremely important that the job is done right.”

Edward Ernest, Concrete Sand Blaster at Superlook

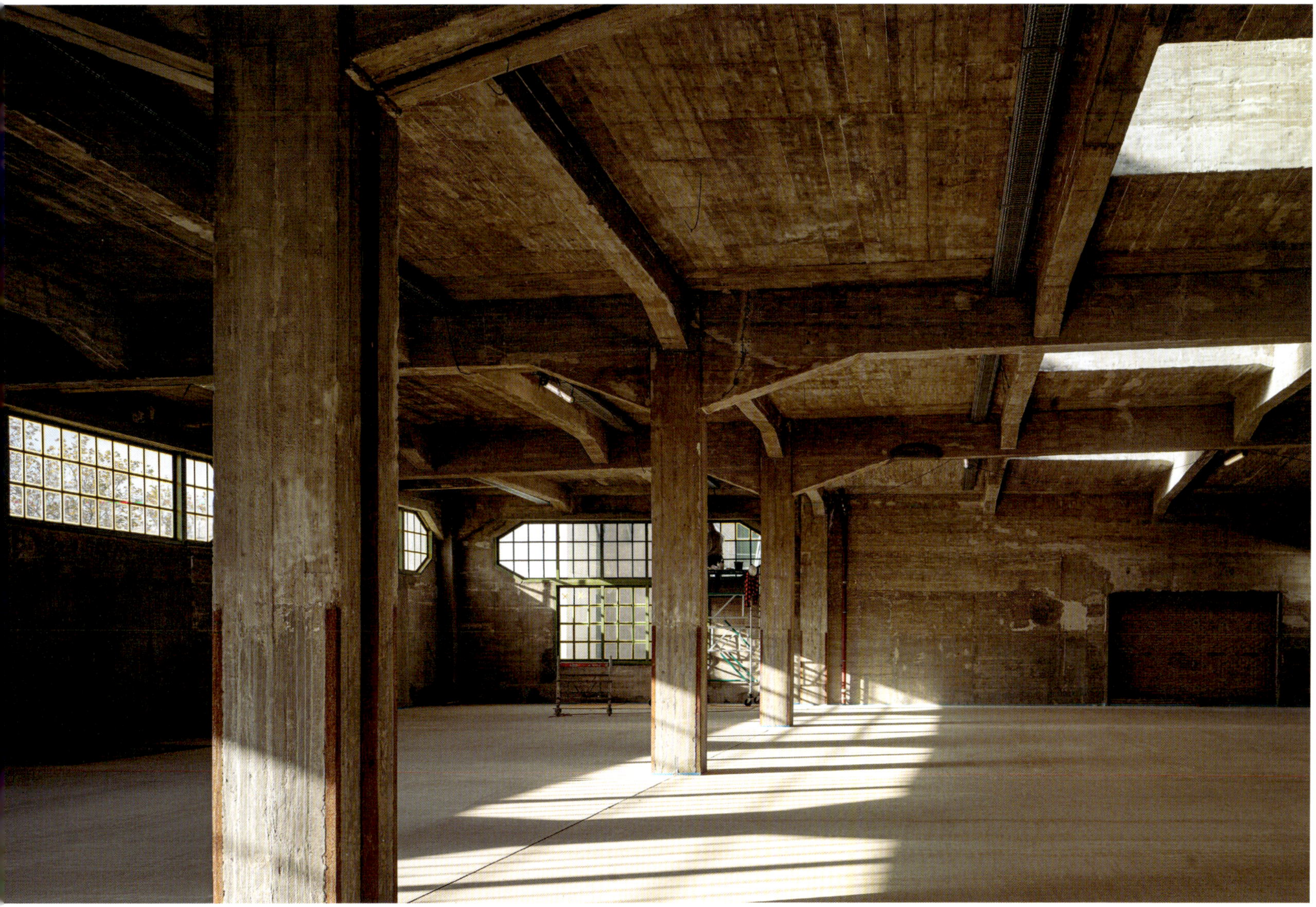

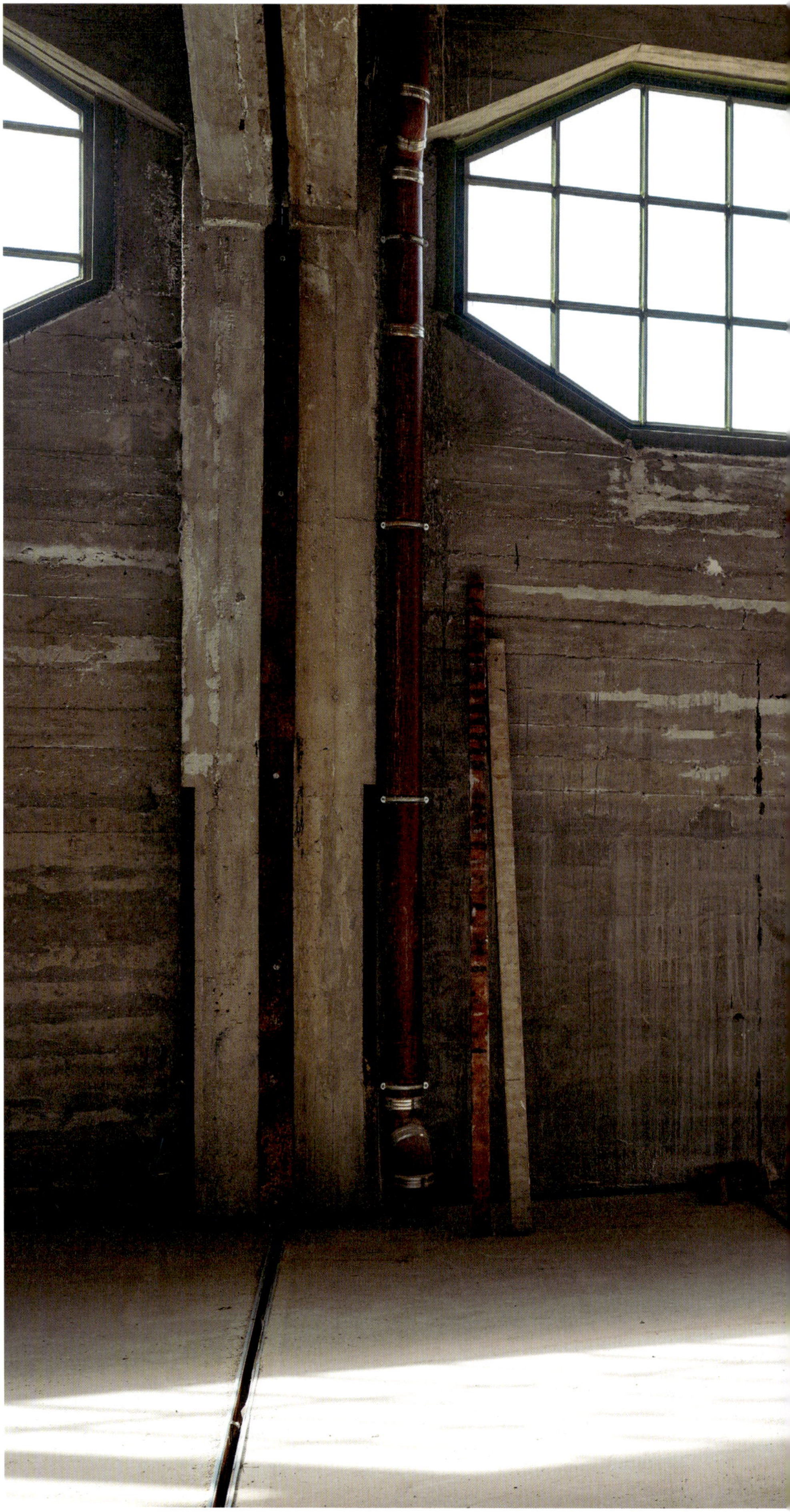

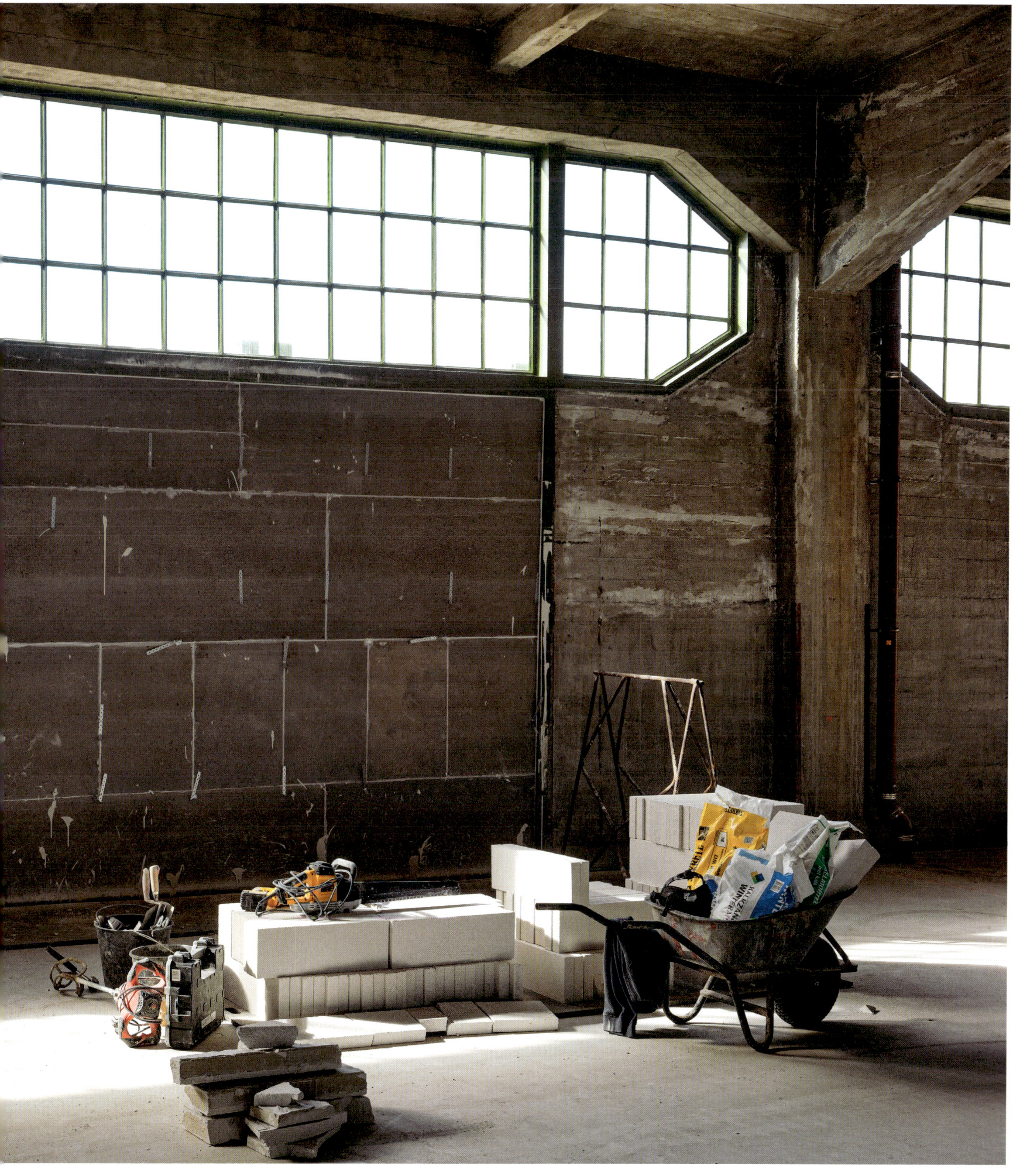

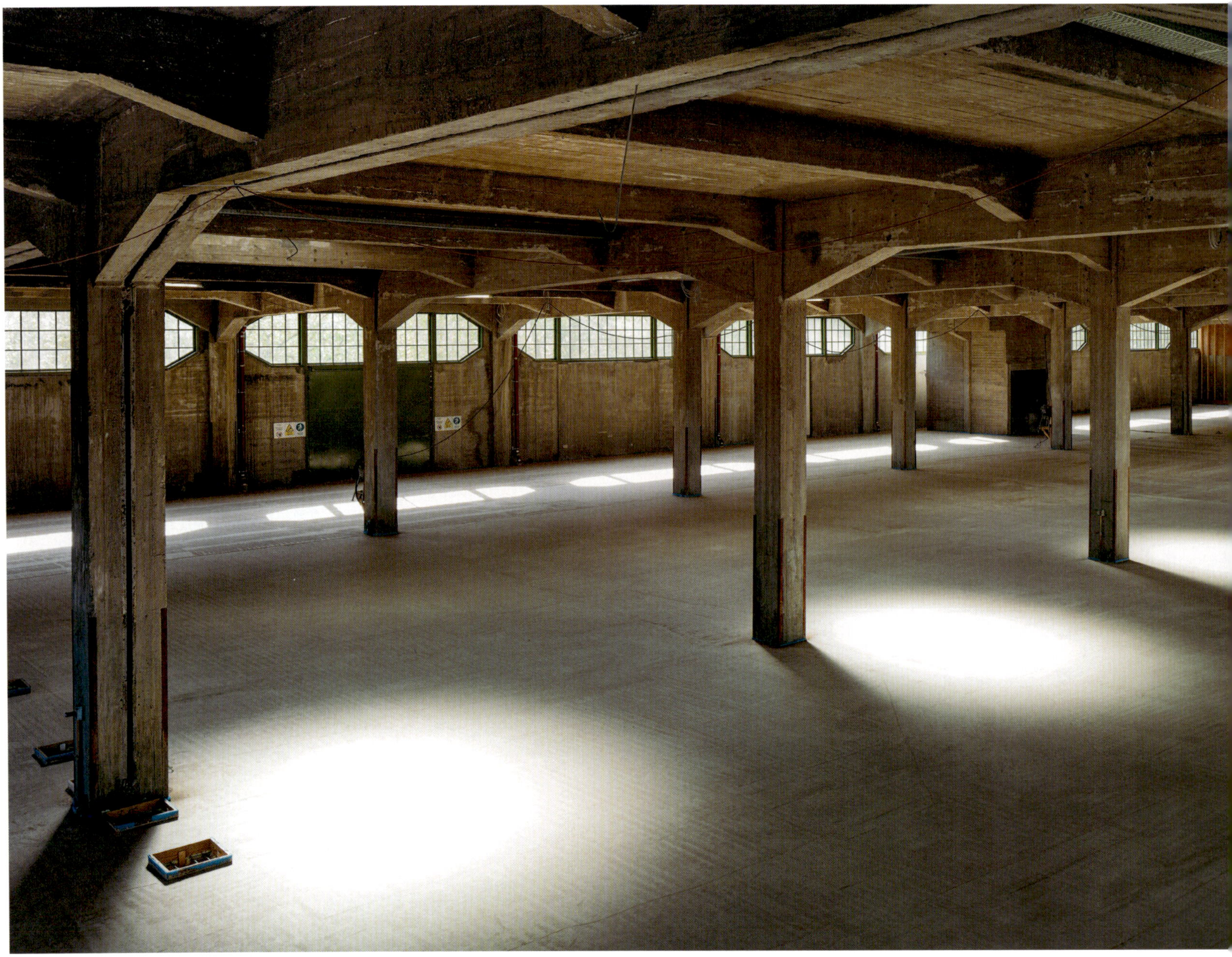

“The scale of Fenix reminds me of where I grew up in Norway, it feels limitless.”

Asgeir Ø Ervik, Project Manager at Bosman

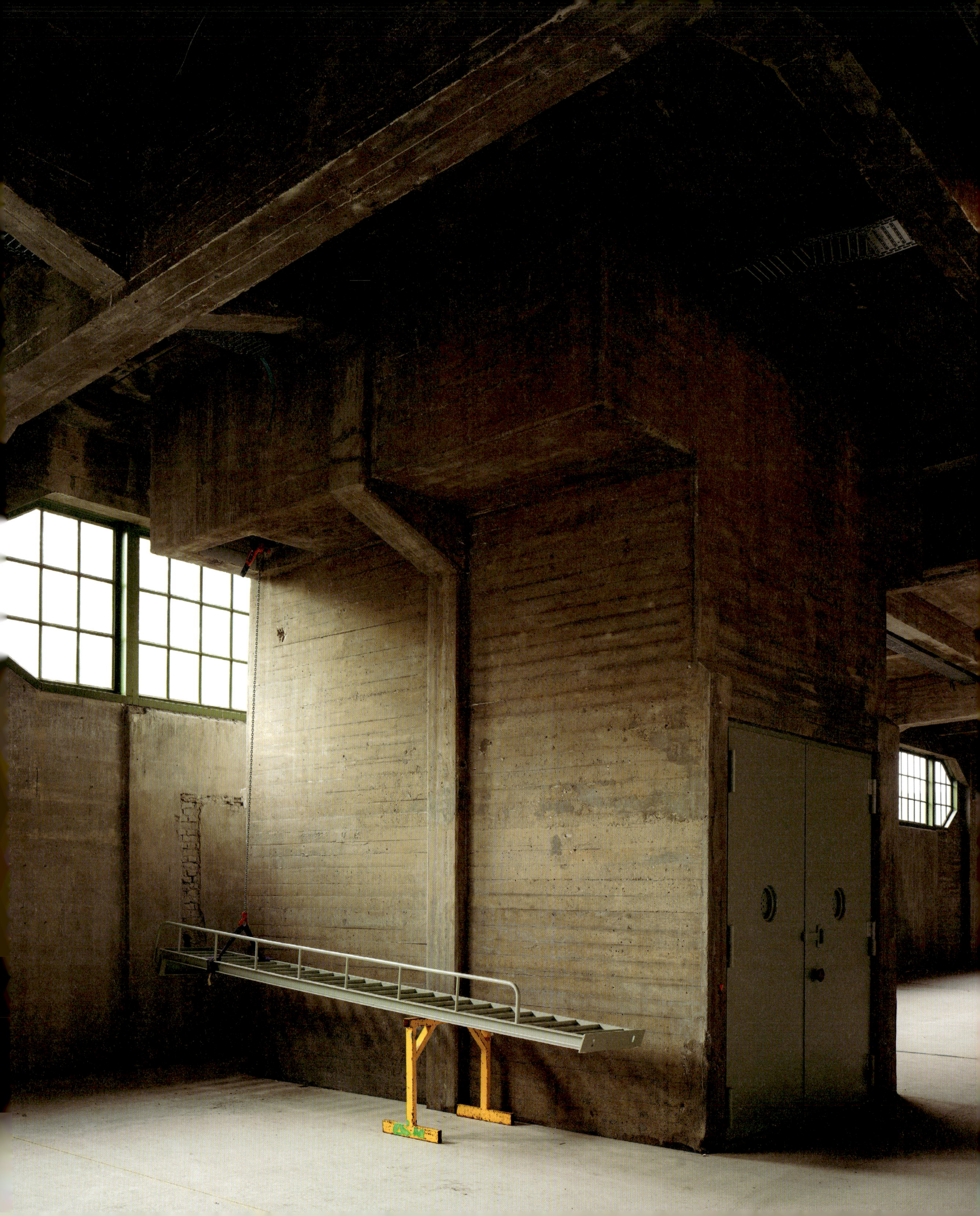

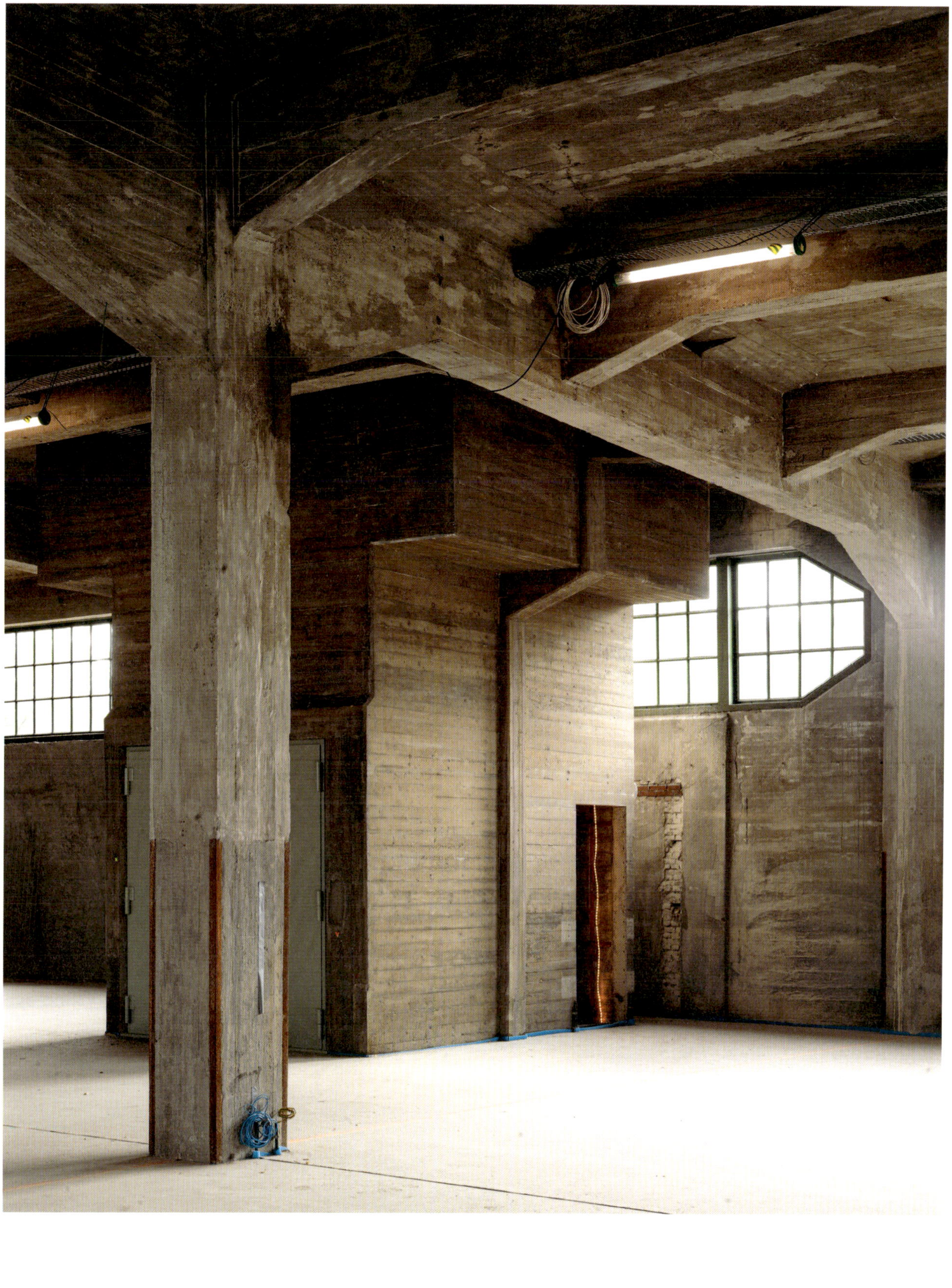

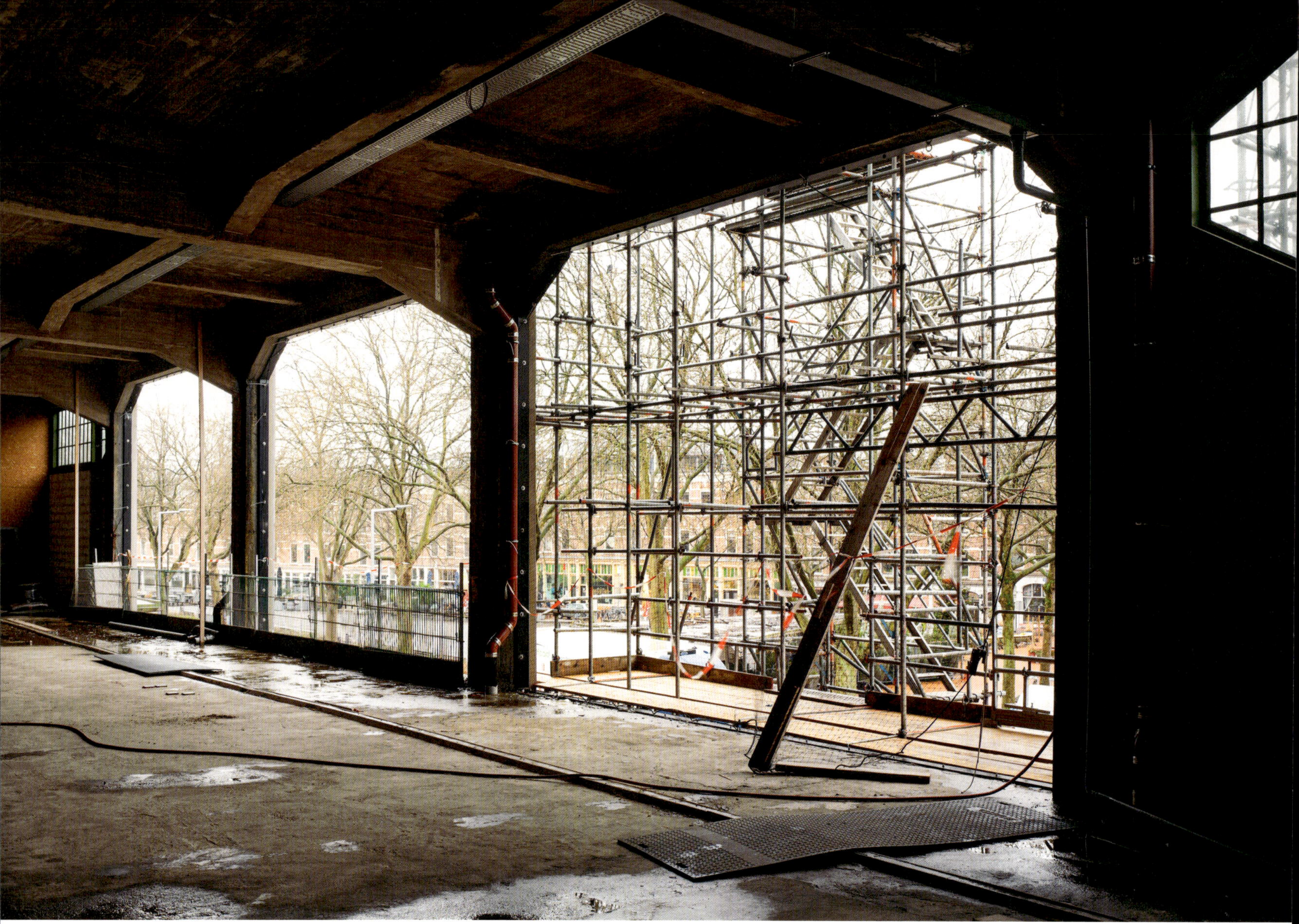

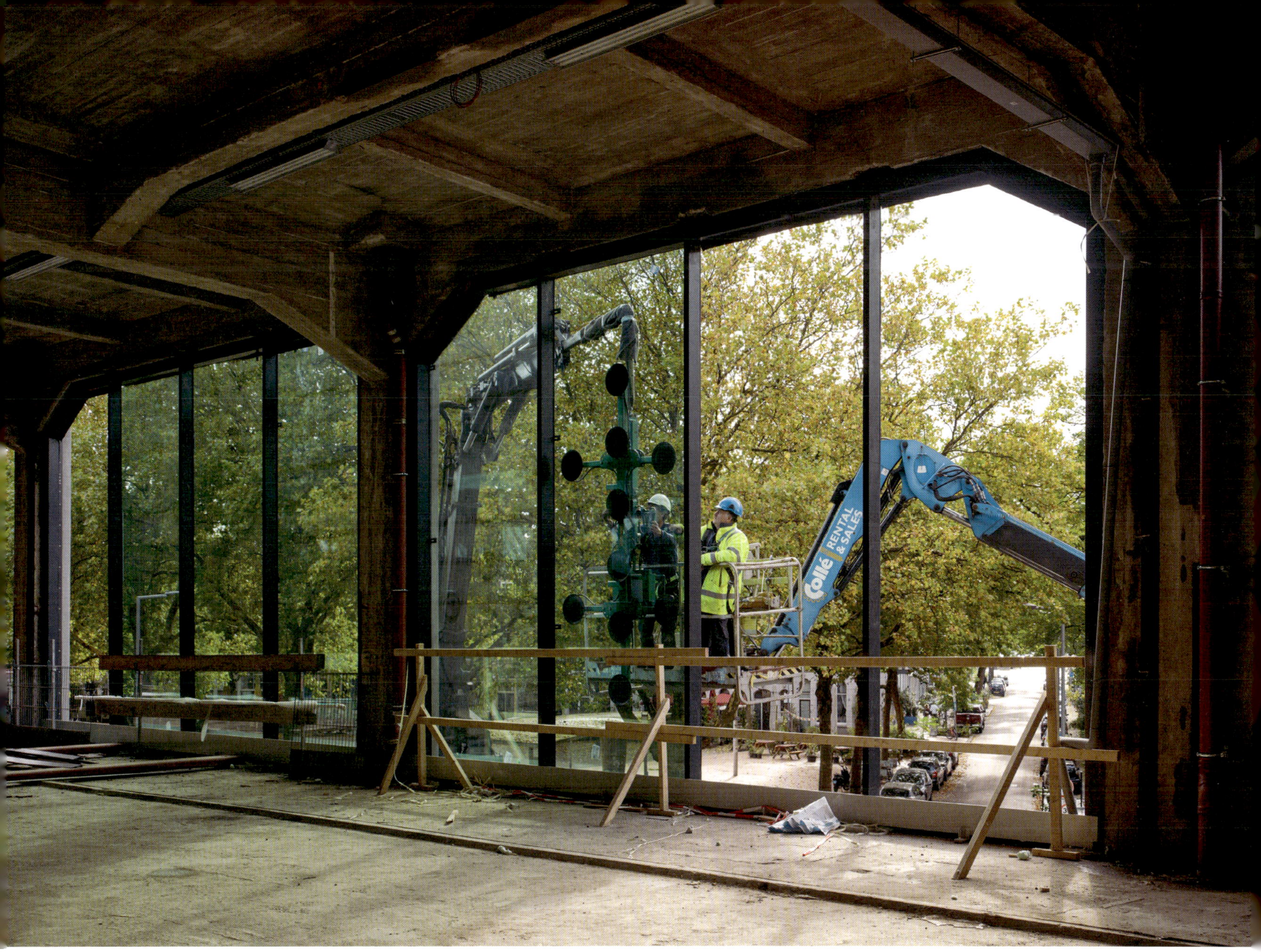
Collé
RENTAL & SALES

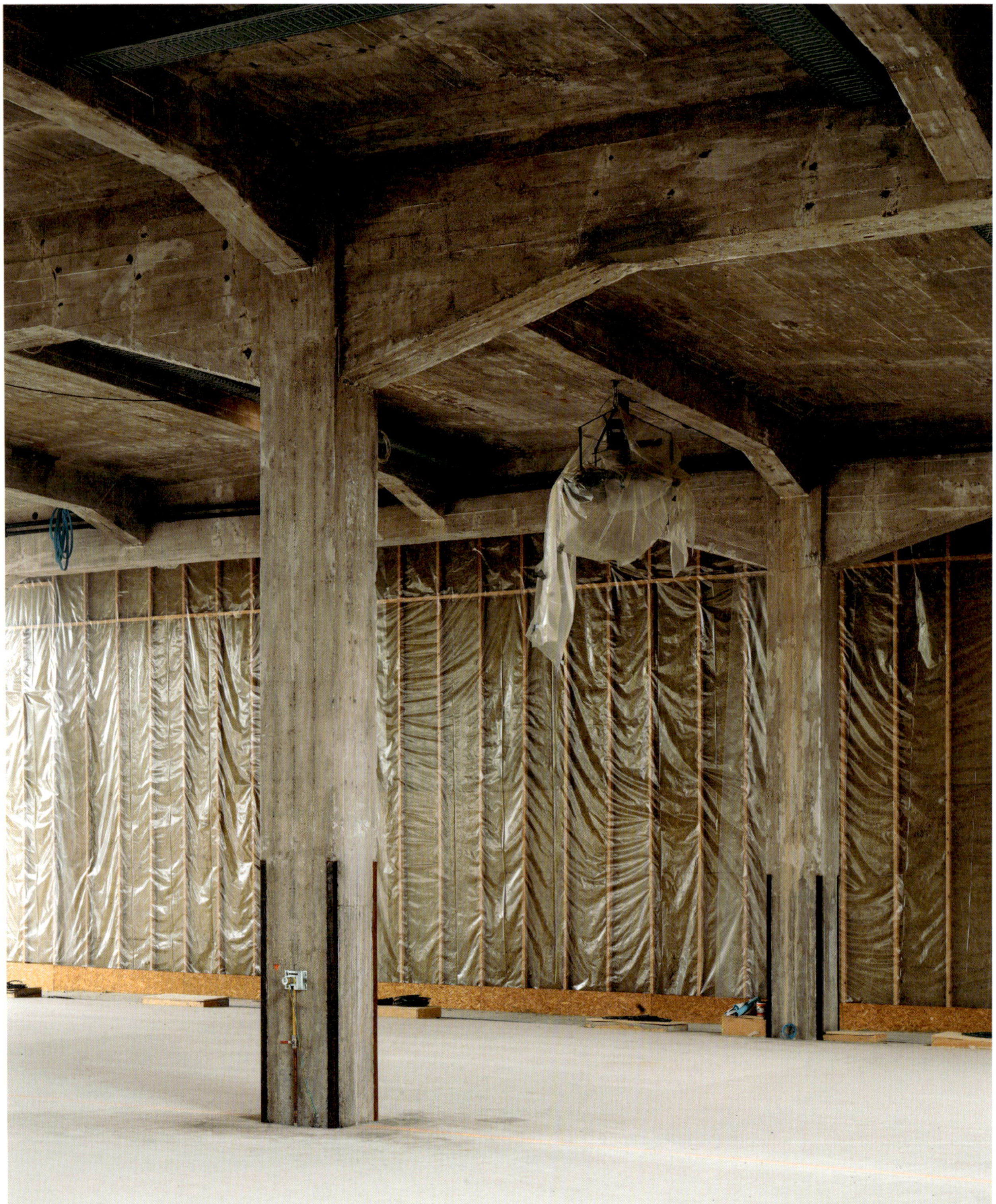

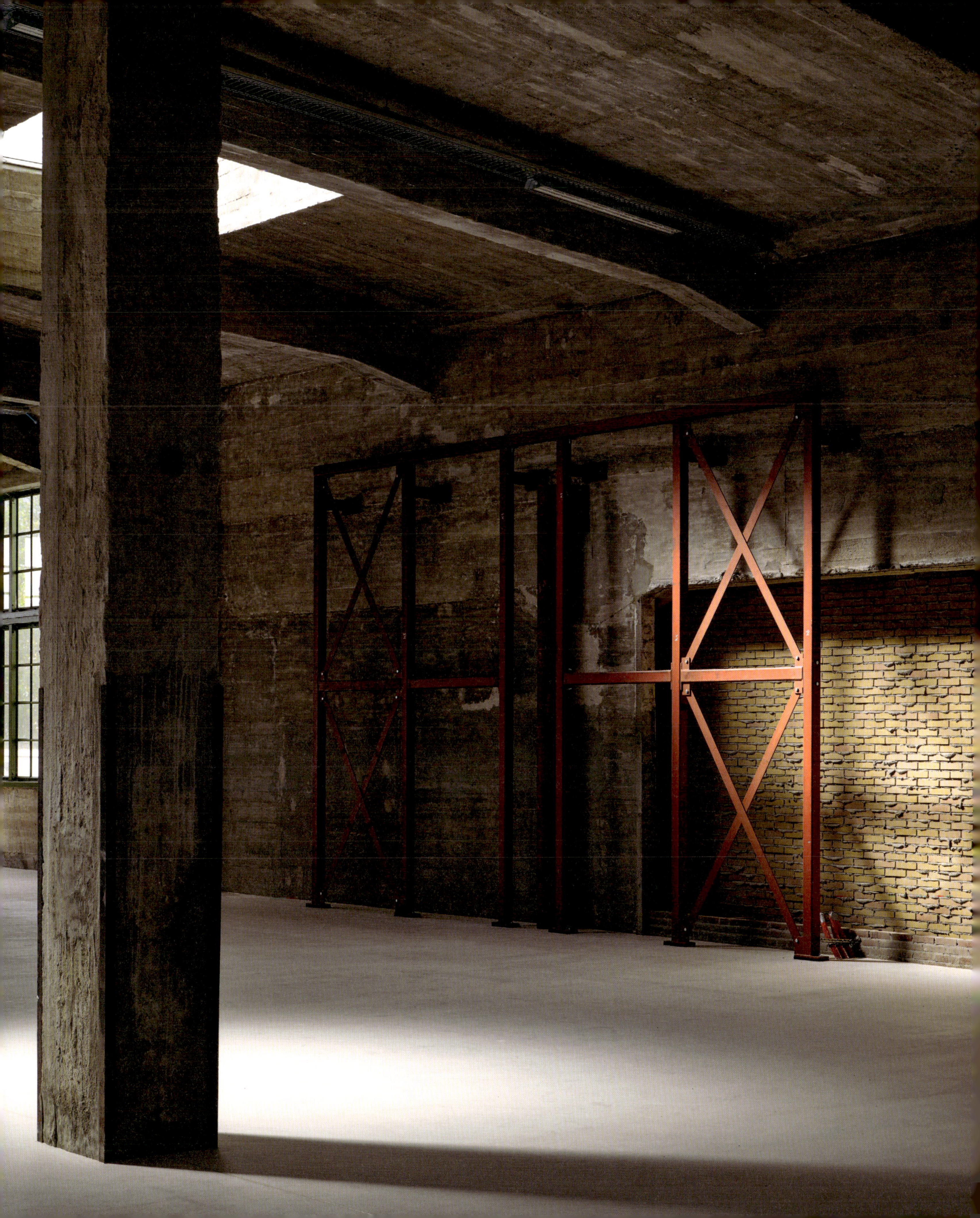

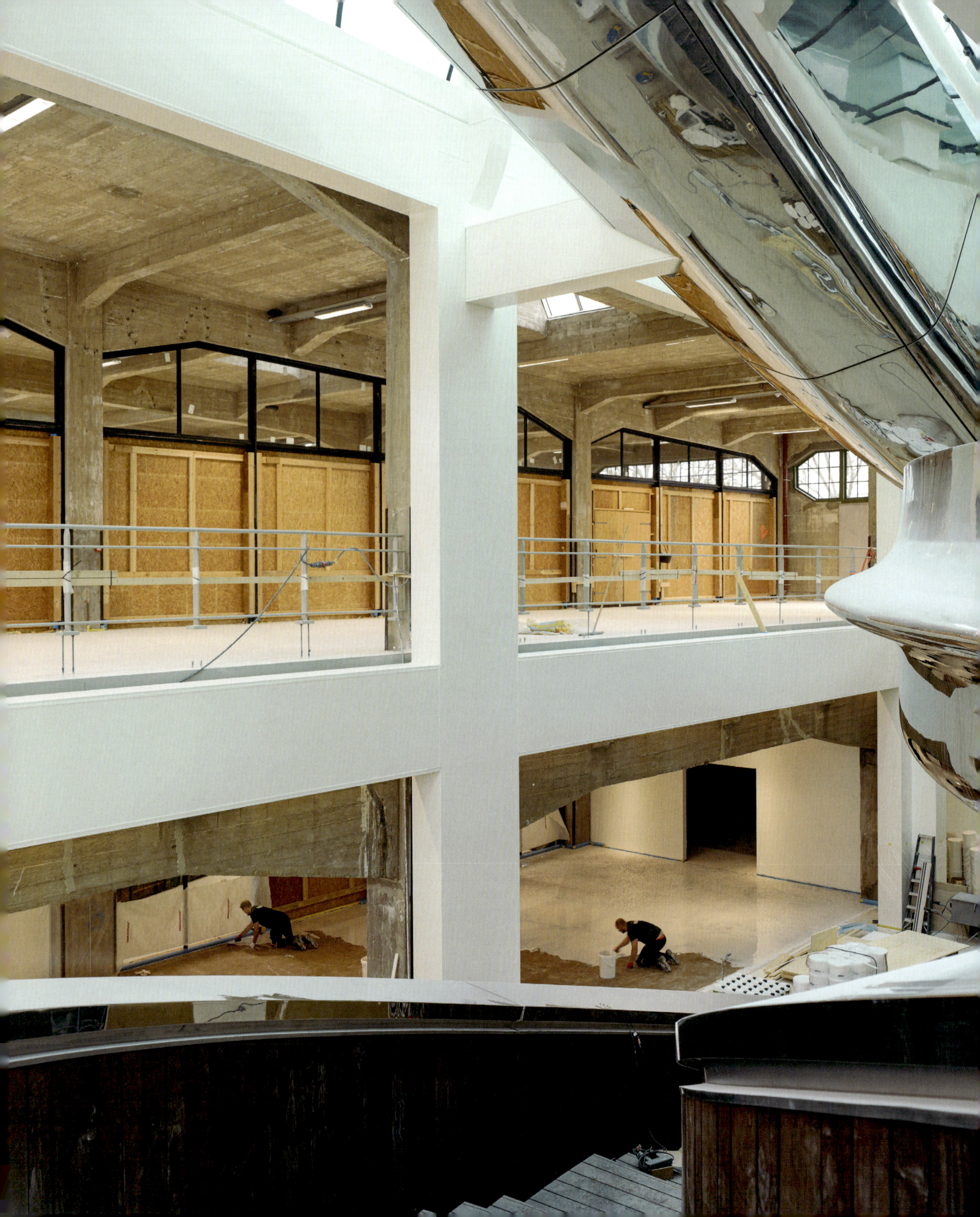

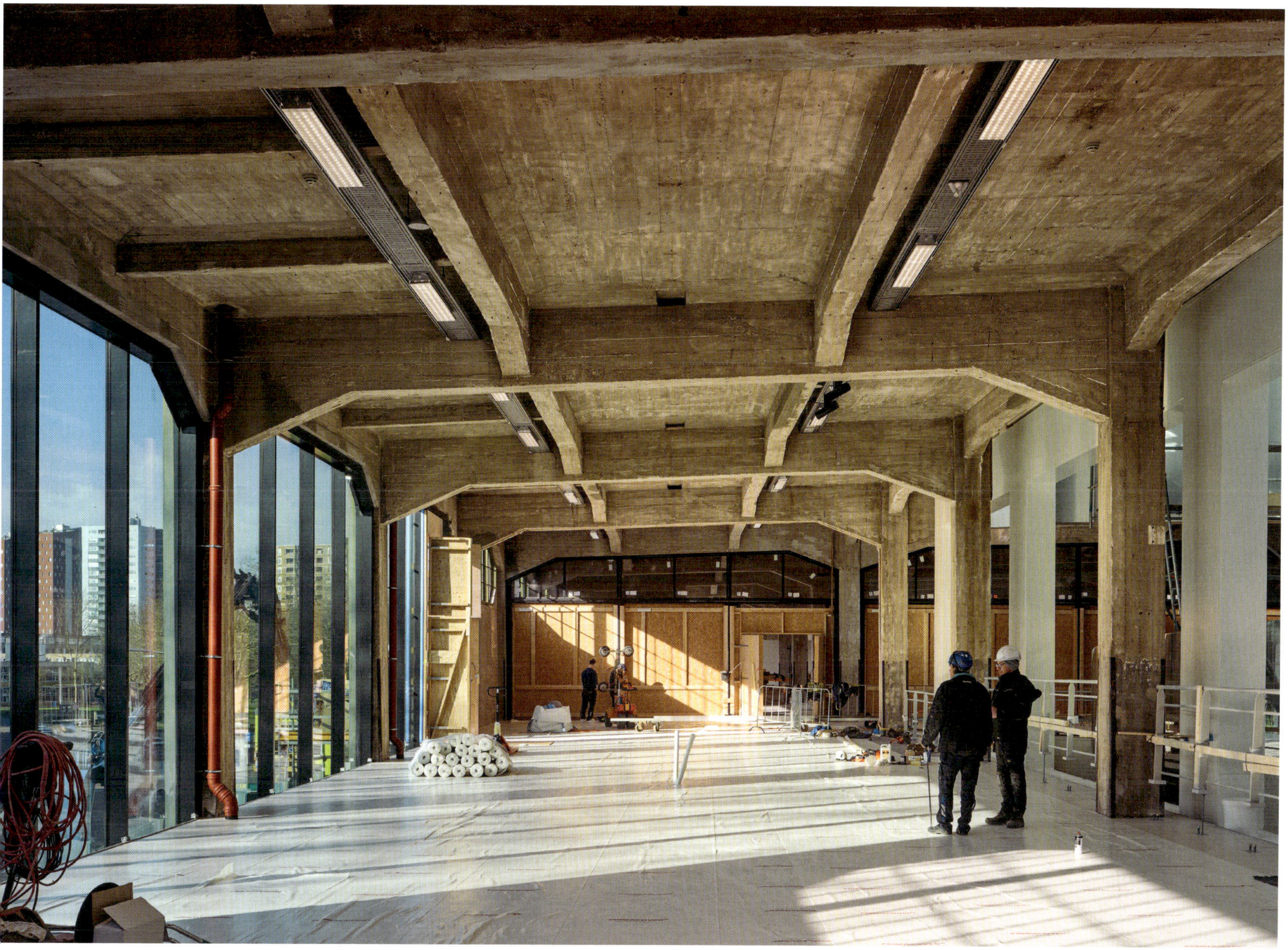

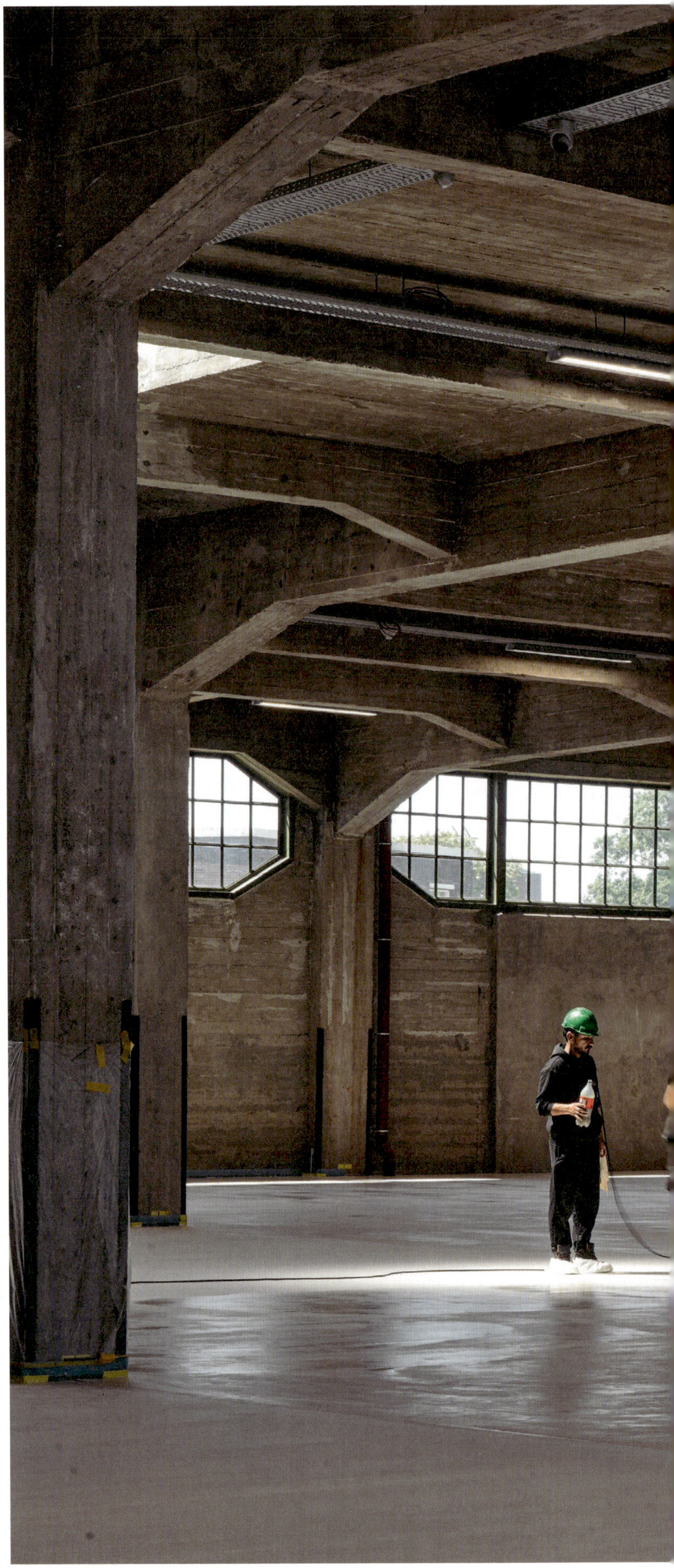

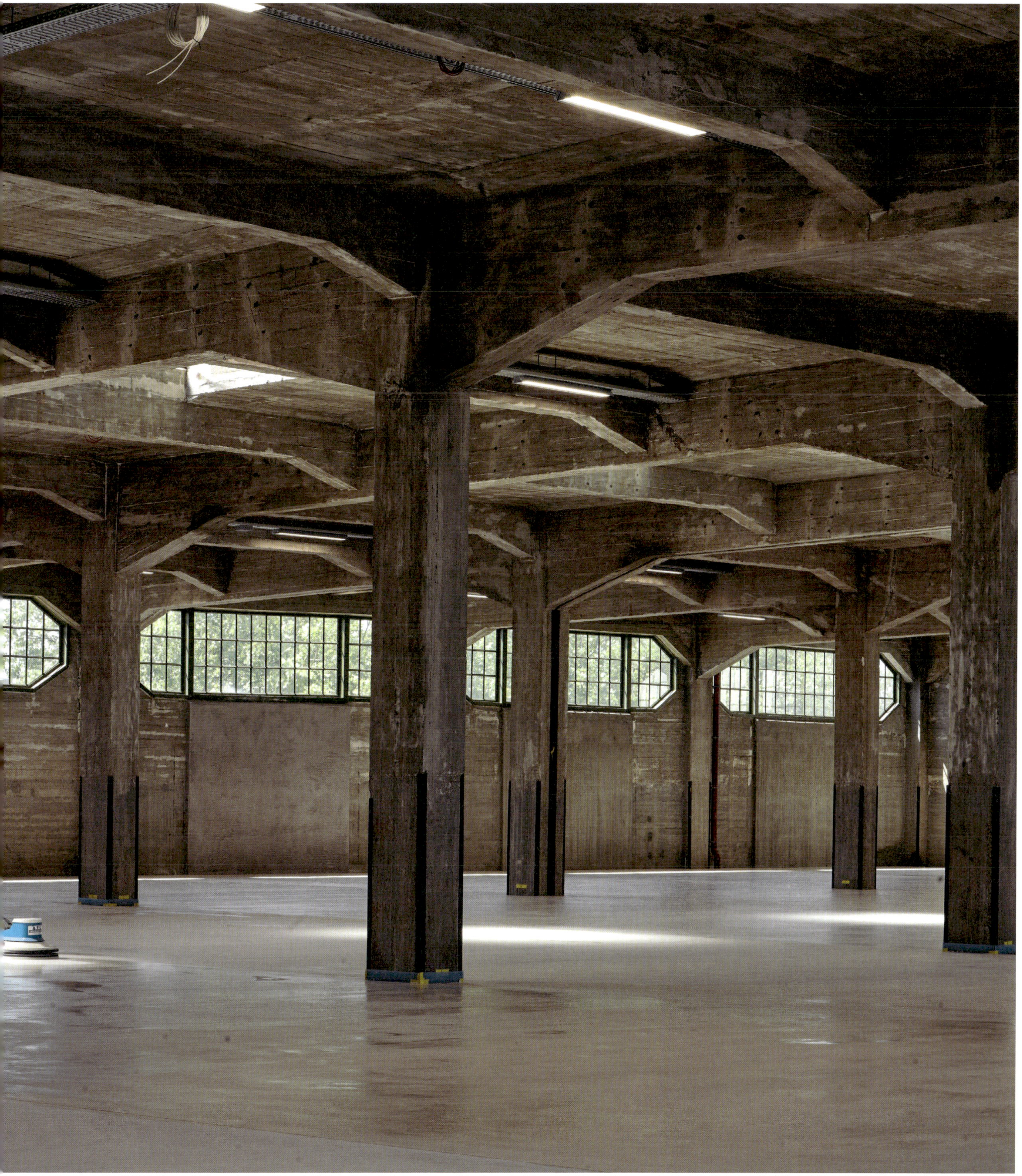

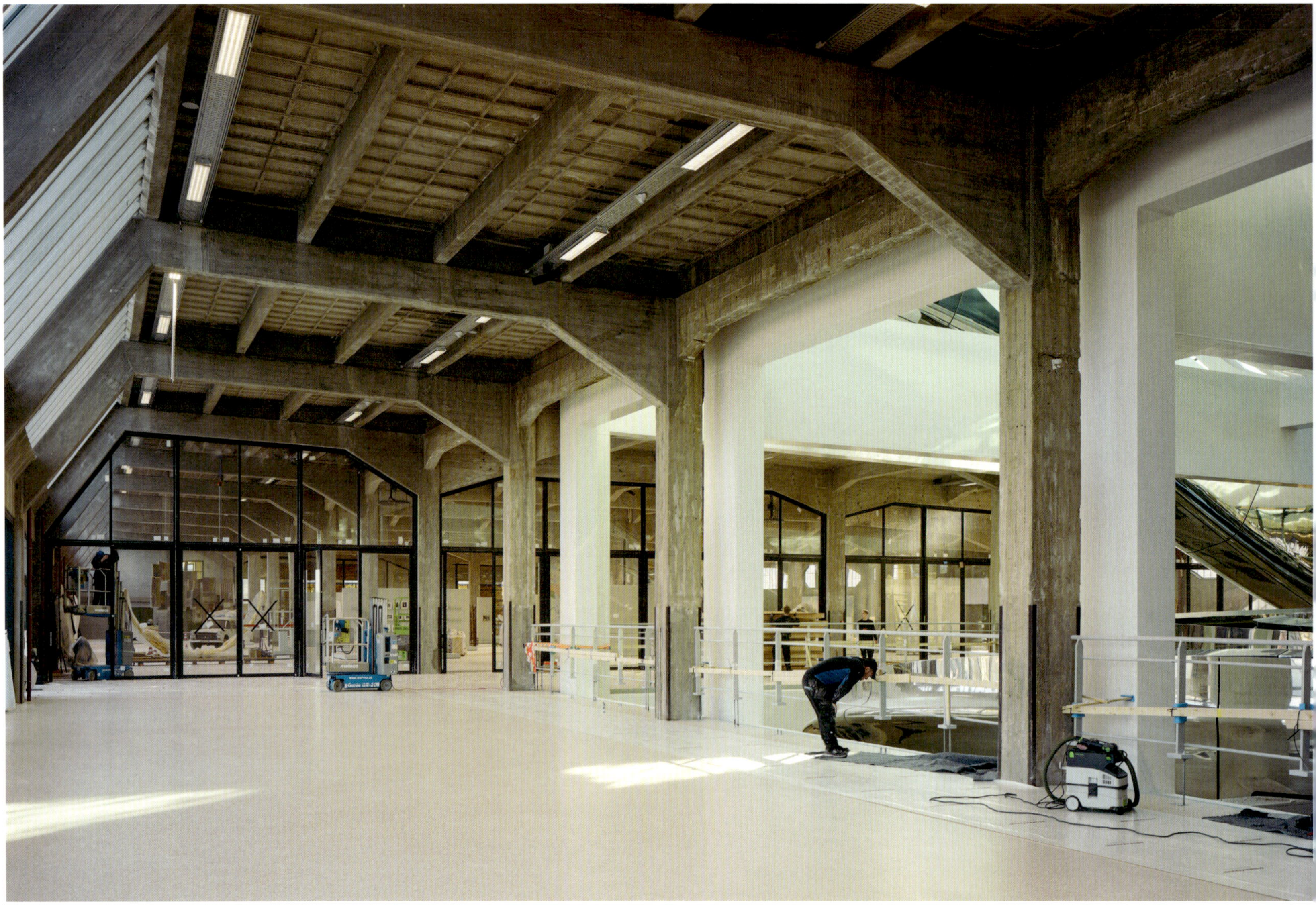

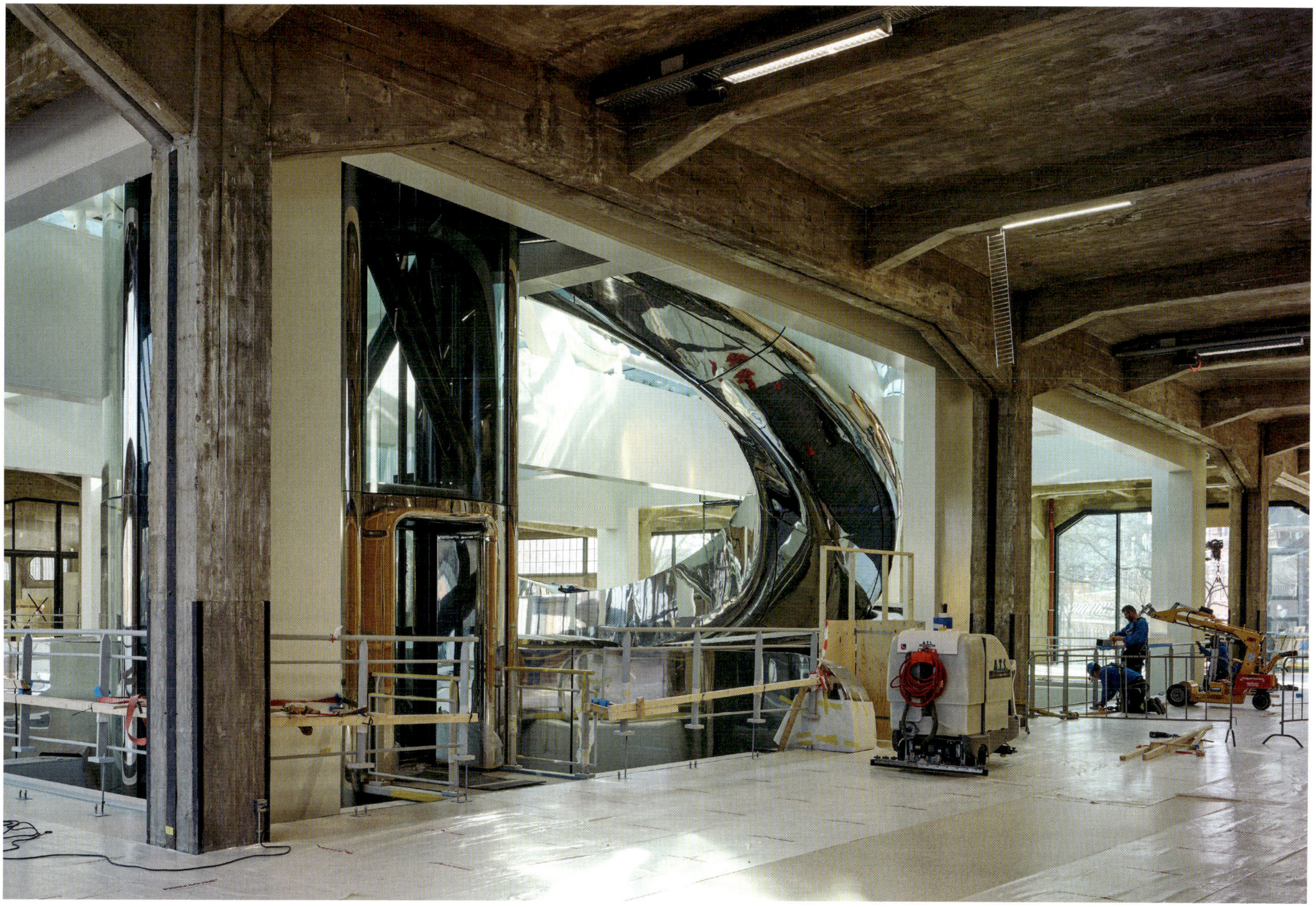

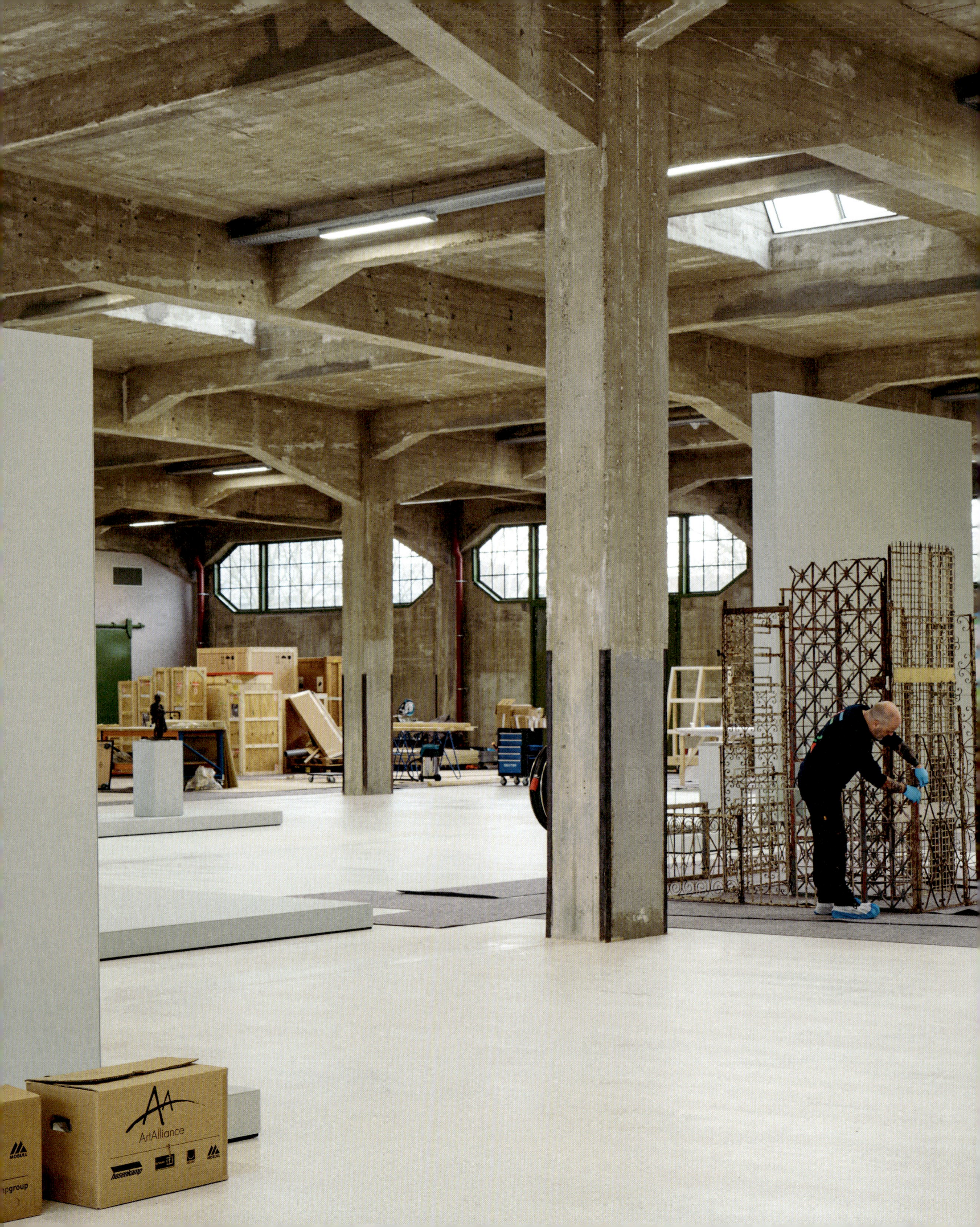
ArtAlliance

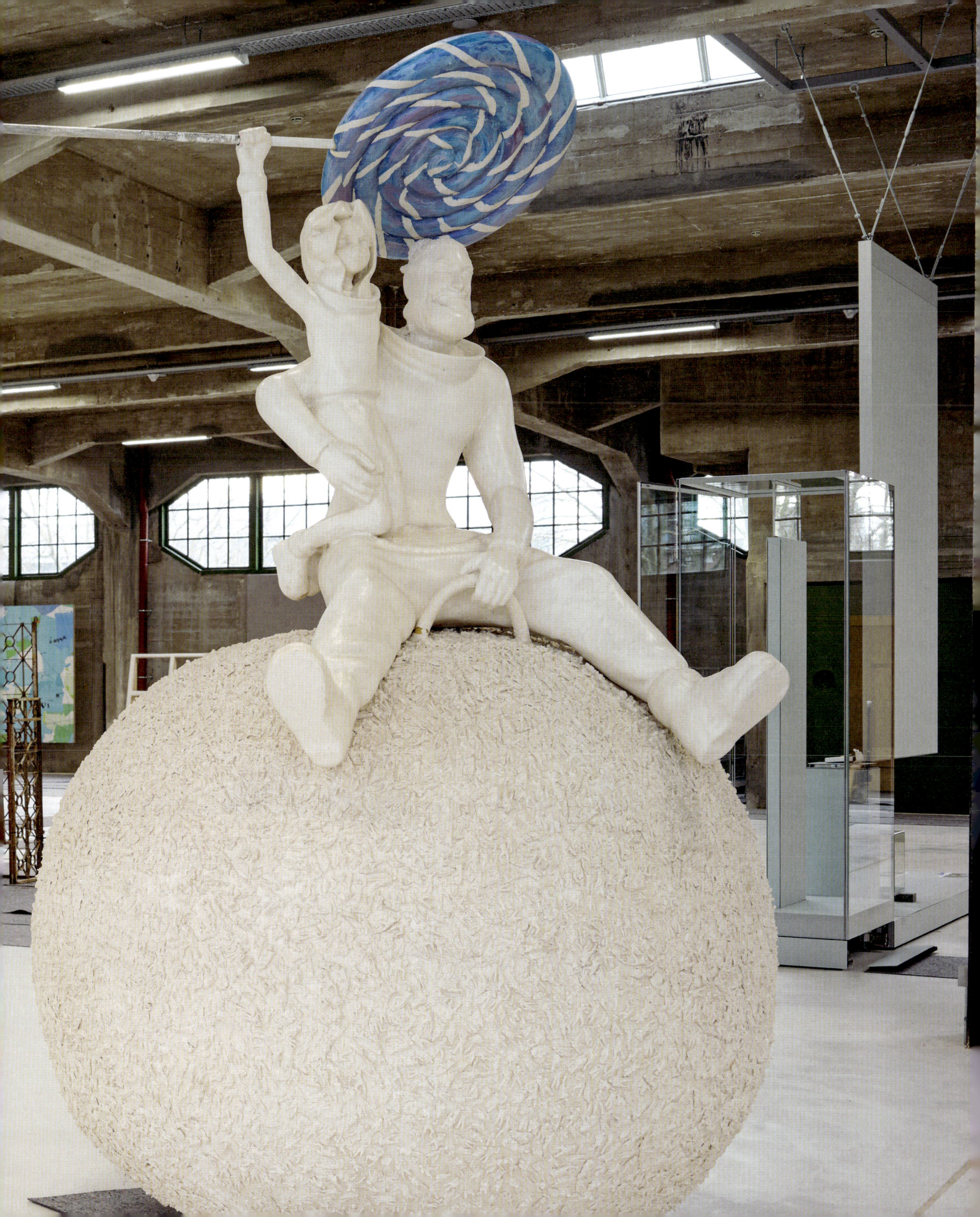

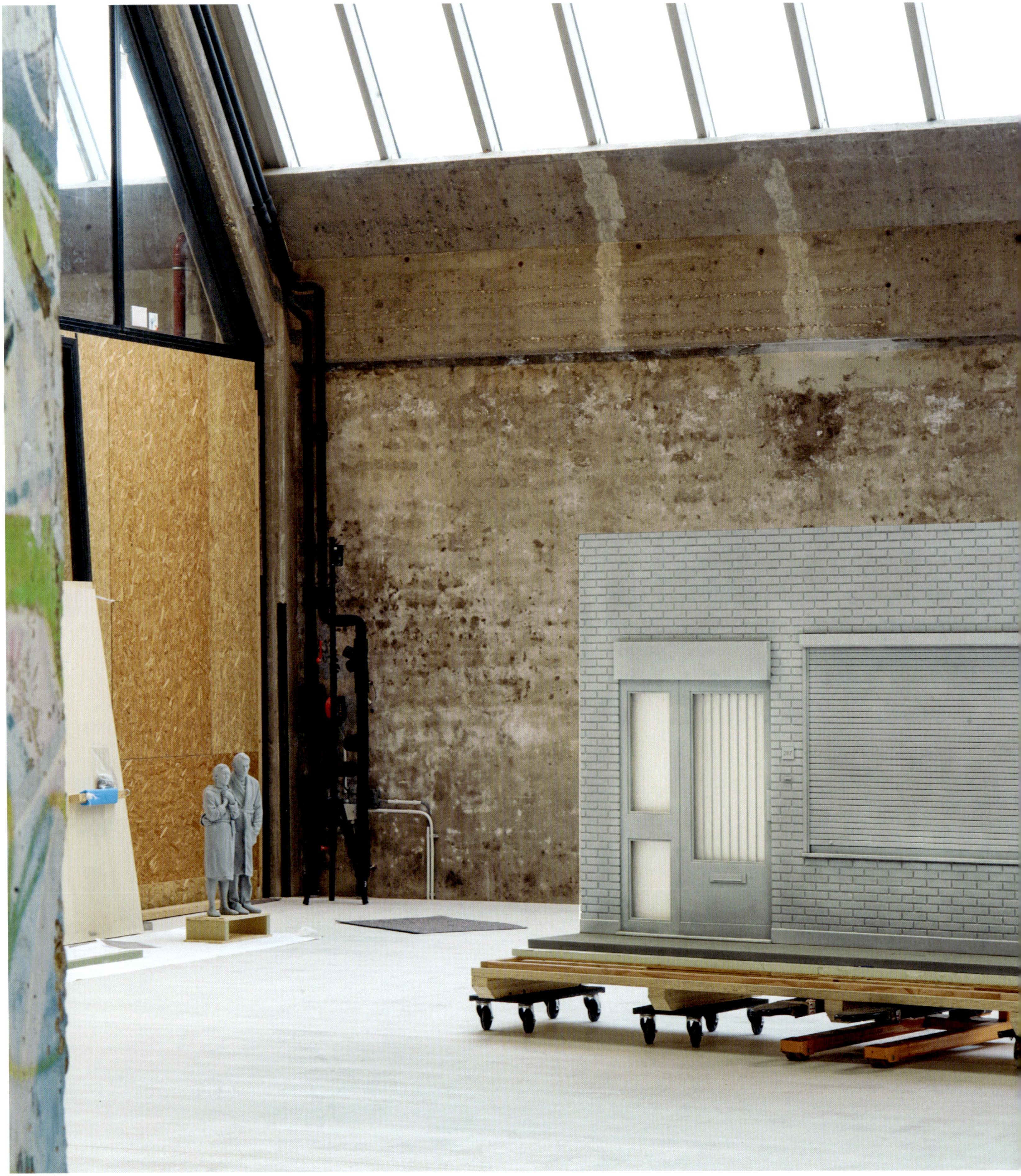

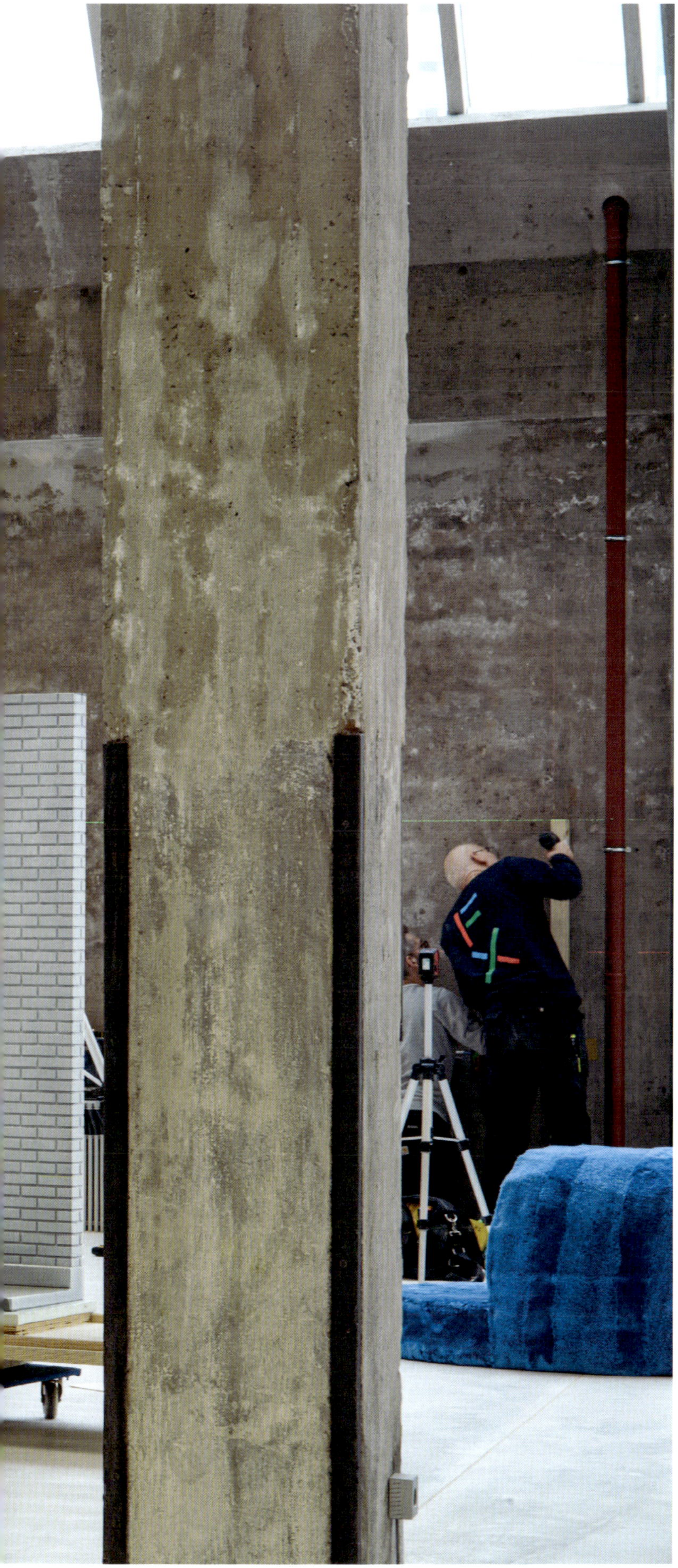

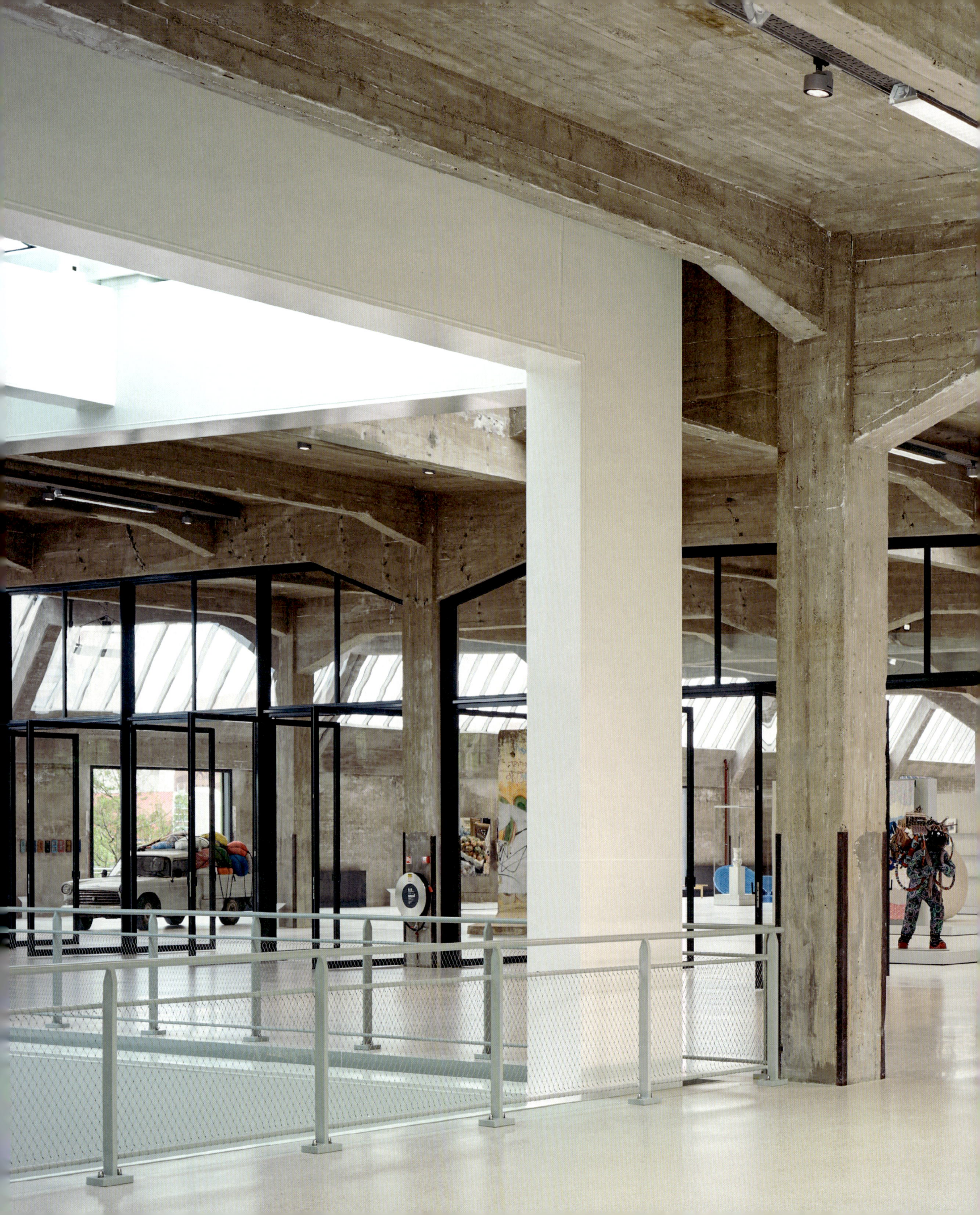

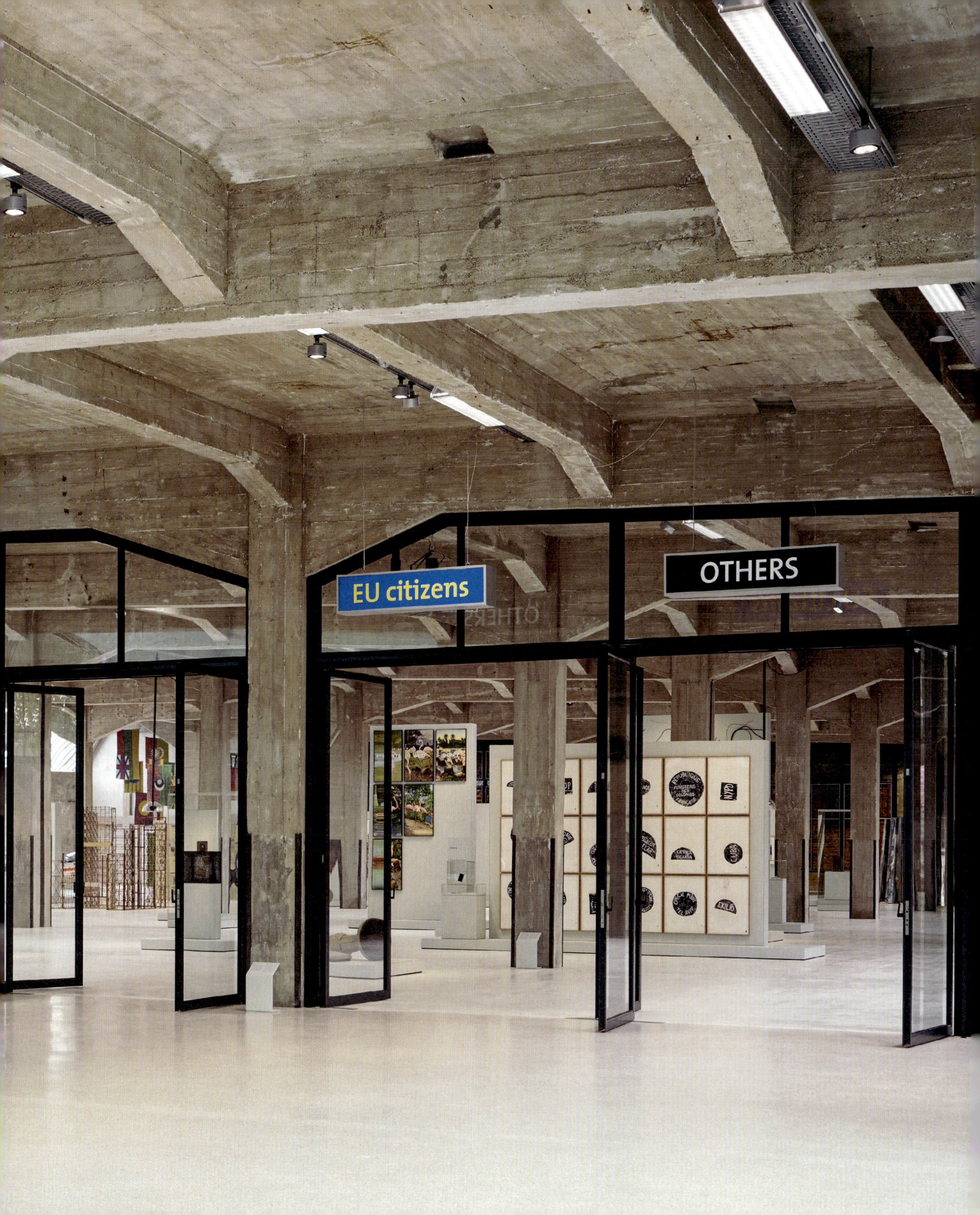
EU citizens
OTHERS

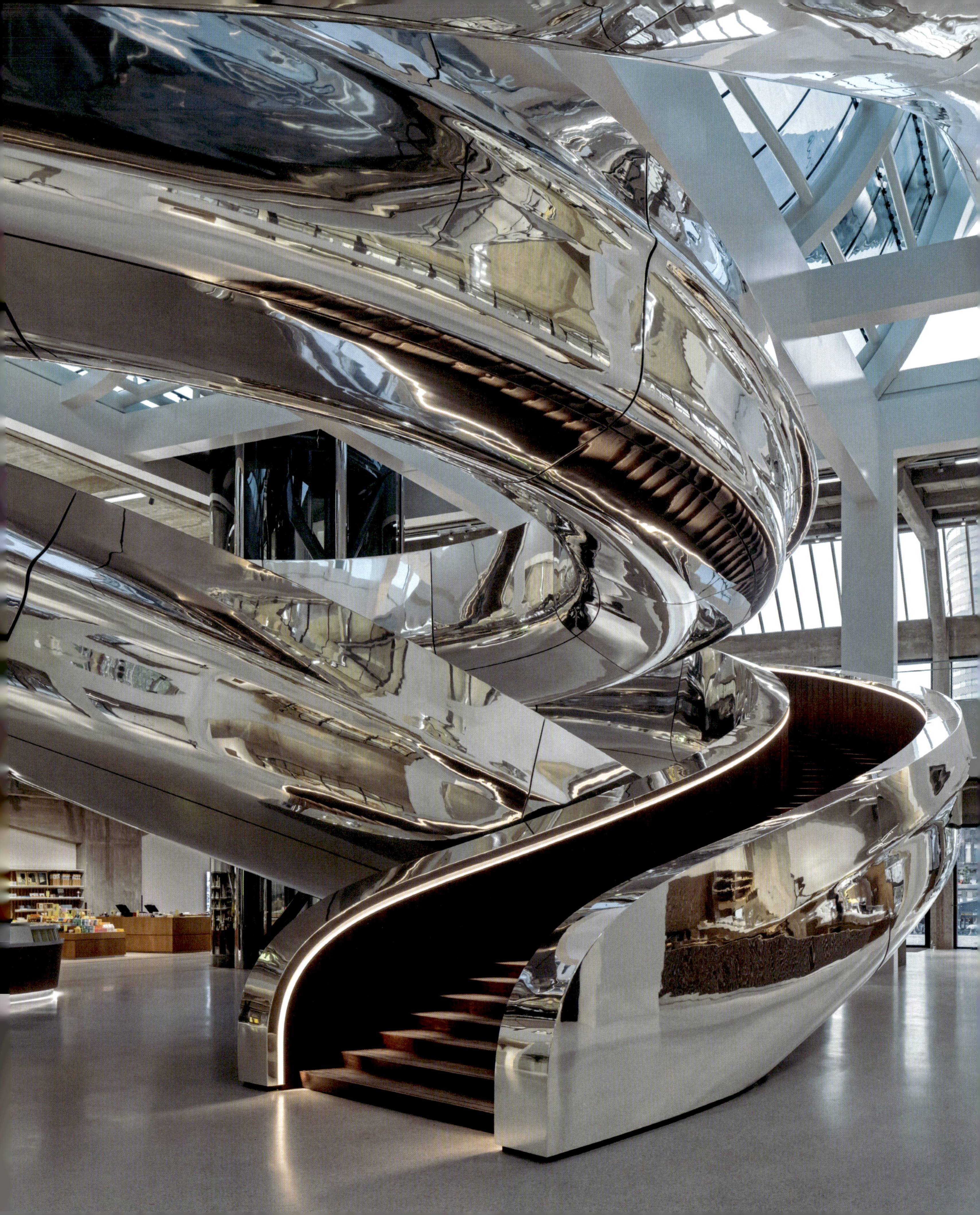

Museum

In a period of over five years, the historic Fenix Warehouse II has been renovated and transformed into a museum. Today, Fenix tells stories of migration. Stories about love and farewells, leaving home and feeling at home, navigating identity or seeking happiness. Stories from the past and present, told through the lens of art. All within the warehouse overlooking the docks where, in past centuries, millions of lives were changed.

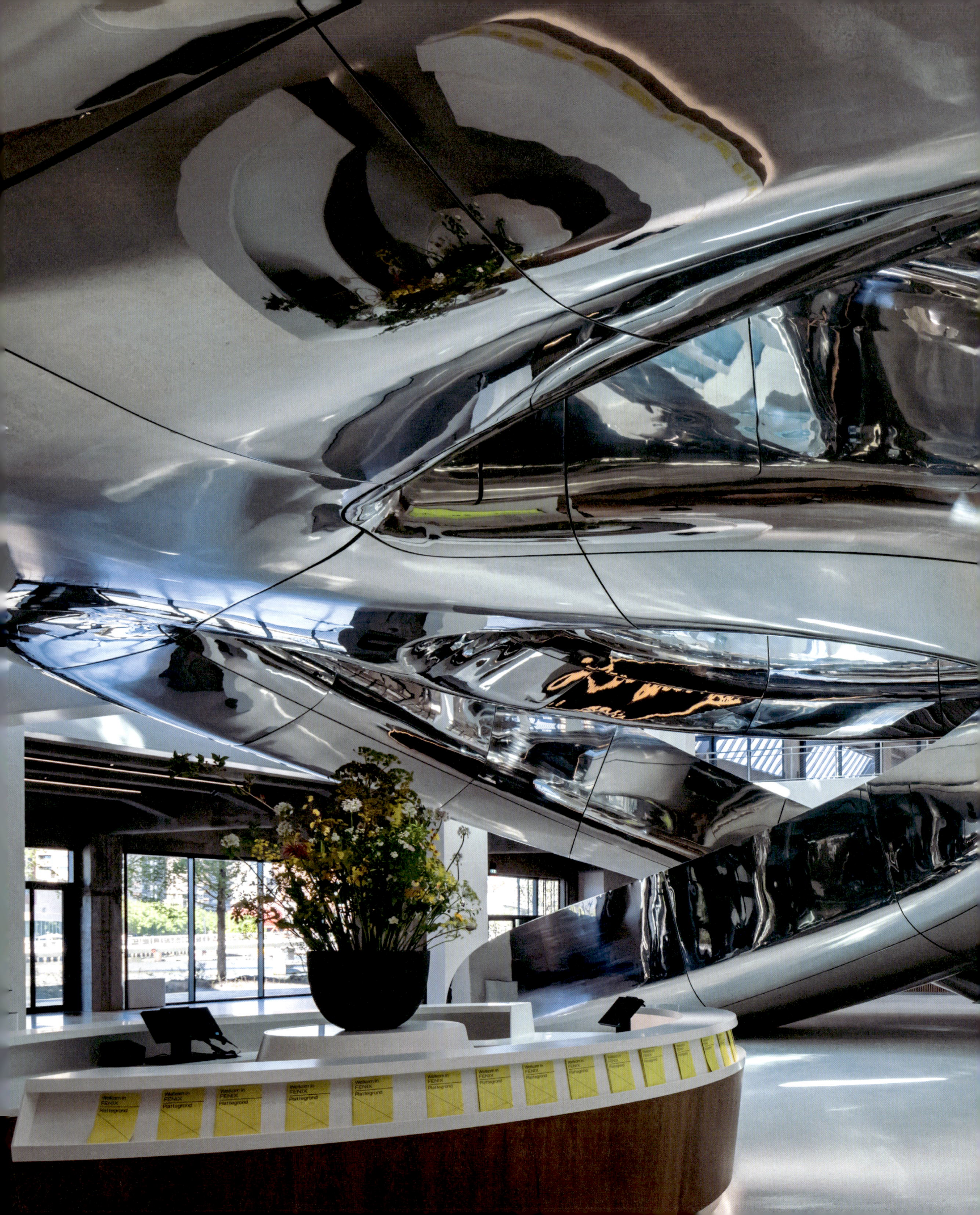
Welkom in
FENIX
Plattegrond

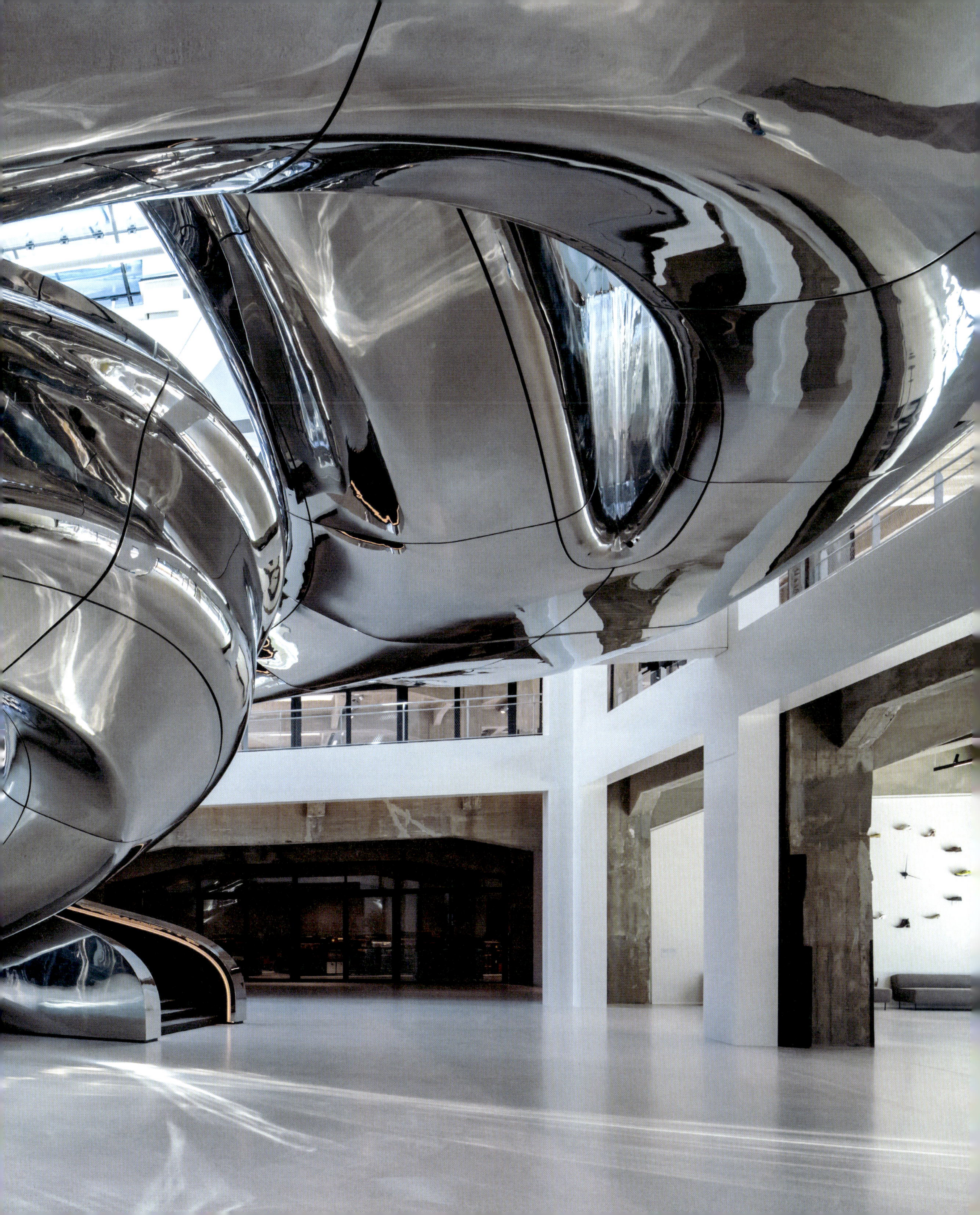

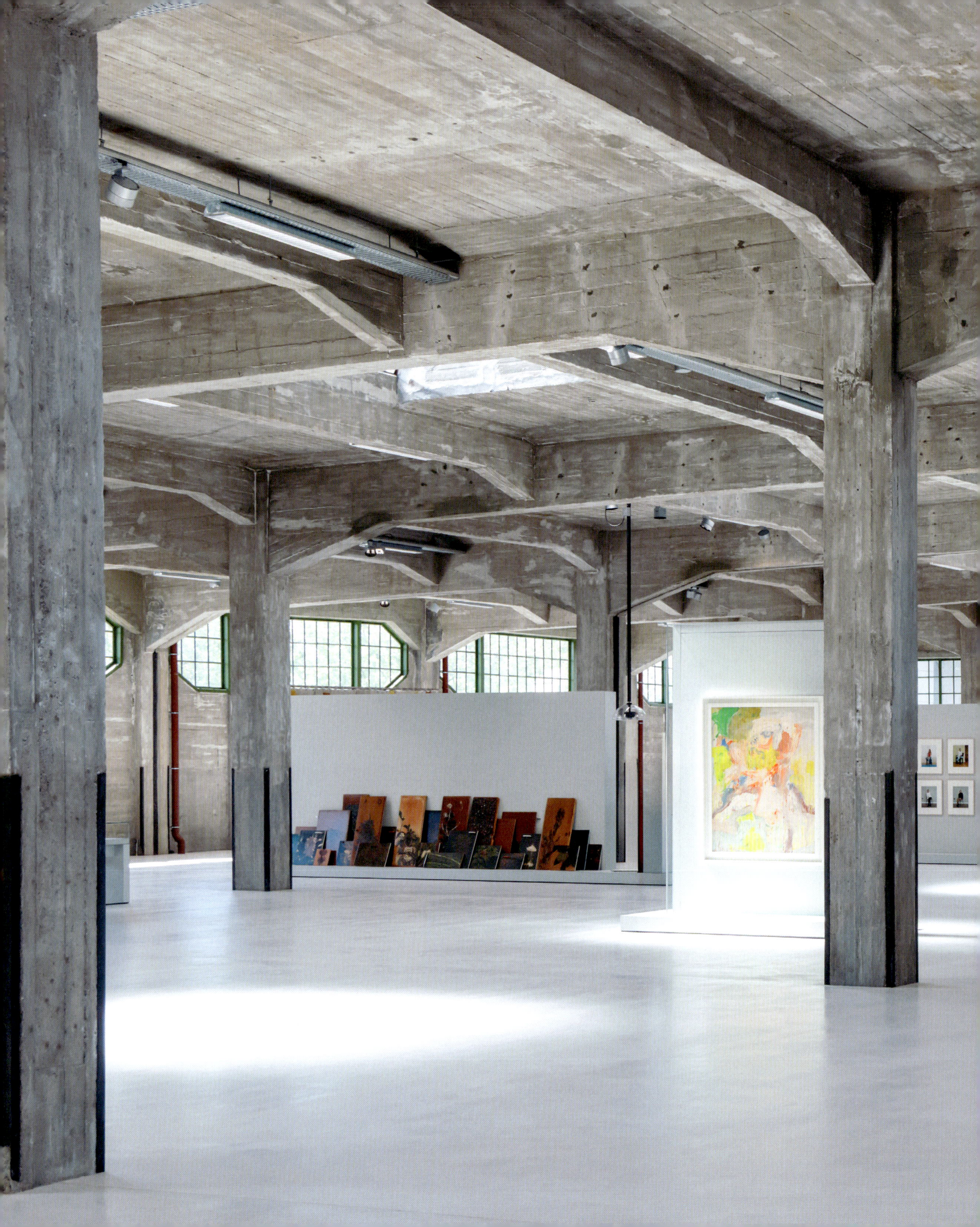

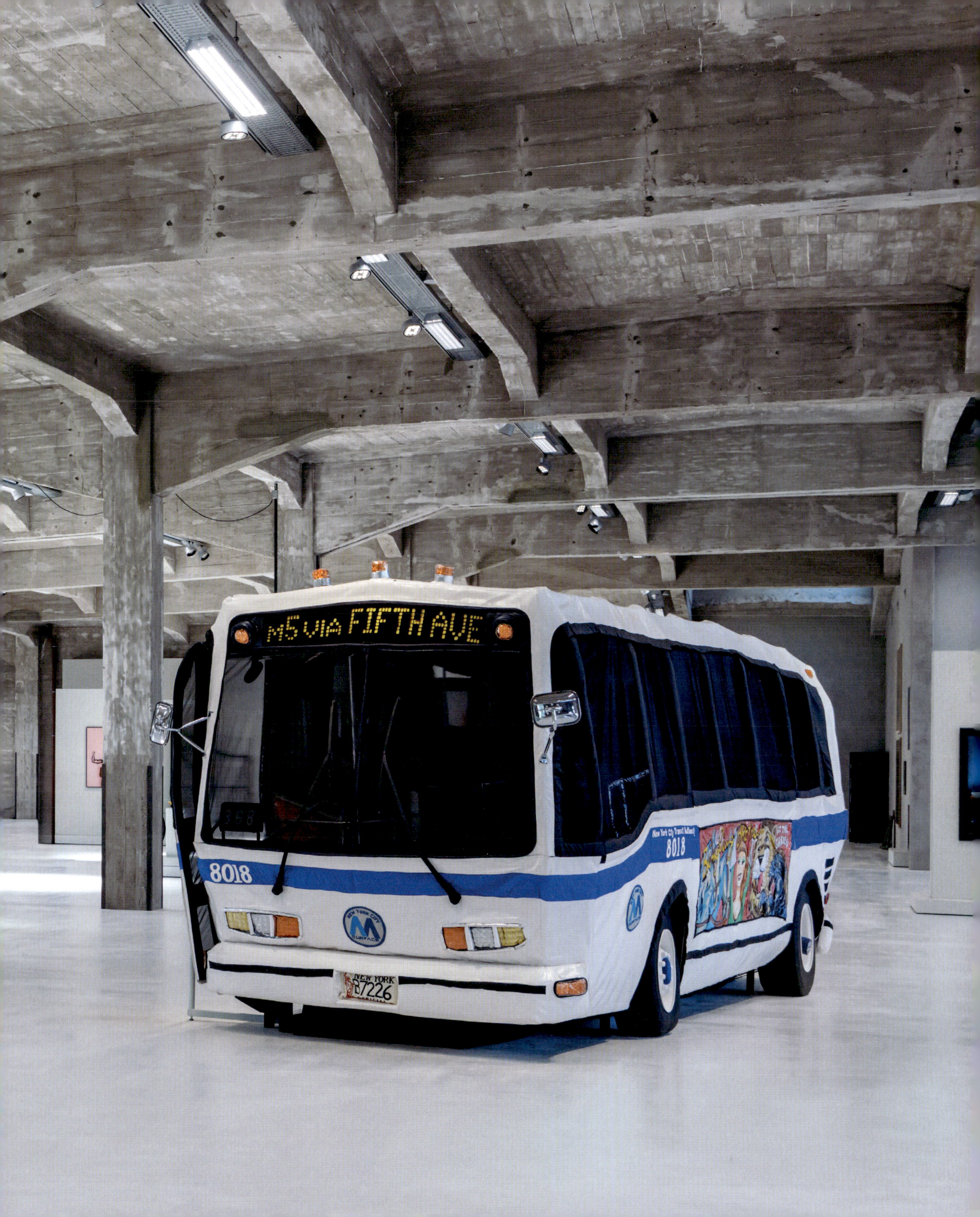
m5 via FIFTH AVE
8018
8018
NEW YORK

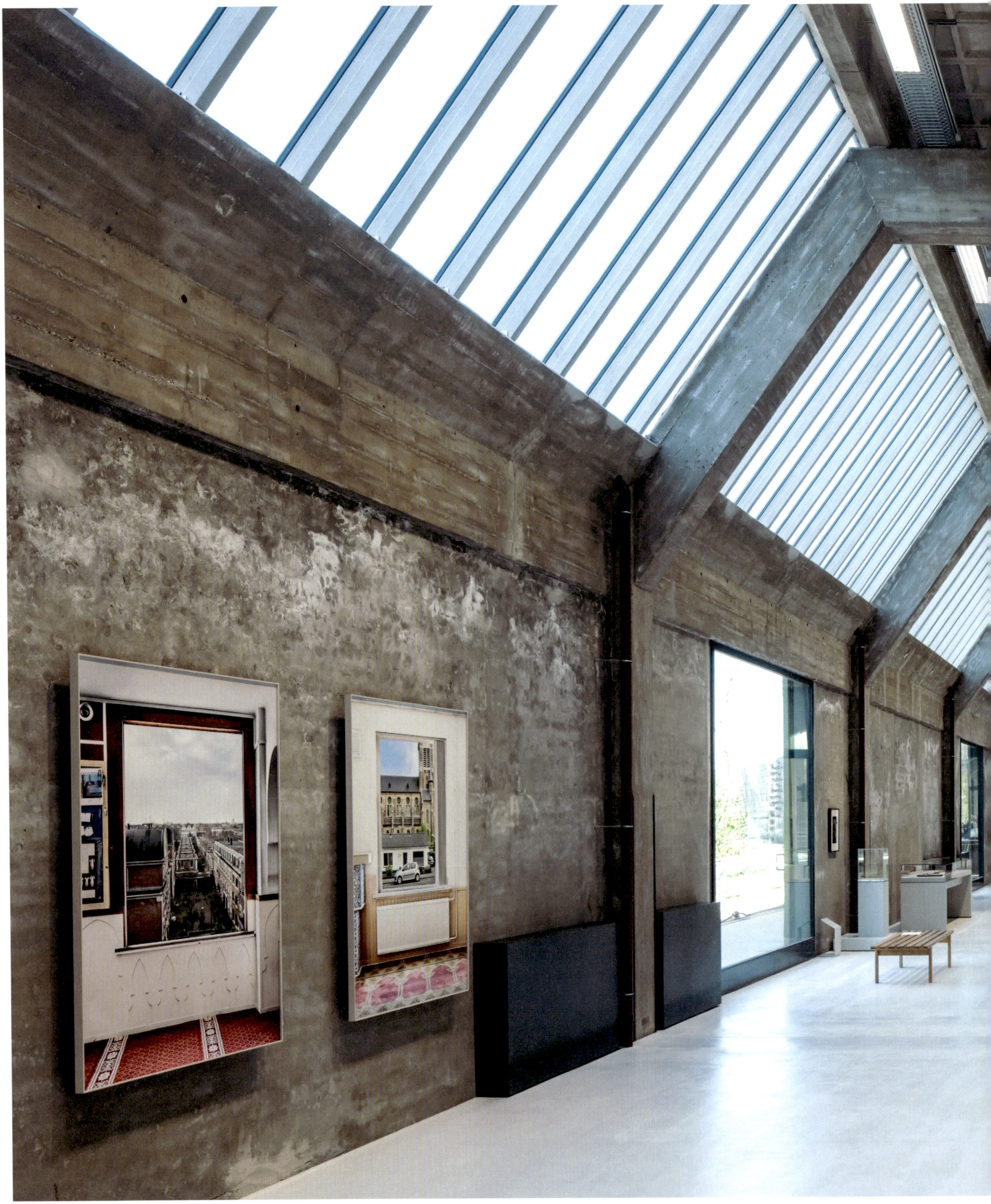

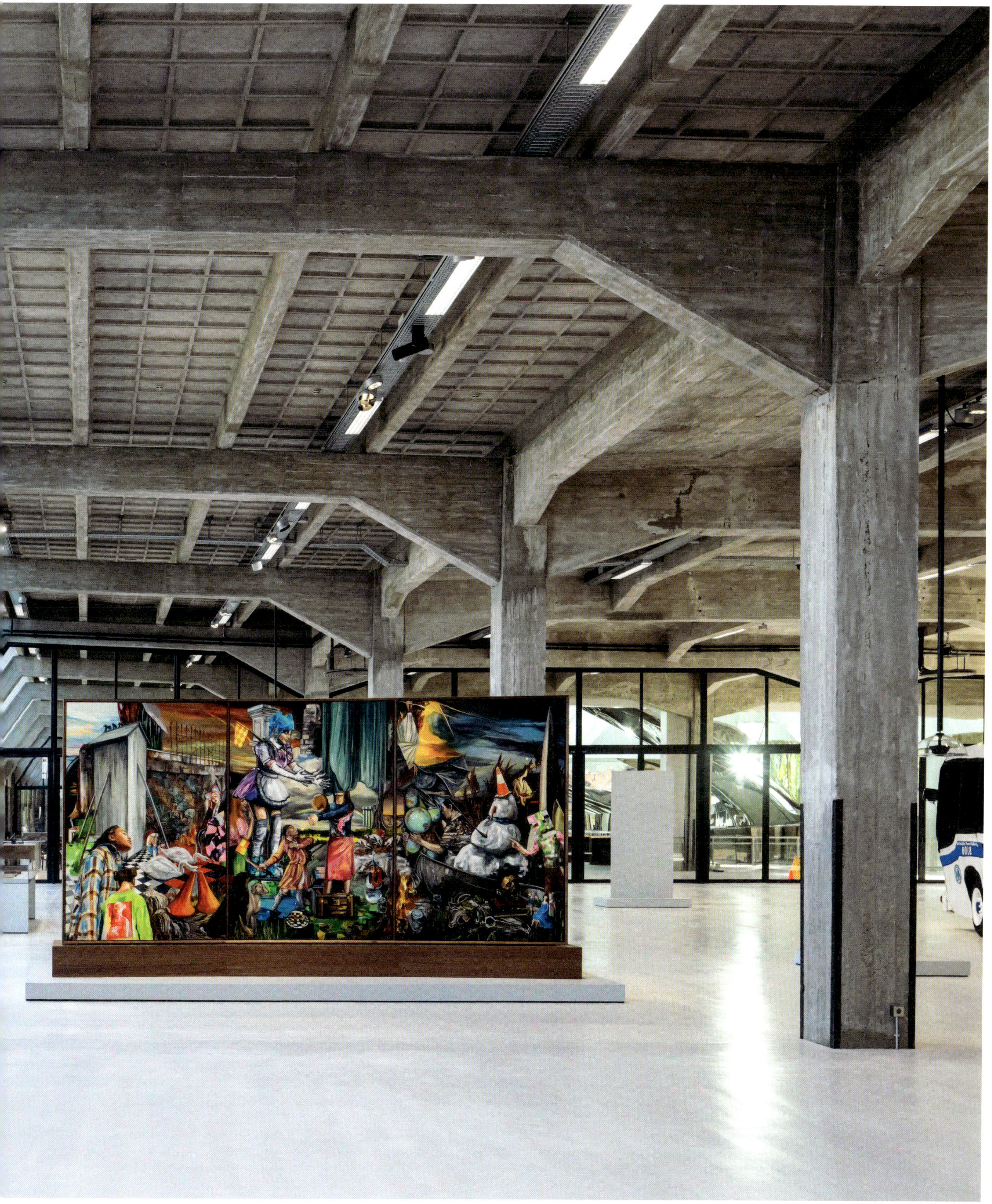

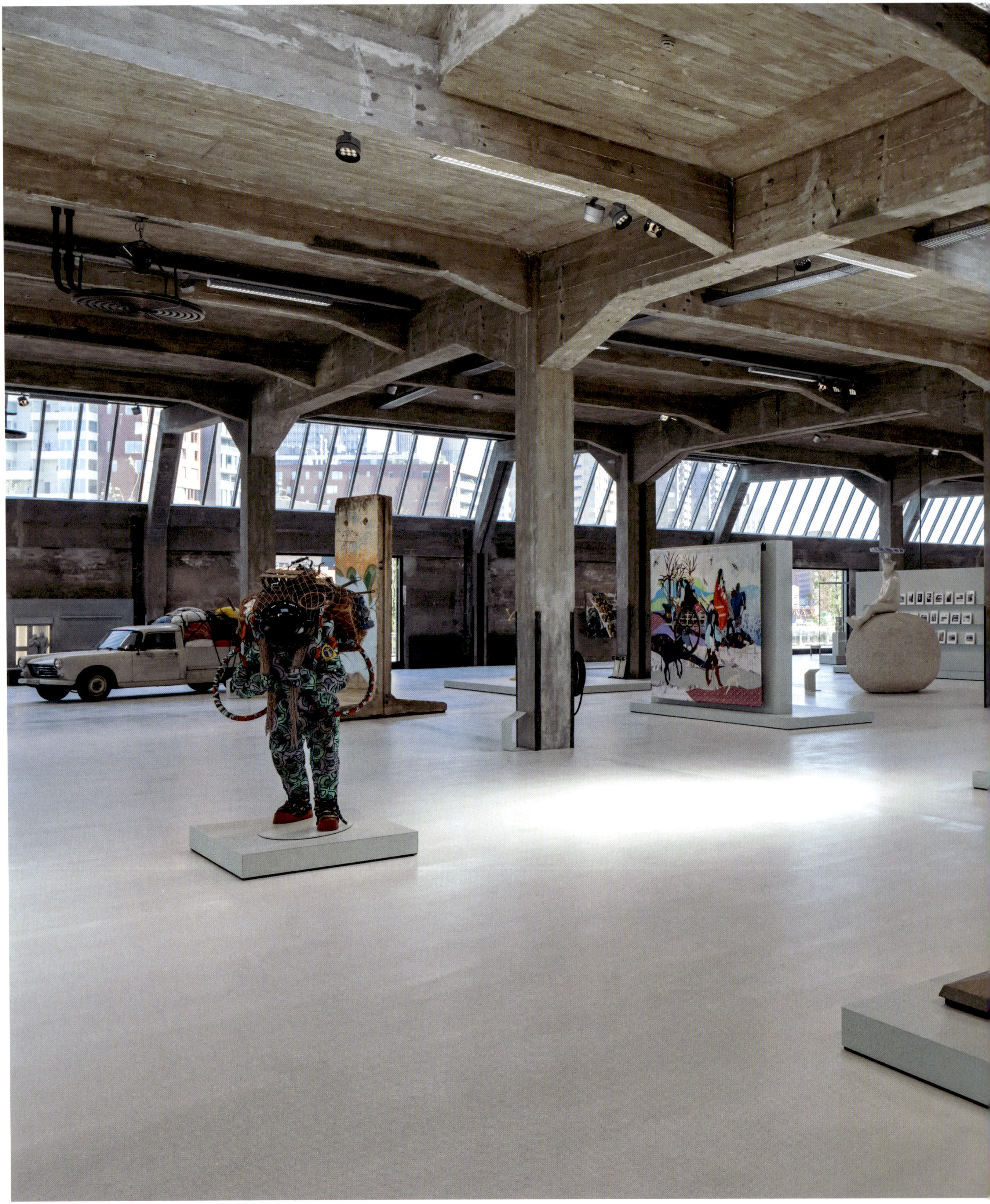

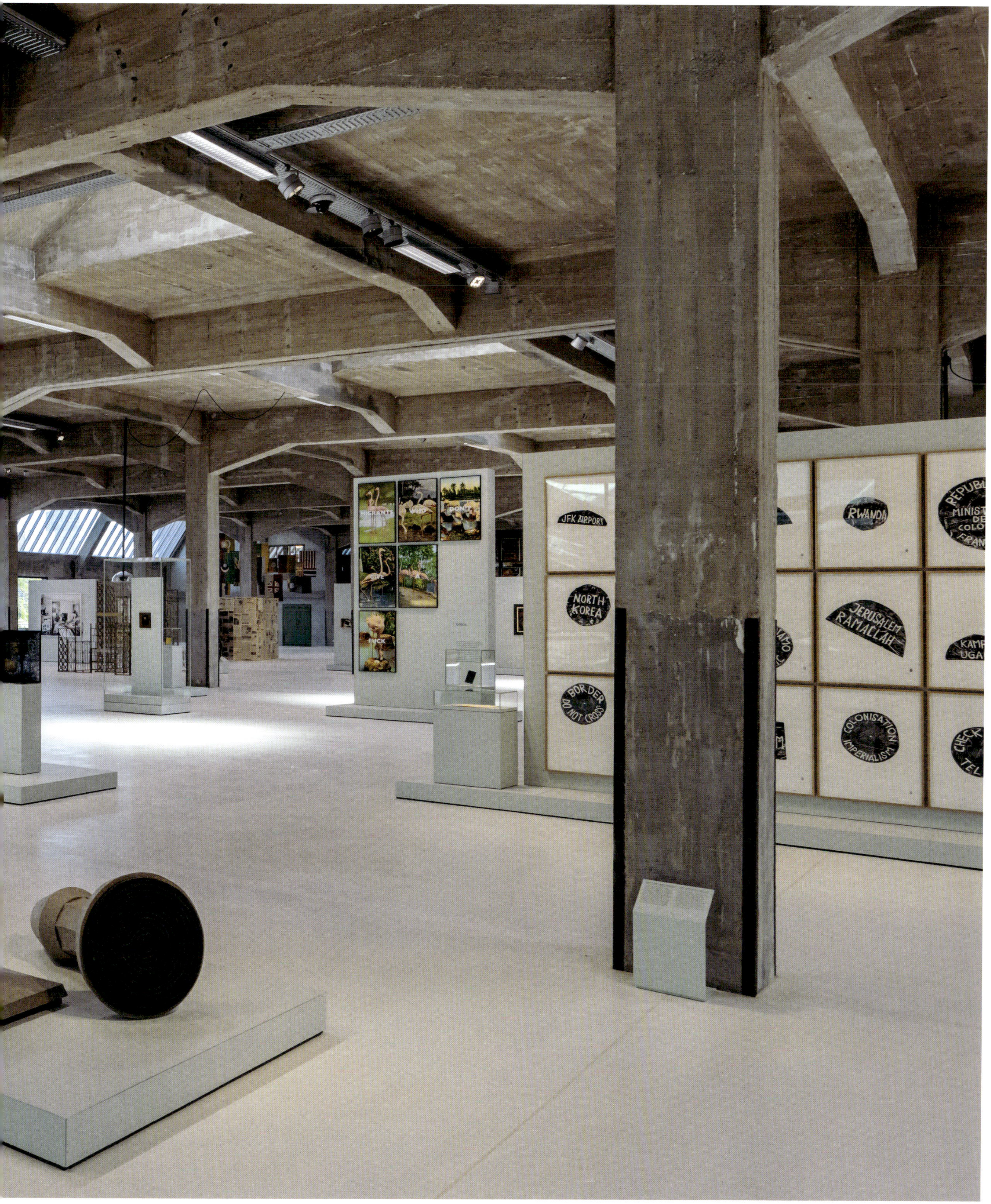
JFK AIRPORT
RWANDA
NORTH KOREA
JERUSALEM RAMALLAH
BORDER DO NOT CROSS
COLONISATION IMPERIALISM
MIGRANTS

“When my team and I started working at Fenix, the exhibition spaces were completely empty. It has been an honor, and challenging at times, to install all the different artworks in this historic warehouse. From a part of the Berlin Wall to a Peugeot 404, to smaller, more fragile artworks. I am very proud of the result.”

Bart Cuppens, Technical Project Leader and Art Handler at Fenix

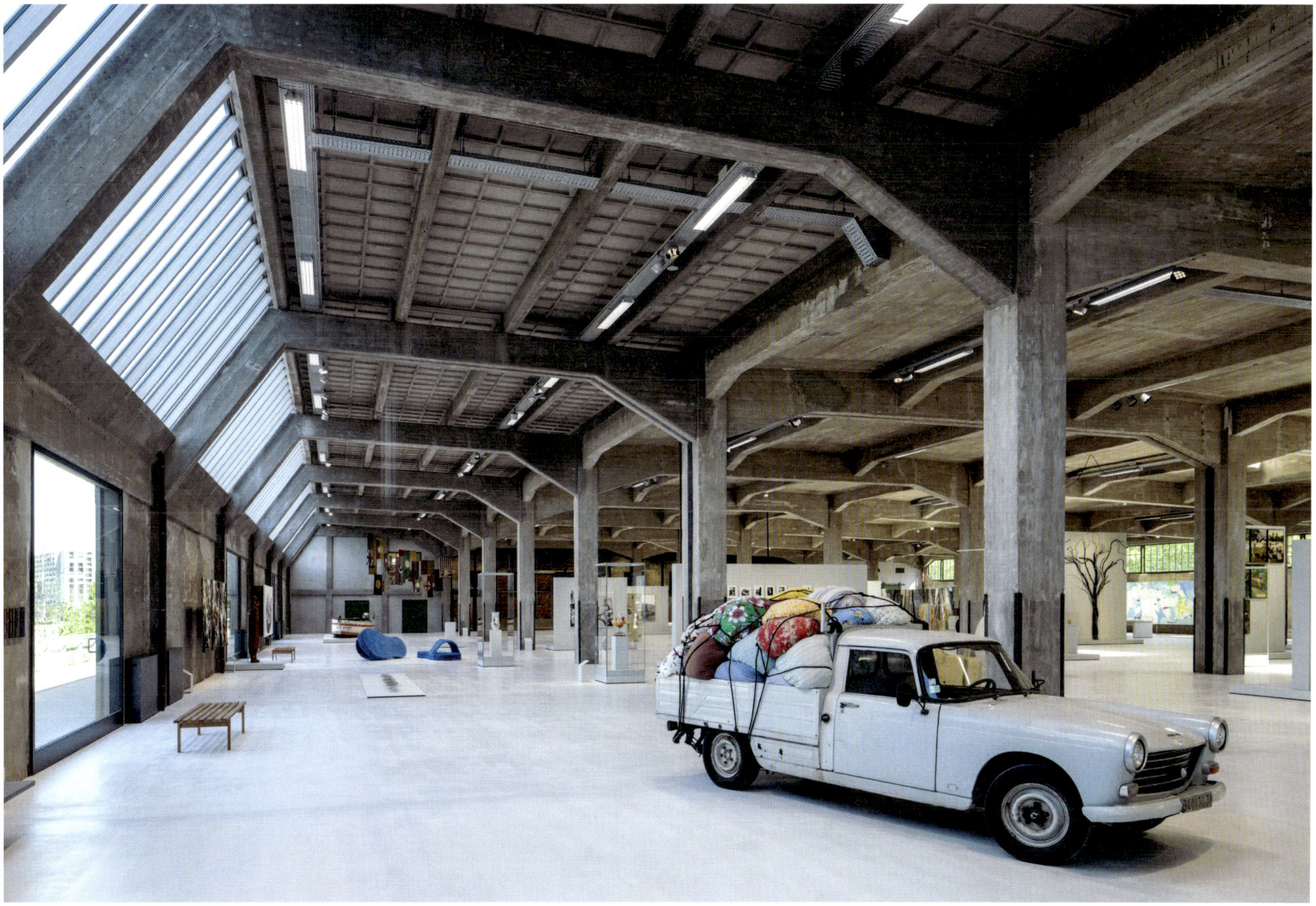

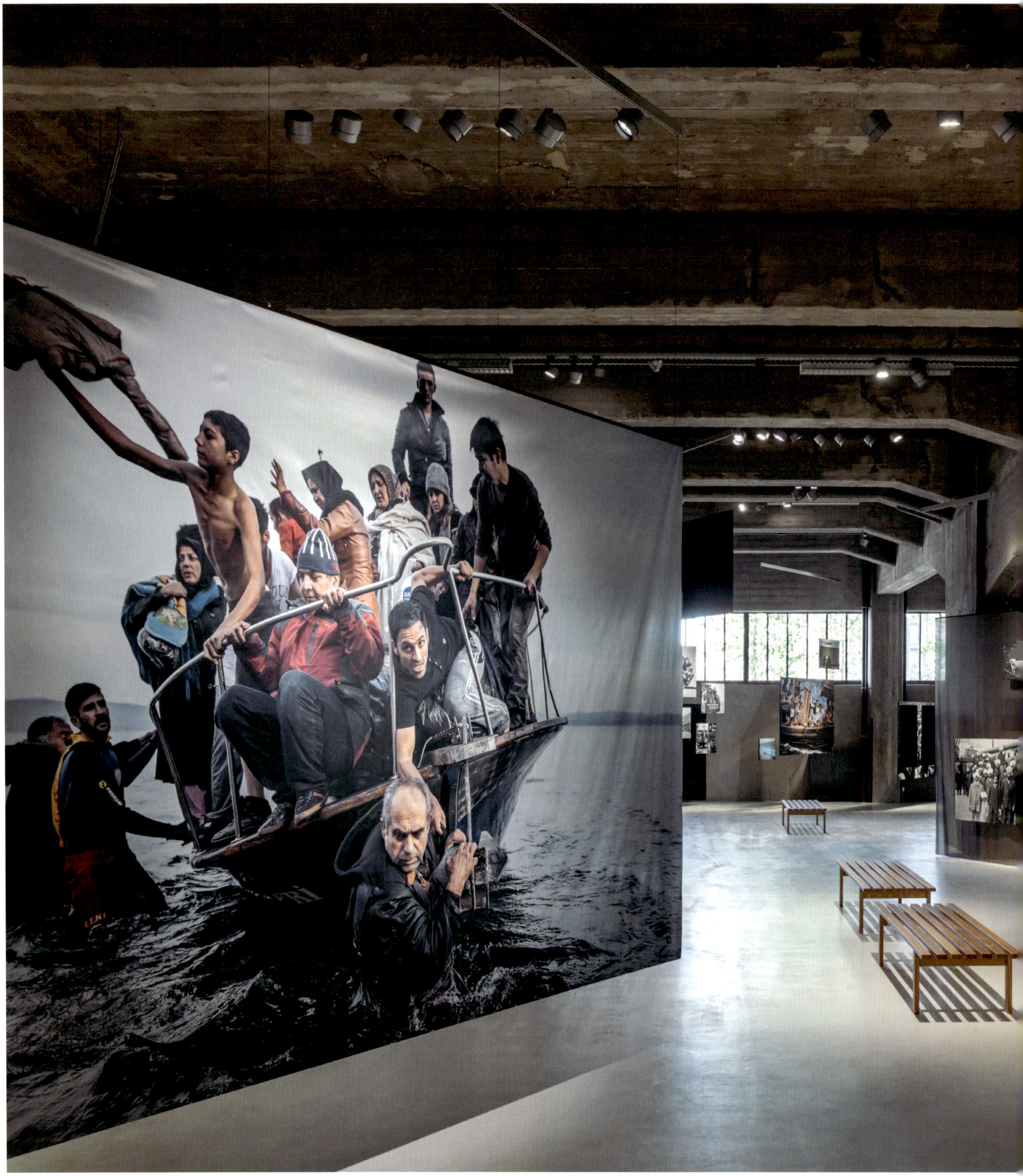

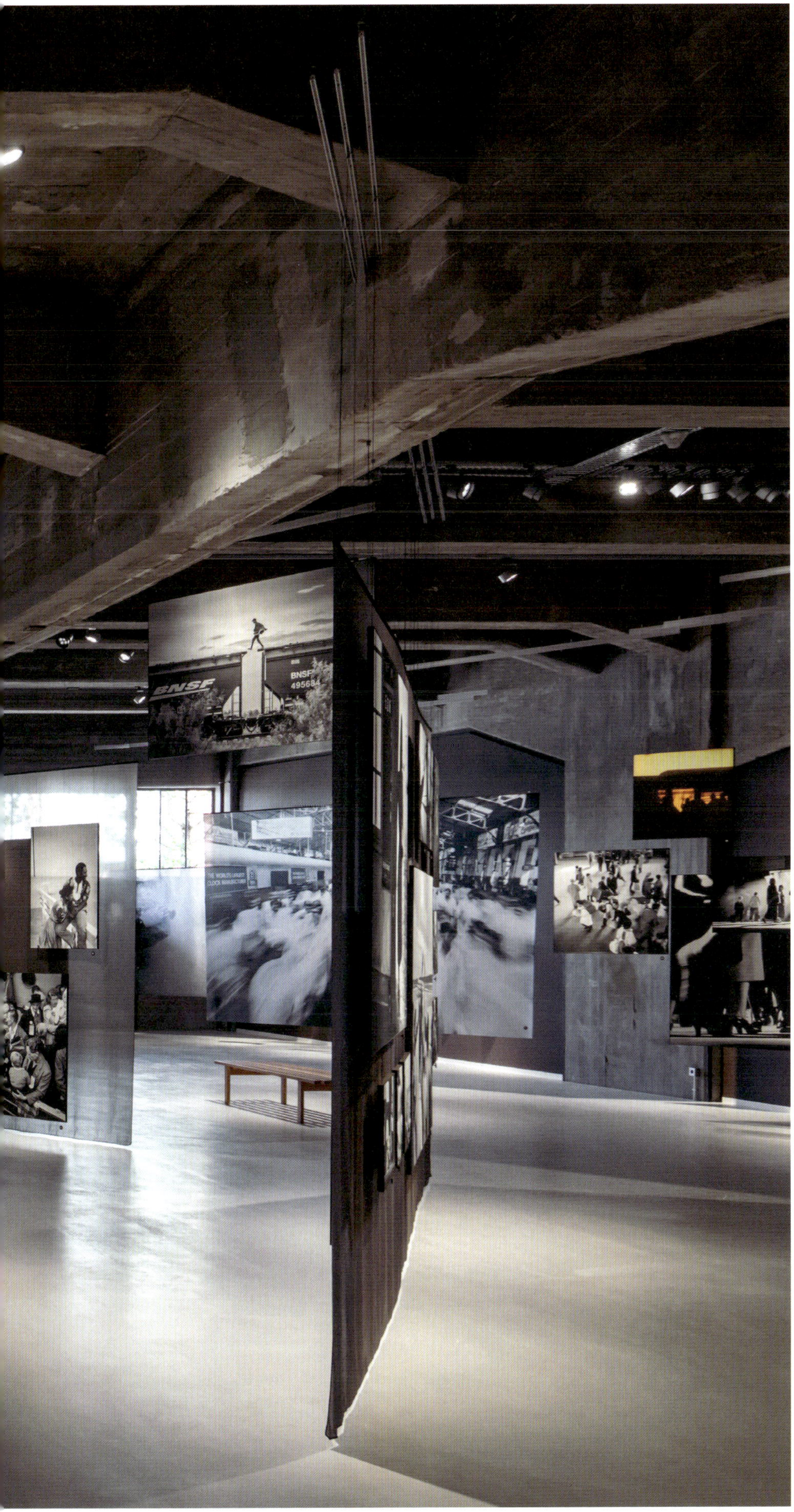

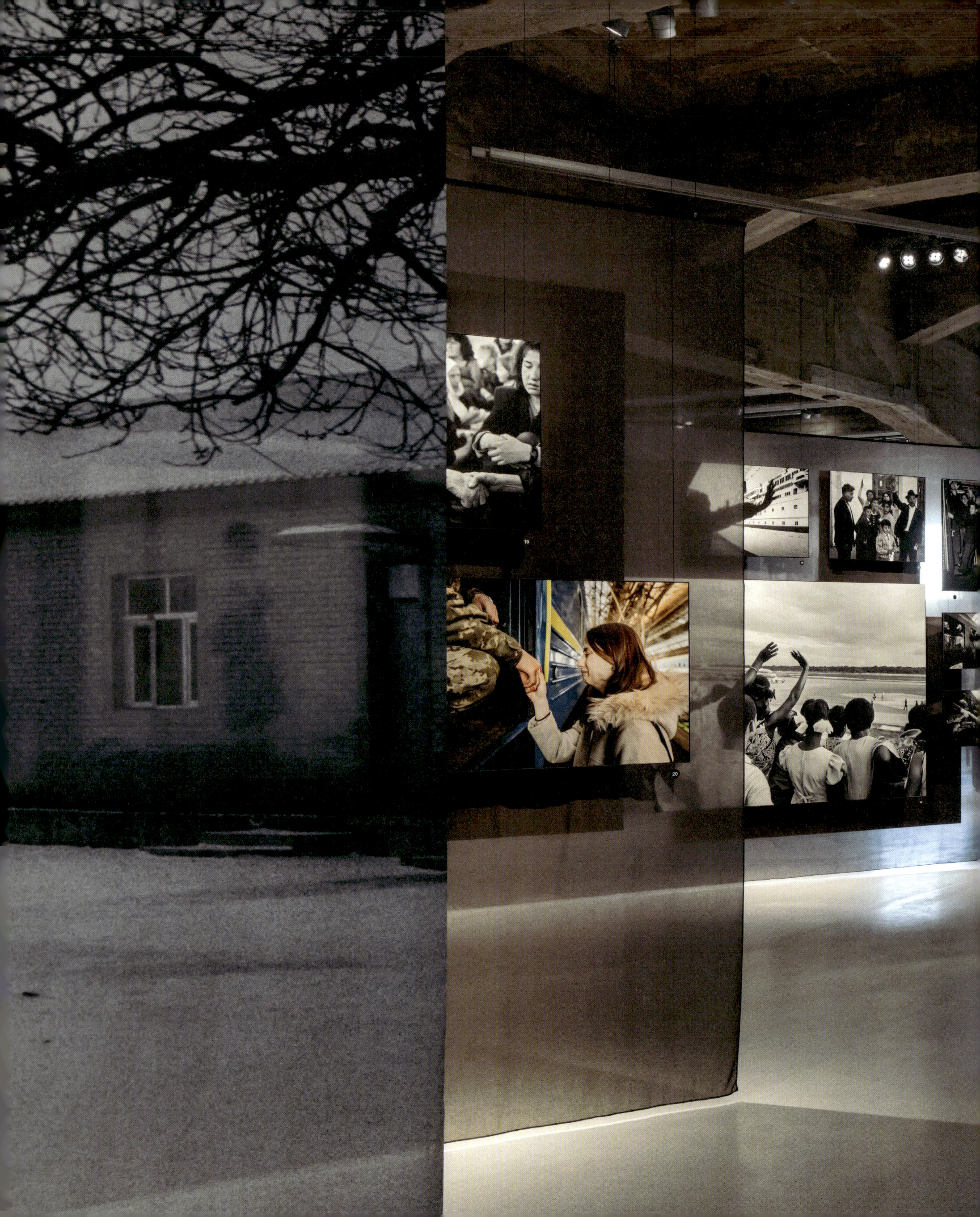

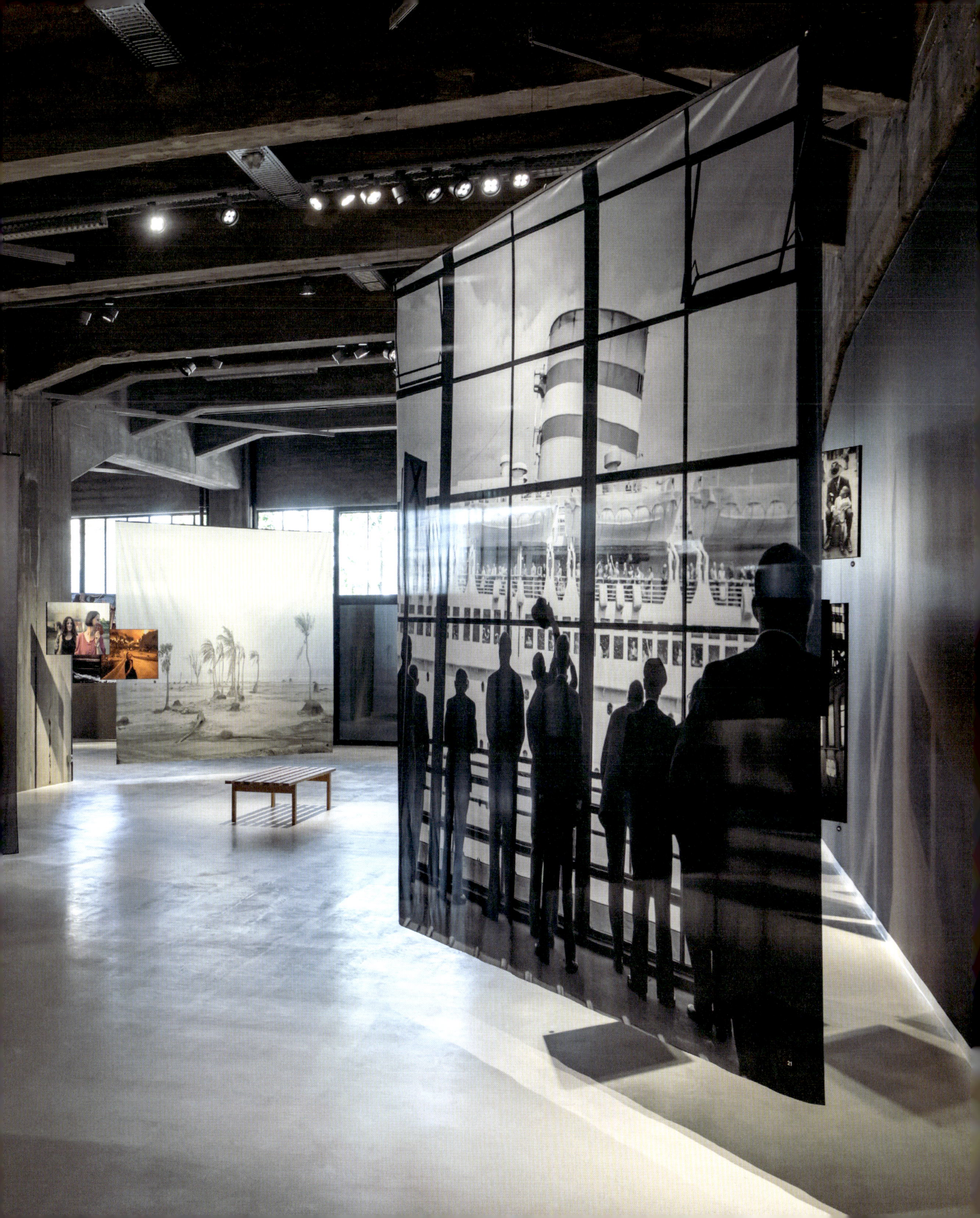

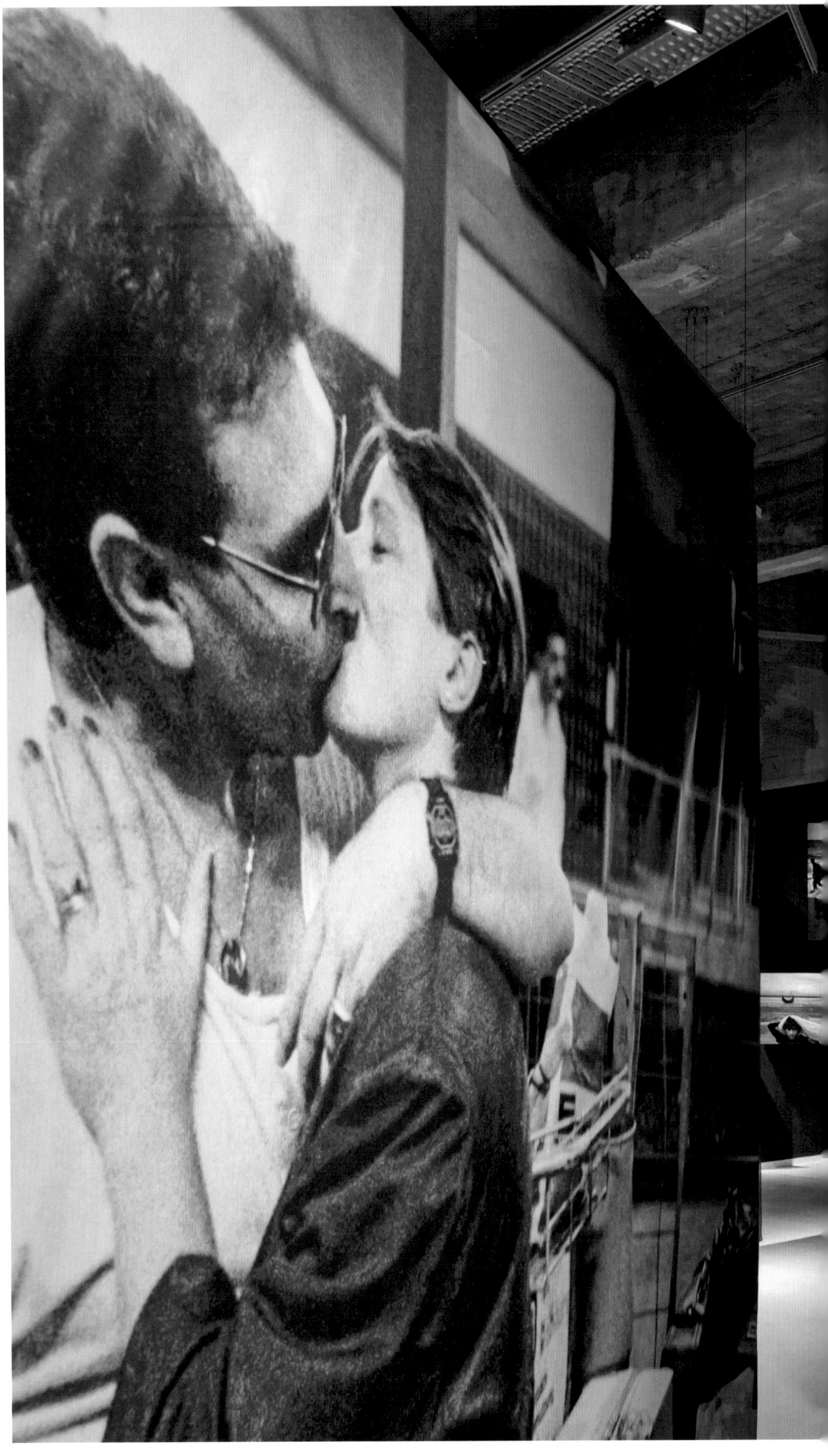

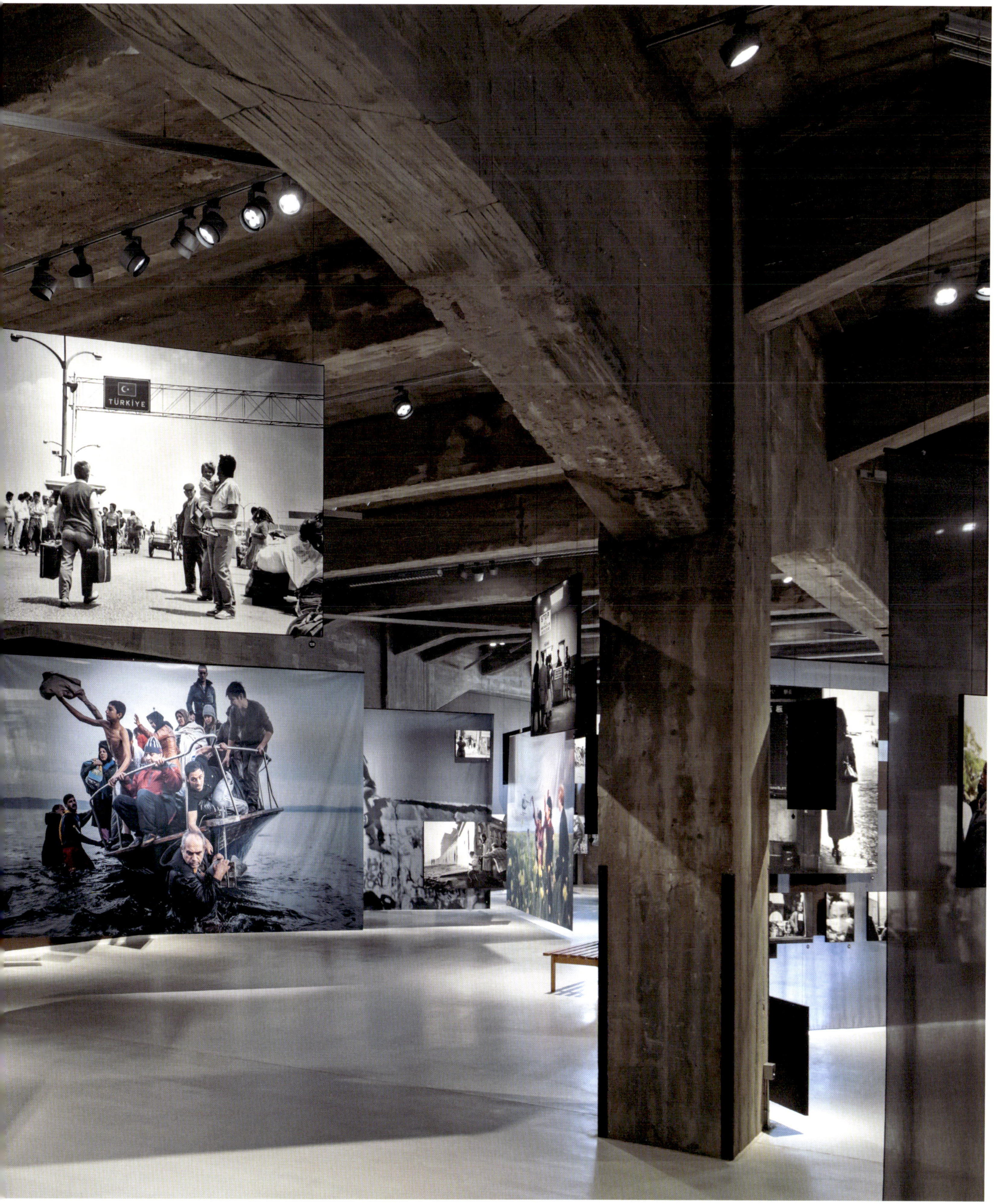
TÜRKIYE

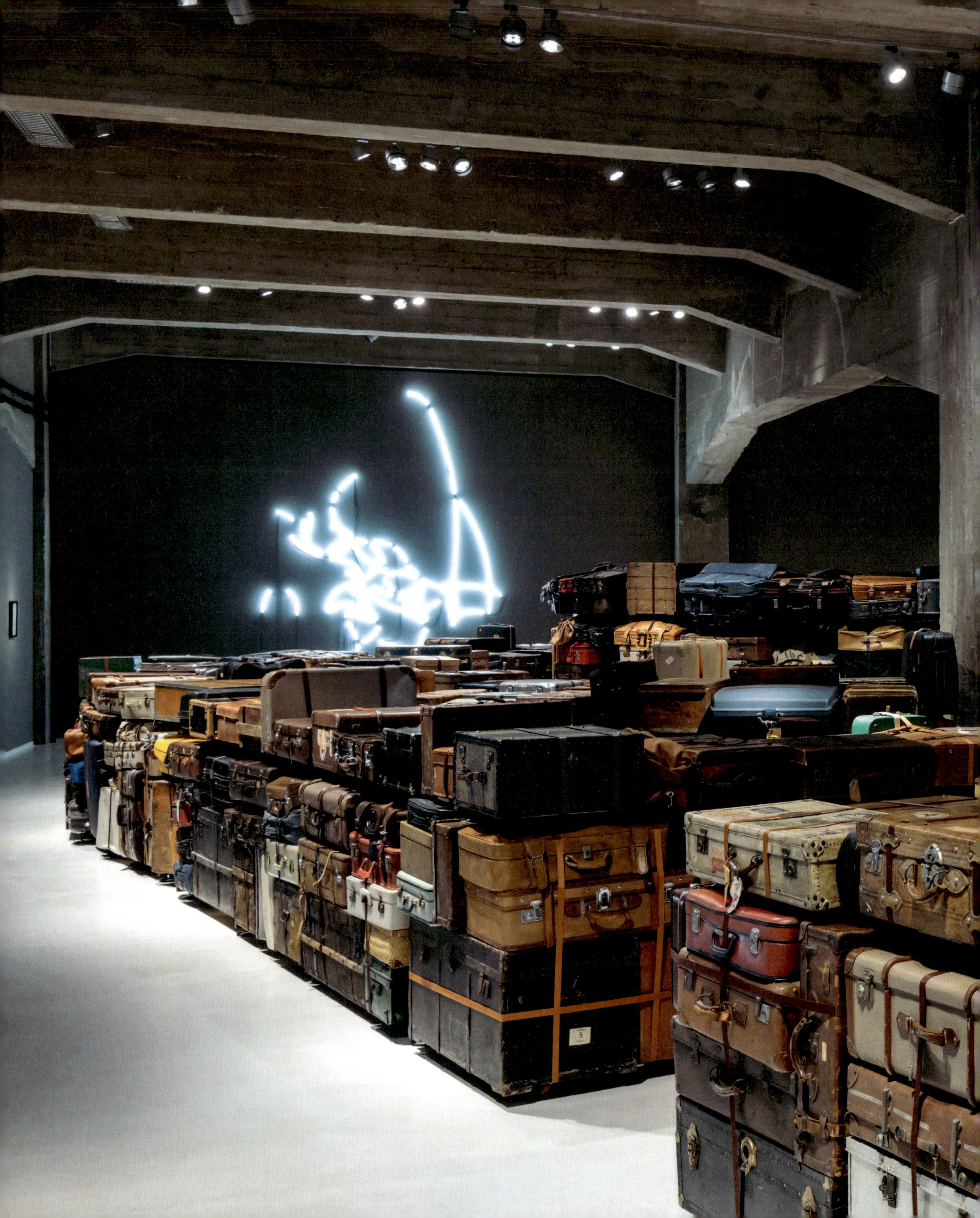

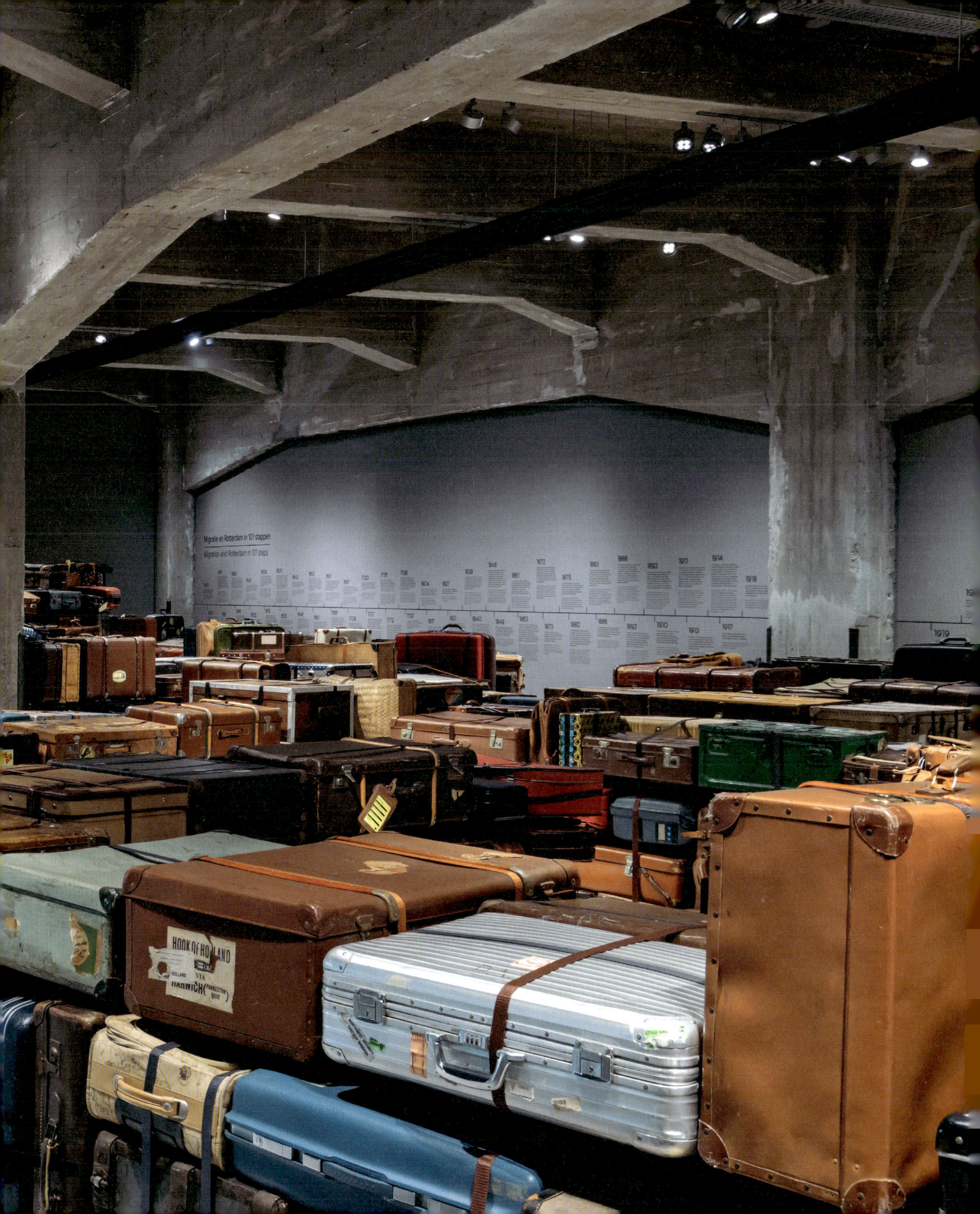
Migratie en Rotterdam in 101 stappen
Migration and Rotterdam in 101 steps
HOOK OF HOLLAND

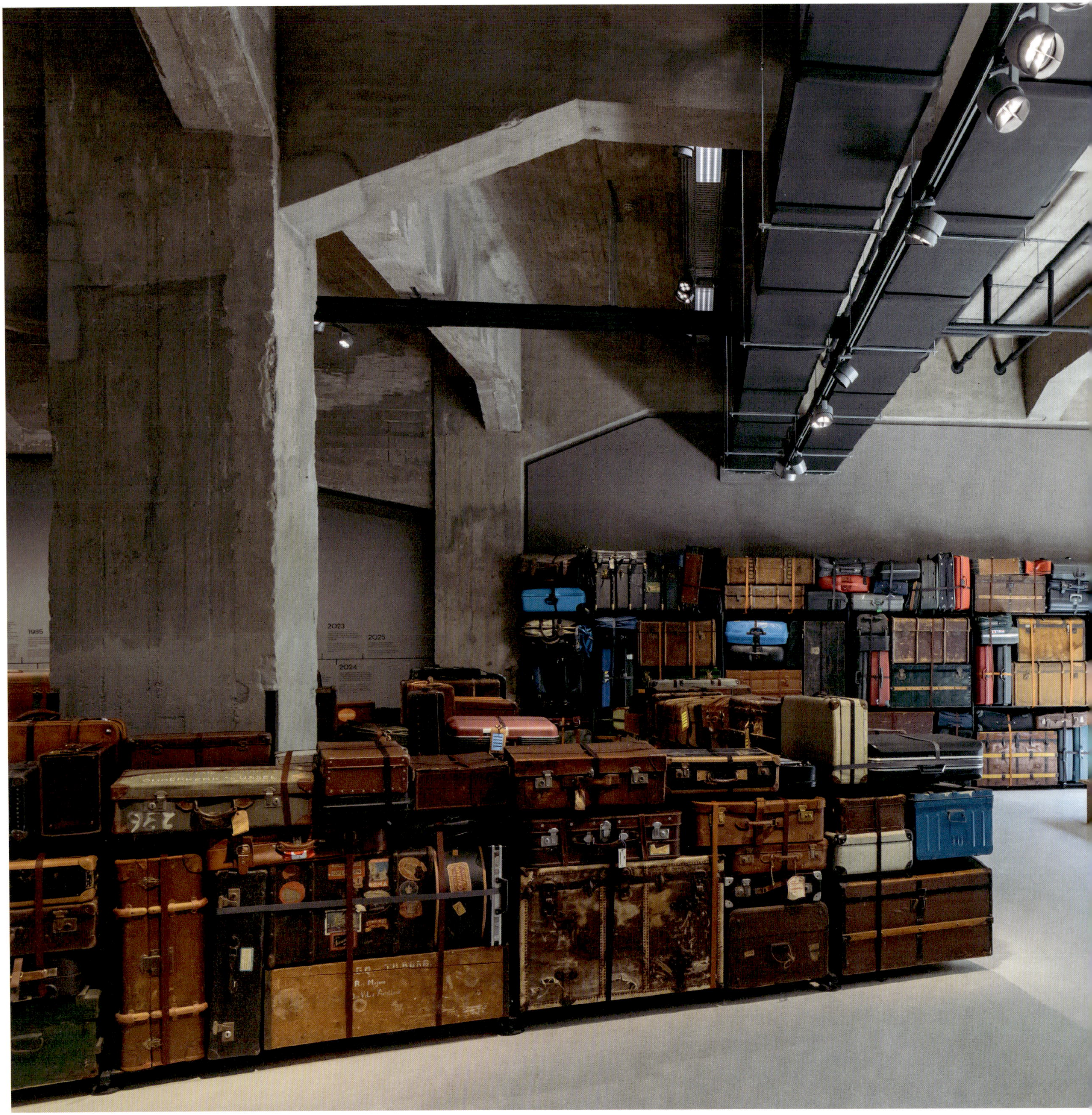

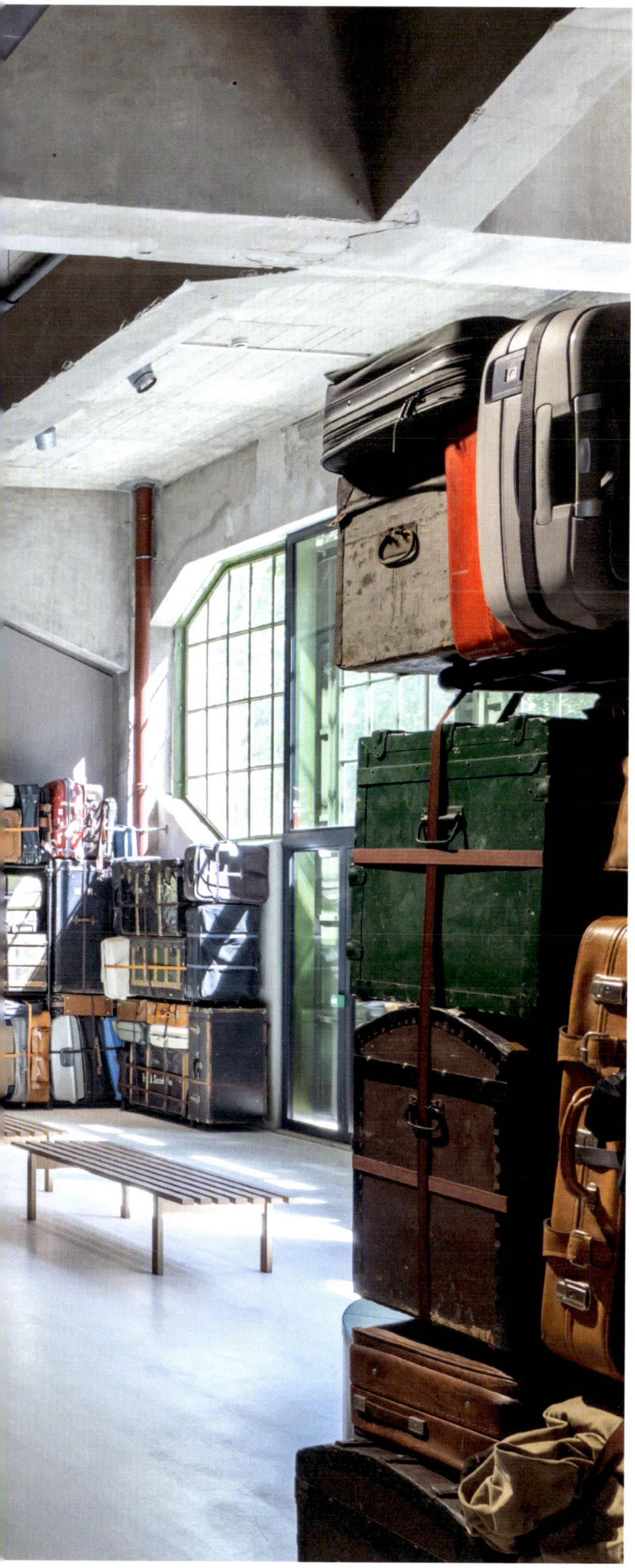

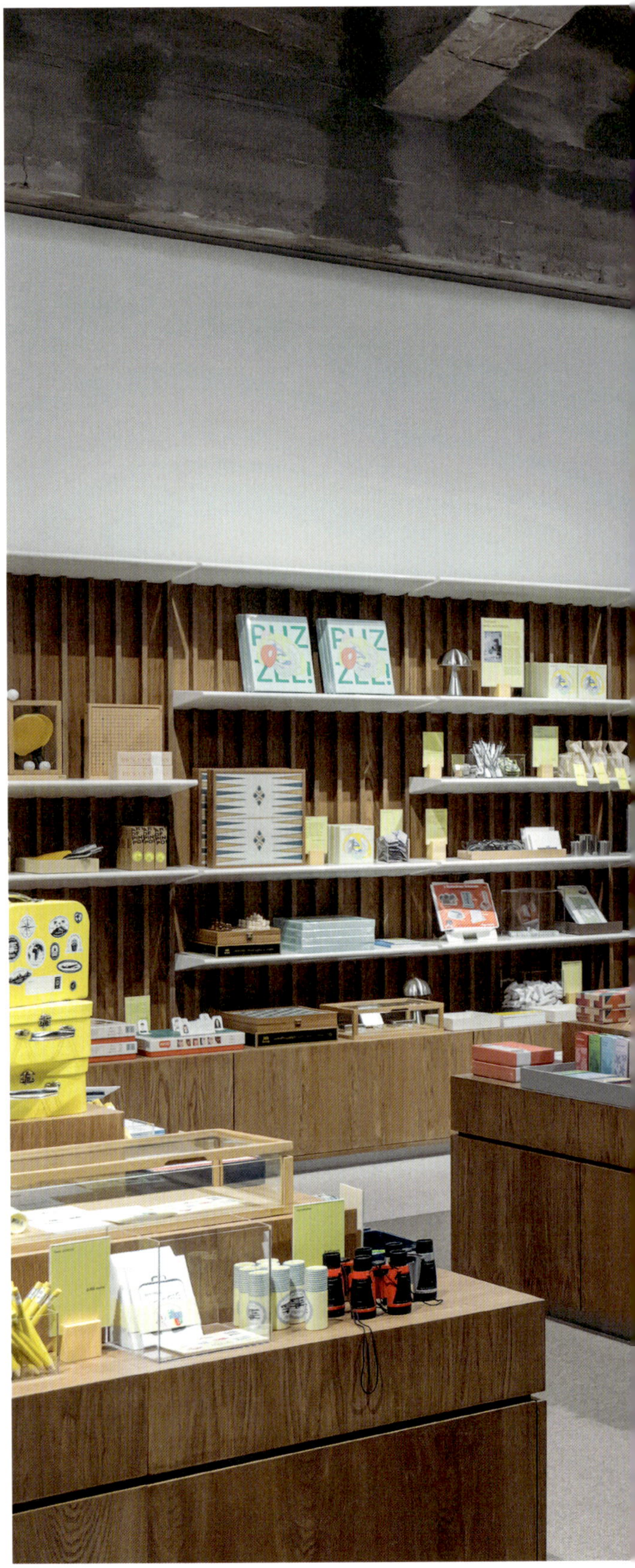

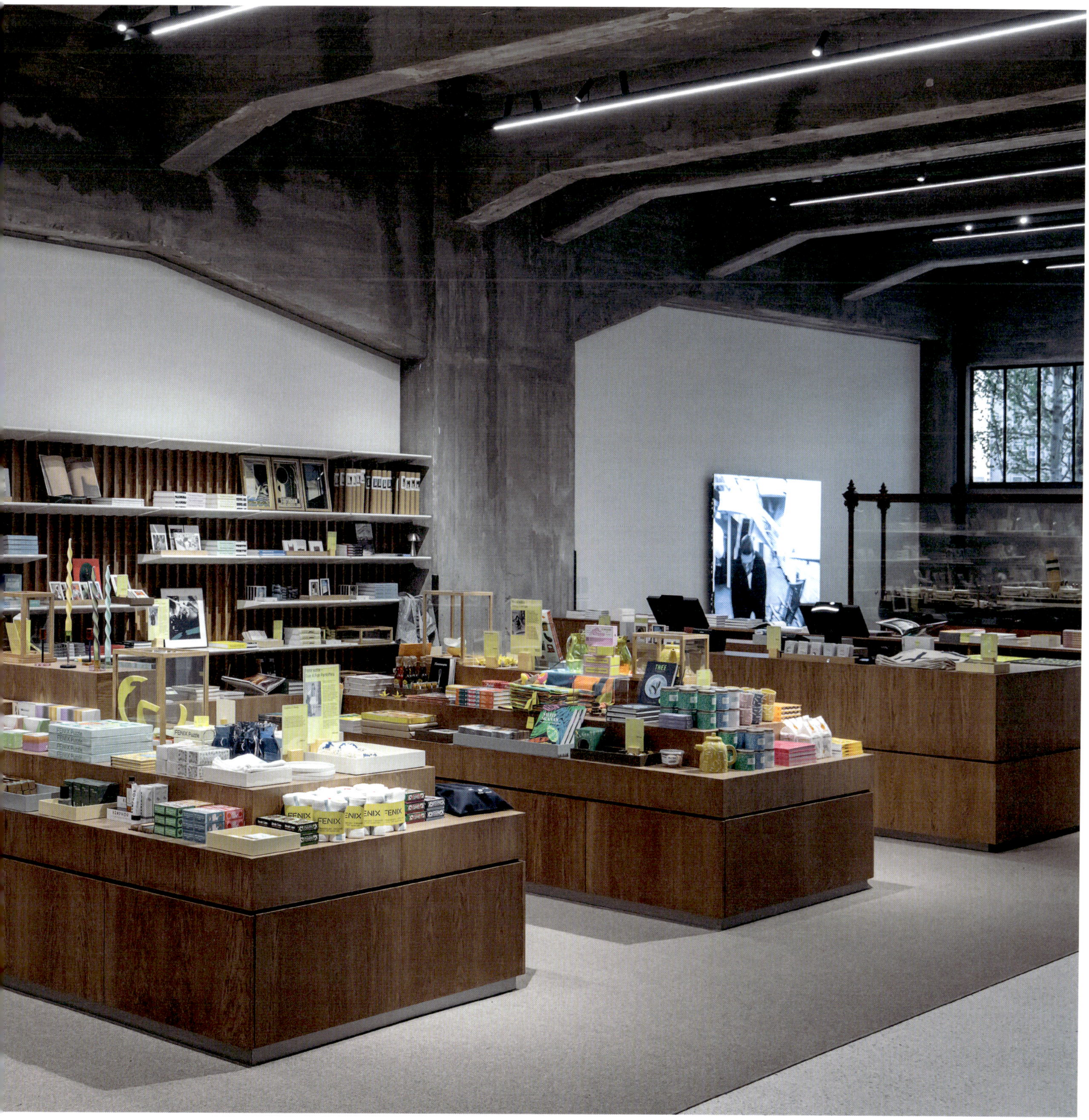
FENIX
FENIX
FENIX
FENIX

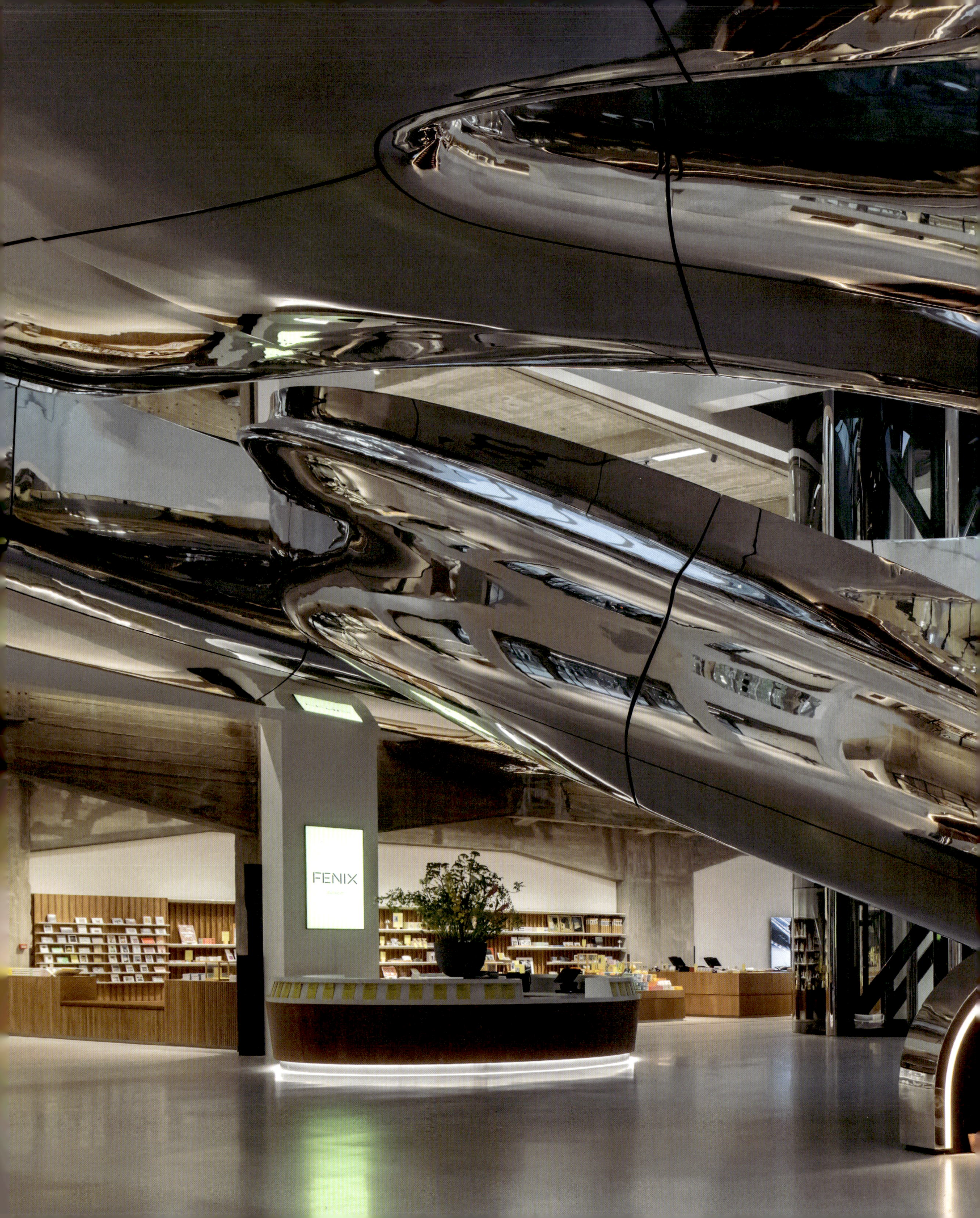
FENIX

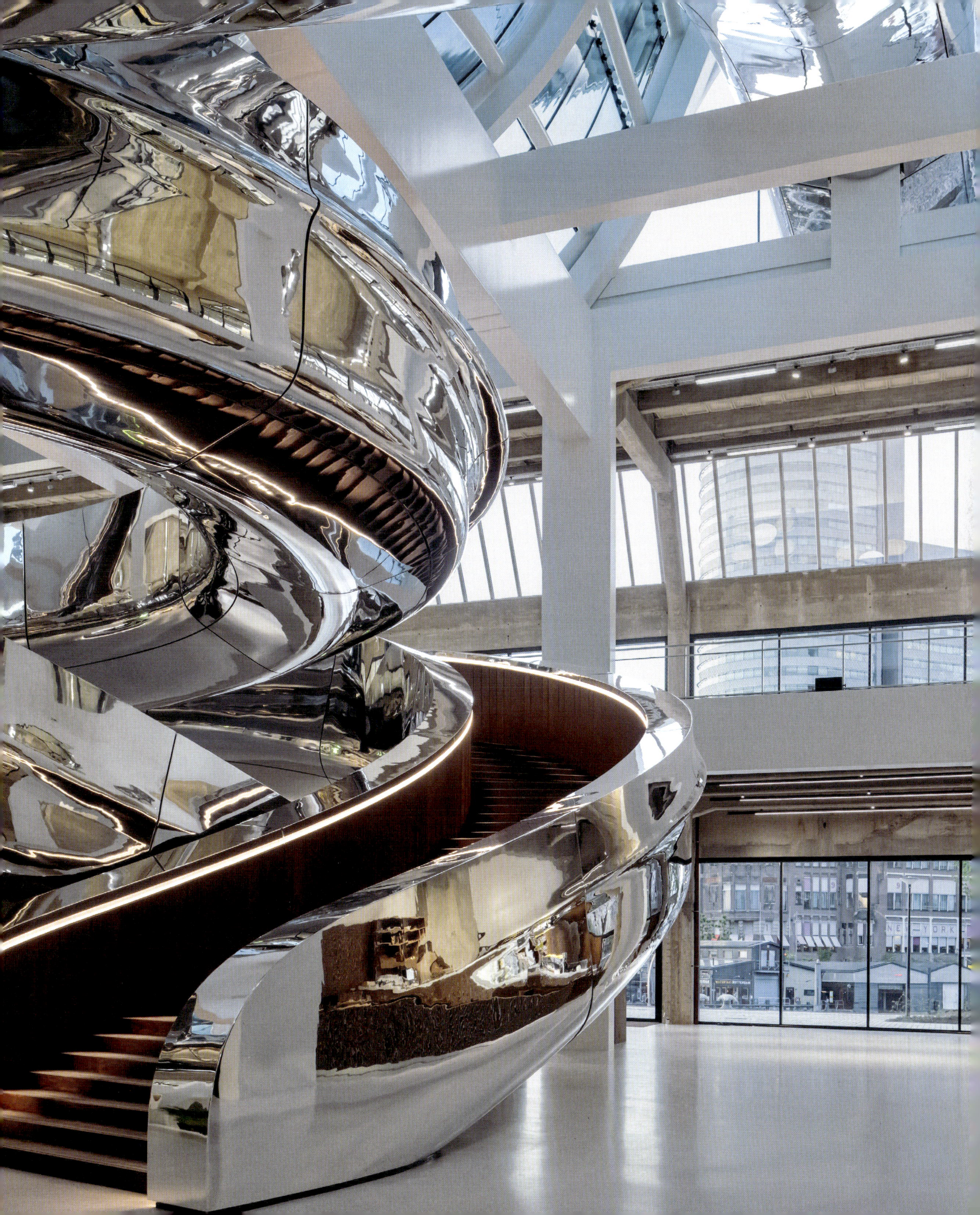
WATERTAXI ROTTERDAM
NEW YORK

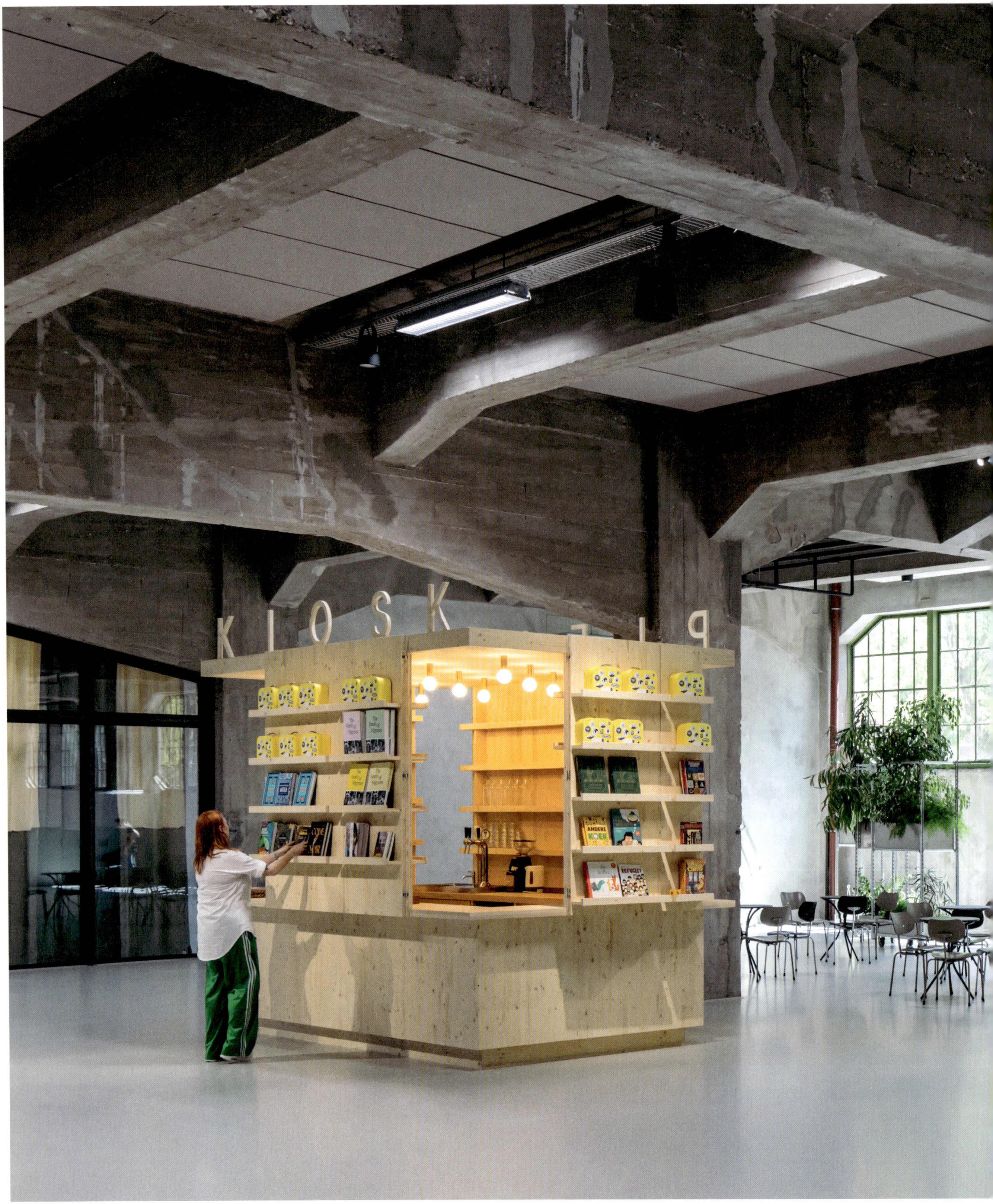
KIOSK

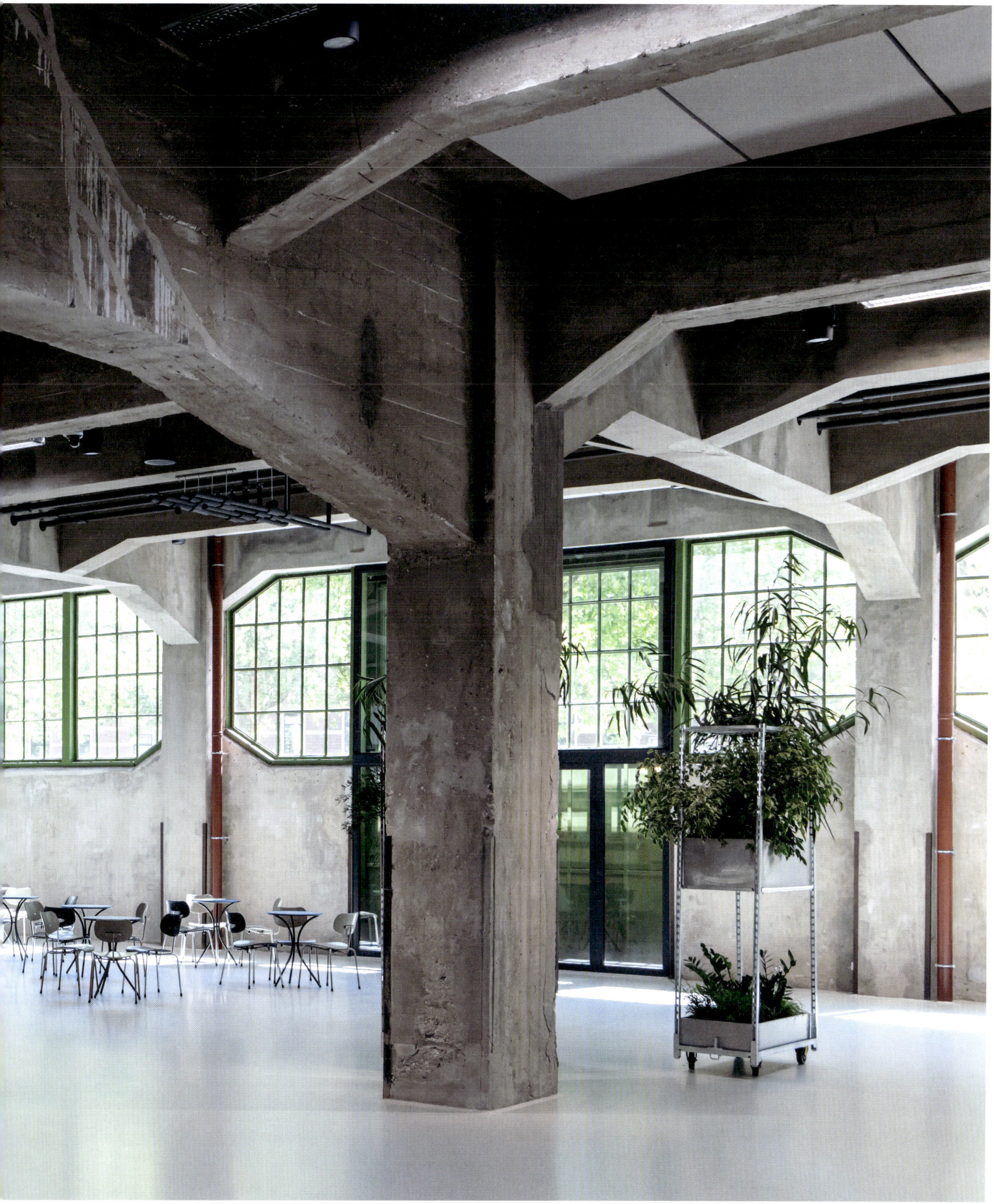

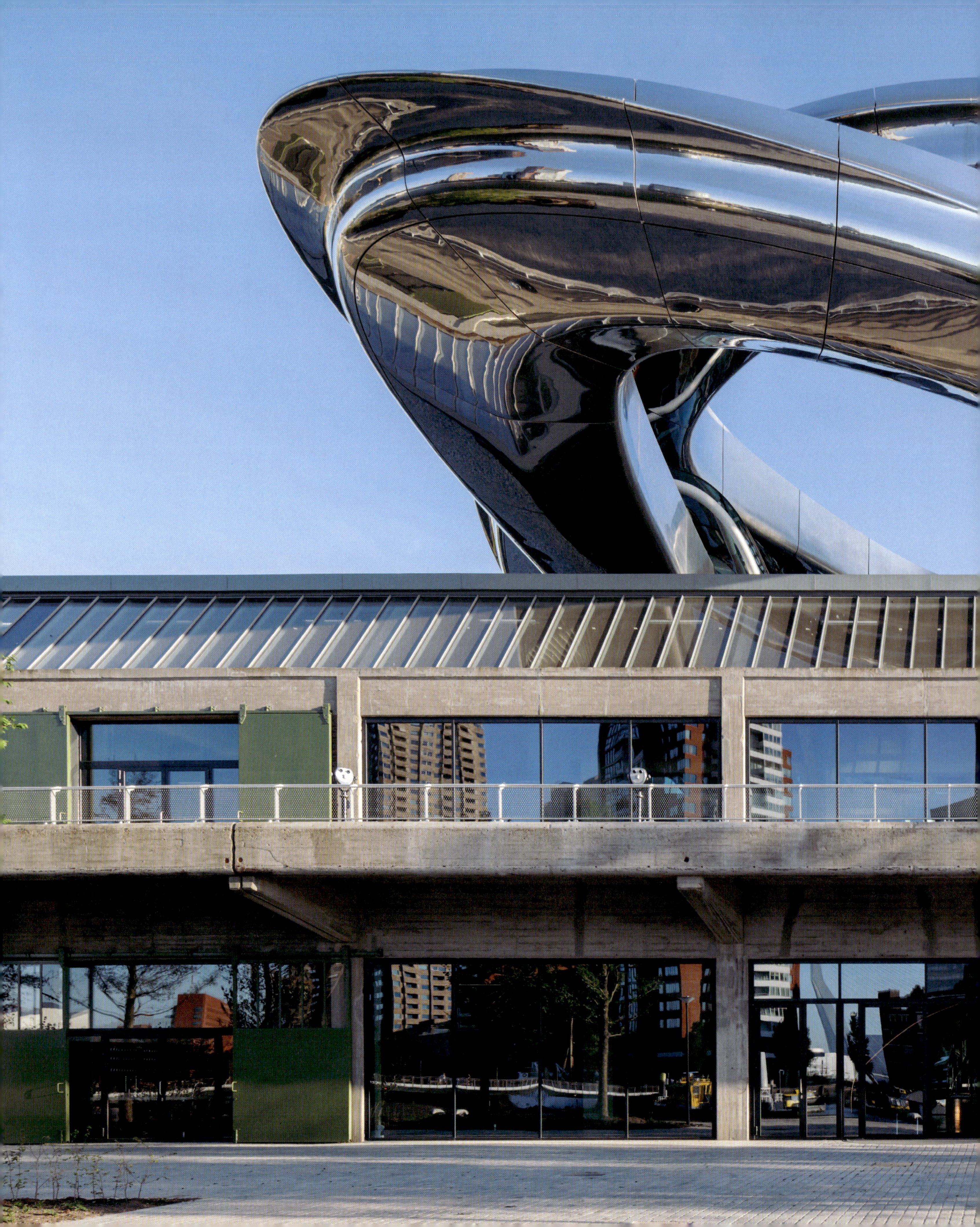

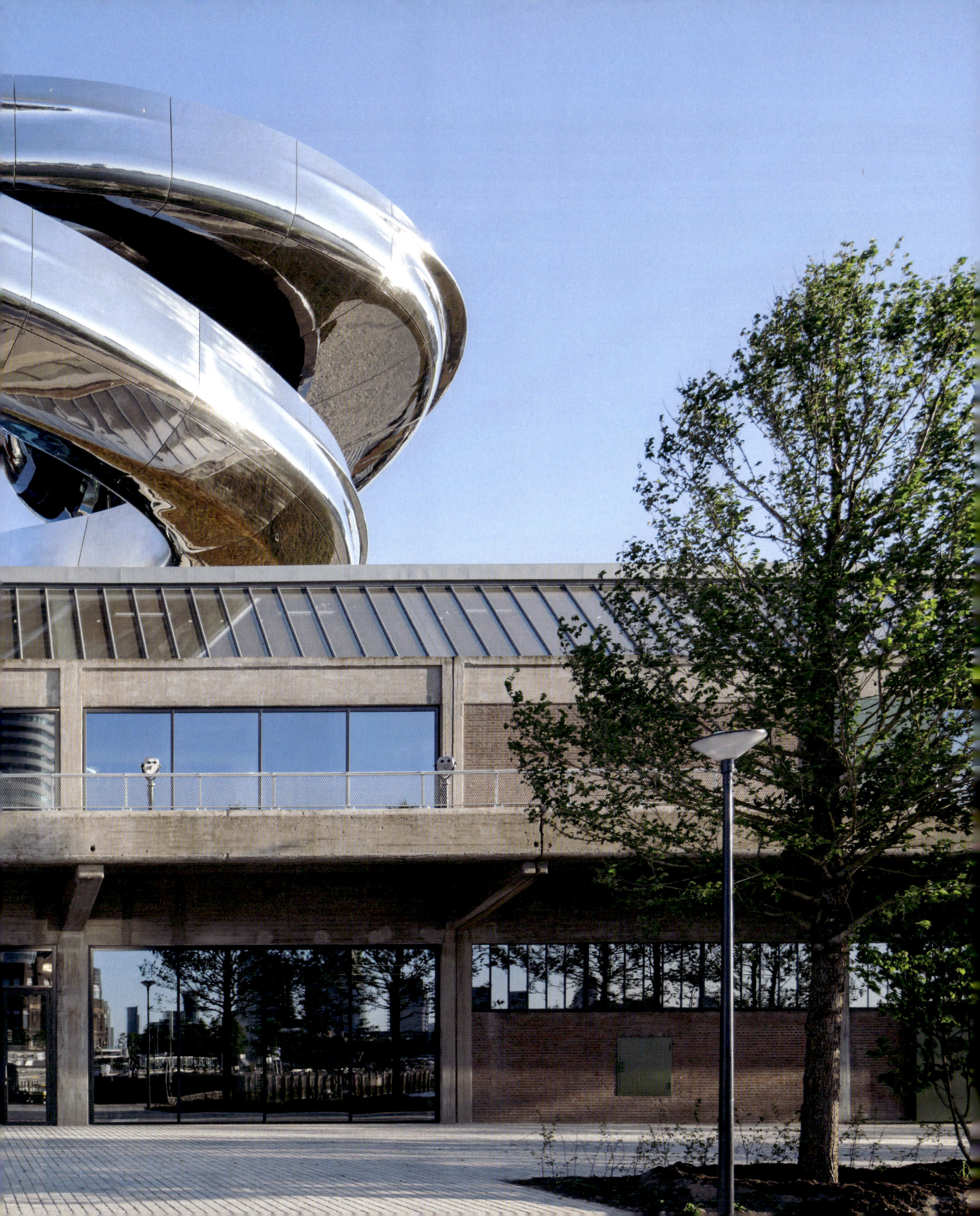

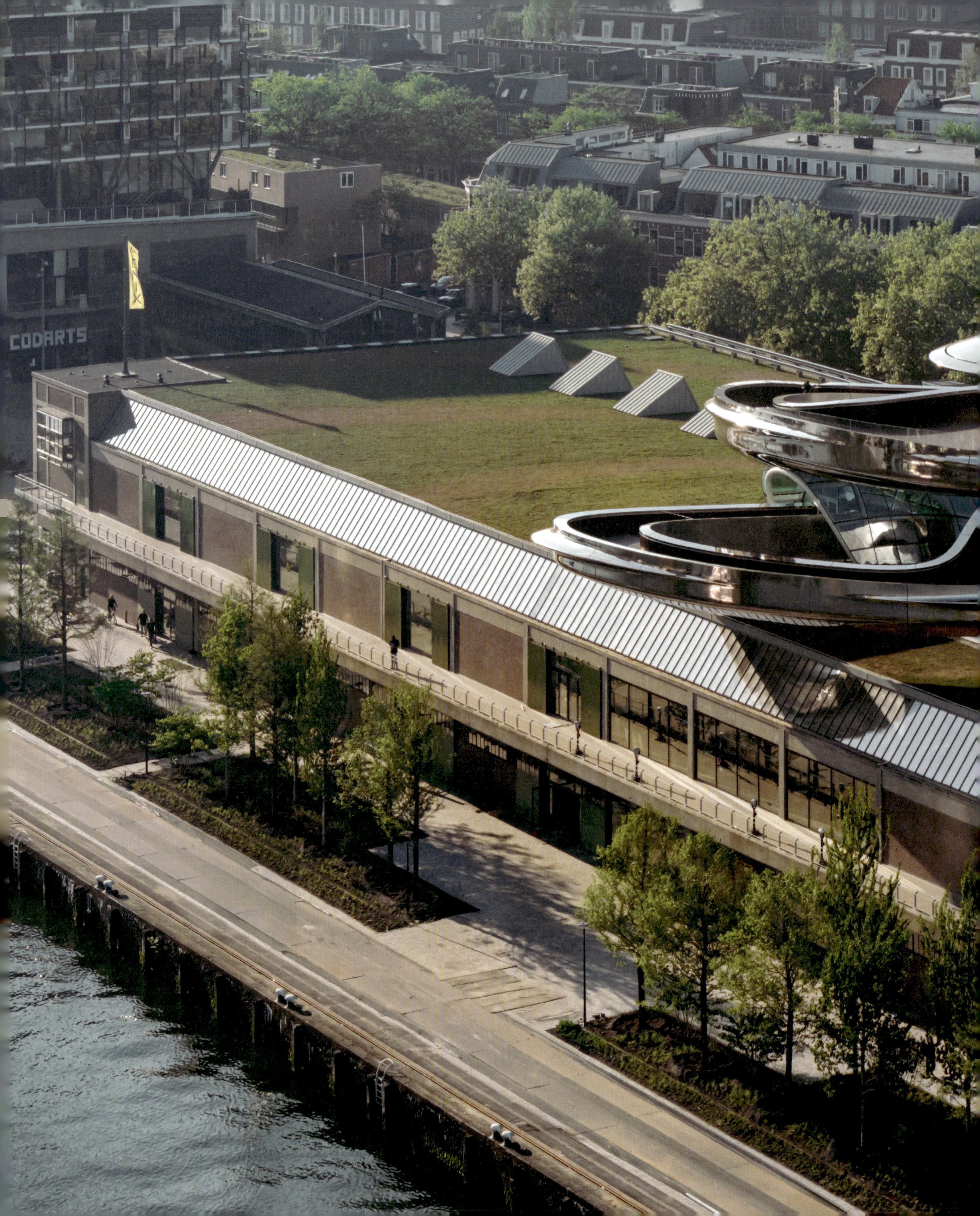
CODARTS

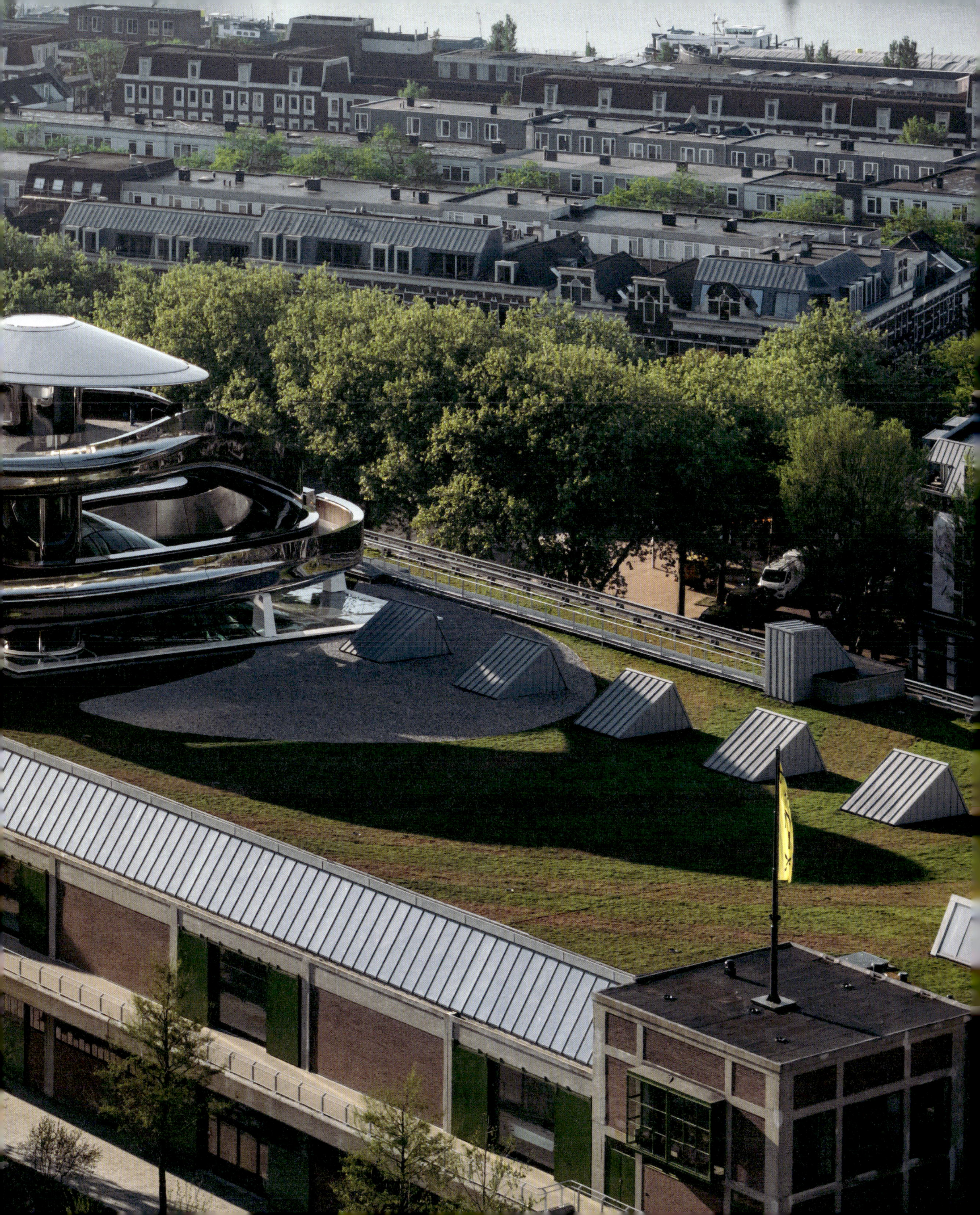

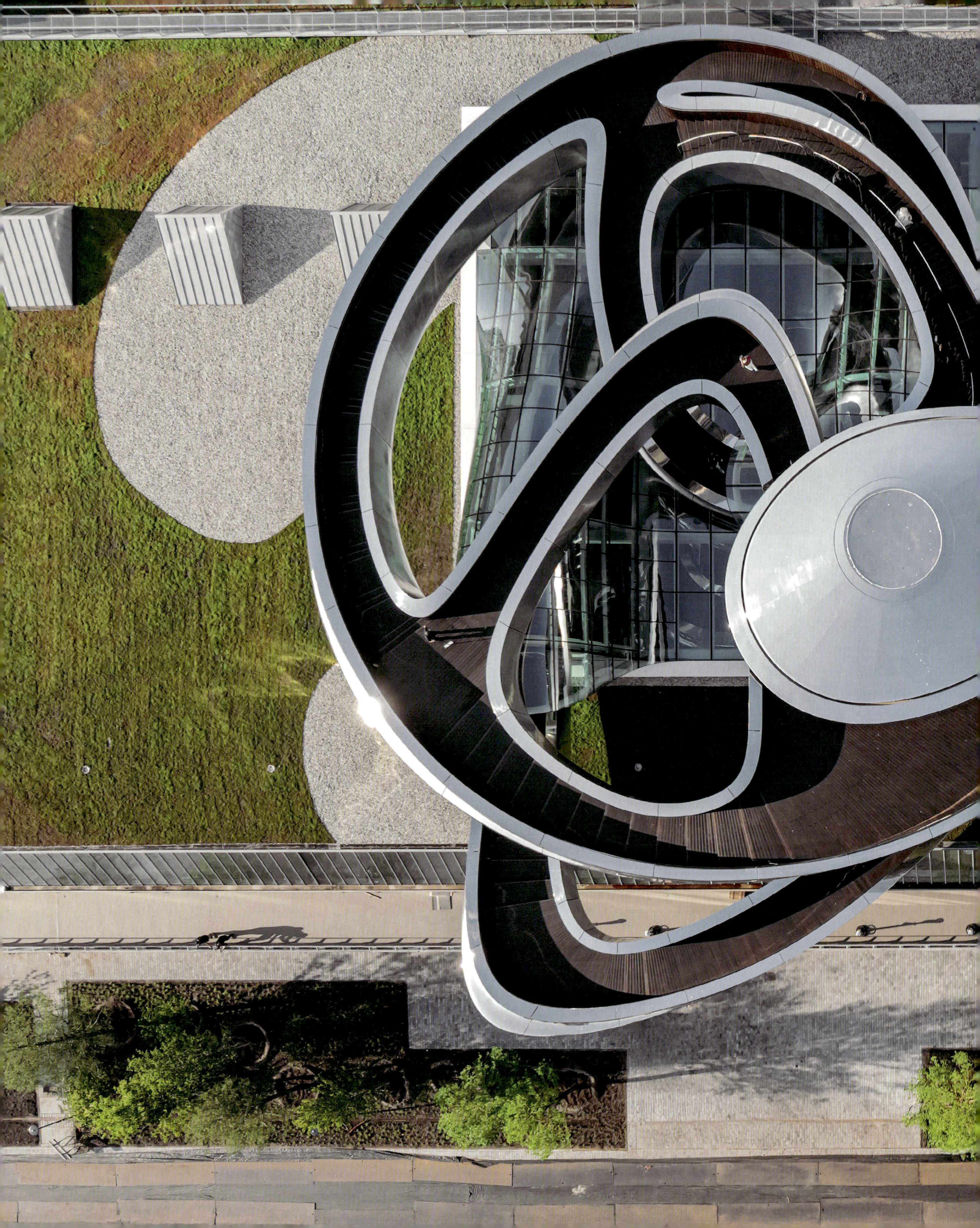

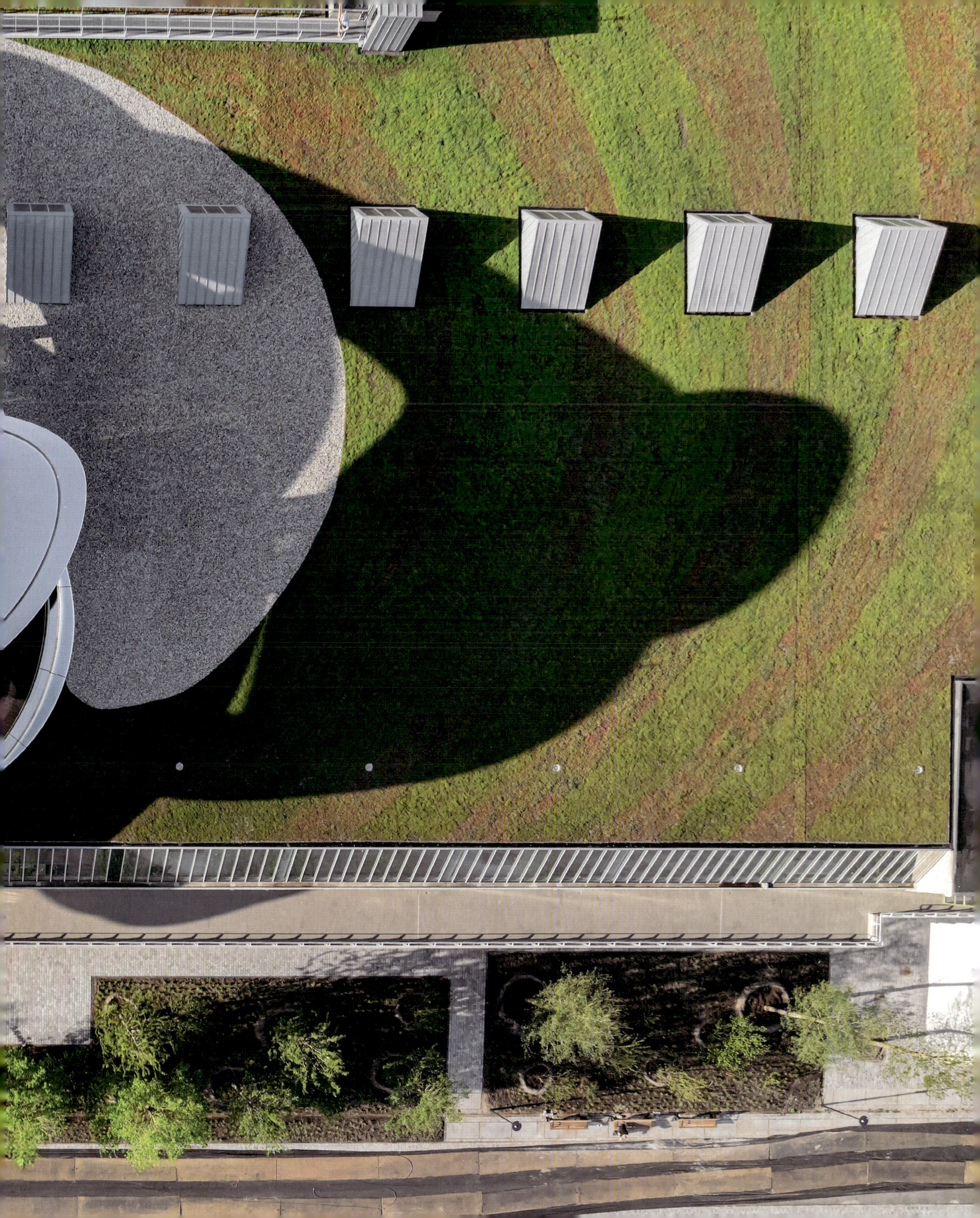

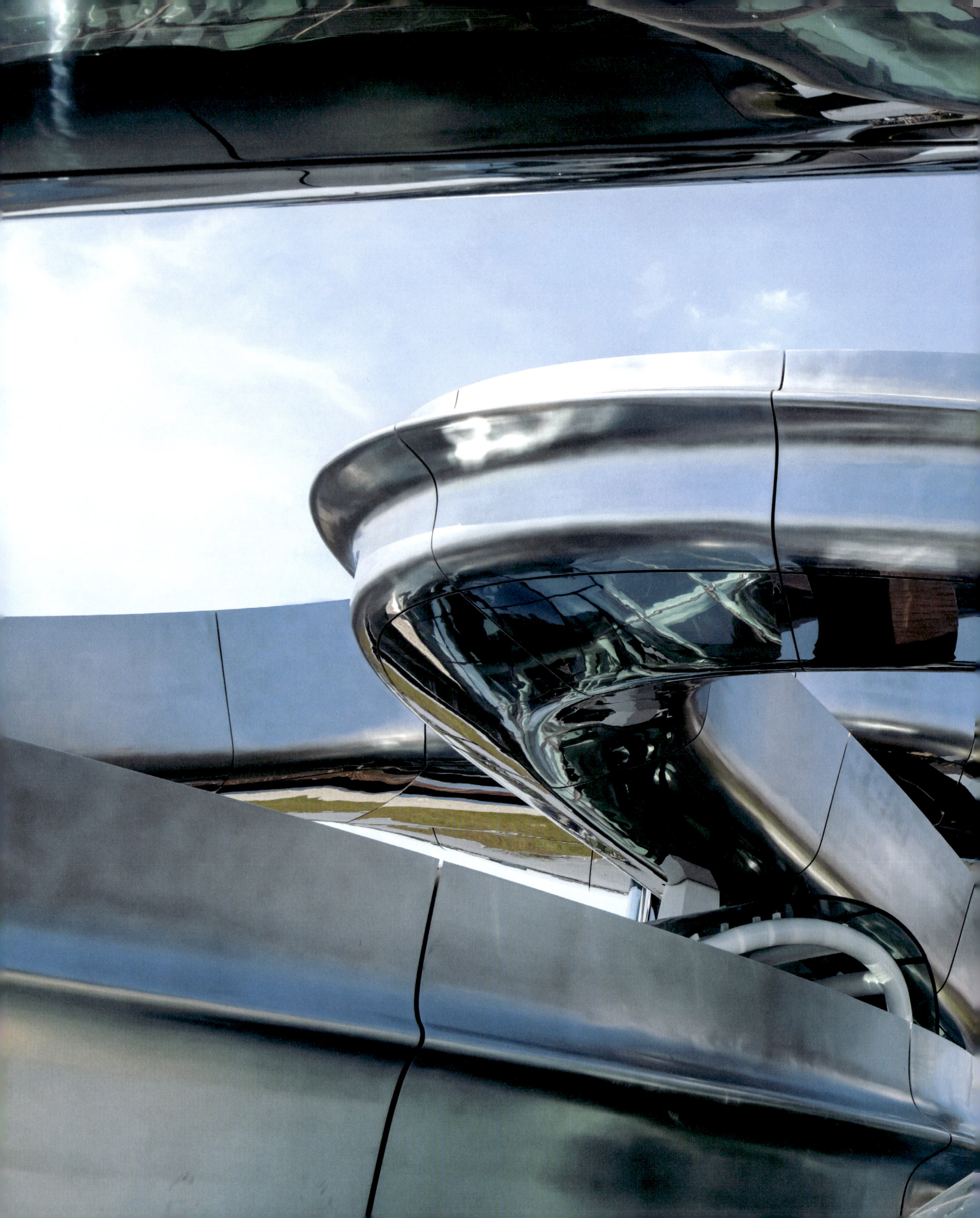

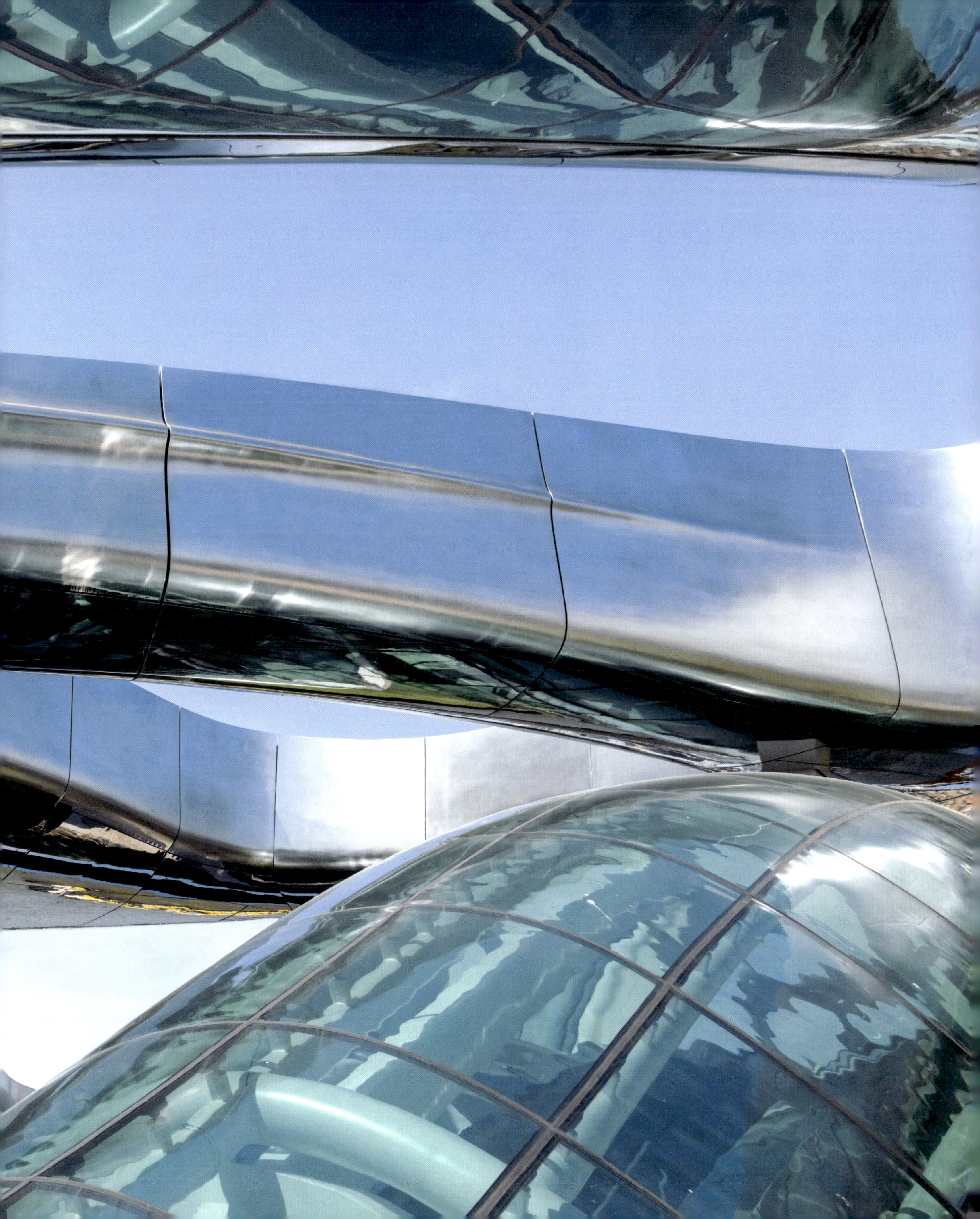

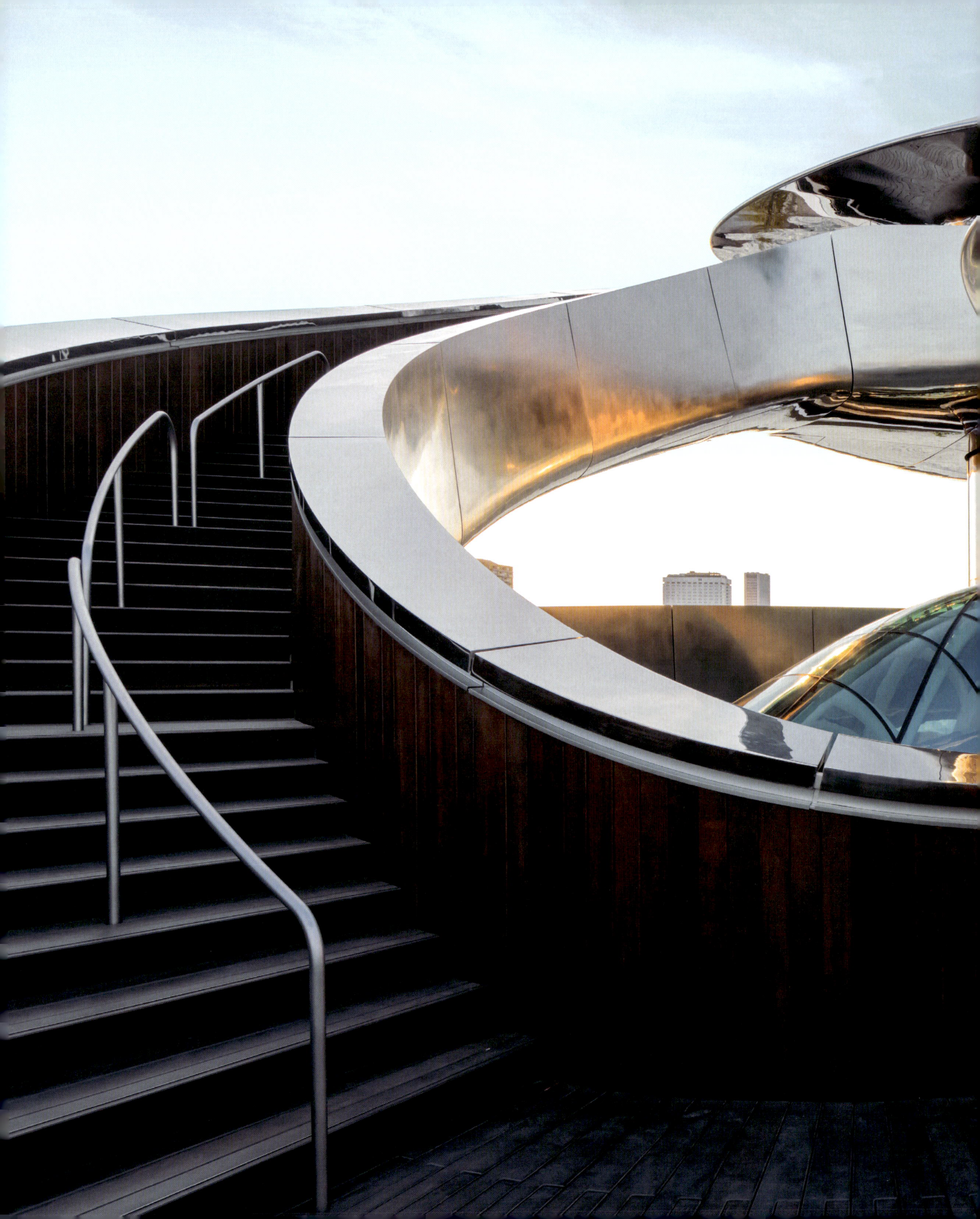

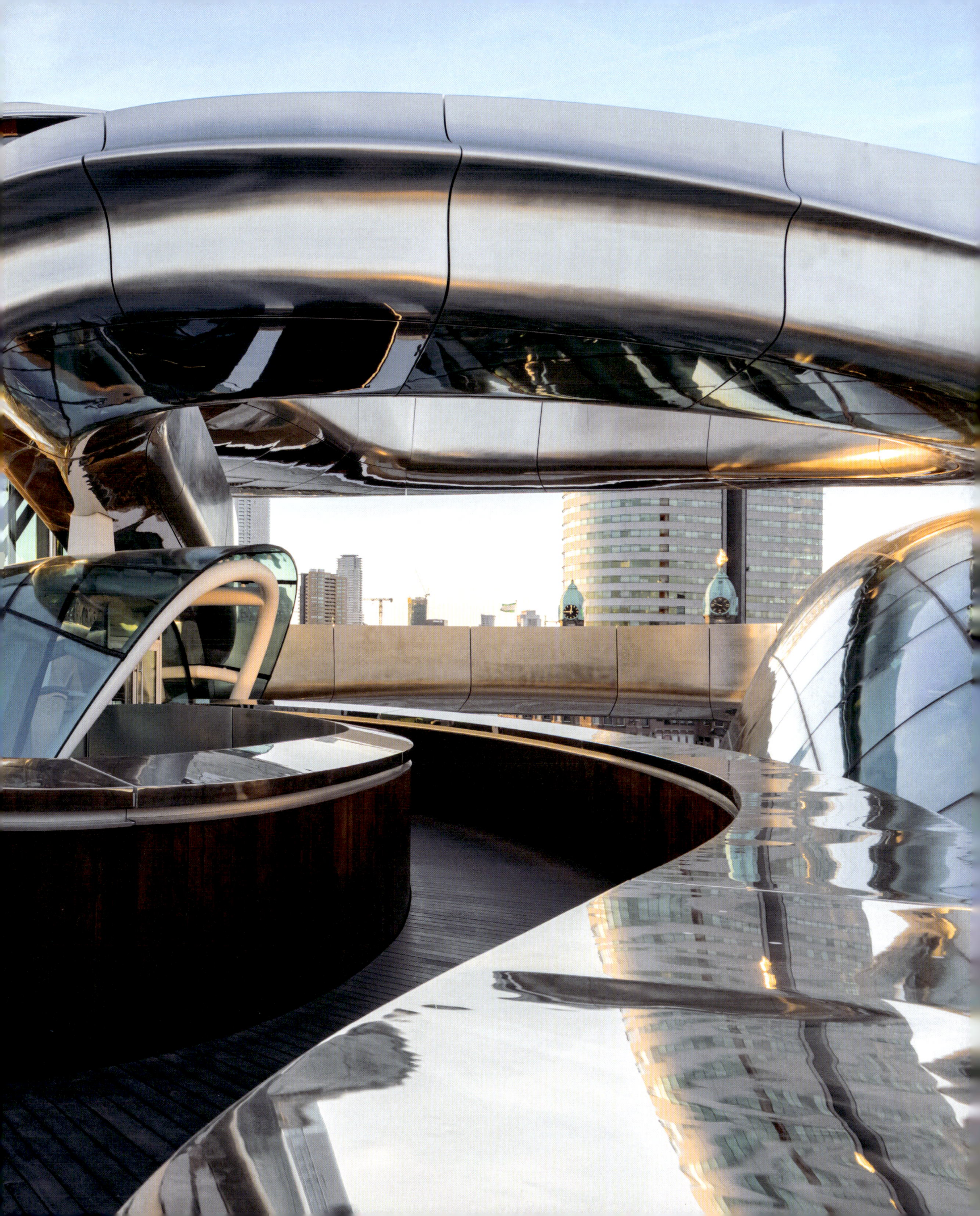

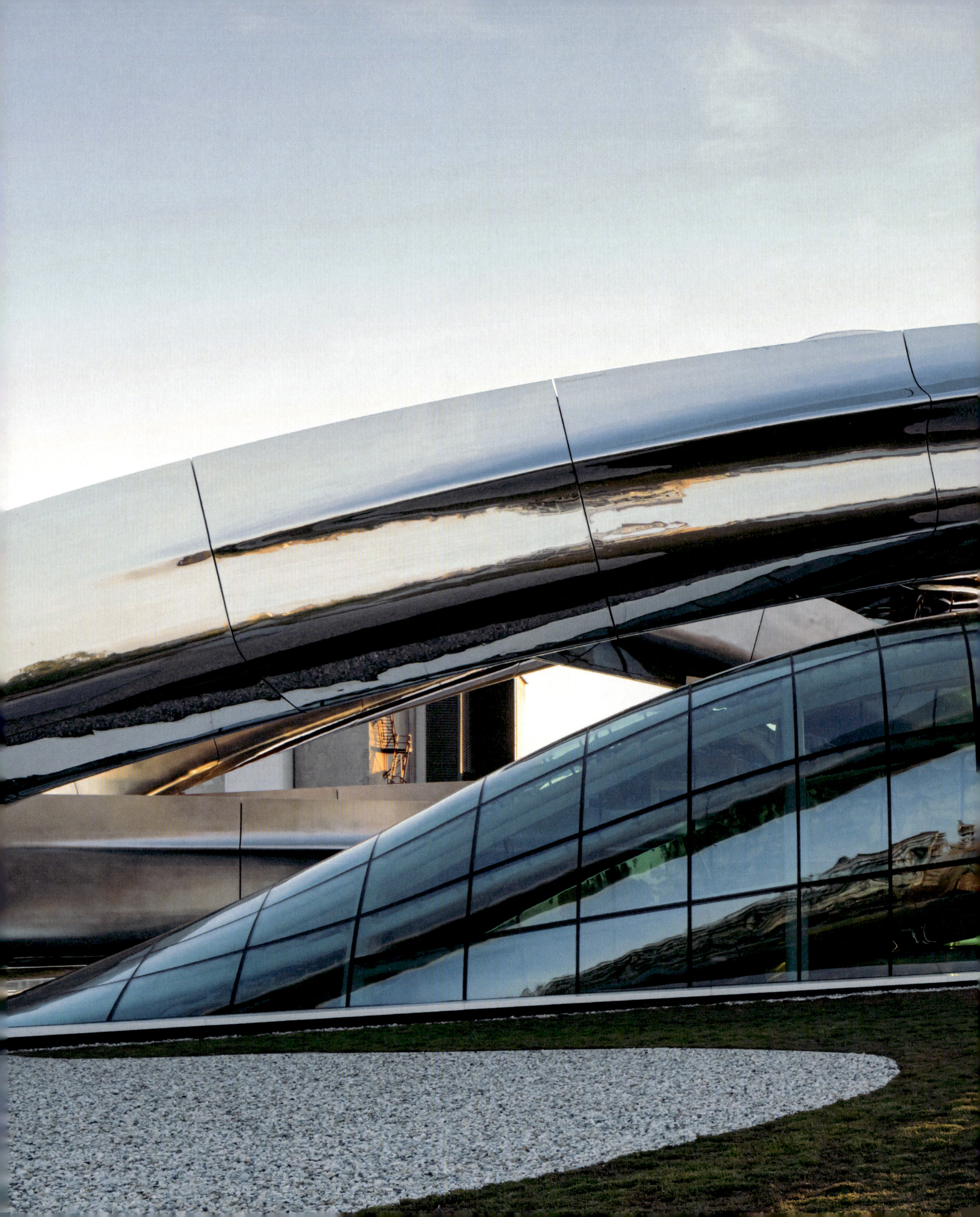

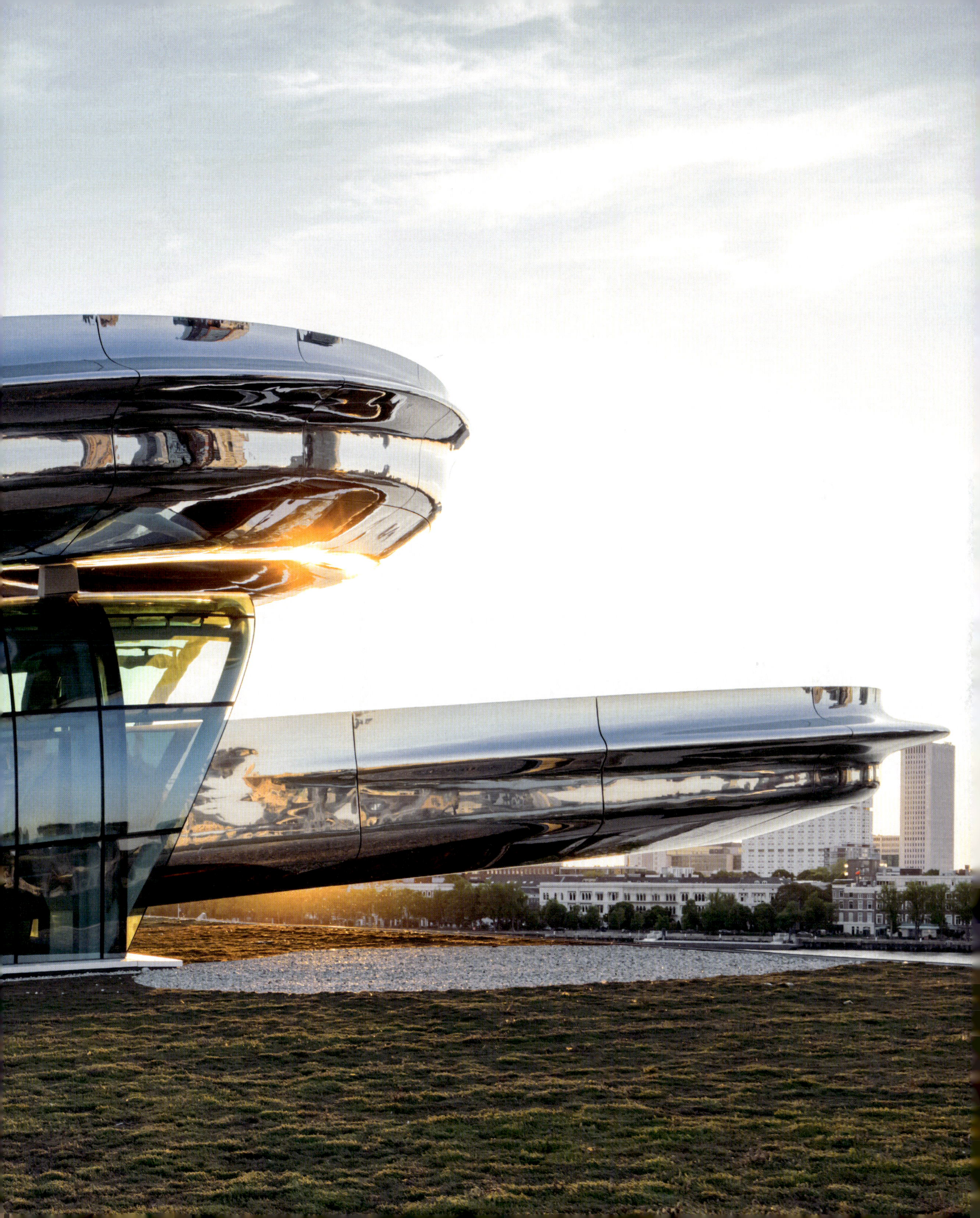

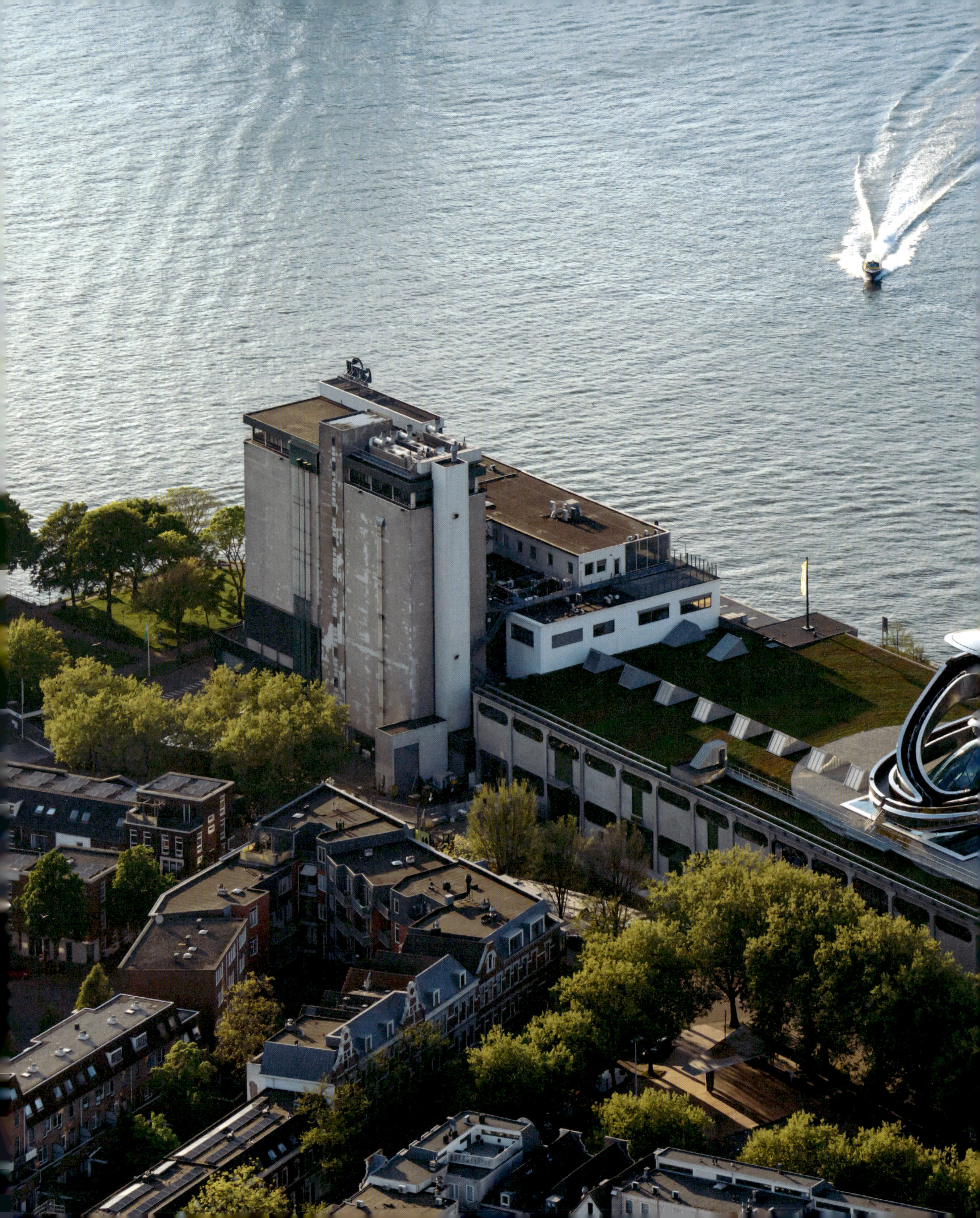

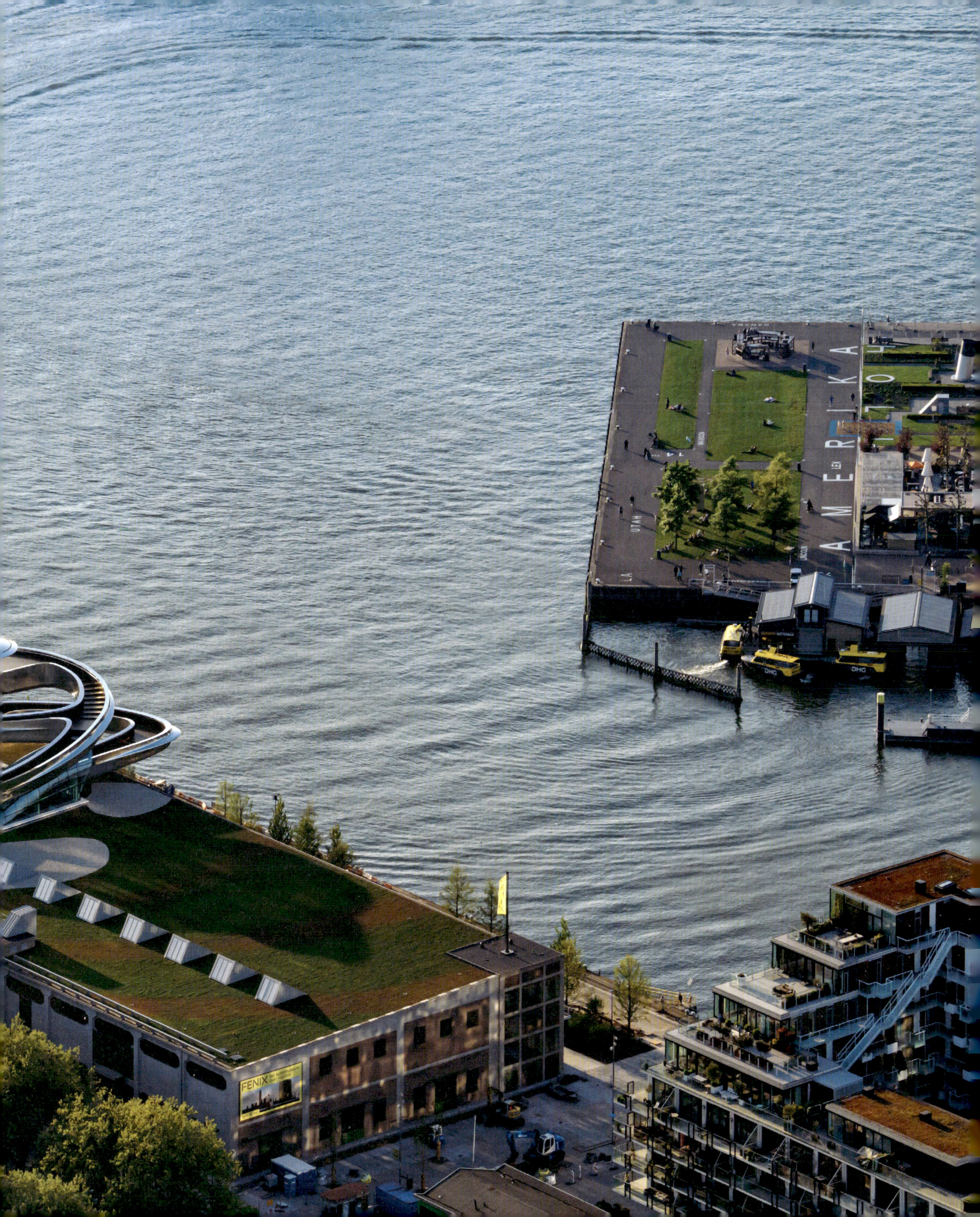
FENIX

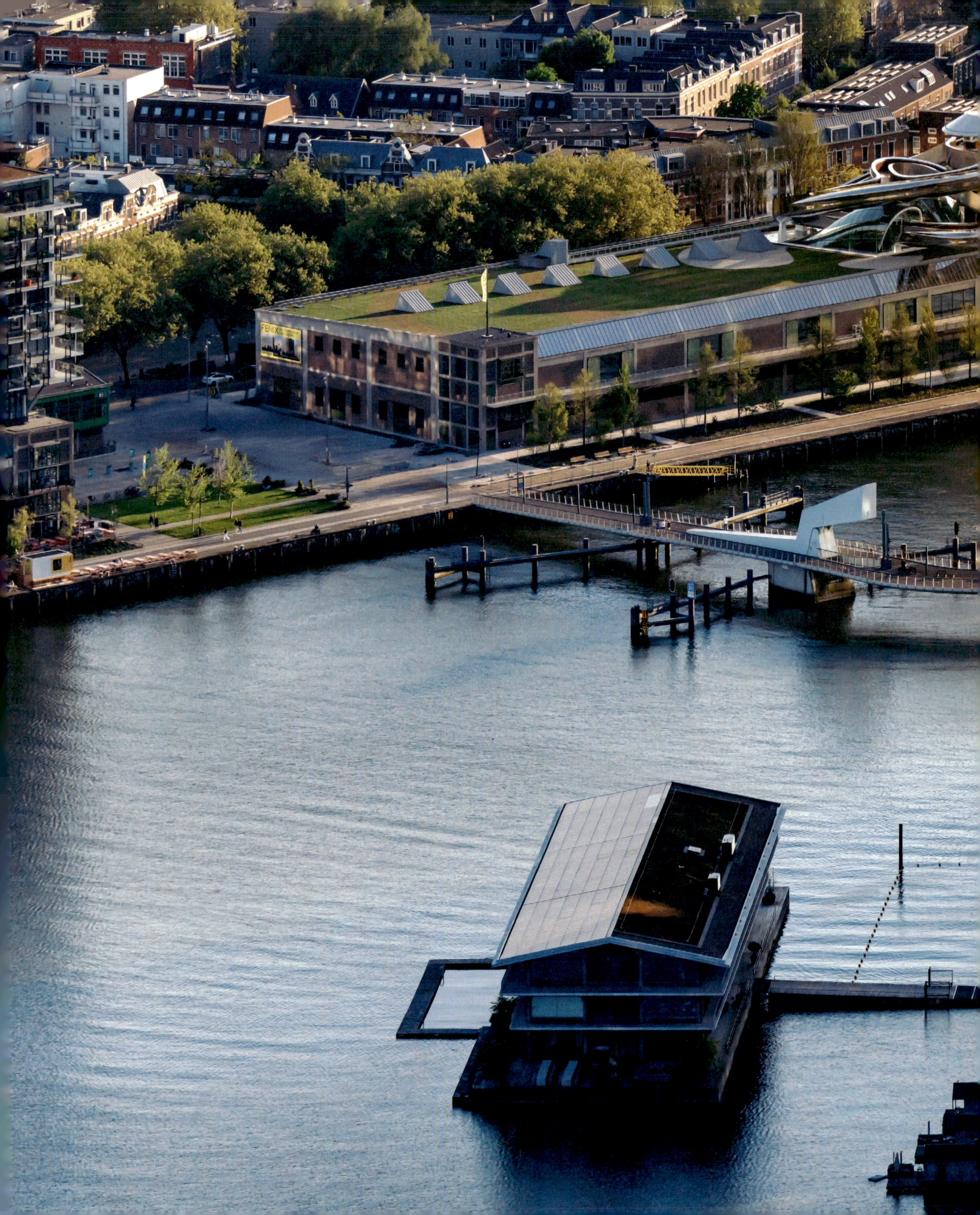

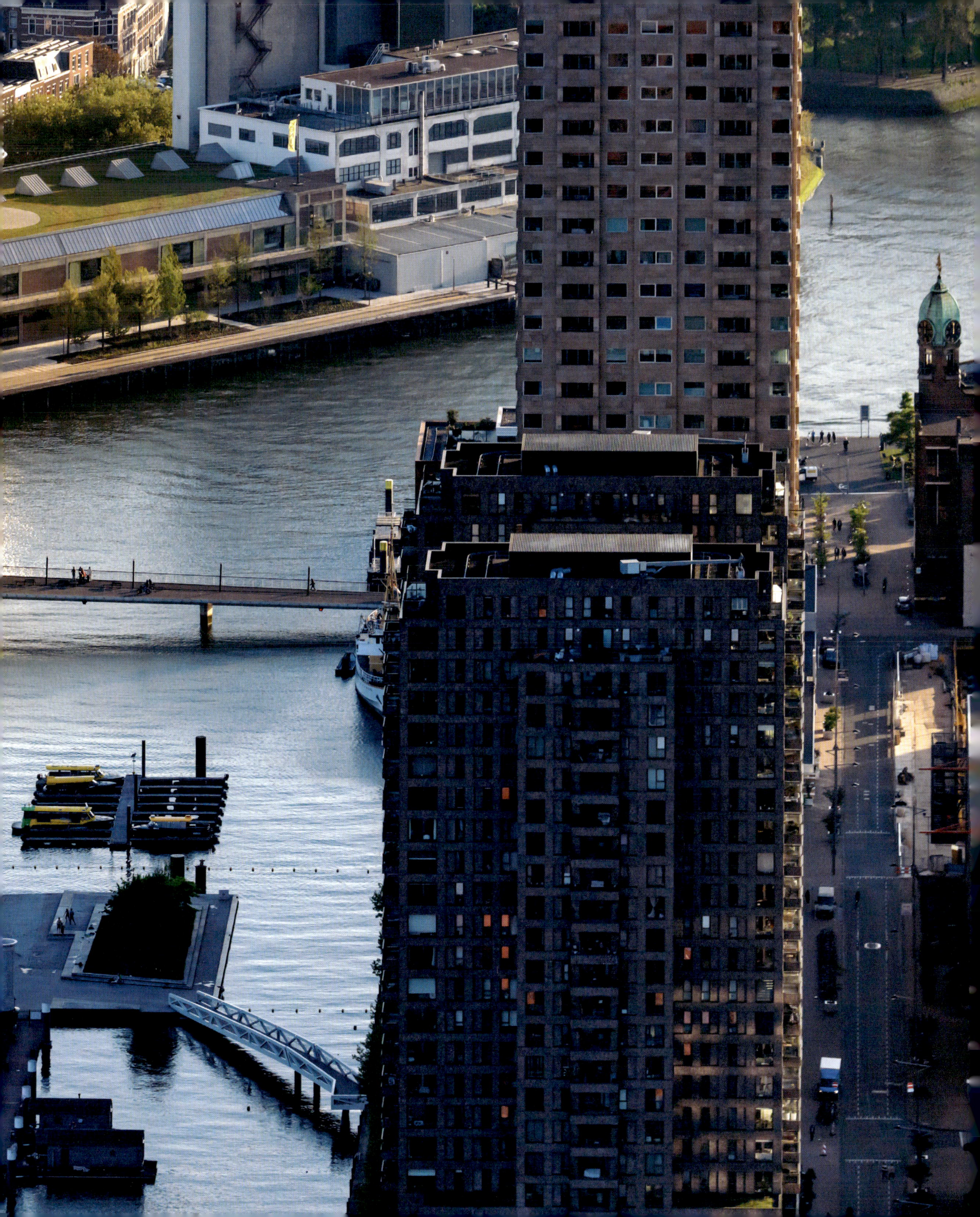

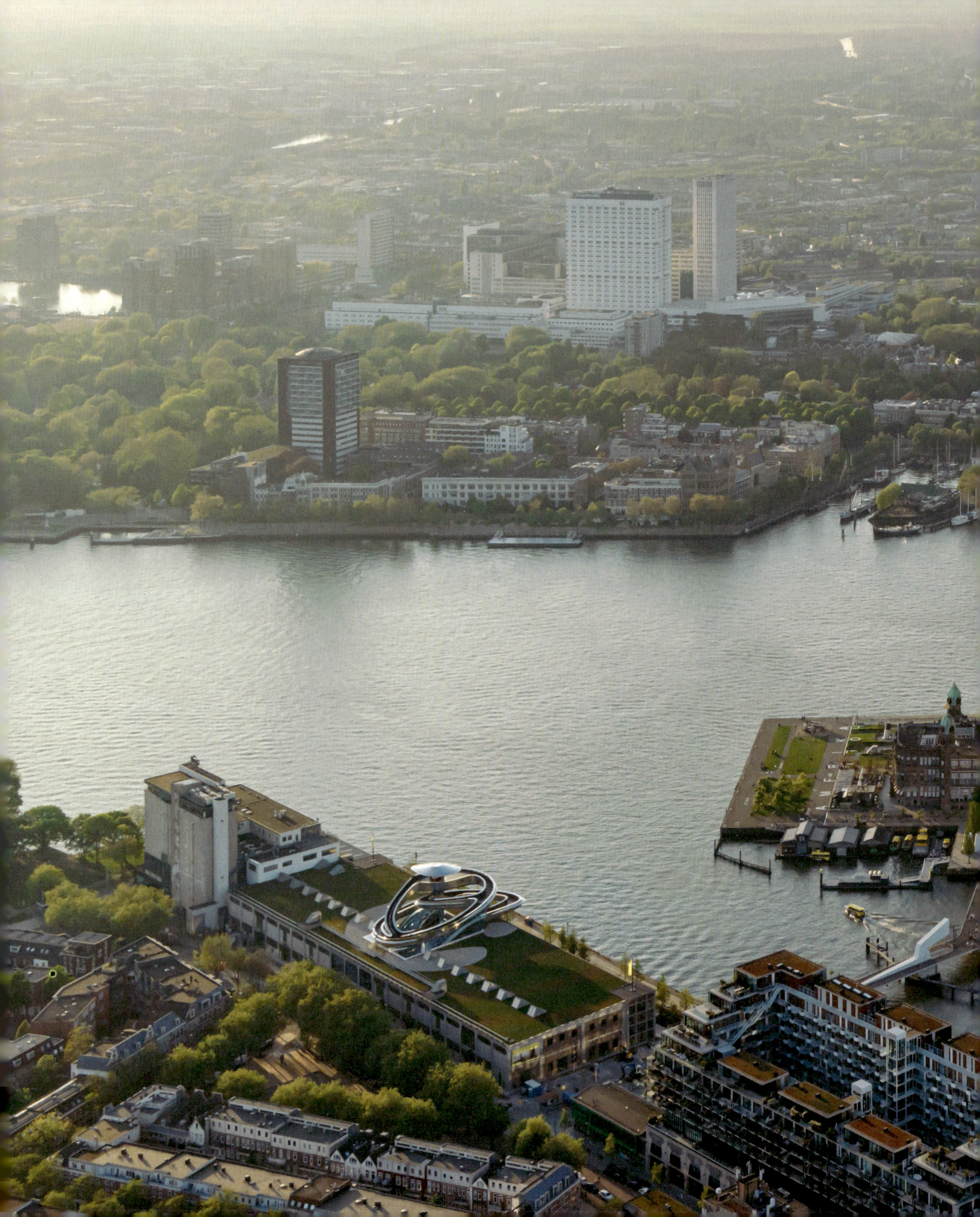

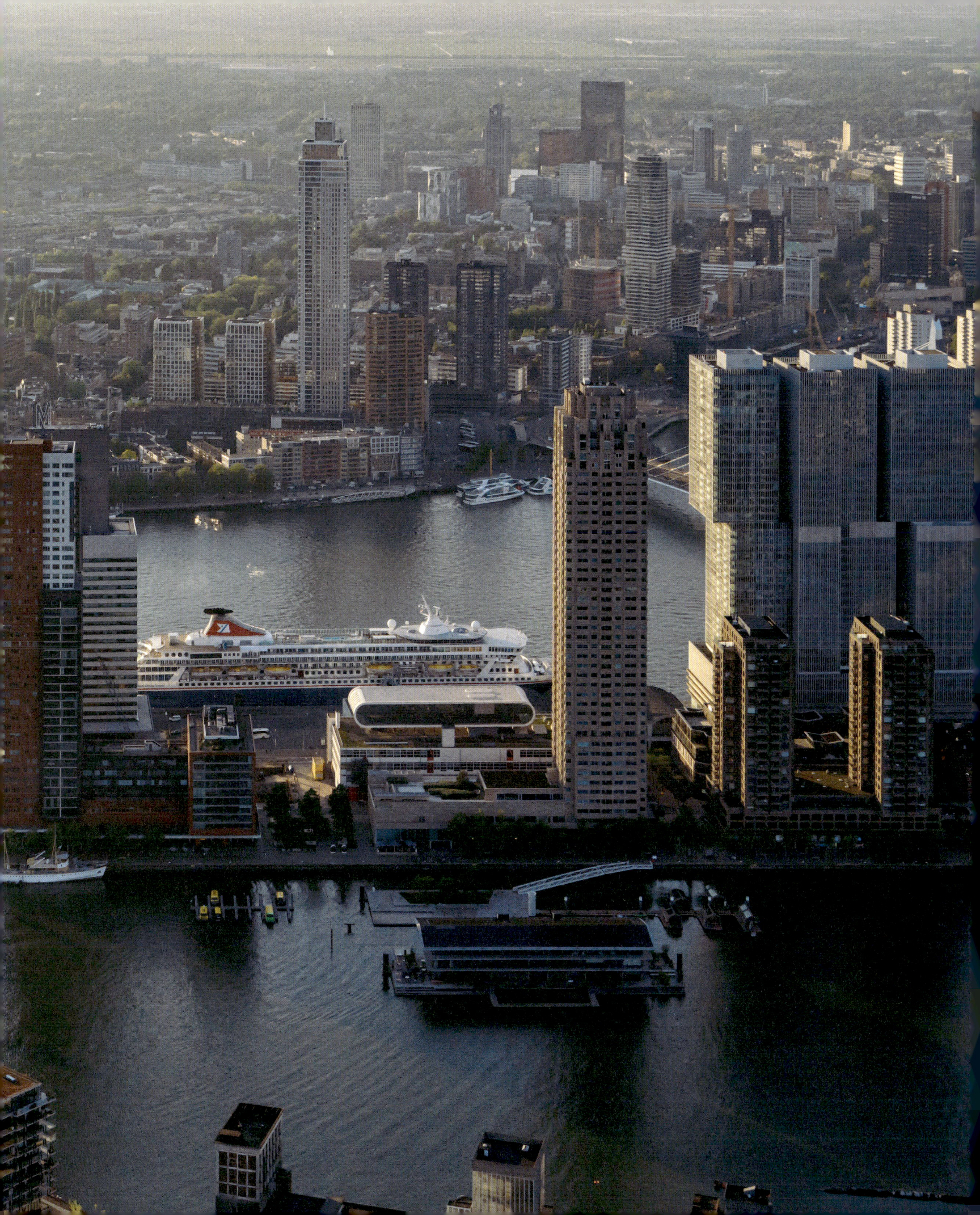

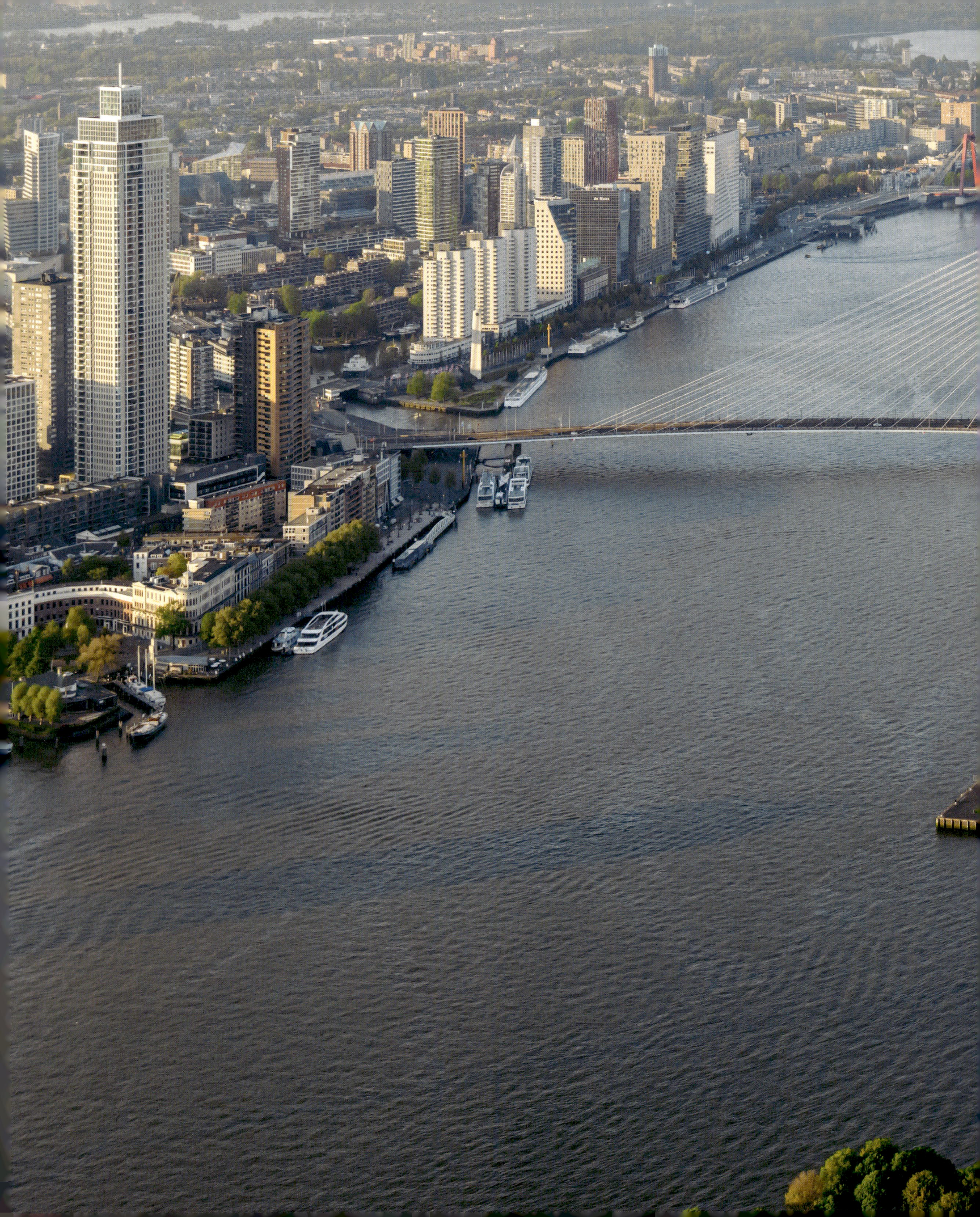

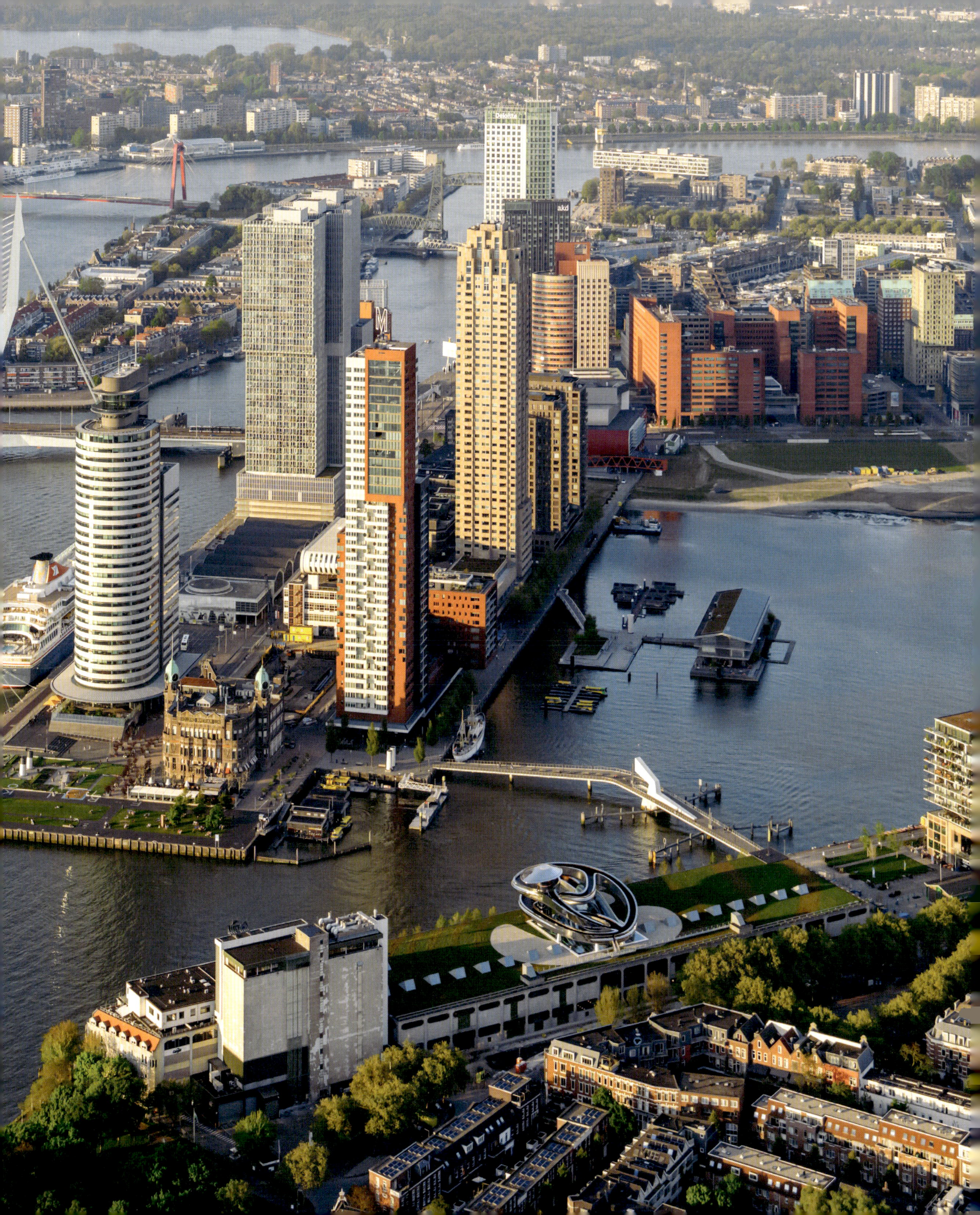
Deloitte
akd

Authors

ANNE KREMERS
Director of Fenix

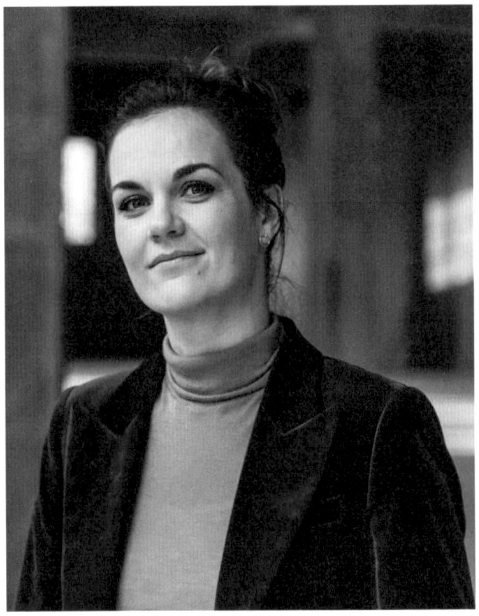

Anne Kremers is the Director of Fenix. Between 2013 and 2017, Anne Kremers led the Museum Villa Mondriaan in Winterswijk in the Eastern Netherlands, appointed at the age of twenty-four, the youngest museum director in the Netherlands at that time. Between 2017 and 2020 she worked for the Chow Tai Fook Art Foundation, designing innovative art and design projects in Hong Kong, before returning to the Netherlands to take up her role at Fenix.

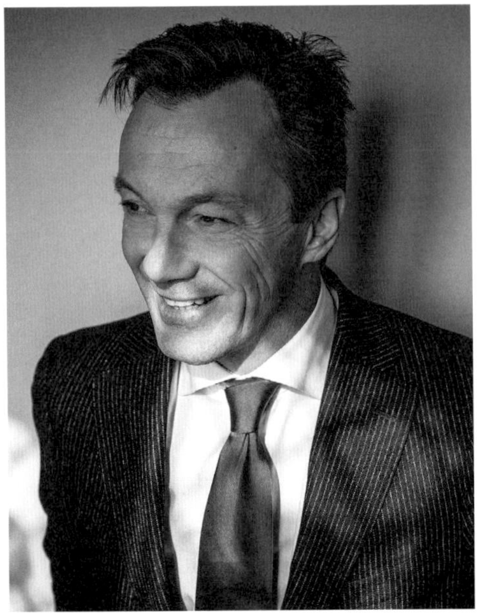

WIM PIJBES
Director of Droom en Daad

Wim Pijbes is an Art Historian and Director of the Rotterdam-based philanthropic foundation Droom en Daad, which supports innovative cultural projects including Fenix. He is the former General Director of the Rijksmuseum, where he led its major transformation and digital strategy, making it the world's largest online museum. He lectures and writes widely on art, museums, and public space, and is the author of several books. Pijbes is a Humanitas Professor at the University of Cambridge and holds board positions at Museum Voorlinden and TEFAF.

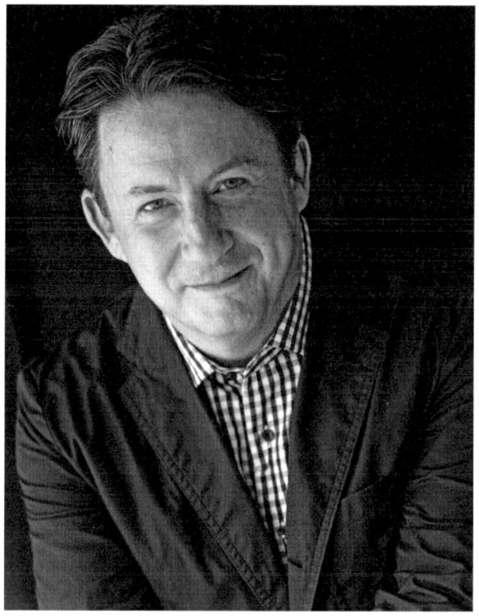

ANDRÁS SZÁNTÓ
Cultural Strategy Advisor

András Szántó, PhD, advises museums, cultural institutions, and leading brands on cultural strategy. An author and editor, his writings have appeared in *The New York Times, Artforum, The Art Newspaper*, and many other publications. Szántó, who lives in Brooklyn, has been conducting conversations with art-world leaders since the early 1990s, including as a frequent moderator of the Art Basel Conversations series. His recent books include *The Future of the Museum: 28 Dialogues* (2020), *Imagining the Future Museum: 21 Dialogues with Architects* (2022), and the forthcoming *The Future of the Art World: 38 Dialogues.*

MA YANSONG
Founder and Principal Partner of MAD

Ma Yansong is the Founder and Principal Partner of the global design firm MAD. MAD featured projects that include the Absolute Towers, Harbin Opera House, and the Lucas Museum of Narrative Arts. Ma's impact extends beyond architectural designs; it permeates the cultural fabric of cities and communities around the world. His extension into solo exhibitions, publications, product design, fashion, and artworks both domestically and internationally underscores the multifaceted nature of his architectural vision. This year, TIME magazine named him to its 2025 list of the 100 Most Influential People.

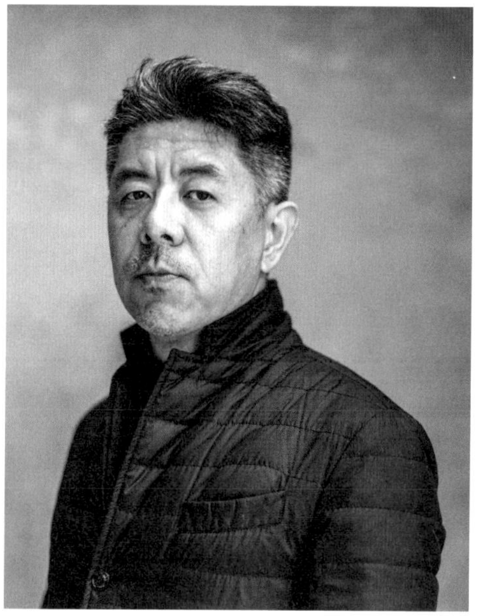

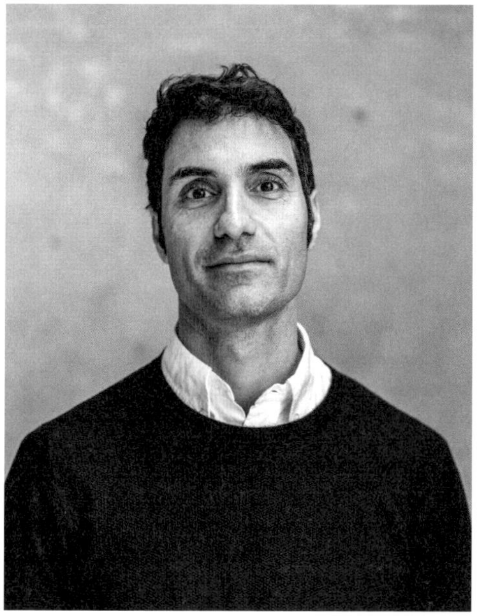

ANDREA D'ANTRASSI
Associate Partner at MAD

Andrea D'Antrassi is a licensed architect in Italy and Switzerland with a Master of Architecture from the Academy of Architecture in Mendrisio. He has solid international project experience across the US, Italy, Australia, China, KSA and UAE. Since joining MAD in 2010, he has contributed to key projects, such as the Boncompagni residential complex in Rome, the Huangshan Mountain Village, the Nanjing Zendai Himalayas Center, and the Lucas Museum of Narrative Art. Over the years, Andrea has also overseen MAD's installations presented during Milan Design Week and Fuorisalone, and he plays a key role in managing the firm's competition entries.

Photographers

IWAN BAAN

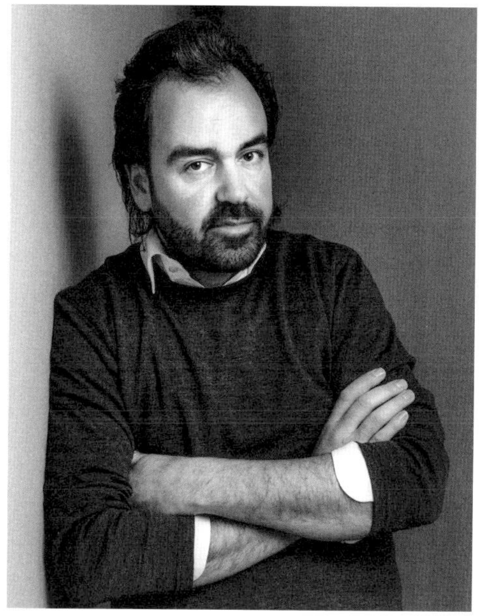

Iwan Baan is a Dutch photographer, primarily known for images that narrate the life and interactions that occur within architecture. Baan studied at the Royal Academy of Art in The Hague and worked in publishing and documentary photography in New York and Europe. Iwan Baan was named one of the 100 most influential people in the contemporary architecture world by the magazine *Il Magazine dell'Architettura* on the occasion of their 100th issue. He is the recipient of the AIA Stephen A. Kliment Oculus Award.

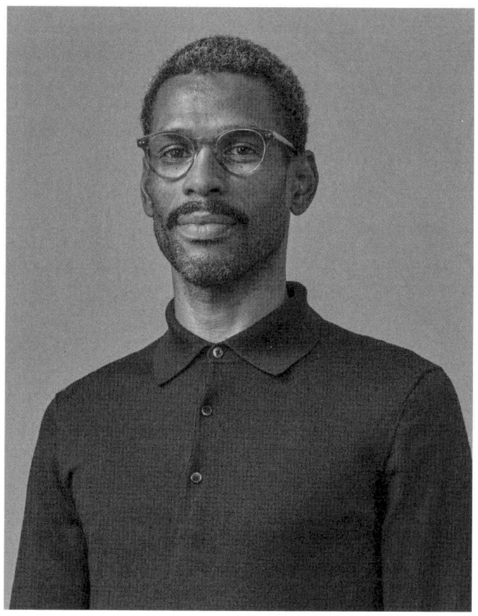

RUBÉN DARIO KLEIMEER

Rubén Dario Kleimeer is a Rotterdam-based photographer. Kleimeer's visual essays have been published in books such as *The Amsterdam Green Architecture Guide* by Arcam and in the past two issues of *Architecture in the Netherlands Yearbook*, by nai010. In addition, he has guest lectured at the Rotterdam Academy of Architecture, the Independent School for the City, and the Berlage in Delft. Kleimeer's work has been exhibited at numerous places nationally and internationally. Over the past six years, he has photographed the transformation of Fenix Warehouse II on Katendrecht, where Fenix came into being.

Fact Sheet

Architect Warehouse San Francisco: **Cornelis Nicolaas van Goor** (1861–1945)
Renovation Fenix Warehouse II: **Bureau Polderman**
Architect Tornado: **MAD**
Warehouse San Francisco completed: **1923**
Post-war reconstruction into two warehouses: **1948–1950**
Original length of façade: **360 metres**
Length façade Fenix Warehouse II: **172 metres**
Total area of the warehouse: **16,000 square metres**
Exhibition galleries: **8,383 square metres**
Plein: **2,275 square metres**
Fenix Shop: **100 square metres**
Height of warehouse: **13.4 metres**
Height of Tornado: **30 metres**
Height of viewing platform: **24 metres**
Height of elevator core: **22 metres**
Weight of the structure of the Tornado: **2,400 tonnes**
Length of stairs of the Tornado: **550 metres**
Number of steps on the Tornado: **336**
12,500 unique wooden planks
100 cubic metres sustainable wood from Norway
297 stainless steel panels
100 hours of polishing per steel panel
255 glass panels on the roof
6,750 square metres green roof

Photo Credits

Iwan Baan: pp. 186; 188-195; 197-213; 218-237
Benny Emmerich: p. 24
Rubén Dario Kleimeer: cover, pp. 25-26; 28-53; 55-60; 64-67; 69-98; 100-101; 103-113; 115; 118; 120-129; 131-149; 150-161; 163-166; 168-185
Jorrit Lousberg: p. 20

Portrait Photos
Anne Kremers: Sylvana Lansu
Wim Pijbes: Vincent Mentzel
András Szántó: Patrice Casanova
Ma Yansong: Mark Bolk
Andrea D'Antrassi: Mark Bolk
Iwan Baan: Jonas Eriksson
Rubén Dario Kleimeer: Pim Top

Acknowledgements

Hundreds of engineers, welders, and carpenters worked together to restore and build Fenix. Behind every bolt, beam, and plank is a person with a story. Fenix wants to thank everybody who worked on the restoration of the warehouse and on making the Tornado a reality.

Head of Business Development
Edoardo Ghizzoni

Project Manager
Costanza de Bellegarde de Saint Lary

Art Director
Luigi Fiore

Design and Layout
Giulia Dolci

Editorial Coordination
Manuela Schiavano, Vincenza Russo

Copy Editor
Laura Colosi

This book is published on the occasion of the opening of Fenix, the new art museum about migration in Rotterdam, on 16 May 2025. Fenix is an initiative of Droom en Daad.

FENIX

First published in June 2025 by
Skira editore spa
via Agnello, 18
20121 Milano
Italy
skira-arte.com

ISBN Skira: 978-88-572-5337-4
ISBN Fenix: 978-88-572-5442-5

This book has been printed by Errestampa s.r.l. on FSC®-certified paper

MIX
Paper | Supporting responsible forestry
FSC® C013389

Distributed in USA, Canada, Central & South America by ARTBOOK | D.A.P., 75 Broad Street, Suite 630, New York, NY 10004, USA.
Distributed elsewhere in the world by Thames and Hudson Ltd., 181A High Holborn, London WC1V 7QX, United Kingdom